A Garland Series

OUTSTANDING
DISSERTATIONS
IN THE

FINE
ARTS

The Western Portal
of
Saint-Loup-de-Naud

Clark Maines

Garland Publishing, Inc., New York & London

1979

All volumes in this series are printed
on acid-free, 250-year-life paper.

Library of Congress Cataloging in Publication Data

Maines, Clark, 1945-
  The western portal of Saint-Loup-de-Naud.

  (Outstanding dissertations in the fine arts)
  Originally presented as the author's thesis,
Pennsylvania State University, 1979.
    1. Saint-Loup-de-Naud (Priory). Portail ouest.
2. Sculpture, French--France--Saint-Loup-de-Naud.
3. Sculpture, Gothic--France--Saint-Loup-de-Naud.
I. Title. II. Series.
NB551.S285M34 1979   730'.944'37   78-74373
ISBN 0-8240-3960-2

193277

Printed in the United States of America

The Pennsylvania State University

The Graduate School

Department of Art History

The Western Portal of Saint-Loup-de-Naud

A Thesis in

Art History

by

Robert Clark Maines

Submitted in Partial Fulfillment
of the Requirements
for the Degree of

Doctor of Philosophy

May 1979

TABLE OF CONTENTS

ACKNOWLEDGEMENTS

Several people and institutions deserve my gratitude
for aiding my research on Saint-Loup-de-Naud. M. Jean
Feray and M. Alain Erlande-Brandenburg facilitated my work
in Paris during 1977 as did Mlle. Odette Merlin in Provins
and Mlle. Lynwine Saulnier in Sens. I am also indebted to
the staff of the Archives des Monuments Historiques in Paris
for making available documents on the restorations at Saint-
Loup and to the staffs of the Musée Romane in Provins, the
Musée du Palais Synodale and the Bibliothèque Municipale in
Sens for permission to photograph sculpture in those collections. Research for this study was supported by grants
from the Samuel H. Kress Foundation, in which regard I am
indebted to Mr. C. Douglas Lewis, from the Pennsyvania
State University and from Wesleyan University. Professors
Anthony Cutler, Walter Cahn and Carl F. Barnes have shared
their ideas and made suggestions which, although they may
not concur in all of its conclusions, have helped to shape
parts of this study. Professor Jan van der Meulen introduced me to medieval art. His willingness to question the
fundamental assumptions of the discipline, his advice and
his criticisms have informed my work. My wife, Pat, and
my sons, Aaron and Joshua, provided the personal support
and encouragement without which I could not have completed
my task.

LIST OF FIGURES

Figures 1-4, 7, 8, 114 and 115 are provided courtesy of Jan
van der Meulen. Figure 111 is provided by the Service
Photographique de la Caisse Nationale des Monuments Historiques. All other illustrations are the author's.

LIST OF TEXT FIGURES

INTRODUCTION

THE MONUMENT, THE PROBLEM, THE METHOD

The former Benedictine priory of Saint-Loup-de-Naud is
located in a tiny hamlet eight kilometers southwest of the
walled town of Provins within the diocese of Troyes (Seine-
et-Marne). Once a dependency of the important Senonais abbey, Saint-Pierre-le-Vif, the priory is now a parish church
and the focus of local rural pride. Saint-Loup's remarkably
well-preserved western portal,[1] long associated stylistically with the group of "Early Gothic"[2] portals centered on
Chartres West, has brought continuing scholarly attention to
the monument which the architecture itself could not have
hoped to command. In spite of its renown, or perhaps because of it, only four monographic studies have concentrated
on Saint-Loup-de-Naud and its portal.[3] The excellent state
of preservation of the sculpture, the high quality of its
carving and the complexity of its iconography, however, urge
the new monographic treatment which this study undertakes.
The portal is considered from each of three interrelated
methodological perspectives against the background of a reassessment of the history of the priory and an analysis of
the architecture of the church "behind" the sculpture which

are presented in the first and second chapters respectively.

One approaches the portal of Saint-Loup-de-Naud through a single-bay vaulted porch which is open on three sides (fig. 10). Framed by wall buttresses supporting the porch (fig. 22), the splayed embrasures of the portal step back into the wall to receive six figured columns. Paired across the portal, these figured columns correspond to three figured archivolts which enframe the central focus of the sculptural ensemble: the tympanum and lintel which, in turn, receive support from a figured trumeau below.

Within the portal complex several compositional foci are immediately evident. The greater size and projection forward into space distinguish the central figure of the tympanum from the figures surrounding it. Analogously, on the lintel below, the central figure is physically bigger and projects further forward into space than the eight, essentially mural, relief figures which flank it symmetrically in groups of four; in turn, these eight figures distinguish themselves from the adjacent archivolt figures by being larger in size. The trumeau figure, while stylistically close to the column-figures, which are all equal in size and rigidly frontal, stands apart from them through being noticeably taller and by turning its head slightly out of axis to our left. Finally, the bottom voussoir figures in the two outer archivolts differentiate themselves from

the remaining voussoir figures in both size and in degree
of plasticity.

The vertical alignment of the central figures on the
tympanum and lintel and the figure on the trumeau forcefully
establishes the central axis of the composition and creates
a bilateral symmetry. The distinction in size between these
three figures and those to their immediate right and left
draws still more attention to the central axis. A secondary,
horizontal axis is established by the plastic distinction in
the lowest voussoirs of the outer archivolts and the central
figure on the lintel.

Significantly, these compositional emphases are related
to the three distinct but interwoven iconographies which focus upon each of the three figures of the central, vertical
axis. First, the tympanum forms an iconographic whole with
the eight, essentially mural figures on the lintel, with the
inner archivolt and with the innermost pair of figured columns which carry it. The Maiestas Domini is enthroned above
an exceptionally abbreviated college of disputatious apostles
and, together with them, is enframed by a cordon of the
angelic host; the easily recognizable figures of Saint Peter
and Saint Paul, which are missing from the lintel, appear
below instead as the innermost column-figures. Second, the
central figure on the lintel relates directly to the bottom
voussoirs of the second and third archivolts which, as we

have seen, are correspondingly larger, and probably also to
the column-figures beneath them. The enthroned Virgin at
the center of the lintel is thus the iconographic focus of a
unique combination of three Nativity scenes represented on
the voussoirs: Annunciation, Visitation and Magi before
Herod. Each of these scenes is most probably prefigured in
the Old Testament images on the columns below. Finally, the
trumeau relates to the smaller, animated figures on the voussoirs of the two outer archivolts. All apparently represent
episodes taken from the life and miracles of the priory's
patron, Saint Loup of Sens.[4]

The composite nature of the portal iconography at Saint-
Loup-de-Naud has been implicitly recognized from the outset
and, recently, has even been stressed,[5] but its implications
for the programmatic interpretation of the sculptural ensemble have never been considered. For example, the portal has
been contradictorily typed as both a _Maiestas_ portal and a
Saints portal.[6] This dilemma is entirely understandable.
The theme of the architectural focus of the portal--the tym-
panum--together with its theological preponderance argue for
the former. On the other hand, the visibility of the large
trumeau together with the extended _vita_ cycle in the archivolts argue for the latter. Given the sculptural emphasis
of the Virgin on the lintel, one almost expects a "minority
opinion" categorizing Saint-Loup as a "Virgin's Portal."
Simply stated, Saint-Loup fits all three categories or none

of them individually. Traditional typological terminology
ultimately has to be reconsidered.[7] Moreover, the possible
architectural implications of the iconographic compositeness
have never been explored at all. Instead, the ensemble and
its sculptural style have been characterized as "...une
tranquille harmonie,...une unité si fortement sentie qu'elle
domine toujours l'éclatante perfection de tel ou tel dé-
tail..."[8] Nevertheless, the compositional/iconographic distinctions do raise necessary questions about the physical
and iconographic integrity of the ensemble as a whole. Why
are there distinctions in size: between column-figures and
trumeau?[9] between lintel and voussoirs?[10] between voussoirs and voussoirs?[11] If these are to be explained solely
as iconographically motivated distinctions, then why are
Saint Peter and Saint Paul not distinguished from the other
column-figures as they are, for example, at Le Mans? One
may pose other, related questions: Why are there only eight
apostles on the lintel? Why do the column-figures occupy
the entire space between their bases and capitals instead of
allowing upper and lower sections of their shafts to be visually effective as in other comparable portals? To put the
issue another way, do these distinctions (also?) represent
changes from the original or intended emplacement? Are some
of these sculptures "spoils" reused from another design context?[12] If some of the sculpture can be shown to be reused,

what are the implications of that fact for any possible programmatic interpretation of the ensemble and for its relative stylistic unity?

Recognition of the reuse of works of art in contexts
for which they were not designed has a long tradition in
medieval art history, particularly in the minor arts. The
issue has even been articulated systematically for monumental sculpture at least since Kunze.[13] However, those who
would elevate the examination of the physical integrity of
medieval monumental sculpture to the status of a primary
principle of investigation have been in the clear minority.[14] The evidence provided by earlier studies together
with the distinctions in the portal's composition call for
a careful, thorough-going analysis of the physical and visual structure of the sculptural ensemble at Saint-Loup-de-
Naud. The third chapter of this study undertakes this investigation. It demonstrates that much of the sculpture, including the tympanum, the lintel, the column-figures and some
of the voussoirs, cannot have been designed for their present emplacement at Saint-Loup-de-Naud. (With respect to
spolia, it is important to point out that none of the sculptures at Saint-Loup-de-Naud is carved from stone which is
native to the region.[14]) The third chapter also contains
initial remarks on iconography and style which are included
to convey the interrelationship of placement, theme and style.

The broad outlines of an overall iconographic program were sketched briefly by Salet in 1933: "Les divers éléments s'organisent et rayonnent autour de l'image du Christ-Juge qui s'affirme au centre de la composition. Au-dessous, la Vierge se détache en avant des apôtres, médiatrice, à mi-chemin entre le divin et la terre. Plus bas, enfin, saint Loup represente l'emouvante figure de la sainteté humaine et raidis aux montants de la porte, les personnages des Deux Testaments composent au roi de ciel une admirable garde."[15] The fourth chapter of this study investigates the iconographic program of the portal of Saint-Loup-de-Naud in the light of the physical evidence. The subtlety of the two-fold iconographic program, in which are presented the roles of Christ, Mary and Saint Loup as intercessors and as types of the Church in the divine plan for mankind's redemption, mirrors the subtlety with which the physical assemblage of disparate pieces of sculpture has been accomplished.

The sculptural ensemble of Saint-Loup-de-Naud has always been considered to be stylistically homogeneous. Sources for its style have been postulated in Chartres and in Burgundy. In the light of the pastiche nature of the portal's assemblage, the fifth chapter of this study shows how the sculpture may nevertheless be relatively unified in style and from where the reused pieces, as well as the atelier which erected the portal in its final form, may have come. Sculptures sent from the metropolitan center of Sens,

together with a Senonais workshop, are postulated on the
basis of comparison to surviving works in Sens and on historical information. Implicit in this discussion is a re-
valuation of the artistic position of the city of Sens
during the Middle Ages.

Underlying the entire methodological approach to the
portal ensemble is an exhaustive, rational description of
each piece of sculpture.[17] This "data base" constitutes
Appendix C; it includes stylistic and compositional analyses
as well as the identifications for individual figures and
scenes. To as great an extent as has been possible, each
of the core chapters can be read independently of (in spite
of their dependence on) the information given in this
descriptive catalogue. Readers may want to refer to the
catalogue occasionally as we consider the portal of Saint-
Loup-de-Naud from each of the three different methodological perspectives: physical and visual structure, iconography and style.

FOOTNOTES

NB Complete citations are given for the first time a work
is cited. Thereafter, the author's last name and the
date of publication refer to the full citation which is
listed in the bibliography.

1. Appendix A provides a systematic discussion of the
state of preservation of Saint-Loup-de-Naud with particular
emphasis on the portal sculpture. Apart from very recent,
minor repairs, no evidence, physical or documentary, can be
found to establish (or to postulate) any restorative work
on the portal sculpture at all.

2. The term "Early Gothic" is used here and throughout as a convention to designate that group of column-fig-
ured portals in and around the Ile-de-France which are
traditionally dated c.1155 (± fifteen years). For methodological reasons which will become clear as the study proceeds, the absolute chronological implications of "Early
Gothic" are abandoned herein.

3. Fundamental to any investigation of the portal are:
F. Bourquelot, "Notice historique et archéologique sur le
prieuré de Saint-Loup-de-Naud," Bibliothèque de l'École des
Chartes, II (1840/41), pp. 244-271; A. Aufauvre and C.
Fichot, "Saint-Loup-de-Naud," Les Monuments de Seine-et-
Marne, Paris and Melun, 1854-1858, pp. 139-143; L. Roblot-

Delondre, "Saint-Loup-de-Naud," Monuments Piot, 21 (1913),
pp. 111-144 and F. Salet, "Saint-Loup-de-Naud," Bulletin
monumental, 92 (1933), pp. 129-169.

4. Saint Loup, or Lupus, was archbishop of Sens
during the Merovingian period. He was active about 610
and was canonized for the holiness of his life. Saint
Loup's anonymous, ninth-century (?) vita has been published
in Acta Sanctorum, 1 September, pp. 255-267. A brief collection of his miracles appears in Catalogus Codicum Hagio-
graphicorum Latinorum, II, Brussels, 1890, pp. 311-312.

5. Bourquelot, 1840/41, pp. 251-255, first correctly
identified several elements of each cycle. Salet, 1933,
p. 167, speaks of the organization of the portal's diverse
elements (see below, p. xxi.

6. E. Mâle, L'Art religieux du XIIe siècle en France,
2nd ed., Paris, 1924, pp. 222-223, discusses Saint-Loup as
a Saints Portal (preceded as such only by the southern portal of Saint-Denis West). Later (p. 382), Mâle discusses
Saint-Loup as one of a group of portals (Chartres, Le Mans,
Moissac, et. al.) whose central theme is the Maiestas of
Revelations 4 and 5.

7. A glance at merely the single portal ensembles of
the so-called Maiestas Domini type within the Île-de-France
and regions contiguous to it--e.g., the now-destoyed church
of Saint-Thibault in Provins, Saint-Ayoul in the same town,
Vermenton (Burgundy), Le Mans (Maine)--reveals that the

composite nature of the iconography of Saint-Loup is the rule rather than the exception. Moreover, the ancillary iconographic cycles of each of the Maiestas-type portals are different from each other. To the extent that surrounding iconographic contexts determine the final interpretation given to any general theme, portal typology as traditionally practiced is rendered virtually meaningless (In regard to this reciprocity, see J. van der Meulen, "Schöpfer, Schöpfung," L.C.I., IV (1972), col. 100).

8. Salet, 1933, p. 167.

9. Surviving comparanda are hard to come by, but if the central portals of the west facade of Sens Cathedral and the two transepts at Chartres are any indication, one would expect the trumeau and the column-figures at Saint-Loup to be the same size. See also the discussion of trumeaux in Appendix C, n. 31.

10. At Saint-Ayoul in Provins, Le Mans, Chartres West (central portal), Angers and Notre-Dame-en-Vaux in Châlons-sur-Marne the lintel and lowest voussoirs are equal in height.

11. While there are often differences in size between the lowest voussoirs in a portal and those above them [e.g., Chartres West (central portal), Angers], there appears to be only one comparable example in which there exists a differentiation in size within the lowest voussoirs of a portal-- that of Saint-Ayoul in Provins.

12. It must be acknowledged that wherever differences in size of this nature occur, those circumstances must themselves be investigated from the point of view of spolia.

13. H. Kunze, Das Fassadenproblem der französischen Früh- und Hochgotik, Leipzig, 1912.

14. For a summary of the question antecedent to a discussion of the circumstances of the transepts of Chartres Cathedral, see J. van der Meulen, Sculpture and Its Architectural Context at Chartres Around 1200," The Year 1200, III: A Symposium, New York, 1975, pp. 509-514; Notre-Dame de Chartres: die vorromanische Ostanlage, Berlin, 1975, pp. 13f and 17. The issue has more recently been critically appraised for the Mediterranean area by F. Deichmann, "Die Spolien in der spätantiken Architektur," Bayerische Akademie der Wissenschaften, Sitzungberichte, 1975/76, pp. 3-101 and expanded upon by van der Meulen, "Chartres: die Weltschöpfung in historischer Sicht," Francia, V (1978), passim and "Die Abteikirche von Saint-Denis und die Entwicklung der Frühgotik," Kunstchronik, 30, no.2 (1977), pp. 60-61.

15. Marquise de Maillé, Provins, les monuments religieux, 2 vols., Paris, 1939, II, p. 87, n.2. Thus, the blocks had to be imported whether they were already carved or not.

16. Salet, 1933, p. 167.

17. The author was first introduced to this methodological imperative and convinced of its efficacy in a
seminar on Chartres Cathedral given by J. van der Meulen
at the Pennsylvania State University in 1969. The method
remains as central to the author's approach as it does to
van der Meulen's.

CHAPTER I

TOWARDS A HISTORY OF THE PRIORY

I. Introduction

Like most surviving medieval ecclesiastical foundations, the priory church of Saint-Loup-de-Naud exists
today denuded of most of its surrounding architectural
complex[1] and devoid of any of the monastic records once
kept in its archives or library.[2] Such historical information as survives fragmentarily from a variety of scat-
tered sources cannot be expected to provide a complete
history of the priory.[3] Nevertheless, the few surviving
records merit critical reconsideration; they are collected
in Appendix B.[4] These records contain less information
than has sometimes been supposed about absolute chronologies for the architecture and sculpture, but they also
provide more information than has been realized about the
religious and political contexts within which the works
of art must be understood.

This chapter reconsiders the circumstances of the
priory's foundation, its relationship to the parent abbey,
the great controversy surrounding the relics of its patron
saint and the ultimate decline of the priory. Along the

1

way, points will be made and questions raised to which we will return in the art historical chapters which follow.

For the convenience of the reader, all references to documentation will be made by document number parenthetically within the text (e.g., Doc. VIII) rather than in footnotes. In Appendix B, they have been arranged and numbered in chronological order and are preceded by a chronological table which is numbered according to the documents themselves. When essential to the argument, passages from the documents will be quoted in the text.

II. The Circumstances of Foundation

Evidently either a chapel or a parish church dedicated to Saint Loup was present at Naud prior to the establishment of the Benedictine monastic community which was founded as a dependency of the abbey Saint-Pierre-le-Vif in Sens during or shortly after the year 980 A.D. (Doc. I):[5] the twelfth-century and later copies of the original tenth-century charter speak of an "altare quod est... in pago pruvinensi, in villa que dicitur Naudus, in honore sancti Lupi consecratum, ..." and tell us that the grant was made "...ad supplementum victus et vestitus..." so that there were apparently lands and revenues attendant to it.[6]

We know, moreover, that the Benedictine foundation was made in the course of church reform. During the middle years of the tenth century the region of Sens was

involved in local feudal wars.[7] The parent abbey, Saint-
Pierre-le-Vif, was itself subject to military leadership
from 957 to 974 and was abused by the archbishop,
Archambaud (†968).[8] Reform began late in the tenth century, particularly under Archbishop Sewinus (978-999),[9]
who raised his nephew, Rainardus, to the abbacy of Saint-
Pierre-le-Vif in 979[10] and who, the following year, made
the original grant of Saint-Loup to him. We may assume
that what the archbishop ceded to the abbey was probably
a personal prebend inadequately served by secular clergy
in exchange for which--in the spirit of reform--it would
establish a resident community and "...in eis fideles
sacerdotes ad serviendum Deo omnipotenti digne constituant."
The attendant lands and revenues assured the first monks
the wherewithal to accomplish their task and assures us
that the priory possessed a material basis from its very
inception.

We know, too, that the spirit of reform was a recurrent (and, therefore, necessary?) theme at the parent
abbey. Saint-Pierre-le-Vif was reformed by Abbot Odo of
Cluny (926-944)[11] and in 1149 again accepted the rule of
Cluny although it never came under the ecclesiastical
jurisdiction of that great abbey.[12] We may reasonably
assume that this second reform affected the parent abbey's
dependencies as well.

From an art historical standpoint we can probably

conclude that new building programs were a possibility (financially) for the monastic community from the time of its foundation.[13] We can also conclude that there exists an historical basis to seek stylistic ties with Burgundy.[14]

III. Relations Between Parent Abbey and Priory

Relations between Saint-Pierre-le-Vif and its priory in Saint-Loup-de-Naud appear to have been consistently close. We know that the parent abbey sought and obtained confirmations of its possessions on a regular basis (Docs. III and V). At least once in the twelfth century (and presumably a good deal more often) the abbot of Saint-Pierre exercised his rights of visitation (Doc. IV) and at least by the thirteenth century the abbey held regular meetings with representatives from its dependencies in attendance.[15] There appears to have been at least one instance in which a monk moved from the priory community to that of the parent abbey.[16] It may have been also that the priory was a sort of administrative training post insofar as the first two priors known to us by name became abbots of Saint-Pierre-le-Vif.[17]

We know, too, that (at least in the eleventh century) the parent abbey held the important privilege of administering justice in all its domains.[18] This privilege was first established by the abbot Ermenalde (†1046) under King Henry I and was confirmed under his successor, Abbot

Gerbert (†1079).[19] Given the profitable nature of justice in the Middle Ages, we may consider that the abbey guarded this privilege as long as possible in the face of the ultimately dominant royal power. The privilege is another indication of continuous active involvement in its domains.

Finally, and perhaps most compellingly, among the transactions, exchanges and agreements of which we have record, no examples exist in which the priory enters into any arrangement without the involvement of the parent abbey (Docs. VII, VIII and IX).[20]

Beyond monastic interests in its own dependency, Saint-Pierre-le-Vif had good economic and political reason for continued involvement with Saint-Loup-de-Naud. The priory lies just eight kilometers from the important medieval fair town of Provins[21] which was also a residence of the counts of Champagne.[22] The parent abbey held properties there[23] and, not surprisingly, the archbishopric of Sens and the other major Benedictine abbey in the city, Sainte-Colombe, had dealings with Provins as well.[24] For a see and city of the pretension of Sens, particularly in the twelfth century, involvement with a city such as Provins would have been a necessity.[25]

Each of these evidences of continued ties between parent abbey and priory reinforces the others. It would not be unreasonable to say that in all things Saint-Loup-de-Naud looked to Sens. Given the manifold historical

links of their ecclesiastical structures, connections in
the visual arts may be expected as well.

IV.   The Controversy Over Relics

In the year 1161 the priory of Saint-Loup-de-Naud
received important relics of its patron, the sainted
archbishop Lupus of Sens (Doc. VI). These relics, which
included a "partem de capite et de reliquiis corporis"
and a "particula capsule," were given to the priory
community by the archbishop, Hugh of Toucy, who received
them from the abbey of Sainte-Colombe on (or after) the
occasion of an elevation of the corpus. Hugh gave these
relics to the priory "...pro evidentissimus miraculis,
que per merita dicti confessoris frequentius fiebant in
ecclesia ejusdem confessoris Lupi de No,...". Subsequently,
the abbey of Saint-Colombe again claimed to possess the
entire corpus of Saint Loup and initiated a controversy
that was to drag on for more than two hundred years.[26]

The arrival of these relics at the priory in 1161
must have constituted the major event of the century for
the monastic community and its surrounding countryside,
although we have no evidence at all of how the relics were
received there. The charter of Archbishop Hugh (Doc. VI)
attests to the existence of a prior, efficacious cult of
Saint-Loup in the village of Naud and it is probable that
the priory already laid claim to some, presumably minor,

relics of the saint.[27]   That this was so, can be inferred
from another, somewhat earlier charter of this same Hugh.[28]
The document reports that Archbishop Hugh went to Sainte-
Colombe on two occasions between 1148 and 1160 to view and
witness to the integrity of the corpus of the saint which
was interred in that abbey and which formed the basis of
one of its two major cults.[29]   This charter is vague about
the circumstances concerning the integrity of Saint-Loup's
relics stating only that with this action "...tota ulterius
cessaret ambiguitas, omnisque ex inde aborta sopiretur
contentio."[30]   Bouvier has already made the logical connection between the two documents and held the source of the
"rumors" about the "incomplete" nature of the relics at
Sainte-Colombe to be the community at Saint-Loup-de-Naud.[31]

Consideration of the ecclesiastico-political circumstances within Sens sheds more light on why Hughs apparently
chose to stifle the rumors by providing a legitimate basis
for them.   As the two major Benedictine houses in Sens,
Saint-Pierre-le-Vif and Sainte-Colombe were natural rivals
for power and influence, competing, for example, for burial
privileges for the archbishops of Sens.[32]   Around the time
of the gift of the relics to Saint-Loup-de-Naud, the abbey
of Saint-Pierre was clearly allied with the archbishopric,
being claimed among its (i.e., Hugh de Toucy's) possessions.
Sainte-Colombe, on the other hand, was an independent
monastery.[33]   Bearing in mind the primarily religious

aspects, which should not be underestimated, Hugh's gift of relics in 1161 can be considered also to have accomplished two political conditions. It must have weakened Saint Loup's cult at Sainte-Colombe by dispersing the relics and it must have further extended Senonais influence--in the party of Saint-Pierre-le-Vif and by extension the archbishopric--into the important provinois region by reinforcing the cult at Saint-Loup-de-Naud. One is tempted to see in the role which the monks of Sainte-Colombe played a few years later in the canonization of Saint Thibault, whose relics were in Provins, a response to the cult of Saint Loup in Naud.[34] If the traditional identification of a statue, at present in the Grange-aux-Dîmes in Provins, as an image of Saint Thibault is correct, then there is more than a passing iconographic similarity between the two trumeau ecclesiastics which each stood below a _Maiestas_ tympanum.[35]

The date of the gift of the relics has always been mentioned[36] but only recently has it been directly associated with the extensive iconographic cycle dedicated to the saint's life and miracles.[37] However, the date of 1161 has not been universally accepted as a stylistic _terminus post quem_ for the portal sculpture.[38] Indeed, the date should not be accepted as pertaining necessarily to the portal sculpture at all. As the documents make clear, prior to 1161 there already existed a strong thaumaturgic cult of Saint Loup in Naud and a claim to the possession of some relics of the saint. Therefore, we must conclude that the sculptures can have been carved either in relation to the cult and to the relics already claimed by the monks of the priory, or, in response to the gift of 1161. While there is reason to believe that the arrival of the head of Saint Anne in Chartres precipitated the carving of the monumental trumeau figure in the middle portal of the north transept after 1204,[39] no cult of Saint Anne existed prior to the arrival to the relics.[40] Chartres, therefore, provides no analogy to Saint-Loup.

V.   The Decline of the Priory

Presumably the priory of Saint-Loup-de-Naud prospered during the course of the thirteenth century. Surprisingly, however, we actually know less from this century than we do from the twelfth. Records survive for several exchanges similar to that of Henri le libéral's agreement in 1167 (Doc. IX). A dispute over rights and privileges between the monks of Saint-Loup and the village curé which was adjudicated by Pierre de Corbeil, the archbishop of Sens, gives us an insight into the stresses of secular and cloistered religious life in a rural hamlet like Saint-Loup where one church had to serve both needs (Doc. X).[41] The document also provides information on major liturgical feasts for both the secular and the monastic clergy; but, regrettably, it tells us nothing of where various altars may have been located.

We must imagine that as the French royal house and the city of Paris rose in importance during the thirteenth century, centers like Sens, and by extension their dependencies, must have decreased in relative importance. The troubles which beset France from the end of the thirteenth century onward also had their effect on Saint-Loup-de-Naud. While we have virtually no information on the priory for the entire fourteenth century, we do have records from the first part of the fifteenth which indicate that the Hundred Years War was particularly harsh on it. In 1438 the prior made supplication to the king, who in response wrote to assign "bonnes personnes souffisant et convenables" for the temporal administration of Saint-Loup (Doc. XI).

We may consider the history of the medieval priory to end at this point. The damage done during the Hundred Years War and, later, during the Wars of Religion concerns us only in regard to the state of preservation.[42]

VI. Summary

In reviewing the scanty information available for Saint-Loup, we find historical evidence to expect artistic ties with Sens and Burgundy and to assert that the priory possessed the material basis to embark on new building campaigns from the time of its foundation. We also pointed

out the absence of any necessary relationship between the
relic gift of 1161 and the portal sculpture.[43]

CHAPTER I

FOOTNOTES

1. Ruins of a dining hall (?) and a kitchen (?)
survive to the north of the church (see the plan in Chapter
II, n. 41). The foundations of a monastic structure probably still exist beneath the private house located beside
the northern absidiole, but all other structures have
been destroyed and their precise locations lost. The
architecture of the church and the surrounding conventual
buildings are discussed in Chapter II.

2. It is not certain when they were destroyed, but
the most likely time appears to be in the sixteenth century
during the Wars of Religion. See Bourquelot, 1840/41,
p. 260.

3. Because the priory was a dependency of the important Senonais abbey of Saint-Pierre-le-Vif, one might
have hoped for substantial surviving records there; but
these, too, have been destroyed along with the monastic
buildings and even the church itself. See H. Bouvier,
"Histoire de Saint-Pierre-le-Vif," Société des sciences
historiques et naturelles de l'Yonne, Bulletin, 45 (1891),
pp. 5-212. Little else has been written on the abbey
which remains, just under the soil, a ripe target for

archeological investigation.

4. The documents have been published or excerpted
by Bourquelot, 1840/41, pp. 244-271 (Docs. I, VI, VIII -
XI and a translated excerpt of IV) and by Salet, 1933,
pp. 129-169 (excerpts of Docs. I - III, V and VII).
Neither study however, considers all of the relevant
documents.

5. It was certainly founded by the time of Archbishop Sewinus' death in 999 because the original grant
is confirmed in his testament (see Doc. II).

6. See Doc. I, Comments and nn. 3-5.

7. Bouvier, 1891, pp. 70-71. See also, H. Bouvier,
Histoire de l'église et de l'ancien archdiocèse de Sens,
Paris and Amiens, 1906, T. I: Des origines à l'an 1122,
passim.

8. Bouvier, 1891, pp. 71-72.

9. Ibid., pp. 73-78.

10. Ibid., p. 74. Bouvier describes Rainardus as a
builder, restorer and colonizer, but does not cite his
sources for this description (presumably they are among
those listed in his bibliography, pp. 9-10.). He might
simply have quoted the thirteenth-century Sénonais chronicler,
Geoffrey of Courlon, who wrote succinctly of Rainardus,
"Restauravit monasterium et claustrum Sancti Petri,
monachos revocavit, terras et predia redemit" (Geoffroy
de Courlon, Le livre des reliques de l'abbaye de Saint-

Pierre-le-Vif-de-Sens, publié avec plusiers appendices par G. Julliot and M. Prou, Sens, 1877, p. 74).

11.   Ibid., p. 67 and J. Evans, The Romanesque Architecture of the Order of Cluny, Cambridge, 1938, p. 4, n. 2.   Odo actually held the abbacy of Saint-Pierre-le-Vif for a time.

12.   Bouvier, 1891, p. 113 and Evans, loc. cit. In 1147, the monks of Saint-Pierre-le-Vif elected a cluniac monk named Girardus to be their abbot.   Two years later the pope Eugenius IV wrote to urge the monks of Saint-Pierre to accept the rule of Cluny but specifically exempted them from the jurisdiction of the abbot of that great house.   The text of Eugenius' letter appears in M. Quantin, Cartulaire générale de l'Yonne, 2 vols., Auxerre 1854-1860, I, pp. 452-453.

13.   As we will see in Chapter II (esp. pp. 35,36) several scholars have implicitly assumed that any new construction following the foundation had to have been preceded by a period of time during which the community established itself.

14.   Relations with Cluny and Burgundy were close for reasons beyond those of the rule followed.   The archbishop claimed possessions in Burgundy at Valuisant (see the Bull of Hadrian IV in 1156 cited in nn. 24 and 33 below).   H. Bouvier, 1906, II, p. 8 and n. 4. claims that in the late 1120's Archbishop Henri Sanglier took the

abbeys of Saint-Étienne and Saint-Bénigne in Dijon under his protection, but his source remains obscure. Both the abbot of Cluny and the pope advised Archbishop Leotheric to put the city of Sens under the king's protection, which he did c. 1015 (Bouvier, 1891, p. 78). To return to Saint-Pierre-le-Vif, we know of one instance, which must actually have been quite common, in which Abbot Herbert (†1147) attended the pope and the king during their stay in Dijon (Bouvier, 1906-1911, II, p. 52; see also below, Chapter V, p. 242).

15. Bouvier, 1891, p. 132. See also Doc. III and Comments.

16. This appears to be the case for the monk named Clarius mentioned in Doc. IV, Comments, n.3.

17. See Doc. VIII, Comments and n.4.

18. Bouvier, 1891, p. 99.

19. Ibid.

20. Two unpublished thirteenth-century documents mentioned by Salet (see Doc. IX, Comments and nn. 2 and 3) were not accessible. There is no reason to suppose that they break the pattern set by the others.

21. On the fairs of Provins, see F. Bourquelot, Étude sur les foires de Champagne, 2 pties., Paris, 1865 (Mémoires de l'Académie des Inscriptions et de Belles-Lettres, 2nd series., vol. 5).

22. See F. Bourquelot, Histoire de Provins, 2 vols.,
Provins and Paris, 1839-1840, esp. vol. 1, pp. 65-148.
The main seat of the county, within which Saint-Loup lay,
was at Troyes, which was also the priory's diocesan see.
The archdiocesan see for the entire area, which, of course,
was Sens, lay within the royal domain (See R. Fawtier,
The Capetian Kings of France, trans. L. Butler and R. Adam,
London, 1960, p. 14).

23. For example, the transaction with Count Henri
le libéral in 1167 resulted in the acquisition of two
houses in the city for the abbey (see Doc. VII).

24. For example, in 1156 the archbishop of Sens
was confirmed by Pope Hadrian IV in his possession of the
collegiate church of Saint-Quiriace in Provins as well as
a "feudum de Pruvino." These possessions were reconfirmed
in 1157 and 1163 (Quantin, 1854, I, p. 537-540). The
monks of Sainte-Colombe were active in the canonization of
Saint-Thibault of Provins during the reign of Pope
Alexander III (Bouvier, 1906-1911, II, p. 83), and they
also held property in the Provinois area. See the confirmation of possessions issued by the same Hadrian IV in
1157 (Quantin, 1860, II, pp. 86-89). On Sainte-Colombe
see, L. Brullée, Histoire de l'abbaye royale de Sainte-
Colombe-les-Sens, Sens, 1852.

25. There are a variety of ways to measure the
importance of a metropolitan see and its city: for example,

familial ties of its archbishops; special privileges granted; councils attended. In the twelfth century, Sens ranks highly in each of these categories. For example, from 1110 to 1155 the archbishop of Sens attended more royal councils than any other archbishop (see E. Bournazel, Le Gouvernement capétien au XIIe siècle 1108-1180, Paris, 1975, graphs 1 and 2). On the see in general, see Bouvier, 1906, vols. 1 and 2.

26. The later history of this controversy is traced in Appendix B, Doc. VI, Comments.

27. According to Bourquelot, 1840/41, p. 255, n. 2 the Bollandists "...parlent de reliques données en 990 au prieuré de Saint-Loup." It has not been possible to verify this reference.

28. Cf. Doc. VI, Comments, n. 1.

29. Julliot and Prou, 1887, p. 289 "...beatissimi confessoris Lupi integrum corpus cum capite..." and "...pro reverentia et honore sancti patroni sui, Lupi, ..." (italics mine). The other major saint was the virgin martyr, Sainte Colombe. The two saints were entombed near one another and are frequently mentioned together in documents. See, for example, the Bull of Alexander III (1164) concerning the dedication of Sainte-Colombe (at which that pope officiated) which has been published by Quantin, 1860, II pp. 176-177.

30. Julliot and Prou, 1887, p. 288.

31.   Bouvier, 1906-1911, II, p. 60.

32.   See the list of archbishops and their places
of burial given by Geoffrey of Courlon in Julliot and Prou,
1887, pp. 91-98. Saint-Pierre-le-Vif had possession of
the bodies of the first two archbishops (by legend), Saint
Savinian and Saint Potentian; Sainte-Colombe, of course,
had the body of Saint Loup. These three were clearly the
most important in terms of local cults. Saint-Pierre
clearly held the upper hand in number of burial privileges
for the other sainted (i.e., early) archbishops.

33.   In fact, the abbey of Saint-Pierre appears to
have been under the jurisdiction of the archbishop since
847 (See, Quantin, 1854, I, p. 53). Without attempting
here to trace the bond between the two establishments,
it appears that the bond remained in effect, although not
always with perfect harmony (See, Bouvier, 1891, p. 109,
e.g.). A bull of Hadrian IV in 1156 lists Saint-Pierre
among the possessions of Archbishop Hugh of Toucy (See
Quantin, 1854, I, p. 539 and n. 24 above). The bull of
1157 referred to in n. 24 places Saint-Colombe, however,
under the protection of the papacy and precludes any
bishop from holding ordinations or saying mass in the
monastery without the abbots' permission ("Prohibermus...
ordinationes...facere et...missas publicas celebrare..."
p. 88). Presumably this is aimed at the archbishop,
particularly because the text relating to the election of

the abbot goes on to state, "Electus autem ad romanum pontificem, aut ad Senonensem archiepisicopum benedicendus accedat, _vel_ a quocumque maluerit episcopo benedictionem accipiat,..." (p. 88) (Italics mine).

34. See above n. 24.

35. The identification of the statue as Saint Thibault is by no means absolutely certain. In regard to the portal, see, particularly, Maillé, 1939, I, pp. 191-205, esp. 198ff and fig. 121. The visual parallels must have been obvious to anyone who knew the two portals, particularly if the lost and unrecorded archivolts contained scenes of Saint Thibault's life, which is certainly possible.

36. Since Bourquelot, 1840/41, p. 255.

37. L. Pressouyre, "Réflexions sur la sculpture du XIIème siècle en Champagne," _Gesta_, 9 (1970), p. 23.

38. W. Sauerländer, _Gothic Sculpture in France, 1140-1270_, trans. from the German (1970) by J. Sondheimer, New York, 1972, pp. 393-394, continues to adhere to an earlier date of c. 1155-c. 1160. We will return to the questions of style and dating below.

39. On the Sainte Anne figure, see J. van der Meulen, "Recent Literature on the Chronology of Chartres Cathedral," _Art Bulletin_, 49 (1967), p. 154 and nn. 18 and 19 and "Sculpture and its Architectural Context at Chartres around 1200," _The Year 1200_, III, N.Y. 1975, p. 523.

40. Y. Delaporte, <u>L'Ordinaire chartrain du XIII</u>^e
<u>siècle</u> (SAEL-Mémoires, XIX), Chartres, 1952-1953, pp. 54-55.

41. See Doc. X, Comments, for a discussion of the
relationship between the monks and the village curé. How
long the church served both secular and monastic needs
does not concern us here, but it probably goes back at
least to the early part of the twelfth century.

42. See Appendix A.

43. The gift and its context are discussed again,
Chapter IV, pp. 176-178.

CHAPTER II

THE ARCHITECTURE OF THE PRIORY CHURCH

I. Introduction

Before considering the western portal of Saint-Loup-
de-Naud in detail, we must examine the larger architectural
context in which we find it: the architecture of the
church into which it has been built, and the building
history as it has been written.

The complexities of the basic spatial and structural
disposition will be described. New observations and evidence will be presented and a summary of the state of
preservation given. These will be followed by a critical
appraisal of the state of the literature on the building
history which is divided into two sections: the "monographic," or internal, building history and the comparative,
or external, building history.

The purpose of this building "sketch" does not reside
in the presentation of a new, absolute building chronology:
the architectural history of the priory church has already
received a false precision from supposedly reliable dates
misappropriated from slender documentary evidence. Rather,
its purpose resides in an effort to reconsider the portal's

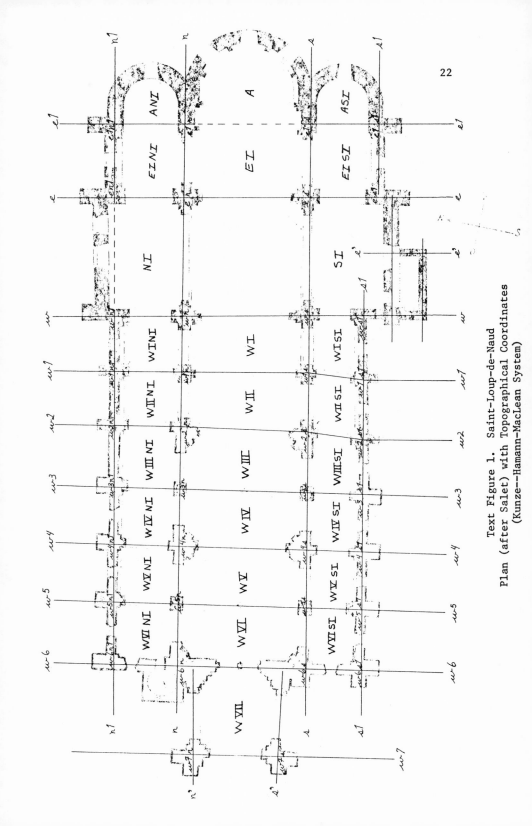

22

Text Figure 1. Saint-Loup-de-Naud
Plan (after Salet) with Topographical Coordinates
(Kunze--Hamann--MacLean System)

context in relative terms. New information and new comparisons will both broaden and narrow our perspective on the actual sequence of construction at Saint-Loup-de-Naud.

II. Basic Spatial Disposition

A. Interior

The priory church of Saint-Loup-de-Naud is a primarily longitudinal, multivesselled structure developed axially around a rectangular, cupolaed crossing bay (text fig. 1, p. 22 and figs. 1, 2).[1] The church is built of petit appareil except for the quoins, salient features and the support members of the main vessel which are constructed of dressed masonry.

West of the crossing, a six-bay nave flanked by groin-vaulted side-aisles extends to a rib-vaulted, trapezoidal entry porch which is open on three sides and is flanked by a stair turret on the north.[2] Before restoration, the irregular alternating support system[3] of the main nave rose to carry barrel vaults above a simple string course in bays WI and WII (fig. 3).[4] In the remaining bays (WIII-WVI) the arcade carries an intervening high wall with blocked, round-headed openings below quadripartite rib vaults spanning two nave bays so that Saint-Loup-de-Naud is today, at least, a hall church (fig. 5).[5] East of the crossing, a barrel vaulted, one-bay long-choir precedes the stilted semicircular apse (fig. 2). The long-choir opens laterally onto the groin-vaulted bays preceding each of two absidioles which combine with the main apse to form an apse en-echelon system (figs. 8, 9). North and south of the crossing, one-bay, barrel-vaulted transept arms project slightly beyond the side aisles and open onto both the aisles and the bays preceding the absidioles (fig. 8).[6]

Returning to the crossing bay, the four massive cruciform piers carry an additional projection on the faces which enframe the crossing itself (figs. 2, 8). These doubled projections rise without bases[7] to simple chamferred imposts from which spring doubled arches. The inner of these doubled projections and their corresponding wall arches express the residual wall of the intersecting transverse volumes while the additional projections and their corresponding underposed arches articulate the crossing as such. Set in the angles of intersection between the spandrels above the doubled arches, doubled squinches transform the rectangle of the crossing bay into the oval of the drum beneath the cupola vault (fig. 7).

The first two bays west of the crossing (WI and WII) continue the latter's rigidly mural form (fig. 3). The cruciform piers, which are conceived as residual intersecting walls, also rise, baseless, to simple chamferred imposts at the springers of the arches which they support.

On the main nave side the projections rise to a cornice
(with which the impost is continuous) just below the vault.
The projections on the other three faces of the piers
correspond to the underposed arches and wall arches of the
nave arcade and the transverse arches of the side aisle
(fig. 4).[8] At piers w2n and w2s the support system changes
so that the original configuration of the main supports
on axis w2 cannot be known for certain. Like the intermediate supports at w1n and w1s, they probably had a cruciform shape, although on the high nave side they may well
have had, like the crossing piers, an extra projection
for doubled transverse arches.[9]

On the lateral walls of the side-aisles rectangular
projections rise without interruption to form wall arches
enframing round-headed windows with simple splayed embrasures and sloping sills (figs. 3, 4).[10] A second,
narrower projection (baseless like the nave piers) rises
to simple chamferred imposts which carry the transverse
arches dividing the vaulting bays.

On the west side of axis w2 the system of articulation changes to a more massive and complex alternation
(fig. 5). The strong support piers consist of an irregular
cruciform core articulated on four sides by engaged semi-
columns.[11] On the high nave side the semi-column and rectangular projection of the pier core rise to the level of
the continuous cornice marking the springing point of the

vaults where they support the doubled transverse arch.
The semi-columns of the other three faces of the pier
correspond to the underposed arches of the nave arcade[12]
and the transverse arches of the side aisles. Set diagonally in the re-entrant angles of the pier on the high
nave side, additional semi-columns (equal in diameter to
those which support the transverse arches) rise to carry
the diagonal ribs of the vaults.[13] The alternate supports
which are either simple columns (on axis w3) or polylobed
piers (on axis w5), relate only to the nave arcade and
the transverse arches of the side-aisles.

The four bays of each side-aisle which correspond
to nave bays WIII-WVI repeat the configuration of the
easternmost side-aisle bays (WINI etc.) except for the
substitution of engaged semi-columns for the rectangular
projections which support the transverse arches (fig. 6).[14]

The plinths of the attic bases of the piers of these
four western nave travées[15] all rest on a chamferred socle.[16]
Underneath most of the nave piers and along the outer walls
of the aisles one can see rough-hewn, irregularly projecting
masonry which does not correspond to the forms carried
(text fig. 2, p. 27 and fig. 19).[17] The presence of this
"sub-structure" material has never before been remarked.
It will figure significantly in the discussion which follows.[18]

Above the relieving arch enframing the western door[19]

Text Figure 2. Saint-Loup-de-Naud
Plan (after Salet) with Pier Widths (in centimeters)
and Areas of Irregular Footing Masonry

AREAS WHERE IRREGULAR
ROUGH-HEWN MASONRY PROJECTS
AT FOOT OF PIERS AND WALLS

27

the continuous cornice separates the otherwise unarticulated end wall from a triforal arcade which opens the
second storey of the nave onto a chapel above the porch
vault (fig. 1). No longer accessible, a small doorway
in the northern corner above the cornice once gave access
to this room.[20]

East of the crossing the long-choir is articulated
by underposed arches set beneath wall arches in the openings to the adjacent bays of the lateral chapels (fig. 2).[21]
East of these openings, the long-choir contains a narrow,
stilted wall arch on each side.[22] Rectangular projections
carrying a transverse arch divide the long-choir from the
slightly stilted apse. The apse is articulated by round-
headed windows[23] enframed by a wall arcade which supports
the semi-dome of the vault.[24]

The outer walls of the two lateral bays adjacent
to the long-choir (EINI and EISI) are each similarly
articulated with a wall arch enframing a round-headed
window (fig. 9).[25] The slightly stilted absidioles are
utterly bare of articulation except for single axial
windows. Today stark and unappealing, these chapels must
once have possessed elaborate fresco cycles like the main
sanctuary itself.[26]

The box-like transept walls, which are also rigidly
mural in conception, carry no articulation except for a
round-arched door in each end wall[27] and a large round-

headed window set just below the barrel vaults (fig. 8).[28]

B. Exterior

From the exterior the visual focus of the church is the relatively tall crossing tower which is articulated on all four sides by an open arcade (figs. 14, 15).[29] West of the tower, the ridge line of the main nave roof continues into that of the two-storied, gabled porch (figs. 10, 12).[30] This long horizontal finds an echo in each of the side-aisle roofs which now extend nearly to the upper limit of the main nave wall.[31] Eastward the massing becomes more complex. The long-choir and apse flanked by chapels terminating in absidioles[32] climb to meet the tower and box-like transept arms[33] (which themselves rise above the nave aisles) at a height lower than the transept roofs so that, seen from the east, there is a sequential stacking of volumes which culminates in the massive focus of the crossing tower itself (figs. 14, 15). At the western end of the church, the central vessel extends in front of the side-aisles so that block-like projections flank the entry porch (fig. 12). An extra buttress, bonded into the central vessel projection, supports it on the south side while rectangular buttresses articulate the outer corners of the side-aisles,[34] thereby broadening the church facade (fig. 11).[35]

Each of the two free-standing (western) piers of the two-storied porch consists of a rectangular core articulated

on the outer faces by stubby buttresses and on the inner
faces by engaged semi-columns (figs. 10, 13). The two
eastern piers attach to the facade of the church and also
carry engaged semi-columns on their inner faces. The bases
of all four piers are articulated by a low chamferred
socle. The bases and capitals of these piers correspond
in style to those in travées WIII to WVI.[36] From the
imposts of the semi-columns spring pointed, underposed
arches of simple rectangular section off-set beneath the
sharp arris of the wall arches which spring from the imposts of the pier cores. These wall arches are flush with
the petit appareil masonry of the second storey walls.
On the inside of the porch, the corresponding pier core
imposts carry the large, simple tori of the rib vault
(figs. 13, 22). Except for the single, round-headed
window on each outer face and the shallow, buttress-like
projection which extends nearly to the roof in the north-
eastern corner,[37] the second storey remains unarticulated
on the exterior (fig. 10).

C. Irregularities: (text figs. 2 and 3, pp. 27 and 31).

Any consideration of the irregularities in the plan
of Saint-Loup-de-Naud must necessarily commence with a
discussion of the site. The church is situated on the
edge of a sharp incline at the foot of which runs the main
road through the village.[38] Hence, at any stage in the
building's history, extension southward presented signifi-

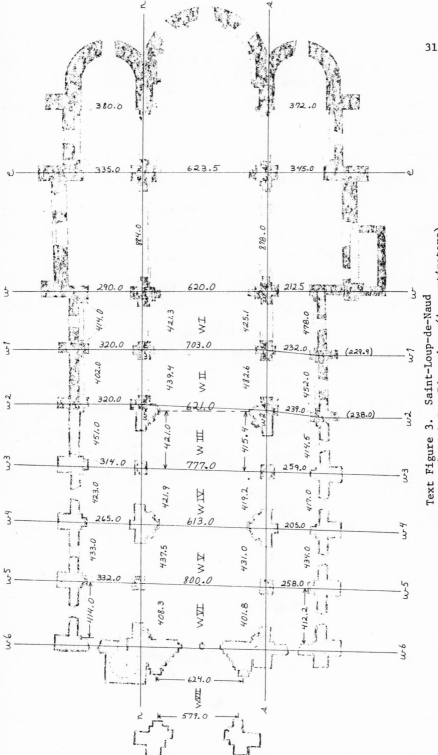

31

Text Figure 3. Saint-Loup-de-Naud
Plan (after Salet) with Bay Dimensions (in centimeters)

cant problems.[39] Documentary evidence, scanty though it may be, gives us reason to believe that a chapel (?) or a small church (?) existed somewhere on the site prior to the foundation of the monastery.[40] Neither this, nor any other, earlier structure has ever been identified with any part of the building now extant, but, of course, may have conditioned the form of the church as we find it today.[41] Other earlier structures may once have existed north of the present church, and may also have (partially) conditioned its present form.[42]

Plan irregularities in Saint-Loup-de-Naud fall into four general categories: differences in size between comparable areas and variation(s) within one area; differences in bay widths; differences in size between comparable members; and deflection of related axes.

The most significant examples of the first category are the overall difference in width between the north side-aisle and the south side-aisle (which obtains in addition to variations in individual bay widths on the e/w axis) and the trapezoidal plan of the tower porch which is far narrower on its western side than it is against the portal (text fig. 3, p. 31).[43]

In a church constructed of petit appareil framed with salient structural features of a rough-hewn masonry of various sizes along the outer walls and rather rough-hewn ashlar in the supporting members of the interior[44]--

all of which was originally plastered--one cannot expect
the mathematical precision of the ashlar churches of the
thirteenth century. Thus the variation in the width of
bays measured in the nave and side-aisles respectively in
travées WIV through WVI (which falls into the second
category) and which is nowhere greater than about 6.5
centimeters indicates an acceptable level of inaccuracy
(text fig. 3, p. 31).[45]

The most significant examples of the third category
are the differences between the size of piers w1n and w1s
and between the dimensions of the eastern portions of
piers w2n and w2s (text fig. 2, p. 27).

Finally, the deflections along axes w1 and w2 fall
into a fourth category (text fig. 3, p. 31).

Each of these plan irregularities is potentially of
great moment for an understanding of the relative building
chronology of Saint-Loup-de-Naud. Each, and particularly
the axial deflections will be returned to in response to
the state of research on the internal building history.

III. State of Preservation

Since Saint-Loup-de-Naud became a national monument
in the nineteenth century its structural fabric has been
subject to various restoration projects. The most re-
grettable of these projects--probably an unavoidable one--
remains the revaulting of the choir and apse and the

consequent loss of the medieval murals. Indeed, the walls,
arches and vaults of much of the eastern part of the building have been significantly rebuilt or substantially repaired. For example, both eastern crossing piers have
been entirely rebuilt. On-site investigation readily
reveals where new ashlar blocks have been inserted elsewhere into the fabric of the building, both on the interior
and on the exterior. Of course, the entire structure has
also been re-roofed. However, in spite of this sometimes
radical repair, the appearance of the building remains
authentic, especially on the interior. More importantly
for any consideration of the building chronology relative
to the western portal the critical parts of the building
(the four western travées--WIII - WVI--and the areas of
axial deflection along w1 and w2 including the side aisle
wall on the south) remain demonstrably unrestored. An
extended discussion of the state of preservation with
reference to archival records appears in Appendix A.

IV. State of (Published) Research

A. Internal Building History

The obvious formal disparity between the eastern
parts of the church, including nave travées WI and WII,
and the remaining western parts of the church (travées
WIII through WVII) has produced a uniformity in the opinion
held about the order of construction and about the dating

of Saint-Loup-de-Naud. From the very beginning of writing
on the architecture, all scholars have adhered to an east
to west order of construction and to dates of "eleventh
or, beginning of the twelfth century" and "twelfth century"
for the two different periods of construction. Writing in
1840/1841, Felix Bourquelot first suggested, apparently
on the basis of form, that the eastern portions of the
church, including the first two nave travées (WI and WII)
were built first and that they dated from the eleventh
century while the remainder of the church was built considerably later, in the twelfth.[46] Only Francis Salet
undertook what can be called a detailed building chronology.[47] Salet argued that construction must have begun
with the peripheral wall along bays WISI and WIISI because,
although the wall there is identical formally with the
eastern parts of the church, its piers, w1s1 and w2s1,
are out of axis with their corresponding nave piers, w1s
and w2s, (text fig. 3, p. 31).[48] Following this "false
start," which Salet saw as a "première campagne" rather
than as a separate period of construction, the remainder
of the eastern parts of the church were constructed.[49]
This work was followed, at some distance in time, by a
third campaign which proceeded sequentially westward to
the porch.[50]

Salet's approach is problematic because it attempts
to deal with only one of the irregularities in the plan

at Saint-Loup. While the "false start" or "première campagne" theory may be a sufficient explanation for the deflection of axes w1 and w2 in the south side aisle, it can hardly be necessary for the explanation of it. Moreover, the theory fails to address the additional deflection of axis w2 in the main nave (text fig. 3, p. 31).

In large measure, Salet's error lies in attempting to account for irregularities solely in terms of extant structure. We know of at least one structure present on the site prior to the construction of either of the (at least) two, major building components which today make up the church of Saint-Loup.[51] We know also that beneath the piers and peripheral walls of most of the western part of the church interior there exist masonry substructures which cannot plausibly be related to the piers or walls which have been placed on top of them (text fig. 2, p. 27).[52] If we assume that this masonry substructure relates to an earlier building on the site and that it has been re-used here as a footing for the present piers and walls,[53] then we can begin to explain the plan irregularities which we find in both the south aisle and the nave.[54]

Construction (of the building in the form which has been preserved) would indeed have begun in the east, but not as an independent building. Erecting the present sanctuary and transept would have required not only demolition of the eastern termination of our earlier building but also some planning and structural adjustment to connect the two building components. Thus, the deflection of axes w2 in the nave can be understood as a result of accommodating the disparate axes of the two building parts in order to unite them (text fig. 3, p. 31). This unification would necessarily produce a shorter wall on one side, which we find in the north aisle[55] and a longer wall on the opposite side, which we find in the south aisle and an accommodation of the travée axes between the walls which occurs along axis w2 in the main nave. Confirmation of this interpretation of the evidence can be found in the dimensions of the nave piers on the axes in question. Pier w1s and the eastern portion of w2s are longer (on their e/w axes) than w1n and the eastern portion of w2n (text fig. 2, p. 27). This increase in size of the two south side nave piers probably served two functions: it helped to mask the deflection in axes w1 and w2 and it reduced the differences in arch spans so that the respective apeces of the nave arcade remain approximately equal in height.[55a]

Although the results of this sequence of construction cannot be said to be pleasing aesthetically, this sequence best explains the evidence and the irregularities. As a sequence of construction, it follows a pattern which may be expected in medieval buildings, namely the elaboration of the eastern end of the church in accordance with

liturgical needs which, in this case, were presumably the
choral requirements of a resident monastic community.[56]

At some later time the older (western) part of the
church must have been demolished (or, have collapsed) and
must have been rebuilt, as we see it today, using the
lower parts of the older piers and walls as footings. The
porch would have been added at this time and, as we will
see, the portal which exists today subsequently fitted
(in two stages) into that structure.

Thus, a reassessment of the data yielded by the
building itself allows us to confirm the generally accepted opinion that the relative sequence of construction
at Saint-Loup-de-Naud proceeded, at least loosely, from
"east to west." However, the actual circumstances of construction were rather more complex than had been previously thought. The utilization of an earlier structure with
parts of the present building affords us a more "medieval"
picture of a site in continuous elaboration over the centuries than the "modern" vision of total demolition and
reconstruction which has always been implicit in earlier
studies. This reassessment of the building history provides no information concerning absolute dates for the
building.

B. Comparative Building History

At first glance, the treatment of Saint-Loup-de-Naud

in comparative architectural history suggests that the
building has been treated in two different ways: by comparison with other buildings, regardless of region, in
terms of analogous building elements (e.g., vault systems,
apse en-echelon, etc.) and by comparison with other
buildings within specified regions in terms of building
elements. Upon second glance, one readily perceives that
the first approach ultimately reduced itself to the second. Thus Anfray's observation of Norman influence at
Saint-Loup in the vaulting ultimately views the priory
through the lens of the so-called Norman Romanesque.[57]
Dehio's assertion that Saint-Loup is the northernmost
example of a church with a barrel-vaulted nave and a
crossing dome ultimately sees the church in relationship
to southern, possibly Poitevin, regional forms.[58] In the
following discussion, therefore, we will concentrate on
the major regional approaches to Saint-Loup-de-Naud and
attempt to ascertain which, if any, adds substantively to
our understanding of the building. In a critical context,
new information and observations will be brought to bear
on the problem.

Perhaps the least successful regional approach was
put forward by de Lasteyrie who proposed that Saint-Loup
belonged to an "école de l'Île-de-France."[59] De Lasteyrie
found it necessary to rationalize the existence and limits
of this school largely because little from the "Romanesque"

period today survives above ground in this region. The
result is an extremely limited group of churches with
which to compare Saint-Loup. De Lasteyrie found himself
with little to say on Saint-Loup save for the fact that
the vaults, in their variety, reveal an "esprit de re-
cherche des constructeurs de l'Île-de-France..."[60]

Enlart saw in Saint-Loup-de-Naud the impact of what
he called the "école du Poitou ou du Sud-Ouest."[61] Although he made other comparisons, to churches in Burgundy
and Normandy for example,[62] Enlart was clearly influenced
by the barrel-vaulted hall cross-section which he saw as
the Poitevin hallmark. As such, its appearance elsewhere
was sufficient to indicate influence. No attempt was made
by Enlart to provide any historical basis for this loose
formal association.

In her second article on Saint-Loup-de-Naud, Roblot-
Delondre refined Enlart's southwestern influence by focus-
ing on a group of Périgordan churches centered around
Cadouin.[63] Here the formal comparison becomes rather more
striking: The churches are three-vesselled hall churches
which possess a projecting transept, crossing cupola and
an apse en-echelon system which terminates the structure
to the east.[64] The lack of structural correspondences--
such as the method of supporting the cupola (squinches at
Saint-Loup, pendentives in the Périgordan churches)--does
not overly concern Roblot-Delondre; her hypothetical

travelling master merely passes through the Anjou, in effect picking up squinches as he goes on his way to the Champagne.[65] Perhaps a more critical problem for Roblot-Delondre is the fact that these three Périgordan churches are something of an exception within their own region.[66] Since they were not major ecclesiastical centers, do they not represent the results of an importation of architectural style rather than a basis for an exportation of it?[67] These problems are compounded by the lack of any real historical basis for the formal links.[68]

Salet, writing in 1933, discussed three aspects. He eliminated, on the basis of formal comparisons, analogies between Saint-Loup-de-Naud and churches in the Île-de-France and the Champagne.[69] He pointed out certain similarities in plan form between Saint-Loup and its parent abbey, Saint-Pierre-le-Vif in Sens[70] and emphasized formal correspondences between Saint-Loup and Burgundian churches such as Ameugny, Saint-Hippolyte and, most particularly, Iguerande.[71] Further, Salet pointed out that a cupola borne on double squinches, as at Saint-Loup, is also found in Burgundy at Avallon and at La Charité.[72] Without disavowing the influence of Saint-Pierre-le-Vif,[73] Salet went on to conclude that Saint-Loup-de-Naud "...est un édifice bourguignon."[74]

Salet's assessment of Saint-Loup clearly provides the most satisfactory results thus far; but it also raises some problems. Emphasizing the Burgundian properties of Saint-Loup has the effect of disguising the relationship between the priory and its parent abbey, not to mention misrepresenting the relative importance of Sens as an artistic center.[75] Moreover, Salet's assessment depends heavily on the cupola form which exists in several instances in Burgundy (while ignoring other building elements such as pier forms, support systems, etc.). This emphasis on extant forms and structures necessarily underplays the role of the city of Sens since so many of its major monuments have been destroyed.[76] For example, while it is true that no known documentary evidence refers to Saint-Pierre-le-Vif as having a cupola, we do know on the basis of written evidence that, from the ninth century, the church of the rival abbey of Sainte-Colombe did contain one.[77] Given the geographic proximity of Burgundian examples, we may assume that it was borne by squinches. There exists nothing in the 1656 plan of Saint-Pierre-le-Vif to exclude the possibility of its having had a crossing cupola also.[78] Thus, without altering Salet's observations, it might be more correct to alter their emphasis and conclude that the architecture of Sens (once) revealed a marked relationship with Burgundy[79] and that this fact is reflected in the eastern parts of Saint-Loup which was a Senonais church.

By now it will have become clear that comparative studies have concerned themselves all but exclusively with

the older, so-called eleventh-century parts of Saint-Loup
to the neglect of the architecture of the western parts
of the church. Norman influence has been seen in the rib
vaulting of bays WIII-WVI.[80] Salet has made comparisons
between the alternating system of support at Saint-Loup
and those in the Île-de-France[81] and between detail forms
at Saint-Loup and those of other local churches.[82] Only
Severens has specifically remarked the presence of the
alternating support system at Saint-Loup in relationship
to the alternating system found at Sens Cathedral.[83]
Severens also summarily compared the capital sculpture in
the two churches,[84] but he concluded that "the Senonais
borrowings did little to alter the strongly provincial
character of the design"[85] (of the western parts of Saint-
Loup). If, however, we carefully re-examine the relationship between the western parts of Saint-Loup and the older parts of Sens Cathedral,[86] we will find comparisons
which tie Saint-Loup more closely to the city of its
parent abbey.

Along the northern choir aisle of Sens, attic bases
rest on low plinths which surmount a chamferred socle, as
at Saint-Loup, and the relatively low and flat lower torus
is similarly anchored at the corners by spurs. A particularly instructive comparison can be made between the base
of the major shaft of pier elnl, at Sens and the eastern
and southern bases of w4s at Saint-Loup where even the

converging incisions of the spurs correspond closely
(figs. 19, 20).

Comparison of capitals from Sens Cathedral with
several from Saint-Loup produced equally striking results.
Within the variety of capital types at Sens, there are a
number which are essentially block-like in form and bear
incisions to articulate large, thick foliation which occasionally congeals into lumps of vegetal form that project from the surface of the capital.

The nave arcade capital of pier ws and the diagonal
respond capital at pier w6n in Sens Cathedral correspond
closely to the aisle transverse arch capital of pier w4s
and to the western diagonal respond capital of pier w4n
of Saint-Loup in the shape of the broad, flat leaves, in
the patterns formed by the incisions and in the way the
leaf tips become lumpy masses which project from the surface of the capital (figs. 6, 16, 17, 18). The twin
capitals of pier els at Sens correspond closely to the
diagonal respond capital of pier w2s and to the nave
arcade capital on the same pier at Saint-Loup in their
almost complete absence of articulation and in the shape
and thickness of their large palmette leaves (figs. 5,
21).[87]

Finally, the profile of the side-aisle rib vaults
at Sens differs from the rib profiles at Saint-Loup-de-
Naud only in the form of the off-setting groove above the

tori:

Text Figure 4. Comparison of Rib-Vault Profiles
from the Side-Aisles of Sens Cathedral (left)
and the Nave of Saint-Loup-de-Naud (right).

Thus in all respects, from plan-form to major architectural elements like the cupola, to details such as
bases and rib profiles, the forms found at Saint-Loup-de-
Naud can be closely associated with forms found or documented in the city of its parent abbey.

Given the close historical ties between priory and
parent abbey, we need not look further, not to the Périgord, not even to Burgundy. Saint-Loup-de-Naud was a
Senonais dependency and its church an expression of
Senonais architectural forms.[88]

V. Summary

In the preceding discussion of the architecture of
Saint-Loup-de-Naud consideration of the placement of an
earlier structure on the site, traceable in the masonry
substructure beneath the western piers and walls, explained
many of the plan irregularities and provided a more compre-

hensible building chronology. A reconsideration of documentary evidence and surviving architectural forms from the city of Sens allowed Saint-Loup-de-Naud to be "oriented" toward the artistic ambience of that important city. This orientation will prove helpful as we consider the portal in detail.

Issues of absolute chronology have been avoided wherever possible. A selection of fixed dates, superficially applied to the relative chronology of Saint-Loup is neither useful in terms of the information which thereby might be provided, nor justifiable in the light of surviving documentary evidence.

CHAPTER II

FOOTNOTES

1. The topographical coordinate system used throughout this study was first proposed by Georges Durand and
improved by Hans Kunze and Richard Hamann-MacLean. See
especially, R. Hamann-MacLean, "System einer topographischen
Orientierung in Bauwerken," Jahrbuch des Marburger Universitätsbund, (1965) pp. 1-35 and J. van der Meulen, "Die
topographische Bezeichnung von Raumteilen und Detailformen
nach dem Koordinatensystem Kunze/Hamann-MacLean," in J. van
der Meulen, Über die Kathedrale von Chartres, a pirate
edition published by the Société archéologique d'Eure-et-
Loir, Chartres, 1974.

2. The stairway is entered through a door in the
western wall of the north side-aisle.

3. This will be described in detail immediately
below.

4. WI was rebuilt with a groin vault in the nineteenth century. The supporting high walls were constructed
at that time. See Appendix A, p. 292 and n. 54.

5. The openings are still visible through the
plaster in the high nave wall above bays WIII/WIV and
WV/WVI. Whether they once opened onto the exterior or only

under the side-aisle roofs remains unclear because the aisle roofs have been rebuilt (see Appendix A, p. 291). It is no longer possible, because of rotting timbers, to enter the passage above the aisle vaults to make a determination of the original condition. Both the author and van der Meulen are of the opinion that this part of the building may have originally had a basilican section. Moreover, bays WI and WII can also once have had a basilican section (and a wooden roof) which was later sacrificed for the security of barrel-vaults.

6. Off the south arm there is a small, one-storey room, which is now used as a vestry. It appears to be integral with the transept.

7. This rigidly mural system has its origin in Roman architecture in structures like the Pont-du-Gard near Nîmes and its medieval continuity in structures like Saint-Michael's in Hildesheim, Nivelles and Chateau-Landon. Van der Meulen questions whether we are concerned at Saint-Loup (and elsewhere) with a rising floor level and, hence, with buried bases. The author believes that, because of the traces of an earlier structure visible beneath the western parts of the nave (see below, text fig. 2, p. 27 and p. 36), this is unlikely for Saint-Loup, but it is certainly not impossible (see also, n. 14).

8. These arches have a simple rectangular section.

9. On the main nave side of piers w2n and w2s there

exists a gap where the simple chamferred cornice in the two eastern nave bays gives way to the moulded form of the cornice of the western bays (fig. 1). This gap also exists in the imposts of the nave arcade and is clearly related to the reworking of the piers. See below, n. 52.

10. Bays WIINI and WIIINI contain no windows in their outer walls, a circumstance which may have resulted from the presence of existing (or planned) buildings on the exterior (see below, n. 14, on other structures on the site).

11. Only the piers on axis w4 present the complete system. Those on axis w2 are subject to the earlier forms on their eastern sides and those on axis w6 are truncated by the western wall of the nave.

12. The impost above the semi-column capitals of the nave arcade extends onto the pier core to support the wall arches.

13. Two small tori flanking an arrissed fillet articulate the intrados of the ribs.

14. The aisle windows west of axis w2 are placed higher than those east of it. A rising ground level (see above, n. 7) or lighting requirements in the central vessel might explain this shift. Each side-aisle terminal wall contains a window: a small oculus in the north and a round-headed window in the south. Salet, 1933, p. 154, thought that the exceptionally high placement of the window

in bay WIVNI was necessitated by the presence of a cloister
on the exterior. Surprisingly, Salet does not mention the
existence of a small door, of uncertain date, located in
the adjacent bay (WVNI). It is now walled shut but presumably once gave access to a cloister. See above, n. 10
and below, nn. 41-42, on other structures on the site.

15. Travée is used to distinguish three-bay transverse segments (central vessel plus side-aisles) from single
bays.

16. The bases themselves consist of a wide flat
torus ("anchored" at the angles of the plinth by spurs)
off-set from a shallow scotia surmounted by a small upper
torus (fig. 19). The capitals of these piers are essentially
block-like with a variety of incised foliate patterns (fig.
6). In some cases this "engraved" foliation congeals into
fleshy vegetal forms which project in lieu of volutes from
the capital mass, but the bulk of the foliation adheres
two-dimensionally to the core. The capitals' original
painted appearance must have yielded a rather different
impression.

17. On the high nave and eastern sides of pier w4s
the masonry below the socle does not project beyond it.

18. See below, pp. 36-38.

19. The flattened form of this basket arch raises
questions about whether or not it has been rebuilt.

20. Van der Meulen has suggested that access may have

been by the stair turret entered in bay WVINI through the roof space and then by gantry out over the nave to the chapel.

21. Here, as in the two eastern nave bays, the pilasters and projections rise baseless to simple chamferred imposts.

22. Unlike the two eastern nave bays no cornice separates the wall from the barrel-vault.

23. The windows, which have been reconstructed (see below, Appendix A, nn. 48, 54), were probably smaller originally.

24. Although this arcade was substantially rebuilt in the nineteenth century (see below, Appendix A, nn. 48, 54) an examination of the first arch on the south side of the apse, which still contains its medieval fresco on the wall within the arch, assures that the restorers reconstructed an original form.

25. In bay EISI, springers of a now replaced rib-vault still exist at piers es and elsl. They may represent either the start of an intended revaulting or the remains of a rib-vault which may have replaced a still earlier (presumably) groin-vault.

26. See Appendix A, n. 48.

27. In the south arm the door leads to the vestry. On the north it opens to the outside and presumably once gave access to conventual buildings, perhaps to the

cloister or dormitory.

28.   There also exists a round-arched opening in the
eastern wall of the north arm above the arch (fig. 2).   This
apparently lighted a passage above the northern lateral
chapel and may have given access to the crossing tower.
Whether it ever had a stairway to the ground (the choir?)
remains unknown.

29.   A corbelled cornice carries the open arcade.
Each baseless cruciform pier of the arcade bears a chamferred impost course from which spring both the wall arches
of the arcade itself and the underposed arches within them.
The arches on three sides are round; on the eastern face
they are pointed.   A second corbelled cornice articulates
the upper wall just below the eaves.

30.   This continuous ridge-line may be a convenience
effected during the nineteenth century when all roofs were
rebuilt (see also below, n. 50).

31.   Less than a meter of masonry appears above the
aisle roofs.   See above, n. 5.

32.   The straight exterior walls of the flanking
chapels contain projecting buttresses on axis el (see text
fig. 1, p. 22).   Otherwise, this portion of the building,
which was heavily restored in the nineteenth century
[see below, pp. 33-34 (briefly) and Appendix A], remains
pure wall mass.

33.   Except for simple buttresses at the corners,

the transept arms are unarticulated.

34.   The lateral walls of the side-aisles also carry buttresses which correspond in position to the transverse arches of the aisles on the interior.   The form of the buttress thickens from axis w3 westward in correspondence with the change in support system on the interior (see text fig. 1, p. 22).

35.   The western buttress on the north end of the church facade has been cut off.   Presumably this was done to accommodate the addition of a low structure in front of the north side-aisle.   Still visible in old nineteenth-century photographs, traces of this structure can be seen on the facade and on the stair turret wall.   Here and on the south side there appears to have been at least one horizontal string course articulating the church facade.

36.   See above, n. 16.

37.   The origin of this projection is hidden by the stair turret.

38.   It is not known if the present roadbed is also the medieval one.   While medieval roads are known to wander, the slope of the hill, which drops off still more sharply south of the road, increases the possibility that the modern road occupies the same place as the medieval one.

39.   Construction southward was certainly not im-possible but, entirely apart from the road, it clearly would have required extra foundation work and buttressing.

40.   See above, p. 2 and Appendix B, Doc. I.

41.   We will argue that an earlier structure did condition the shape of the present building.   See below, pp. 36-38.   Moreover, a rectangular volume thought to be a crypt is known to exist under the present sanctuary. This narrow, rectangular "crypt" is indicated by dotted lines beneath part of the choir and apse in an inaccurate plan published by Roblot-Delondre, 1913, p. 112 (see figure below).   Apparently it was entered through a much narrower passage which extended northward beneath the flanking choir chapel.   The "crypt" bears no axial relationship to the church itself.   Today inaccessible, it was "remise à jour" by M. Louis Delondre (Ibid., pp. 126-127), then owner of the adjacent lands and a relative of Roblot-Delondre.   Cut into the hard clay soil of the terrace north of the church are several "souterrains," or subterranean tunnels, which I have explored through the courtesy M. Hubert Deroo, the present owner.   Whether Delondre found an actual architectural structure, or merely another "souterrain" (the dates of which are uncertain) is not at all clear.   If a souterrain, then some supporting members must be present where the volumes pass beneath the foundations of the present sanctuary. If the volume entered is in fact a crypt, then the building history of Saint-Loup-de-Naud is still more complex than has been thought.   What relationship this crypt, if

it is one, bears to the present church remains to be determined.

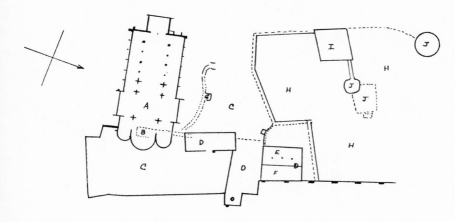

Plan of the priory showing the location
of the "souterrains" (marked G) and the
"crypt" (marked B) (after Roblot-Delondre)

42.   The monastic buildings all lay, as far as one
can tell from surviving evidence and the slope of the
land, to the north of the present church.   Two fragmentary
structures still remain north and east of the church.
They appear to have been a refectory and a kitchen and
were published by Roblot-Delondre, 1913, pp. 140-142 and
figs. 13 and 14 (see n. 41, plan, E and F).   On the basis
of style, Roblot-Delondre dates these structures in the
Gothic period.   The large house immediately north of the
sanctuary, which is now the property of M. Hubert Deroo
(see n. 41, plan, D), clearly uses materials from the
priory buildings if not the actual foundations of one of
its structures.   Presumably any buildings attendant to

the church before it became a priory (if any existed)
would also have stood on the north side.

43. The state of preservation of the bays east of
the crossing [see below, pp. 33-34 (briefly) and Appendix
A] precludes measurements of a reliability equal to those
taken in the nave; however, their exclusion will not
affect our discussion.

44. Most of the dressed masonry should probably be
called moyen appareil, although some of it, especially on
the western end and in the main support piers, could be
called ashlar.

45. The variation between the bay lengths of WV
and WVI becomes insignificant when the two are added
and compared to the vaulting bay which is WIII plus WIV
(839.4cm: 838.8cm). Actually, only WIV and WV are
strictly comparable (420.6cm: 434.3cm) because both WIII
and WVI are subject to externally imposed irregularities:
namely, the nature of the pier configuration at w2n and
w2s and the west wall of the nave, respectively. [NB-In
each case, the dimensions given represent a "central"
dimension arrived at by averaging the pair of dimensions
found on text fig. 3 (p. 31).]

46. Bourquelot, 1840-1841, pp. 249-250, who is
followed by Aufauvre (and Fichot), 1854-1858, pp. 140-141;
G. Leroy, "Une visite à Saint-Loup-de-Naud," Société
archéologique de Seine-et-Marne, Bulletin, 1867, pp. 125-

126; E. Lefevre-Pontalis, "Église de Saint-Loup-de-Naud,"
Congrès archéologique, 69 (1903), pp. 82-85; Roblot-
Delondre, 1913, pp. 119-121 and 125-128; R. de Lasteyrie,
L'architecture religieuse en France à l'époque romane,
Paris, 1929 (2nd. ed.), p. 540 and Salet, 1933, pp. 136-
156. Aufauvre refined the dating from Bourquelot's
eleventh century and twelfth century to the beginning of
the eleventh century and end of the twelfth century.
Lefevre-Pontalis suggested that the western parts should
be dated "vers milieu" of the twelfth century. Roblot-
Delondre followed C. Enlart, Manuel d'archéologie
française, vol. 1, Paris, 1913 (1st ed.), passim, in
explicitly assigning dates of beginning of the twelfth
century for the eastern parts, 1140 for the nave and
1150 for the porch. Enlart himself does not discuss the
building as an entity but does assign fixed dates as he
discusses each part individually within the larger morpho-
logical structure of his Manuel. (Enlart, in the second,
standard edition, 1919, I, p. 497, refined his chronology
to 1144-1178, evidently on the basis of supposed documentary evidence. For a refutation, see Salet, 1933, p. 148,
n. 1). De Lasteyrie puts the choir "peut-être" in the
eleventh century, the transept "presque aussi ancien" and
the nave west of axis w2 between the beginning and the
middle of the twelfth. Salet dates the two parts of the
building from the end of the eleventh century and after

1167 respectively. With the exception of Salet, who uses supposed documentation for the date "after 1167" (on which, see above, Chapter I, p. 5 and Appendix A, Doc. VII), all these dates are arrived at by (usually implicit) analogy to the forms of other supposedly securely dated structures. However, the dates of these structures are themselves, at best, hypotheses.

47. Salet, 1933, pp. 136-156, which can be considered the standard study; subsequently the architecture has not been discussed in detail.

48. Salet, 1933, p. 139, "Ces deux travées (bays WISI and WIISI) sont, en effet, plus étroites que les autres et les pilastres engagés dans le mur extérieur ne sont pas placés vis-à-vis piles de la nef qui leur font face...les dispositions ne peuvent s'expliquer, si l'on n'admet que le mur extérieur de ces duex travées de la nef (the side-aisle wall) est antérieur au reste de la construction." One might well observe that literally commencing with a peripheral wall ought to produce a deflection of axes insofar as a cruciform structure, at least conceptually, must begin with the location of the cross axes -- i.e., with the location of the crossing piers. Evidently Salet was unaware of the further deflection of axis w2 between nave piers w2n and w2s.

49. Salet, 1933, p. 139, "Il semble que la première campagne n'ait pas été menée d'une seule traite et qu'elle

se soit arrêtée quelque temps après la plantation des
deux travées du bas-côté sud, ..."

50. Ibid., pp. 148-156. On the porch, Enlart,
1919, I, p. 538 and n. 7, first suggested that a tower
was intended to surmount the second storey. G. Fleury,
Études sur les portails imagés du XIIe siècle, Mamers,
1904, p. 21, n. 2, who did not otherwise write on the
architecture, argued the piers are "trop faibles" to
support a heavier structure. Salet (pp. 154-155) re-
capitulates the problem without resolving it. Surprisingly no one has mentioned the shallow buttress-like projection on the north side of the porch in this context.
While the issue cannot now be decided, it can be pointed
out that merely raising the ridge-line of the porch half
a meter would sufficiently distinguish its volume from
that of the nave to term it a tower-porch.

51. That earlier structure is described by the
phrase "altare...sancti Lupi" in the priory's foundation
charter discussed in Chapter I, pp. 2-3.

52. The single exception (circled A, with inset,
on text fig. 2, p. 27) is located in the major re-entrant
angle of the eastern side of pier w2s. There, nearly flush
with the floor, a slab, which was apparently once rectangular, projects out of the pier core to within 49.5cm
of the eastern arris of the pier. This compares closely
to the 48cm (west side) and 46cm (east side) of the cor-

responding northern faces on the intermediate support
pier, wls (inset B, text fig. 2, p. 27). This correspondence allows us to reconstruct hypothetically the major
support piers, now seen only fragmentarily at w2n and
w2s, as cruciform piers. The gap between the impost
and the pier core and the gap in the chamferred cornice
above must have related to the now-missing projection.
Whether or not w2n and w2s ever had additional projections
on the main nave side as do the crossing piers cannot now
be determined. Insofar as we will argue that the other
masonry sub-structures--all of which lie, significantly,
west of axis w2 (text fig. 2, p. 27)--reflect an earlier
building to which the eastern parts of the present structure were attached, one must question whether piers w2n
and w2s were ever actually completed in the form which
we find on their eastern halves. The juncture between the
two existing building parts is probably identical to the
juncture between the eastern parts of the present structure and the earlier building.

53. The huge size implied by the projections beneath w4n and particularly w4s suggest a strongly mural
system for this earlier structure and would seem to indicate a western massing above travées WV and WVI. Perhaps
this monumental western termination found liturgical
continuity in the porch which belongs to the structure
which replaced it.

54. One irregularity, which will not be discussed further, is "removed" but not explained by this hypothesis: the difference in width between the northern and southern side aisles in the present building was determined by a similar difference in the earlier structure. The reason for the irregularity in that structure remains, however, unresolved. Any combination of buildings extant to the north, liturgial requirements, the ground slope to the south could have been factors in creating it. Van der Meulen believes the best explanation for the irregularly trapezoidal plan of the entry porch lies in the re-use of masonry from an (earlier) porch of a span narrower than present portal form. Such a porch would not (and need not necessarily) correspond to the earlier building reflected in the masonry substructures.

55. Whether or not the length of bay WIII NI is conditioned by this juncture or stands in need of a separate explanation remains a moot point (text fig. 3, p. 31). Since the masonry substructure terminates along the wall west of pier w2n1 (text fig. 2, p. 27) the circumstances at the juncture between the proposed original (or earlier) western part of the nave and the eastern part of the present structure cannot be ascertained without excavation. Whether the fact that this bay and the adjacent bay WII NI do not have windows reflects an effort to strengthen the lateral walls at the intersection

of the two building parts or the presence of another structure so close in the north as to make fenestration unnecessary also remains unknown.

55a. This latter function was suggested by J. van der Meulen in conversation with the author. In fact, the spans between w1n and w1s and the western crossing piers are nearly equal: approximately 244cm and 248cm, respectively. However, the spans between w1n and w2n and w1s and w2s differ by some 17cm: 275cm and 258cm, respectively.

56. Comparable monastic establishments elaborated to the east include, for example, the priory of Charlieu and the new cruciform church of 814 at Saint-Philibert-de-Grandlieu. The phenomenon was common to major houses like Saint-Martin at Tours and Saint-Rémi in Reims as well. It would be interesting to know how pressing the choral requirements were. Did the monks embark on the elaboration of the sanctuary end of the church soon after they arrived, or only later as their community (presumably) grew larger? It should be remembered that the material means to build existed since the foundation of the priory (see above, Chapter I, pp. 2-4 and Appendix B, Doc. I).

57. M. Anfray, L'Architecture normande: son influence dans le nord de la France aux XIe et XIIe siècles, Paris, 1939, p. 327. K. Conant, Carolingian and Romanesque Architecture, Baltimore, 1959, p. 277 follows this opinion.

58. G. Dehio and G. von Bezold, Die Kirchliche
Baukunst des Abendlandes, 7 vols., Stuttgart, 1887-1901,
I, p. 419, n. 1. More recently, this same notion has been
echoed by H. Kubach, Romanesque Architecture, New York,
1975, p. 210.

59. De Lasteyrie, 1929 (2nd. ed.), pp. 531-545.
Given the brevity of his treatment, it is not clear
whether F. Benoît, L'Architecture: l'occident médiéval,
I, Du romain au roman, Paris, 1933, p. 414 should be
included with de Lasteyrie or not.

60. De Lasteyrie, 1929 (2nd. ed.), p. 540. A.W.
Clapham Romanesque Architecture in Western Europe, Oxford,
1936, p. 89, who follows de Lasteyrie's definition of
an Île-de-France school, echoes but depreciates this
idea by referring to Saint-Loup's use of the barrel vault
as a "tentative experiment."

61. Enlart, 1919, I, pp. 226-227, defined the
region as broadly as possible including Anjou, Maine, the
Touraine, "une grande partie" of Brittany, the Angoumois
and Saintonge. In fact, little is omitted!

62. Enlart, 1919, I, p. 250 and n.5.

63. L. Roblot-Delondre, "Notes sur l'église de
Saint-Loup-de-Naud," Revue archéologique, 30 (1929),
pp. 58-63. On the churches which, in addition to Cadouin,
include Bussière-Badil and Saint-Privat-des-Prés, see
M. Aubert, "Cadouin" and "Les églises romanes du Périgord"

in Congrès archéologique, 90 (1927), pp. 176-183 and
pp. 392-401 respectively. It should be pointed out that,
apart from its own merits and/or drawbacks, Roblot-
Delondre's article sets out with the explicit bias of
attempting to demonstrate "oriental influence" at Saint-
Loup-de-Naud, an assertion which the author had originally
put forward in 1913. Since, even for Roblot-Delondre,
these purported eastern influences are at best several
steps removed, we will not consider them further.

64. Specifically, Roblot-Delondre, 1929, p. 61,
compared Saint-Loup to the plan of Cadouin, the nave of
Bussière-Badil and the "aspect général" of Saint-Privat-
des-Prés. As remarked above, n.5, the present hall church
cross section at Saint-Loup may be somewhat misleading.

65. Ibid., pp. 61-62.

66. M. Aubert, 1927 (II), p. 392. Of the two types
Aubert defines, the Cadouin group is "...de beaucoup les
moins nombreuses..."

67. Can they share a common source of inspiration?

68. Roblot-Delondre, 1929, pp. 62-63, made an
attempt to establish historical connections. Because
Cadouin was a Cistercian house [Aubert, 1927 (I), p. 176]
and a dependency of Pontigny, because Thibault-the-Great,
count of Brie and Champagne, founded Pontigny and because
his heir, Henry-the-Liberal, made donations to Saint-
Pierre-le-Vif and Saint-Loup one can allow the possibility

of "...un point de contact quelconque..." between Saint-
Loup and Cadouin. Such a connection is theoretically
possible, but tenuous links of this sort could be made
to relate almost any two churches in France. Probability
is another matter.

      69. Salet, 1933, p. 148.

      70. Ibid., pp. 140-141. Specifically, like Saint-
Loup, Saint-Pierre-le-Vif was a three-vesselled building
with a projecting tower structure on the west, a large,
projecting transept and a short choir terminated by an
apse en-echelon system. This plan presumably dates from
before 1015 in its general outlines, although the building
was apparently rebuilt early in the thirteenth century.
On Saint-Pierre, see H. Bouvier, 1891, pp. 5-212, J.
Hubert, L'art préroman, 2nd ed. (1st ed., 1938), Chartres,
1974, pp. 32-33 and pl. 1, fig. d. and R. Branner, Burgundian
Gothic Architecture, London, 1960, pp. 183-184. Cf.
Chapter I, n. 3.

      71. Salet, 1933, p. 140. Only Iguerande is truly
comparable to Saint-Loup, having three vessels, a
cupolaed crossing and an apse en-echelon system. Ameugny,
for example, is a single-vesselled hall church with a
cupola over the central crossing bay. On these buildings
see, J. Virey, L'architecture romane dans l'ancien diocèse
de Mâcon, Paris, 1892.

      72. Salet, 1933, p. 143. As Salet points out, the

form also occurs outside Burgundy as, for example, at Saint-Benoît-sur-Loire.

73. Ibid., p. 147, "Si l'église de Saint-Pierre-le-Vif présentait des analogies avec celle de Saint-Loup-de-Naud, il n'est pas défendu de penser que l'abbaye mère a pu envoyer son architecte bâtir le prieuré." Because Salet dates Saint-Pierre to "avant 1015" (p. 140) and the eastern parts of Saint-Loup to "la fin du XIe siècle" (p. 136), he clearly does not intend the same architect for both buildings.

74. Ibid., p. 148. Earlier, Salet modified the passage quoted in n. 73 by saying "Nous verrons d'ailleurs, que notre église, par bien des caractères, se rattache à la Bourgogne" (ibid., p. 141).

75. The relative importance of Sens is a secondary concern of this study and will occupy us in the chapters which follow.

76. A partial list of churches in and immediately around Sens--which, of course, includes Saint-Pierre-le-Vif and Sainte-Colombe--can be found in E. Vaudin-Bataille, Fastes de la Sénonie, monumentale et historique, Paris, 2nd ed. (rev., cor. et aug.), 1898, pp. 176-181 (églises détruites) and pp. 181-185 (églises conservées). Vaudin-Bataille does not mention the Benedictine abbey of Saint-Rémi which is known through documents (see the chronicle of the monk Clarius published by L.M. Duru, Bibliothèque

historique de l'Yonne, 2 vols., Auxerre and Paris, II, 1863, pp. 471, 472 and 516).

77. Hubert, (1938) 1974, p. 177.

78. The crossing piers in the 1656 plan, which are presumably thirteenth-century although perhaps older at the foundations, are of large size relative to most other piers on the plan. Given the other large piers immediately adjacent in the choir, transept and nave, a cupola is certainly not out of the question particularly if the outlines of this plan (and its intercolumniations) accurately reflect the older disposition.

79. K. Severens, The Cathedral of Sens and its Influence in the Twelfth Century, unpubl. dissertation, The Johns Hopkins University, 1968, p. 31, wrote, "If a change in plan had not occurred in the course of the peripheral construction, Sens would have emerged as a Burgundian Romanesque cathedral." See also below, n. 86. On the relationship at the beginning of the Gothic period, Branner, 1960, p. 16, states that "Sens was not at this time (prior to 1180) a funnel to the south but an out-post of the Île-de-France." Ecclesiastical relationships were discussed in Chapter I, pp. 3-4 and n. 13. Stylistic relationships will be re-examined in Chapter V. The entire question, with particular reference to destroyed monuments, awaits re-examination.

80. See above, p. 39 and n. 58.

81. Salet, 1933, p. 149, is surprisingly vague, stating that alternation is "...très fréquente dans toute l'Île-de-France." Although he perhaps considered the church to be subsumed under "Île-de-France," it is rather surprising that Sens Cathedral received no special mention.

82. Ibid., pp. 150-151. Salet saw the spurs on bases at Saint-Quiriace in Provins as "très proche" to some at Saint-Loup. (He did not specify which bases.) He found "frappantes analogies" between the earlier capitals at Chalautre-la-Petite (near Provins) and Saint-Loup.

83. Severens, 1968, p. 116.

84. Ibid., pp. 116-117, "The capital sculpture with broad flat leaves and overhanging foliate knobs refers both to Sens and St. Quiriace." On the relationship between Saint-Loup and Saint-Quiriace, see below, n. 88.

85. Ibid., p. 117. Perhaps Severens was influenced by Branner, 1960, pp. 20-22, who insisted on separating Saint-Loup from Sens and tying it to "...a small group of (provincial!) churches..." including Bellefontaine in the Soissonais and the nearby Voulton. In so doing, Branner in effect denies the "reduced copy" relationship between the architecture of a major center and that of its dependency which he himself articulated for Cluny and Paray-le-Monial (p. 11).

86. Sens Cathedral, on which the literature is large but not insurmountable, is thought to have been reconstructed

in the second quarter of the twelfth century and substantially modified thereafter. Most recently see, K.
Severens, 1968, whose bibliography is largely complete,
although available only in the footnotes. Without wishing
to enter into the fray over whether "twelfth-century Sens"
began c. 1130 or c. 1140, or even to enter into the matter
of absolute chronology, suffice it to say that with a
single exception, no scholar has dealt with the existing
building in terms of its forerunners besides R. Hamann,
"Ottonische Kapitelle im Chor der Kathedrale von Sens,"
in Festschift für Hans Jantzen, Berlin, 1951, pp. 92-96.
Because Branner, 1960, p. 182, dismissed his ideas with
the remark "...the dating of the capitals is hardly
acceptable..." Hamann's contribution has not been
mentioned in the subsequent literature on the church and
the issues which Hamann raised remain unresolved. "Eine
Arbeit über die Kapitelle der Kathedrale in Sens unter
Berücksichtigung dieses Gesichtspunktes wäre sehr
erwünscht" (Hamann, op. cit., p. 92).

87. One might also remark that the eastern apse-
arcade capital of pier aln at Sens compares closely to
the capital of pier w5sl at Saint-Loup in its two-tiered
arrangement, the shape and fleshiness of its foliation and
the depth of relief. [NB-None of the capitals from Sens
used in the preceding discussion was among those considered
to be "ottonisch" by Hamann.]

88. Clearly, the preceding survey of comparisons
between Saint-Loup and Sens is neither so detailed nor
so extensive as to rule out other possible formal relationships: e.g., those Salet indicated with Saint-Quiriace
in Provins (see above, n. 82). Rather than seeking simple
formal relationships as they can be found more or less
at random, the foregoing survey proceeds from the assumption that formal parallels should be sought along ecclesio-
political lines first. Far from ruling out formal links
to Saint-Quiriace, it should be remarked that transactions
between Saint-Quiriace, Saint-Loup and Saint-Pierre-le-
Vif date back at least to 1160 (see Appendix B, Doc. VIII,
sect. C, n. 2). Moreover, a Bull of Hadrian IV from 1156
lists Saint-Quiriace among the possessions of the archbishop of Sens (see, Quantin, 1860, I, pp. 537-539)! One
should therefore expect formal links between Saint-Quiriace
and Saint-Loup. To be understood fully, however, those
ties must be seen in the light of the ties both churches
had with the city of Sens. Salet, himself, moved closer
to this position in a later article on another local church:
see, F. Salet, "Voulton," Bulletin monumental, 102 (1944),
pp. 91-115 and esp. p. 114, n. 1, "Elle se remarque, en
effet, dans la partie gothique de Saint-Loup-de-Naud,
construite vers 1170, ou elle procède des traditions
bourguignonnes par l'influence de Saint-Pierre-le-Vif de
Sens." Throughout this study, Salet finds more Senonais

influence in the Provinois region than he had previously. In this regard he has presumably been influenced by the work of Maillé (1939).

CHAPTER III

AN ANALYSIS OF THE PHYSICAL AND VISUAL STRUCTURE

OF THE WESTERN PORTAL OF SAINT-LOUP-DE-NAUD

I. Introduction

Medieval monumental sculpture exists in an architectural context.[1] It has, by definition, a physical
and visual structure relative to its architectural location. It is the thesis of this chapter that sculpture
can and should be analyzed structurally in a way anala-
gous to the way in which, ideally, we approach architecture itself. Such an approach can potentially yield a
wealth of information about how and in what order a
portal complex was assembled. Logically, a "structural
analysis" of a portal complex should precede iconographic
or stylistic analysis but it should not be conceived of
as prior in an hierarchical sense. Each methodological
approach brings its own set of questions; each approach
produces different but hardly independent answers.

This chapter, then, explores the physical and
visual structure of the western portal complex of Saint-
Loup-de-Naud. Based on measurements and on-site observations, the analysis of the physical and visual structure

treats the sculpture in its portal setting as if it were
architecture. Tolerance limits taken from the "unsculpted
architecture" are used as controls for evaluating tolerance limits for the "sculpted architecture." Using this
approach, it will be shown that nearly one-half of the
portal sculpture, including the tympanum, lintel, column
figures and several of the voussoirs were designed for a
different architectural location. The remainder of the
sculpture will be shown to have been designed for an
emplacement of the dimensions found at Saint-Loup-de-Naud,
not, however, as an integral unit but as parts of at
least two successive portals which may have evolved on
the site.[2]

The descriptive approach to the portal will follow
the iconographic imperative: tympanum, then lintel, both
from the center outward; trumeau; embrasures from the
inside outward; and each archivolt from each side at the
bottom to the apex. The outermost pair of archivolts
will be discussed together for iconographic clarity later
in Chapter IV.[3] Each piece of sculpture will be "identified" using the topographical designations proposed by
Hamann-MacLean (text fig. 5, p. 74).[4]

The following discussion is based on the descriptive
catalogue of the sculpture of the western portal contained
in Appendix C, wherein each piece is described fully and
identified within a full critical framework. Here we

k
n/7
s/7
n/6
s/6
n/5
s/5
n/4
s/4
n/3
s/3
TYMPANUM
n/2
s/2
n/1
s/1
n/4 n/3 n/2 n/1 M s/1 s/2 s/3 s/4
LINTEL
WM3
WM2
WM1
WM1
WM2
WM3
3/n 2/n 1/n n
s 1/s 2/s 3/s
TRUMEAU
3-n 2-n 1-n n
s 1-s 2-s 3-s
3/n 2/n 1/n
1/s 2/s 3/s

Text Figure 5. Saint-Loup-de-Naud
Western Portal (WM) with Sculpture Designations
(Hamann-MacLean system) (corresponds to fig. 22)

will limit ourselves to summary remarks about attributes
and style to facilitate the discussion in the succeeding
chapters of the interrelationships of iconographic theme
and of the relative stylistic unity among these physically disparate elements. Some repetition is not only
inevitable but will be seen to be necessary.

II. Tympanum: Maiestas Domini

The tympanum represents the traditional, western
Maiestas Domini (fig. 23). It consists of five, large
figured blocks of which the largest, in the center, depicts the cross-nimbed Deity enthroned in glory. Each of
the four lateral blocks contains a "living being" or
"Evangelist Symbol." All four creatures are nimbate,
winged and carry a book, except for the eagle which grasps
a scroll. All face or turn their heads toward the central
Maiestas. Lines, realized by blunted incisions, dominate the drapery of the two human figures. Nominally
related to an additively conceived anatomy, the drapery
is decorative in a restrained way and little undercut.
All five figures manifest a strong sense of the block.

Each of the four lateral blocks is bordered by an
undulating band intended to represent cloud-like, form-
less matter. This band, or border, appears to be continuous along its lower and outer edges, except at the apex
of the tympanum where the upper edge of the central block

(the nimbus of the Deity) interrupts the outer border of each of the two upper, lateral blocks (fig. 74).

Comparison with other tympana where the cloud-border is a continuous band reveals that the interruption of the frame above the central block at Saint-Loup-de-Naud is unique.[5] In light of this fact, several other circumstances at Saint-Loup take on added significance (text fig. 6, p. 77): First, the rising masses of cloud-like matter along the outer edges of each of the two lower blocks (the lion and ox) actually extend slightly beyond the horizontal upper limits of those blocks. Second, the undulating border beneath the eagle does not continue behind the ox's head (fig. 75). Significantly, the corresponding border on the other side of the tympanum, beneath the winged man, does continue uninterrupted into the outer border. Third, at the juncture along the outer edge of the two blocks on the right (the eagle and ox), two rising masses of cloud-like matter very nearly touch one another with no intervening depression (cf. figs. 76, 77). Fourth, in comparison to their lower wings, the upper wings of the eagle and the man appear to be truncated.

Comparison with other tympana having similarly formed cloud bands reveals that the first circumstance is unique.[6] The second takes on significance in the light of the third. Comparison of the borders at the intersection of the lower and outer edges of each lateral block reveals that the

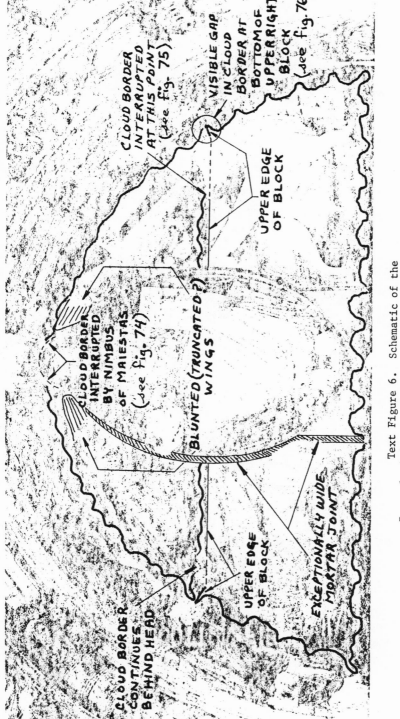

Text Figure 6. Schematic of the
Irregularities in the Borders of the Tympanum Blocks
(corresponds to fig. 23)

border normally continues around the "corner" with a depression in the cloud-like matter immediately flanked
on each side by rising masses (fig. 23). The analogy of
other tympana having similar cloud borders supports this
internal evidence without exception.[7] In aggregate,
these facts strongly suggest that the tympanum of Saint-
Loup-de-Naud has been reduced from at least a slightly
larger original size.

By conceptually increasing the size of the tympanum
by the extent of two complete undulations,[8] each of the
idiosyncracies cited above can be readily explained.
Increasing the size of the tympanum would require shift-
ing the upper blocks slightly upward and outward and the
lower blocks slightly outward (the upward shift of the
former automatically extends the radius of their outer
borders thus requiring the outward shift of the latter).
As a consequence of these shifts, the area of all four
lateral blocks would be increased along their inner edges
(next to the central block) and along the upper edges of
the two lower blocks. The following could then occur:
First, the undulating cloud band could continue uninterrupted above the Maiestas; second, the lower border beneath the eagle could continue without interruption behind the ox's head into the border along the outer edge
of the block; third, the horizontal upper edges of the
two lower blocks would be higher so that the rising masses

of cloud-like matter which now extend beyond those edges
would fall within their limits; fourth, the upper wings
of the man and the eagle could be extended slightly and
thus appear more in proportion with their lower wings.[8a]

The obvious internal and analogical logic of this
hypothesis requires its adoption: In its original execution, the tympanum at Saint-Loup-de-Naud was slightly
larger and must have been intended for a different architectural setting.[9] The decision to re-use the tympanum
in its present location necessitated its reduction and
the consequent manipulation. While it can be argued
that the discrepancies noted may simply represent minor
"workshop" errors, it is ultimately not a matter of so
many centimeters one way or the other, but the violation
of the integrity of the iconography (evidenced in the
physical discrepancies) which requires the conclusion
that the tympanum is a spolium.

III. Lintel: the Virgin and Apostles Enthroned
The lintel zone is composed of three blocks (fig.
23). The central, smaller block contains an image of
the Virgin enthroned whose remarkable accumulation of
attributes, including a throne with a mandorla-like back,
will concern us later. Two tiny angels in the upper
spandrels of the central block each reach down with one
arm to touch the Virgin's throne-back beside her shoulders

and reach up with the other arm which rests on the rim of her nimbus. The central block is among the least well-preserved in the portal complex; amid other damage, the head of the Virgin has been broken off and replaced-- apparently with the original.[10] The two lateral blocks each contain four enthroned, nimbate apostles seated within a richly decorated arcade surmounted by architectural forms. Each of eight apostles holds either a book or a scroll and places his bare feet on a small footstool. The three outer figures on each block enter into dialogue with a neighbor either by pose or gesture or both. The inner two which flank the Virgin are isolated from the others by their rigidly frontal poses.

The figure of the Virgin, which is axially aligned with the Godhead above and the figure of Saint Loup below, is considerably larger than the apostles on either side and projects forward in front of them. Whereas she is realized in front of the block from which she was carved, they are cut into the surface. Blunted incisions establish linear patterns in the drapery of all the figures. The drapery is, however, arranged relatively calmly in keeping with the generally restrained frontal poses. The additive conception of the figures' anatomy is enhanced by a lesser emphasis on a more overtly decorative handling which can be seen in each figure in the tendency to separate anatomical forms into ovoid compartments.

A.   The Central Block

The representation of the enthroned Virgin takes
up virtually the full width and height of the relatively
narrow block (figs. 24-26). Indeed, the breadth of the
figure masks nearly all of the vertical edges of the
block so that the relationship between figure, block and
adjacent slabs becomes difficult to discern. Nevertheless, several observations can be made which question
whether this is the original intended location of the
sculpture. The edges of the block, where they are visible
above and below the tiny angels and beside the throne,
reveal a marked mortar joint (fig. 24). This joint, and
therefore the edges of the block itself, are overlapped
by both the mandorla-like back (at its widest extension
just above and below the throne bench) and by both little
angels in the upper corners.[11] Moreover, in contrast to
the edges beside the throne, which are straight, the
upper edge of the block just below and just above the
tiny angel on the left is damaged and irregular. Addition-
ally, the placement of the little angels behind the mandorla results in their actually coming into contact with
the adjacent architectural forms of the two lintel slabs
(figs. 80, 81).[12] Their resultant "pinched position" in
the spandrel area is awkward. Finally, the correspondence

of fold lines on the Virgin's veil and on her right
shoulder (fig. 78)[13] indicates that in repositioning the
head, it has been placed lower and further forward.
While one cannot be certain, it is entirely possible
that repositioning this head to align the veil folds
would bring it into direct contact with the tympanum
border above.

No one of the foregoing observations conclusively
establishes whether or not the central block on the lintel was designed for its present emplacement. Taken
together, however, they strongly suggest the possibility
that it was not.

B. The Lateral Blocks

The arcade in which the apostles sit consists of
a series of decorated arches surmounted by architectural
motifs (fig. 23). The paired or single colonettes of
each arch consist of a base, which rests on a low plinth,
a spirally fluted shaft and a capital surmounted by both
an abacus and an impost block.

Except for the crack running through the architecture to the right of figure s/1 and some damage at the
base of the slab below that figure (which were repaired
in 1967),[14] the arcade enframing the apostles appears,
at first, to be in an excellent state of preservation.
However, closer consideration of the colonettes demon-

strates conclusively that both lateral blocks have been significantly shortened on their inner ends.

The shafts of the colonnettes at the inner ends of the blocks are slightly smaller in diameter than those at the outer ends (fig. 23). Moreover, they are approximately one-half of the diameter of both the single and coupled shafts of the remaining, interior colonnettes. The six interior capitals consist of a variety of symmetrical acanthus arrangements, surmounted by a complete abacus (figs. 23, 82).[15] Each of the outer end capitals (n/5 and s/5) consists of an abbreviated but identical form (figs. 79, 82). Taking account of their end or "corner" positions, the sculptor has carved these capitals almost three-quarter round so that the symmetrical foliate pattern has been begun, even though it could not have been completed. In both of these capitals, the abacus consists of two bosses framing a concave moulding, i.e., an abbreviated but nevertheless visually complete form.

In contrast, the capitals at n/1 and s/1 bear only half of a regular pattern (figs. 80, 81). The acanthus patterns in both cases are asymmetrical. Were they mirrored, they would produce symmetrical patterns like all the other inner capitals. They are not three-quarters of a complete pattern as occurs at the outer ends. Moreover, the abaci of these innermost capitals are also of the undulating type, but only half of it. The break comes

precisely at the point of maximum convex curvature.
Similarly, whereas the outer bases (n/5 and s/5) are
three-quarter round, those at n/1 and s/1 are only half
a base (fig. 23). Cutting the lateral blocks also ac-
counts for the variation in profile on the colonnette
shafts from rich and undulating to nearly straight on
the two sides of shafts n/1 and s/1.

At first glance, the architectural motifs above
colonettes n/1 and s/1 show no evidence of cutting as
we would expect (fig. 23). However, the motif above
s/1 can be understood as half of a form like that above
s/4, so that cutting it in two would have been no more
complex than cutting one of the twin colonettes.[16]
Alone among all of the structures above the colonettes,
the round building above n/1 does show subtle signs of
having been re-cut. Only this structure tilts (to the
left) out of the vertical. To the right of the single
arch in its lower storey are traces of an adjacent arch,
just visible as a shallow depression (fig. 80). Together,
these observations urge the conclusion that this must
originally have been a larger, probably circular building
subsequently reduced to its present form.

Thus, an analysis of the arcades of the two lateral
lintel blocks necessitates the conclusion that these two
slabs have been truncated on their inner sides and that
they cannot have been designed for their present archi-

tectural context. Comparisons with similar monuments reaffirm these conclusions.[17] The situation at Saint-Loup-de-Naud is unique.

C. Lintel: Summary

Truncation of the left and right blocks of the lintel implies an original, probably twelve-figure configuration,[18] consisting either of two blocks with six figures or one with twelve. Each of the present blocks measures nearly 140 cm., so that a twelve-figure lintel would have measured approximately 420 cm. This dimension compares favorably with the jamb widths given for other "Early Gothic" portals by G. Fleury:[19] Only Étampes (240 cm.) is narrower than the present 312.5 cm. (including the central block) of Saint-Loup. The widest of the group, Notre-Dame-en-Vaux, is only 450 cm.[20] Thus the estimated length of the "original lintel" leaves it related in size to comparable monuments and well below the length of such "Romanesque" lintels as Vézelay, which is approximately 700 cm.

Establishing that the lateral blocks of the lintel are themselves spoils increases the value of the observations made concerning the central block. While it is still possible that the latter was carved for its present emplacement, the likelihood of this is diminished by establishing the composite nature of the surrounding elements.

IV.   Trumeau

The trumeau at Saint-Loup-de-Naud consists of four blocks (fig. 27). The largest, central one carries the monumental sculpted figure and its console. Behind the figure, the stone is carved as a half-column which steps outward slightly to form an undecorated pilaster-like block at the back. A base for this large, figured half-column/pilaster, its capital and impost comprise the three remaining blocks of the trumeau.

A.   Trumeau Figure: Saint Loup

The trumeau figure represents an over-life-sized image of the priory's patron, Saint Loup of Sens (fig. 27). Dressed in archiepiscopal garb, the nimbed saint stands precariously on two badly weathered, fantastic winged creatures. Save for his head, which is turned out of axis to our left, the figure of Saint Loup is disposed frontally, with one hand raised in blessing and the other extending across the hip to support a now-broken crozier (?) as a symbol of pastoral rank and duties.

This tall, slender ecclesiastic figure is articulated within the strict architectonic of the doorpost. To this end, the saint's archiepiscopal garb has been arranged in the symmetrical patterns to which it is so readily subject. There is relatively little depth of

carving and a minimum interruption of lateral contours.
This architectural conception of the figure is varied
only in the contrapuntal positions of the arms (where
the greatest amount of undercutting appears) and, more
strikingly, in the aforementioned turn of the head.
Also surprising is the eccentric placement of the figure
with respect to the block behind it: the trumeau figure
projects beyond the pilaster markedly further on the
right side than on the left.

B.   Trumeau Base

The socle zone is composed of a badly weathered,
cavettoed plinth (corresponding to the sill course of
the threshold), surmounted by a low die and an attic base
(fig. 22). The base profile consists of a large torus
bound to the plinth by spurs, a scotia set off sharply
above and below, and a small upper torus nearly indistinguishable from the upper off-set. This distorted
attic profile continues back over the pilaster section
of the base and, as we will see, is virtually identical
with those of the embrasure bases. The lowest off-set
of the trumeau base corresponds to a course which continues into the embrasures on both sides of the portal.

C.   Trumeau Capital and Impost

The historiated capital, which bears a scene drawn
from the life of Saint Loup, is divided into two sections

(fig. 27). The forward section, corresponding to the half-column of the main block, contains the narrative. The rear section, which corresponds to the pilaster below, has been left in the boss (unlike the corresponding section of the base which is carved to continue the profile of the half-column base).

The large impost block has almost the same vertical dimension as the capital. Its off-set fillet is carried on an enormous chamfer decorated with a foliate pattern.

The historiated capital and the impost block correspond horizontally (that is, they are of equal vertical dimension) to the capital and impost courses of the embrasures (text fig. 9, p. 105). The impost projects unusually far in front of the lintel to accomodate the protruding figure of the Virgin in the center immediately above.

D. Trumeau: Summary

The physical evidence suggests that the trumeau was designed for its present architectural emplacement. It relates to the embrasures and, coincidently, to the central block of the lintel above.

V. The Jambs and Embrasures

Each of the two strongly projecting jambs rises baseless to foliate capitals (fig. 22). The stepped embrasures each contain three rigidly frontal, monumental figured columns[21] which stand on sloping ring-consoles set, with no visible intervening shaft, between modified attic bases and inhabited capitals.[22] A continuous foliate impost extends over each jamb and embrasure.

A. The Column-Figures: Saint Peter, Saint Paul and Old Testament Personages

Each of the six column-figures holds, or once held, an object relevant to its identification. However, of the one female and five male personages represented, the identity of only the innermost pair can be established: Saint Peter and Saint Paul (figs. 31, 32).

Each column-figure reveals a strict adherence to the lateral contours of its block. Except in the area of the attribute, they also manifest little undercutting. The handling of the hip areas and the relationship between arms and torsoes demonstrates little concern for anatomical structure, in spite of the general appearance of correct proportions.[23] Blunted incisions are used to form the drapery of the figures which does little to reveal the body underneath it. The multitude of folds produces, instead, a decorative effect which is somewhat muted by the generally convincing arrangement of the garments. Minor areas, like shoulders or knees, often receive a more overtly decorative treatment.

All six column-figures show evidence of having been adjusted to fit into an architectural context for which they were not designed. The vertical axis of each shaft has been deflected off-center with respect to the axis defined conceptually by a vertical line running from the center of the bases to the center of the capitals (text fig. 7, p. 91).[24] The amount of these shaft displacements varies from 1.5 cm. (3-n) to 2.1 cm. (3-s),[25] dimensions which, against a shaft diameter of approximately 18 cm., seem insignificant. However, each of these displacements takes place to accommodate the widths of figures which are nevertheless still too large for the narrow steps in which they stand (shaving off even 1.5 cm. from the side of a figure--the only alternative--would, of course, have had a catastrophic result): To cite one example, figure 1-n has been shifted forward to minimize contact with the jamb on the right and to allow that figure to pass in front (at the elbows) of figure 2-n which has correspondingly been shifted diagonally backward, away from 1-n (text fig. 7, p. 91 and figs. 83, 84, 87, 88, 89). In spite of these axial shifts, both the innermost and outermost pairs of figured columns still abut the jamb or buttress flank beside them (text fig. 7, p. 91 and figs. 85, 95). Three of the figured columns, 1-n, 2-n and 1-s, overlap the arrisses of the embrasure step beside them (text fig. 7, p. 91 and figs. 84, 86, 95)

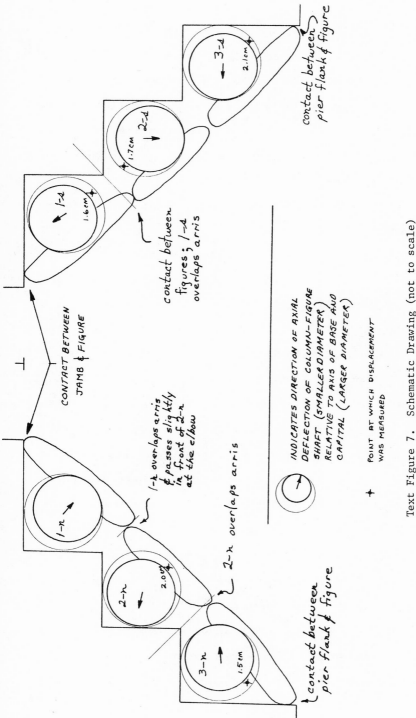

Text Figure 7. Schematic Drawing (not to scale) Showing the Relationships Between Column-Figures and Embrasures

and one of these, 1-s, actually "bumps into" his neighbor
(fig. 95). Finally, three column-figures, 3-n, 1-s, and
2-s, were also apparently once too tall for this architectural setting; their haloes have been cropped to allow
them to pass beneath the astragals of the capitals above
their heads (figs. 90, 94, 98).

Any one of these observations might be dismissed as
an unimportant discrepancy. In concert, however, they
can only be understood as the visible consequences of the
subtle manipulations which permitted statuary not designed
for Saint-Loup-de-Naud to be emplaced there.

Discrepancies analogous to those observed in the
column-figures at Saint-Loup occur in two other surviving
portals: Provins, Saint-Ayoul WM and Ivry-la-Bataille.[26]

The middle portal of the west facade of Saint-Ayoul
in Provins (fig. 116)[27] has suffered heavily over the
course of time. Of this large, once impressive sculptural
ensemble, the eight column-figures have been severely
battered and are today headless[28] but, together with their
capitals, they remain in place (figs. 117, 118). A trumeau, said not to be the (?) original, has been removed,[29]
as have the lintel and the lower half of the tympanum.[30]
The upper half survives but is damaged (fig. 116). Individual figures of the four figured archivolts stand, or
sit, headless at best or, worse, leave mere traces of
their form against the shallow curves of the voussoir

blocks (fig. 125).

The stepped socle of the portal rests on a simple, chamferred ground course (fig. 119). Like the portal at Saint-Loup it carries no decoration; instead bare masonry rises to a molded course which carries the plinths supporting the bases of the three innermost column-figures of each embrasure. This molded course abuts the masonry of the bare projecting jamb[31] and does not continue onto the outer stepped socle below the fourth column-figure, but simply abuts that also. The equivalent course on the fourth stepped recess (on both sides) is chamferred back to the plinth. The column-figures rise from their consoles to terminate at badly weathered, once richly foliated capitals which contrast with the inhabited capitals adjacent on the jambs (figs. 117, 118). Between the inner three figures in each embrasure shallow channeling replaces the arrisses. For all cases, save the arris between capital 1/s and 2/s which has been left undecorated, this channeling, or cavetto, extends into the zones of the bases and the capitals where its sides angle forward to terminate in a point on the line of the arris itself. Between the third and fourth column-figures of each embrasure, however, the arris is retained, visually isolating the outermost figures from the others.

The immediate conclusion to be drawn from the termination of the molding courses at the edge of the third stepped recess and the projecting arrisses between the third and fourth column-figures in each embrasure is that we are concerned with a portal originally designed, or executed, to hold six column-figures and not the eight which we now see.[32] The bases at 4-n and 4-s, which are too large for the shaft of their figured columns and are also larger than any of the six inner bases, also indicate that the present eight-figure composition does not represent the original design (figs. 117, 118, 121). Although these "separating" features have been remarked before,[33] no writer has pursued their logical implications for a revised portal chronology.

Of the eight column-figures, only one today clearly stands on a console (figure 3-s)[34] and no shaft exists between that and the base below. Although the absence of the short intervening shafts has been remarked for Saint-Ayoul,[35] it has never suggested that, for this or any other reason, the figured column(s) belonged within a different architectural context. Yet there is a surprising amount of corroborative physical evidence to suggest that none of the figured columns was designed for their present location.

The axis of the shaft of column-figure 3-s has been shifted 1.5 cm. backward and to the right (fig. 120). Column-figure 2-s also exhibits an axial deflection (at least 1.4 cm.) toward the right. Moreover, the axis of the shaft of figure 1-n lacks any clear correspondence with the axis of its capital (figs. 122, 123).[36] Three of the column-figures have been rotated slightly on axis: 1-n and 1-s inward and 3-s outward (figs. 117, 118). Why this should have occurred is not entirely clear, although it may have had to do with the original size and projection of the console figures. Finally, and perhaps most compellingly, for column-figures 1-n (left side), 1-s (right side), 2-s (left side) and 3-s (left side) the surfaces of these figures tangential to the reentrant sides of the recesses have been chiselled away, or "scalloped out" apparently to allow the statues to be seated further in toward the reentrant angles (fig. 124).[37] The two outer figured columns, 4-n and 4-s which stand in the broader embrasure step have not had to be "scalloped" because the larger space allows them to project further.

Clearly the sum of these manipulations and adjustments represents an accommodation of statuary to an architectural emplacement for which they were not originally intended.[38] Maillé has already pointed out that the treatment of the channeling between the figures makes "...l'arrêt...parfois gauchement..."[39] (for example, the two in the right embrasure beside capital 2/s, fig. 118). One is tempted to speculate whether or not the arrisses were cut back decoratively at the time the figures themselves were added to the portal. It would indeed be in-

teresting to establish whether the figures could have
been emplaced if the arrisses had not been cut back and
if the six inner figures retained their full volume.

In conclusion, the original design of the central
portal of the west facade of Saint-Ayoul in Provins did
not contain, or foresee, (these) column-figures in the
embrasures; quite probably the original portal complex
contained simple shafts like the lateral portals of the
same facade (fig. 116).[40]

Commonly associated with the group of portals surrounding Chartres West, the portal at Ivry-la-Bataille
survives today only in a fragmentary and damaged condition.[41] Of the once highly decorated portal, an earlier
condition of which is known from an eighteenth-century
description,[42] only the three battered archivolts (two
figurative, one decorative), the six embrasure capitals
and one column-figure still survive.

The stepped socle zone at Ivry, which is presumably
undecorated, today lies hidden below ground.[43] The one
remaining column-figure (3-s) fills the entire space,
without intervening shaft, between the base (on which the
ring console directly rests)[44] and the shaft ring of the
capital above. Stark, undecorated arrisses enframe the
figure on each side stressing the architectonic aspect
of the setting.

Although the area around the base has weathered too

severely to be able, on the basis of photographs, to make any assessment of the relationship between it and the console, it appears--from photographs--that the halo has been cropped to accommodate the figure to its present setting.[45] Moreover, one can say with certainty, even on the basis of photographs, that the column has been so reduced in diameter that both the halo and even part of the head are set inside the circumference of the shaft ring at the base of the capital.[46]

When questions about the integrity of an architectural emplacement have occasionally been raised for "Early Gothic" portal sculpture, Ivry-la-Bataille has been one of the few locations for which there has been general agreement that the present condition of the archivolt zone does not represent the original intention.[47] Yet in spite of all the attention paid to the archivolts, only one author, Fleury, has seriously questioned the physical integrity of the embrasure zone as well.[48]

Fleury suggested that the column-figures described in the eighteenth century were not part of the original portal design, but that they replaced simple shafts. He based his argument on: one, the (incorrect) observation that the extant column-figure had no shaft behind it and thus cannot have been designed for a setting (between base and capital) which requires one; two, the observation that the style of the embrasure capitals corresponds not to the style of the portal sculpture but to that of the nave capitals (presumed to be earlier);[49] and, three (implicitly), on his conclusions that the upper zone had also been reworked. All of Fleury's evidence relating to the embrasure zone is analogical with the exception of his observation about the missing shaft which is, however, incorrect: The shaft, as we have seen, has been so reduced in diameter, that Fleury could not see it and hence concluded it to be missing. This observation permits us to reaffirm Fleury's original conclusion that the portal was designed to have bare shafts in the embrasure steps, and not to have column-figures at all.[50]

One general conclusion can be drawn from our analysis of the figured columns at Saint-Loup, Saint-Ayoul and Ivry. In all three portals, evidence of adjustments to an unforeseen architectural setting exists independently of the fact that the figures' consoles rests directly on bases with no intervening shafts. The composition of the figured column unit at Chartres West and Le Mans S suggests that the console form requires at least some intervening shaft between it and the base below. That the figured columns of the three portals in question probably also possessed intervening shafts in their original design settings should be borne in mind when considering early engravings or drawings of destroyed portals.[51]

B. Bases

Although the bases of the south embrasure have
weathered almost beyond recognition, enough remains to
assert that all embrasure base units consist of a modified attic base set on a plinth or die-block which surmounts an independently cut molding course (figs. 31, 32).
The profiles of all the bases are nearly identical, but
the lower torus of 3/n is considerably higher and thicker
than its neighbors. Presumably the same condition once
obtained for 3/s. The first and second plinths in each
embrasure form rectangles rather than squares (and the
lower tori of their bases ellipses rather than circles).
The outer plinth in each embrasure is slightly larger and
more nearly square (and the base more nearly circular--
see text fig. 11, p. 107).[52]

In both embrasures, the two innermost bases are cut
from one block and extend laterally behind the outer
bases (toward the core of the adjacent porch pier).[53]
Although they correspond in height to the coursing of the
jambs (text fig. 9, p.105), the two base blocks are not
bonded into them (text fig. 8, p. 100). The correspondence
in coursing heights, in spite of the absence of bonding,
relates the blocks directly to their present architectural
context and, with the socles below them, fixes the absolute dimensions of the stepped recesses of the embrasures.
The outer bases (3/n and 3/s) are each cut from separate

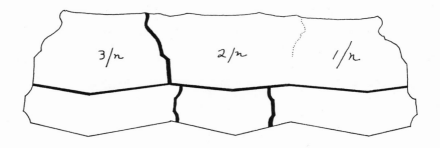

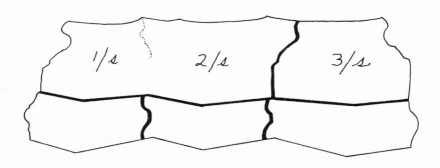

Text Figure 8.   The Configuration
of the Base and Moulding Courses

stones and are also not bonded into the masonry of the
pier mass (text fig. 8, p.100).

Stoddard--the only other author to discuss the
"architectural system" of the portal--points out that the
overlapping course technique used here is the same one
used, for example, at Chartres West, Saint-Denis, and
Le Mans.[54] In principle this is true. Yet within the
system, all courses must be bonded into an adjacent wall
mass (alternately, toward the jambs and toward the projecting facade buttresses) as they do at Chartres West,
for example. That none of the bases at Saint-Loup do so
is a structural anomaly. They can only be explained by
the chronological relationship between portal and porch
posited in the discussion of the architecture of the
embrasures below.

The molded course immediately below the bases and
plinths is separate from them. In each embrasure the
course consists of three separate blocks although their
size and direction of bonding into embrasure core varies.
In the north embrasure the blocks below 3/n and 1/n penetrate into the embrasure core behind the (smaller) block
below 2/n. In the south embrasure the blocks below 2/s
and 3/s both penetrate toward the jamb (text fig. 8,
p.100). Thus in each embrasure one block of the molding
course remains entirely unbonded thereby creating the same
structurally anomalous situation as we find in the base

blocks above. As with the bases, this anomaly will be discussed below.

C. Jamb Capitals

The capitals which surmount the undecorated jambs are each cut from two blocks which include the astragal at their base and the abacus which surmounts them (figs. 33, 34). The larger of the two blocks includes the jamb face and outer two-thirds of the capital. The second block is a narrow filler which is inserted between the first block and the inner edge of the capitals n/1 and s/1 (which extend onto the jamb). The "filler-block" on each side matches the foliation of the main block so that there is no reason to suppose anything but design unity.

D. Embrasure Capitals

Composite beasts inhabit all six capitals (figs. 33, 34). As in the base blocks below, the innermost pair of capitals in each embrasure are carved from the same block. The outermost capitals are separate. The carving itself is continuous only from the jamb surfaces through the innermost capitals in each embrasure. Stark arrisses separate the capitals between the stepped recesses.

The fact that the innermost pairs of capitals are carved from a single block fixes their relationship to each other and to stepped recesses of the dimensions found at Saint-Loup. As the abaci reveal, the capitals also reflect the rectangular and square "plans" found in the bases below (cf. text fig. 11, p.107). On their outer sides, all six abaci bear three bosses and two concavities. On the inner sides of the four innermost capitals, the abaci bear two bosses and one concavity, thus reflecting their rectangular configuration. The abaci of the two outermost capitals also bear two bosses and one concavity on their inner faces, but the concavity has been attenuated to reflect these capitals' more nearly square plan.[55]

E. Imposts

The physical composition of the foliate impost course is identical in both embrasures (figs. 33, 34). Two large blocks, each extending over two capitals are separated by a small, narrow filler-block set above the outer face of the innermost capital of each embrasure. On the north, the filler-block continues the foliate patterns on either side of it; on the south, it relates only to the inner impost block. Like the capitals below, the impost blocks, by extending over more than one embrasure step, relate directly to the embrasure dimensions found at Saint-Loup.

F. The Architecture of the Embrasures

In considering the architecture of the portal and its surrounding porch it will be recalled that it has been customary to argue that the western nave bays, the portal and the porch constitute a design entity constructed sequentially from the east.[56] Exceptionally, the Marquise de Maillé argued that the "...portail (i.e., its sculpture) fut encastré après coup sous un porche à moitié erigé..."[57] To support this conclusion, she cited the irregularity in the southern porch pier coursing at the level of the capital and suggested an irregularity in the coursing at the level of the base block as well.[58] Surprisingly, the implications of Maillé's observations have never been considered. A precise analysis of the masonry relationships within the embrasures and between the embrasures and the porch piers will confirm Maillé's ideas (although for different reasons) and will go beyond them to yield new information leading, as we will see at the end of the chapter, to a reformulated relative chronology for these parts of the building.

The embrasures are composed of dressed ashlar so finely constructed that, in some cases, the amount of mortar between the blocks is less than half a centimeter. Within the embrasures themselves, the running dimensions, across the full width of each splay from jamb to outermost step, never vary more than 0.9 cm. within any given course.[59] The maximum variation between any two courses taken together, again across the full width of each splay, is $\pm$ 0.35 cm. (text fig. 9, p.105).

In the light of this remarkable consistency within

Text Figure 9. Running Dimensions
(in centimeters) of Rising Portal
Masonry (corresponds to fig. 22)

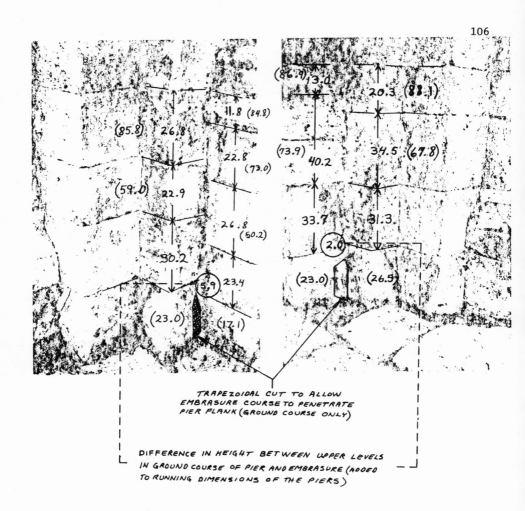

Text Figure 10. Juncture Between
Porch Piers and Portal Embrasures
at the Socle Zone

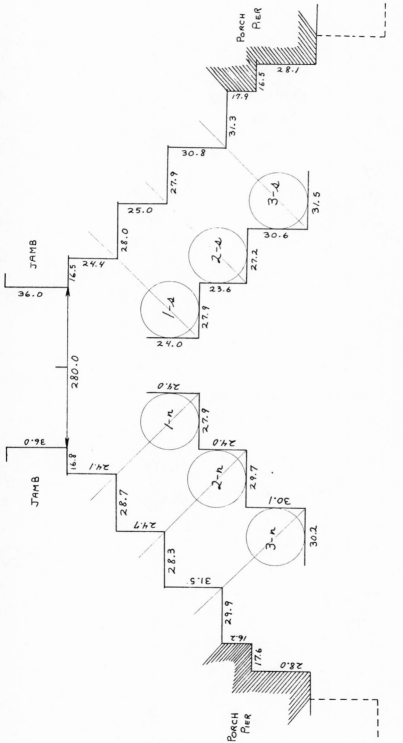

Text Figure 11. Plan of the Portal
(at a height of approximately 0.5M; not to scale)
All Dimensions in Centimeters
Inset Shows Plinths Below Column-Figures

the embrasures, differences in course heights of $\pm$ 2.0 cm.
between the outermost stepped recesses and their adjacent
pier flanks should probably be considered to be significant. On the north, only the third, fifth and ninth
courses can be said to correspond in height,[60] while, on
the south, the first, (third), fourth, fifth, eleventh
and fourteenth correspond.[61] Thus, the running dimensions
present an anomalous picture: On each side of the portal
are two "walls" which appear to be unrelated, but between
which occasional courses do correspond in height. It is
perhaps not coincidence that two of the courses which
correspond on the north are also among those which correspond on the south (third, fifth).

It has been remarked that the base blocks and molding courses at 3-n and 3-s are not bonded into their adjacent pier flanks (text fig. 10, p.106). In fact, none of
the courses in either socle zone (above the sill, or
ground, course) bonds with the pier flanks even though,
on the south, the first courses of each correspond in
height (text fig. 10, p. 106). Moreover, in the sill course
of both pier flanks, a trapezoidal aperture was cut out
(and later wedged shut)., evidently to allow the masons to
work the sill of the embrasure into an already existing
pier mass (figs. 106, 108).[62] Finally, at the capital
level of the south side, courses, which by virtue of their
dimensions (#12-#14), can be said to "originate" in the

jambs, have been inserted into the pier flank with which they do not correspond, thus confirming that even at this level, the embrasure is unrelated to the pier (text fig. 9, p. 105).[63]

Formal evidence produces similar results. No continuity exists between the chamferred ground course of the porch piers and the unarticulated embrasure socles which they simply abut.

Thus, a careful analysis of the fabric of the embrasures in relation to the porch piers suggests that the two were not planned or erected as a single entity and that the porch antedates the portal which was later inserted into it.[64] From the occasional correspondence in coursing heights,[65] it would seem that the masons felt obliged to "anchor" their portal to the piers; presumably, where there is correspondence in course heights, behind column-figures 3-n and 3-s, the embrasures bond into the piers analogously as they are inserted into the pier at the capital level on the south.

VI. Archivolt WMl: Angels and Agnus Dei

The first, or innermost, archivolt at Saint-Loup contains ten standing angels in varied poses of rest and animation and an *Agnus Dei* on the keystone at the apex (fig. 23). All of the angels are nimbate,[66] winged and barefooted. Each holds a liturgical object as an attri-

bute and turns inward toward the tympanum. Except for the
angels at the bottom on each side of the archivolt, which
stand on small convex consoles, each angel stands upon a
small undulant mass of cloud-like matter. Each angel
wears two garments: a long-sleeved, ankle-length tunic
and an outer mantle draped over one or both shoulders and
gathered at the waist to hang downward across the legs.

Stylistically, the angels form a coherent group
which combine idealized, abstract elements with more
naturalistic ones. Drapery seldom reveals anatomy and
although primarily linear and decorative remains restrained. Poses, although sometimes animated are usually
also restrained in their movement.

None of the angels, nor the Agnus Dei on the keystone, exhibit any evidence of recutting or cropping in
order to emplace them. None of the blocks reveals any
adjustments either. Thus, the entire archivolt was evidently made for its present emplacement.

VII. Archivolts WM2 and WM3: Nativity and Saint Loup Cycles
The second and third archivolts must be described
together because of the distribution of their iconographic
elements (fig. 22). The archivolts contain two separate
iconographic cycles. The four voussoirs at the bottom of
the archivolts contain three scenes of an abbreviated
Nativity cycle: Annunciation, Visitation and Magi Before

Herod. The remaining voussoirs, including the keystones,
contain images which apparently derive from the vita of
Saint Loup.[67] This latter cycle can be divided into two
groups: (1) narrative scenes which spread across two or
more adjacent voussoirs and (2) individual, isolated
images which relate to vita episodes in a more symbolic
way. However, of the sixteen scenes and figures, the
identity of only seven can be established with two more
being probable but not certain; four can be plausibly
connected with the vita but four remain entirely unidentified.[68]

All the figures in these archivolts share a number
of formal features. The usually short-waisted, flat-
chested figures show little concern for anatomical structure, as is evidenced in the additive handling of the hip
areas. The linear drapery, which is formed by blunted
incisions, is generally arranged calmly and masks the
body rather than reveals it. Where the body breaks through,
in minor areas, the handling of the folds becomes more
decorative. However, there are also sharp formal differences between the two iconographic groups: The figures of
the Nativity cycle distinguish themselves from the other
voussoirs (and from the angels in the first archivolt) in
their scale, their degree of plasticity and, to a lesser
extent, their more static poses.

For both iconographic and compositional reasons we

will discuss the two cycles separately, beginning with the Nativity scenes.

A. The Nativity Cycle

The voussoir blocks which represent the Annunciation (WM3-n/1, fig. 46), the Visitation (WM2-n/1, fig. 47) and the Magi Before Herod (WM2-s/1 and WM3-s/1, figs. 61, 62) are all too large for their architectural setting. Entirely apart from differences in scale and plasticity relative to the other voussoirs, which could be attributed to an iconographic intention, it is their relationship to the impost blocks beneath them which establishes their spoliate nature. In the Annunciation voussoir, the base on which the figures stand projects slightly beyond the outer face of the impost block and the figure on the left projects even further (figs. 102, 103).[69] In the adjacent Visitation voussoir even more pronounced projections occur (fig. 102).[70] For the two Magi voussoirs, the evidence is even more compelling. On both blocks, the figures' bases project slightly beyond the outer faces of the imposts and the figures on the right of each voussoir project noticeably further (figs. 104, 105).[71] On the inner faces of the imposts, the bases on which the figures stand have been "planed off" flush with the edge of the block, but the figures' feet, which are now broken off, once clearly projected beyond the impost on the inside also (figs. 61, 62).

Not only are the projections of these voussoirs beyond the limits of their impost blocks--the conceptual limit of the cubic space available for any voussoir-- without parallel elsewhere in this portal's archivolts, the projections are without parallel in any voussoir of any comparable figured portal. We must therefore conclude that these four blocks were designed to be emplaced in a larger setting and later re-employed at Saint-Loup.

B. The Saint Loup Cycle

With the exception of one and possibly both keystones, each of the voussoirs of the Saint Loup cycle has evidently been designed for its present emplacement in this portal. All of the figures represented fit comfortably within the limits of their voussoirs. None of the blocks shows any signs of cropping or manipulation (figs. 48-55, 57-59, 63-73).

The keystone of the second archivolt contains a Manus Dei set against a cruciform nimbus (fig. 56). The large, blessing right hand issues from a stylised undulant cloud mass and, uniquely among Manus Dei keystones,[72] projects diagonally downward to the left so that it relates iconographically to the adjacent voussoir (and not to the tympanum).[73] Both sides of the block angle sharply away from the ends of the adjacent voussoirs, leaving clearly visible an increasingly wider mortar joint toward the soffit of the archivolt. Moreover, the intrados of the keystone is cut at a steeper angle than the extrados of the keystone of the first archivolt below it. These relationships clearly indicate that this keystone was designed for an archivolt of steeper pitch than the one in which it has been emplaced at Saint-Loup (text fig. 12, p. 115).[74]

The keystone of the third archivolt contains two bustate, winged angels which protrude from an undulant cloud mass to hold a banderole in front of their chests (fig. 60). Iconographically, this block belongs with the image of the saint on horseback represented on the voussoir to the left.[75] The block has been damaged and repaired, apparently in stone, along the lower left side. The repair continues the undulations of the cloud mass, but it does not repeat the pattern on the right side of the block, which rises higher. Moreover, it is not clear whether the lateral limit of the keystone on the left would have provided sufficient space to repeat the pattern symmetrically. Thus, this keystone may have been designed for another emplacement, trimmed slightly, damaged and repaired.[76] Alternately, the block may never have been absolutely symmetrical and may simply have been damaged and repaired in the process of erecting this archivolt for which it would have been designed.

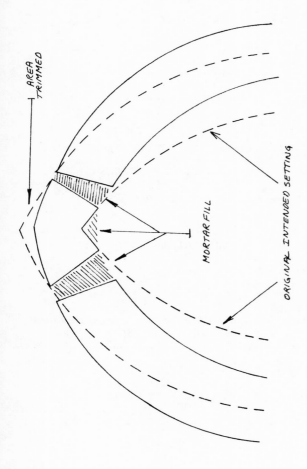

Text Figure 12. Exaggerated Diagram of the
Relationship Between WM2-k and its
Adjacent Voussoirs

VIII. The Architecture of the Upper Zone of the Portal

The massive, complex porch piers rise to profiled imposts from which spring the large tori of the ribbed vault (fig. 13, 22). The portal is enframed, beneath the eastern quadrant of the vault, by a fourth, molded archivolt articulated by a simple cyma profile set off beneath a flat fillet. This archivolt does not continue downward to the imposts but, instead, makes abrupt, awkward right-angle terminations behind the tori at the level of WM3-n/3 and WM3-s/3. We must now consider how the porch above the imposts relates to the portal which we saw, at the lower level, to have been inserted within it.

Surprisingly, the architecture of the upper zone of the porch (and its juncture with the portal) has received more attention than the lower zones. Salet suggested that the porch was designed to carry a groin vault because the ribs "...vient retomber gauchement dans l'angle de deux ressauts des supports..."[77] (cf. fig. 22) and because "...aucun membre d'architecture n'a été prévu pour le(s) recevoir."[78] Based on Salet's observations, Maillé hypothesized that "C'est sans doute au moment de monter le portail que l'architecte changea de parti et que l'actuelle voûte sur croisée d'ogives fut mise en place au-dessus de porche."[79] Salet is certainly right that the porch was not designed to carry rib vaults: In addition to the relation-

ship between ribs and imposts cited by Salet, the raised
fillet, or rectangular underlay, behind the rib tori had
to be suppressed on the sides to allow the tori to fit
into the reentrant angle of the porch arcade (fig. 13,
22). It does not, however, necessarily follow that the
porch was designed to carry a groin vault. Equally, it
could have had a wooden roof.[80] Maillé's hypothesis that
the rib vault was added at the time the portal was built
also seems unlikely. Below the abrupt terminations of
the molded archivolt are narrow triangular areas of rough
mortar fill (fig. 22). These areas would seem to indicate
that the molded archivolt once did continue to the level
of the imposts and that it has been cut back to accomodate
the later insertion of the ribs. Thus, it appears evident
that the present portal was erected before the present
vaulting was added. What the closure was at that time remains unknown.

IX. Conclusion

In summary we have seen that many of the sculptures
from the portal of Saint-Loup-de-Naud are spolia: The
tympanum was originally (at least) slightly larger; the
lateral blocks of the lintel once formed part of a twelve-
(or, perhaps ten-) figure lintel and the central block
was probably also intended for a different setting; the

column-figures and the four voussoirs at the bottom of
the two outer archivolts were all executed for a larger
setting and, finally, the keystone of the second archivolt was carved for an archivolt of steeper pitch. In
contrast the trumeau and the remainder of the voussoirs
(with the possible exception of the keystone of the third
archivolt) all fit comfortably within their present emplacement and show no signs of cropping or adjustment.
Moreover, we have seen that the embrasures, to which the
bases, capitals and imposts necessarily relate, were inserted within an already extant porch and that the present
porch vault post-dates the completion of the present
portal. It is now possible to formulate a new relative
chronology for the western portal of Saint-Loup-de-Naud:

1. a now dismantled or, possibly "hidden", portal
which presumably would have been contemporary with the
construction of the porch (and western nave bays);[81]

2a. replacement of the first portal with a presumably more elaborate, second portal of which the jambs.
embrasure walls, bases, capitals, and imposts still exist
as part of the present portal.[82] The stark architectural
accent given by the bare projecting jambs, the undecorated
socles and the undecorated arrisses of the stepped recesses,
suggests that this second portal had simple colonnettes in
the embrasures (rather than figured columns).[83] The plan
of the embrasures, with its two inner rectangular steps

and one outer, nearly square one (cf. text fig. 11, p.107), would seem to indicate that the innermost pair of archivolts of this "intermediate" portal were fascia-type[84] and that the outer one was a "closure" or frame (analogous to the molded archivolt of the present portal or to the one at Ivry). The tympanum, if there was one, remains an unknown element.

3a. the partial dismantling of the "intermediate" portal to accommodate the insertion of the spoliate sculptures and the remaining sculptures which were carved for their present emplacement. These combine together to form the present portal.

OR

2b./3b. the dismantling of the first portal to accommodate the insertion of parts of at least two separate portals (one of which would consist of all surviving elements of the "intermediate" portal discussed above, including the embrasure core masonry)[85] and those sculptures which were carved for their present setting. These combine together to form the present portal.

4. the erection of the present rib vault after the completion of the portal.
Regrettably, the physical evidence provides no further clues about which sequence of construction actually occurred at Saint-Loup.

CHAPTER III

FOOTNOTES

1. The author was introduced to this fundamental fact during five years of graduate study at the Pennsylvania State University under the direction of Jan van der Meulen to whose own research the method also remains central. See, Introduction, p. iv and n. 12.

2. Yet a third, earlier portal, from which no sculpture survives, will also be shown to have existed.

3. R. Adams, Chartres Cathedral: The Eastern Portal of the North Transept Facade: An Initial Study Towards Defining the Original Sculptural Program of the Cathedral Design of 1194, unpubl. diss., The Pennsylvania State University, 1974, pp. 1-21, has critically assessed the range of descriptive approaches to medieval portals and argued forcefully for beginning at the center of the lower zone. While Adams' method goes far towards clarifying the issue, the circumstances of their genesis prevents any standardization of "approach" to medieval portals. As a note of caution, it must be added that any approach selected may in some unforeseen way bias the interpretation.

4. Hamann-MacLean, 1965, passim.

5. Chartres WM, Le Mans S, Bourges S and Angers WM among surviving portals, and the central portal from Saint-Bénigne among those known through engravings. Even at Saint-Ayoul, where the border takes the form of a simple concave molding, it remains continuous above the Godhead.

6. Chartres WM and Le Mans S.

7. At Chartres WM and Le Mans S the corners of the cloud band are also "turned" by a depression bordered immediately by rising masses on each side.

8. The retention of regular undulation in the cloud border demands that one complete rising mass or one complete depression be truncated on each side. The mortar joint between the central and lateral blocks could fall at the center of a rising mass (as it does at Chartres WM and Le Mans S) as easily as at the center of a depression (as it does here).

8a. In the light of this suggested original condition it is interesting to note the formalist observation of Salet, 1933, p. 157, "...le tympan, assez mal composé, ne laisse qu'un emplacement exigu à ceux qui occupent le registre supérieur, l'ange et l'aigle..."

9. Another possibility is that the tympanum has been reduced by a greater amount than has been suggested here, perhaps even with the loss of additional figures such as the angels which appear beside the Maiestas in

the engraving of Saint-Bénigne. Nothing in the form of
the present tympanum precludes this alternative.

10. Appendix C, pp. 382-383.

11. In fully frontal photographs, the mandorla-like
back appears to abut the adjacent colonnette shafts (cf.
fig. 24). Actually, this is not the case because the
throne-back is carved far enough forward to actually pass
in front of the shafts.

12. The angels do not have wings. Even a very
close, on-site inspection did not determine if they ever
had them because the angels are positioned so close to
the lateral blocks of the lintel that one simply cannot
see.

13. On the other side of the figure this correspondence is obscured by damage.

14. Appendix A, pp. 283-285.

15. The abaci are of two types: the traditional
classical type with three bosses separated by concave
molding (n/3) and a variation in which the central boss
is eliminated to form a concave, convex, concave curve
between the outer two bosses (n/2, n/4, and s/2-s/4).

16. The "ground floor" stories of s/1 and s/4 are
different, indeed necessarily so if the proposed cutting
is to have taken place. In this regard, it should be
noted that the second story of s/1 extends further out onto
the haunch of the arch than any other structure surmounting

a capital. In other words, it appears to have been the largest "double" structure of any above the colonnettes.

17. Since most lintels comprise only one block, the critical capitals for comparison with Saint-Loup are the ones at the outer ends of the lintels: Chartres is not comparable compositionally; at Bourges the "system" is different. Nevertheless, the capital at the right end, while having an asymmetrical foliage pattern, has an abacus, which, although incomplete, is clearly shifted inward. On the left end, there is no abacus but the foliage pattern is adjusted to a three-quarters pattern. Although less "rigorous" than Saint-Loup-de-Naud, both capitals contain some adjustment to their end position. At Le Mans Cathedral every capital in the lintel arcade has both a symmetrical foliage pattern and a complete abacus. The apostle bas-relief from Saint-Denis contains only capitals with symmetrical foliage and complete abaci. The capital at the left end has a three-quarters complete foliage pattern and a complete, but abbreviated abacus! The foliage of the capital at the right end appears at first to be only half a pattern. But it is, in fact, adjusted inward toward the left to become symmetrical with the inner side of the capital. Significantly, the abacus here is complete.

18. From an iconographic point of view, there may also have been ten. See Chapter IV, pp. 149-150 .

19.   Fleury, 1904, p. 46, n. 3.

20.   Ibid. Angers WM is listed at 4m.10 and Bourges (both (?) lateral portals) at 4m.20.

21.   In this study, the terms figured columns and column-figures are used interchangeably. While the terms alternately emphasize the architectural or sculptural aspects and connote diverse origins of the form, these problems must be considered in a separate study. It must however, be pointed out that the term "column" technically refers to both base and capital as well as shaft. Perhaps then, the semantic war should be waged over figured shaft and shaft-figures.

22.   M. Aubert, French Sculpture at the Beginning of the Gothic Period, 1140-1225, Florence, 1929, p. 37, remarked their caryatid-like appearance. (No suggestion of a "medieval renascence" or to any supposed origin of the sculptural form is intended.) The absence of an intervening shaft between the ring-console and the base will concern us below, p. 98.

23.   The proportions of the figured columns are approximately 1:6 for 1-n, 3-n and 3-s and 1:7 for 2-n, 1-s and 2-s. G. Fleury, "Le portail de Saint-Ayoul-de-Provins et l'iconographic des portails du XIIe siècle," Congrès archéologique 69, 1903, p. 486, held that "...à Saint-Loup-de-Naud la tête des statues representer le sixième de la hauteur totale." The radically different

proportions of the trumeau figure, approximately 1:10,
largely result from the attenuation of the legs. A
similar difference in proportions between trumeau and
column-figures apparently once existed in the middle
portal at Saint-Bénigne in Dijon and in the southern
portal of the west facade of Paris Cathedral (the "Porte
Sainte-Anne"). On the other hand, the trumeau in the
southern lateral portal of Notre-Dame-en-Vaux in Châlons-
sur-Marne appears to have been of the same proportion and
size as the adjacent column-figures.

24. The diameter of the shafts is presently smaller
than those of the bases and capitals. Whether they were
always smaller or have been reduced to facilitate the
deflections need not concern us here. Cf. van der Meulen,
1975 (II), p. 520 on axial deflection as evidence of re-
use in the so-called "Confessor" statues in Chartres SE.

25. These measurements have been taken at the
capital level. No measurement could be taken for figure
1-n because the forward shift results in a "gap" hidden
in the reentrant angle behind the figure's halo. The state
of preservation of the south embrasure bases precludes
taking accurate measurements, but the displacements can
nevertheless be seen (cf. figs. 93, 96, 101). In the
north embrasure, the evidence is less obvious, partly
because two of the figures (1-n and 3-n) are shifted
forward so that the "gap" is visible only on the side at

the back and partly because of the size of the console
beneath 2-n. It should be remarked that an intervening
shaft between console and base need not be identical in
diameter to the column-figure shaft.

26. See also below, p. 98 and n. 51.

27. Fundamental for the study of the middle portal
at Saint-Ayoul in Provins remains Maillé, 1939, II, pp.
71 ff. Stoddard, 1952, pp. 32ff, should also be consulted
especially on composition. For style and iconography
reference should be made to W. Vöge, Die Anfänge des
monumentalen Stiles im Mittelalter. Eine Untersuchung
über die erste Blützeit französischer Plastik, Strasburg,
1894, passim; Fleury, 1903, pp. 458-488 and 1904, passim;
Mâle, 1924, p. 382; Aubert, 1929, pp. 40ff; Lapeyre, Des
facades occidentales de Saint-Denis et Chartres aux
portails de Laon, Paris, 1960, 187-193 and Kerber, Burgund
und die Entwicklung der französischen Kathedralskulptur
im zwölften Jahrhundert, Recklinghausen, 1966, p. 62.

28. The head of figure 4-s was discovered in an
excavation in 1911 and arbitrarily positioned on the
statue. Maillé, 1939, II, p. 79, n. 4.

29. Fleury, 1902, p. 459, was of the opinion that
there had been no trumeau but Maillé, 1939, II, p. 77,
has shown convincingly that one once existed. Whether
it was contemporary with the rest of the portal is a
moot point, since the statue has been lost.

30. Maillé, 1939, II, pp. 75-76.

31. It is bonded into the core of the jamb masonry
and corresponds along its upper edge (only) with the
coursing there.

32. No distinction in the style of the figures
suggests that the outer two have to be dated at a different
period. On the contrary, the style of the figures is
quite homogeneous, although Vöge, 1899, p. 204, n. 3 and
Kerber, 1966, p. 62, after him, saw slight differences
between the figures of the north embrasure and those of
the south.

33. Maillé, 1939, II, p. 87 and Stoddard, 1952,
p. 37f.

34. Fleury, 1904, p. 45, stated that "...les
statues de femmes sont supportiés par des feuillages."
Today, figure 3-n (the other female) is too badly damaged
around the feet to determine the nature of the console
form. There is, however, no reason to doubt Fleury.
Figures 2-n, 1-s and 2-s appear to stand on small console
figures; the others are too damaged to determine.

35. For example, Fleury, 1904, p. 45. Part of an
intervening shaft appears below the remains of the
console (figure?) of figure 4-s (fig. 121).

36. The condition of the stone (and in several
cases, the over-hang of the console) precludes a determination for the other figures. That is not to say that

the other shafts do correspond to their bases and capitals.

37. Column-figures 2-n and 3-n may also have been "scalloped" but the mortar filling is so thick here that one would have to remove the statue to be sure.

38. A question about the original interrelationships of these figures (here or elsewhere) can be raised on iconographic grounds: the plausibly identified figures of Saint Peter and Saint Paul (see Maillé, II, p. 79 and n. 3) occupy positions 4-n and 2-n instead of the expected 1-n and 1-s on opposite sides of the jamb as they do at Saint-Loup-de-Naud and almost all other locations. See also Chapter IV, pp. 151-153.

39. Maillé, 1939, II, p. 87.

40. The full implications of these observations remain to be worked out in a more systematic study. Such a study must take into account the probability of a vaulted porch as suggested by Maillé, 1939, II, pp. 72-74 (to which the two over-sized bases in the socle may have been related?) and the sculpture of the upper zones wherein there are also important questions to be raised. Aubert, 1929, p. 34, suggested a stylistic (and chronological) difference between the entire upper zone and the embrasures but he saw no distinction within the upper zone itself. Maillé, 1939, II, pp. 85-86, arbitrarily "refines" Aubert's already arbitrary stylistic chronology to c. 1157-1167 while adhering to its general outlines.

In fact, the archivolt profiles differ: ⌒‾‾‾⟍ for

the first; (‾‾‾‾‾⟍ for the second through the fourth.

The console forms of the figures in the first archivolt

also differ from those of the second, third and fourth

(fig. 125) as do the styles of the two groups. The inner

voussoir figures are stiff and linear in both anatomy

and drapery whereas the outer three archivolts contain

far more animated figures which receive a more plastic

treatment and more broadly handled drapery. The style

of the former more closely allies with the tympanum and

the column figures than does the style of the latter.

The possibility exists that the differences in form and

style between the three outer archivolts and the rest of

the portal are sufficient to postulate separate periods

of carving.

41. The most important recent study on the portal

remains J.P. Suau, "Les débuts de la sculpture gothique

dans l'Eure, I., le portail de l'abbaye Notre-Dame d'Ivry,"

Nouvelles de l'Eure, 49 (1973), pp. 48-59 which also

provides a critical overview of earlier material. For

historical information reference should be made to F.-J.

Mauduit, Histoire d'Ivry-la-Bataille et l'abbaye de Notre-

Dame d'Ivry, ed. anonymously, Evreux, 1899. Among the

older literature, Fleury, 1904, pp. 137-147, must be

consulted. To these should be added: Lapeyre, 1960,

pp. 193-199 and pp. 295-297; Sauerländer, 1972, p. 393

and most recently, L. Musset, Normandie romane, la Haute-Normandie, La Pierre-Qui-Vire, 1974, (ser. la nuit des temps, 41), pp. 291-293.

42. The letter containing the description was written by one Dom Legris to Bernard de Montfaucon in 1726. Suau, 1973, pp. 49-50, quotes the description extensively and considers it critically in relationship to the portal. The text was also quoted by Fleury, 1904, pp. 145-147.

43. The starkness of the architectural aspect of the portal would not lead us to expect a decorated socle zone. The best available photographic documentation is: Bildarchiv Foto Marburg #39506-39509 and L. Musset, 1974, pp. 148-149 to which must be added the early nineteenth-century drawings of R. Bordeaux published by J.-P. Suau, 1973, p. 50.

44. This area has abraded badly and is not really visible in photographs. Reference should be made to Bordeaux's very accurate drawing of the figure in Suau, 1973, p. 50.

45. Bildarchiv Foto Marburg, #39508.

46. Ibid.

47. For an overview of the question of remaniements at Ivry, see Suau, 1973, pp. 54-57. To this must be added to remarks of Musset, 1974, p. 292.

48. Fleury, 1904, pp. 137-147, esp. pp. 141-142.

To this must be added Fleury's letter of 1905 published
only by Suau, 1973, p. 58 n. 35 where he refines his
chronology to include a rebuilding of the archivolts in
the sixteenth century. Suau appears to retreat from
Fleury's position on the embrasures ("...il y a en un
remaniement assez profond du portail au moins dans sa
partie supérieure." (italics mine), p. 55; Musset,
1974, does not consider it.

49. The relationship of the capitals to their
architectural setting may also have to be questioned.
Embrasure capital 2/s (Bildarchiv Foto Marburg #39509)
is an inhabited capital articulated by confronted beasts
whose heads join as one below the projecting angle of the
capital. Symmetrically divided on its inner face the
capital repeats the beast motif in the direction of the
nave. Here, however, the beast is truncated, appearing
to disappear into the wall of the stepped recess of the
embrasure.

50. See n. 48 above. Indeed one should probably
accept Fleury's entire thesis: that the pointed form of
the portal tympanum and the plastic carving of the archivolts, which contrast starkly with the round form and
more mural carving of the blind portal adjacent on the
facade to the right (Bildarchiv Foto Marburg #39506),
represents a rebuilding of an earlier portal more harmonious in conception with the rest of the church. Also

plausible is his suggestion that the present physical
and iconographic chaos in the archivolts represents a
post-medieval (sixteenth-century) reworking. One
problem which remains is the nature of the iconographic
program as Fleury sees it having been rebuilt in the
twelfth (?) century. Three separate cycles (Infancy,
Passion, and Judgement are begun but none is complete;
at least five miscellaneous voussoirs do not fit into
any program. To achieve any iconographic coherence in
the medieval rebuilding, the portal must have included
some voussoirs which no longer survive and excluded some
which do. (On the archivolts see n. 47 above).

51. For example, on the basis of the Montfaucon
engraving (Sauerländer, 1972, ill.10), the lost column-
figures from Saint-Germain-des-Prés appear to occupy the
full height between base and capital with little or no
intervening shaft. Moreover, they also appear to be too
wide for their setting and may have overlapped the
arrises of their stepped recesses. Ultimately, a careful review of all early images of medieval portals--
correlated wherever possible with archeological evidence--
must be undertaken from the point of view of spolia.

52. These dimensions will concern us below, p.118f.

53. It is, of course, impossible to determine how
far inward the stone extends. It may well be that they
simply abut the pier flank behind the embrasures.

54. Stoddard, 1952, p. 35. In this system each successive horizontal course bonds into the wall mass alternately on an e/w axis and a n/s axis.

55. We will return to the plan configuration of the capitals below, pp. 118-119.

56. See above, Chapter II, pp. 34-35 and n. 46.

57. Maillé, 1939, II, p. 90. The point was also made earlier in a passing remark by G. King, "Fact and Inference in the Matter of Jamb Sculpture," Art Studies, 1926, p. 136, when apparently comparing the style of the porch capitals to that of the portal sculpture.

58. Maillé, 1939, II, p. 90. "...au sud, on taillada un des ressauts pour laisser passer le socle d'une des statues et le chapiteau qui la couronne." Maillé seems to be referring to the apparent irregularity at the level of the base block and molding course (cf. fig. 32) rather than to the foot of the actual socle zone itself.

59. The upper surface of the sill, or ground, course of the embrasures was used as the common base from which all measurements were taken.

60. In spite of this correspondence, embrasure course #3 does not bond into the pier flank. Courses #5 and #9 are masked by column-figure 3-n.

61. Courses #1 and #3 do not bond into the pier. Courses #11 and #14 originating in the embrasure are

inserted into the pier flank (see immediately below) but
do not correspond in height to the individual blocks
beside them which originate in the pier. #11 in the
embrasure is 19.3 cm, in the pier 31.3 cm; #14 in the
embrasure is 36.5 cm, in the pier 25.3 cm. Course #5
is masked by column-figure 3-s.

62. The wedge has been lost on the north side where
only the aperture remains. On the south, it can still
be seen.

63. On the north side at the capital level, capital
block 3-n and its impost are inserted into the pier flank
with a smooth vertical edge which gives the appearance
of unity, but, as the more than 2.0 cm difference between
the heights of courses #11-#14 makes clear, the embrasures
do not relate to the pier flank. In this regard we should
also note that the horizontal upper limits of the bottom
voussoirs of the third archivolt do not correspond with
the coursing of the pier flanks beside them.

64. The marked difference in style between the
porch capitals and the portal capitals would seem also
to confirm this sequence (cf. figs. 13, 33); however,
it may also be that the styles reflect their setting:
pure architecture as opposed to decorated portal and
that no chronology can be deduced from them.

65. Perhaps this occasional correspondence results
from the reuse of blocks from an earlier portal (on which

see below, pp. 118-119) and/or part of the pier flanks
themselves. Individual course heights of 27 cm ± 0.5 cm
occur four times in the north pier flank, five times in
the north embrasure, three times in the south embrasure
and twice in the south pier flank. (On the re-use of
unsculpted masonry, see Deichmann, 1975) On the other
hand, the occasional correspondence may simply be coincidental or due to a desire to give the appearance of
unity which can be considered commensurate to the
subtlety with which the spoliate sculptures have been
"accommodated" to their setting.

66. Actually 1/s, 2/s, 3/s and 5/s do not have
nimbi carved on the ground behind their heads probably
never had metal ones inserted there either. However,
these four (and only these four) fold their left wings up
behind their heads so that the wing shoulder enframes
the heads on the side effective for the viewer below.
If we may assume that the wings were painted gold as
the haloes presumably would have been, then these angels,
can also be considered to have haloes.

67. See Introduction, n. 3, on the texts relating
to Saint Loup.

68. Appendix C, pp. 445-458 and 461-476.

69. WM3-n/1: the base projects 0.5 cm over a length
of 4.0 cm; the angel's foot projects another 0.5 cm. The
view from the side reveals that the body of the figure

projects significantly further.

70. WM2-n/1: the base projects 0.8 cm over a
length of 6.0 cm and the projecting foot an additional
0.9 cm. The upper portions of the figure's body project
further still.

71. WM2-s/1: the base projects to 1.1 cm over a
length of 10.9 cm; the right foot of the second Magus
projects an additional 1.9 cm. The view from the side
indicates that the figure projects at least as far.
WM3-s/1: the base projects to 0.9 cm over a length of
11.1 cm; Herod's foot, which is broken at the instep,
still projects an additional 1.0 cm. From the side it is
clear that the figure's knee projects even further.

72. Manus Dei keystones appear at: Le Mans S,
WM1; Provins, Saint-Ayoul, WM2; Sens Cathedral, WM2 and
Chartres, WS1. In the first two cases the hand points
upward, in the second two, downward.

73. (H. Jursch), "Hand Gottes," L.C.I., II, cols.
211-214 and Reau, II, 1, p. 7, the Manus Dei is traditionally associated with various persons of the Trinity
and, therefore, among portals, usually with the tympanum,
which relationship the diagonality here obviates. On
the iconography and problems of the adjacent scene, see
Appendix C, pp. 453-457.

74. That the keystone is a spolium in no way
affects the iconographic relationship with the Saint

Loup scene toward which it points. Originally designed
to relate to another scene (from a life of Christ cycle,
perhaps), it has been re-used here because of its diagonality.

75. Appendix C, pp. 457-458 . Symmetrically paired
angels frequent the keystones of comparable portals, but
those which survive carry attributes other than the
scroll which the angels bear at Saint-Loup: Chartres,
WM3 and Angers, WM3, angels bear a crown; Saint-Denis,
WM4, angels flank a dove; Reims, NW1, angels bear a soul;
Mantes, WM1, angels bear a cross (?). On the two keystones said to be from the original Porte-Sainte-Anne
of Paris Cathedral angels bear the Lamb and the Apocalyptic Christ.

76. Cf. n. 74. This keystone may originally have
related to a tympanum. Changing the inscription painted
on the banderole would have been sufficient to relate to
its present iconographic context.

77. Salet, 1933, p. 155, here must refer only to
the springing of the ribs from the eastern porch piers
where part of the bottom of the torus projects visibly out
over the reentrant angle between the pier projections.
This situation does not obtain at the western piers (cf.
fig. 13).

78. Salet, 1933, p. 156. Salet cites as additional
evidence that "le quartier de route actuel cadre mal avec

le trace des arcades et que la présence des ogives en est
la cause." Presumably he refers here to the rough irregular surface on the inside of the ribs of the eastern two
piers.

79. Maillé, 1939, II, p. 90. Maillé clearly does
not believe that the groin vaults were ever built. It
will be recalled that when she considered the lower zones
she wrote of a porch "à moitié erigée."

80. Given the low height of the tower above, a groin
vault would not have been necessary for structural support.
Perhaps an investigation of the base of the walls in the
upper room would provide more information on the form of
this earlier closure See also Chapter II, n. 50.

81. On the relationship between porch and nave, see
Chapter II, p. 38.

82. In view of the fact that the bases and capitals
relate to embrasures of these dimensions and the fact that
the column-figures do not fit embrasures of these dimensions, we must conclude that the bases, capitals and embrasure walls, on the one hand, and the column-figures,
on the other, never belonged together.

83. Ample analogies to portals of this type abound
in the immediate vicinity of Saint-Loup-de-Naud. The
portals which come most immediately to mind are the two
lateral portals of the west facade of nearby Saint-Ayoul
in Provins (fig. 116). Both contain bare, projecting jambs

articulated only by a simple chamfer on the forward arris, undecorated stepped socles set off from the plinths of the simple colonettes and bare arrisses which, like those of Saint-Loup, extend into the capital zone. It is also worth recalling the proposed original configuration of the embrasures of the central portal at Saint-Ayoul discussed above, pp. 92-96. This same embrasure schema can also be found in a number of small churches in the surrounding countryside: for example, the western portal of the cemetery church at Longueville or, the portal of Saint-Apollinaire at Salins. The form is also common for secondary portals at churches which have figured portals elsewhere: for example, the western portal of Notre-Dame-en-Vaux in Châlons-sur-Marne or, the southern portal of the west facade of Notre-Dame-du-Fort in Étampes.

84. Suggested by J. van der Meulen in discussion with the author.

85. On the re-use of unsculpted masonry, see Deichmann, 1975.

CHAPTER IV

A PROGRAMMATIC APPROACH TO THE ICONOGRAPHY

OF THE WESTERN PORTAL OF SAINT-LOUP-DE-NAUD

I.   Introduction

It will be recalled that as we approach the portal
at Saint-Loup-de-Naud, we are immediately aware of several compositional emphases (fig. 22).   In the tympanum,
the obvious dominance in size and projection of the central figure, over the figures which surround it, is
repeated in the dominance of the two figures arranged
axially beneath it: the central figure on the lintel
projects further forward into space and is physically
bigger than the eight figures which flank it symmetrically in groups of four; the trumeau figure stands apart
from the isocephalic and frontal column figures through
being noticeably taller and by turning its head slightly
out of axis to the left.   The vertical alignment of these
three figures together with their plastic differentia-
tions forcefully stresses the center of the composition
and establishes a bi-lateral symmetry.   Moreover, the
distinction of the central figure on the lintel, together with the distinctions in size and degree of plas-

140

ticity between the bottom voussoir figures in the two outer archivolts and the remaining voussoirs above them, establishes a second, horizontal axis across the width of the portal.

These compositional emphases are related to each of the three separate iconographies found within the portal. First, the Maiestas Domini of the tympanum forms a unit with the abbreviated college of disputatious apostles on the lintel, which, as we will see, must be understood as being "completed" by the images of Saint Peter and Saint Paul borne on the figured columns below. These latter, in their turn, are compositionally related to the remainder of this "inner plane" of the portal's iconographic (and physical) composition, which is the enframing cordon of the angelic host in the inner archivolt. Second, the enthroned Virgin at the center of the lintel is the iconographic culmination of the three Nativity scenes represented on the outermost pairs of bottom voussoirs. The corresponding two outermost column-figures in each embrasure will be shown to relate, by reason of analogy, to the Nativity scenes above them as prefigurations of those scenes. Third, the trumeau figure representing Saint Loup relates to the remaining smaller, animated voussoirs in the two outer archivolts which evidently all contain figures and episodes taken from his life and miracles.[1]

The iconography of the western portal complex at Saint-Loup-de-Naud has been approached only in a general fashion.[2] The "compositeness" of its three distinct themes--_Maiestas_, Virgin, Saint--has long been recognized and, in fact, occasionally even been remarked upon.[3] Any new, detailed study of the portal iconography must now also consider the composite nature of the portal's physical structure.[4]

However, in spite of the apparent iconographic and the actual physical compositeness, it is still reasonable to assume that the portal complex was erected with some iconographic intention.[5] In the case of Saint-Loup-de-Naud, the question immediately arises: Were the use and re-use of various pieces of sculpture, while certainly not at random, iconographically consistent only within the three distinct themes or were their use and re-use effected with an over-riding programmatic intention? In part the answer to this question will depend on the intellectual as well as the physical resources available at any given time. There were, of course, close ties between Saint-Loup-de-Naud and its parent abbey, Saint-Pierre-le-Vif in Sens. Moreover, it will be recalled that the physical unification of the portal ensemble at Saint-Loup occurred with a remarkable degree of subtle-ty. Together these facts suggest the availability of both the intellectual and physical resources necessary to effect a unification of these iconographically and compositionally disparate pieces within a comprehensive programmatic intention.[6]

In order to ascertain any central theme, two crucial questions must be raised: What, if anything, do the individual themes share in common with each other which might reflect a programmatic intention? Do the individual themes express ideas which are related to each other in other media, for example, the writings of the Fathers and/or medieval commentators? With respect of the latter question, it must be emphasized that no "single literary source" will be sought. Indeed, a specific single literary source may well never have existed and, even if it did, its chances for survival and retrieval would still remain largely coincidental. Instead, we assume that an idea exists conceptually independently from the medium through which it finds expression and that, once extant, any idea may find expression in a variety of media. Thus, parallels, not sources, will be sought in exegesis, in commentary, in the liturgy and in other media. Evidence of the expression of an idea in other media will be seen as confirmation of the interpretation of its expression in the sculpture at Saint-Loup. However, in seeking parallels between various other media and the sculptures at Saint-Loup-de-Naud, no attempt will be made to establish fixed chronological relationships

between examples from those other media and the sculptural ensemble. Ideas which find early formulation in
Christian thought and continued expression during the
Middle Ages broaden (not narrow) chronological limits as
they apply to iconography, in a way which parallels the
chronological implications of the presence of spoliate
sculptures. Finally, in any interpretation of a medieval
portal ensemble for which no specific "contemporary"
explanation can be irrefutably adduced, the fallacy of
intention is inevitably risked. In an effort to minimize
this ultimately unavoidable dilemma, the study will stress
major thinkers or widespread ideas. With these questions
and cautions in mind, we turn to an investigation of the
iconography of the present western portal at Saint-Loup-
de-Naud. In it we will discover evidence of a complex
programmatic intention centered on a theme of redemption
which both unifies and transcends the three distinct
iconographic themes within the portal complex.

II. The Maiestas Cycle

The traditional, western <u>Maiestas</u> <u>Domini</u>, although
generally consistent throughout its long history,[7] is
richly varied in its details, even within the group of
so-called Early Gothic portals with allegedly "identical"
tympana. At Saint-Loup, the figure of the Deity sits
enthroned in a glory. He raises his right hand in

blessing and, with his left, rests a richly decorated, large, closed book on his knee. His head is enframed by a cruciform nimbus and his feet rest on a curved, arcuated footstool.[8] The figure of the Deity is surrounded by representations of the four living beings[9] which face inward (man, eagle), or turn their heads (lion, ox), toward him.[10] All four creatures are nimbate,[11] winged[12] and carry closed books, except for the eagle which grasps an open scroll.[13]

Although the textual basis for the tympanum lies in the fourth and fifth chapters of Revelations and in the Old Testament prophecies of Ezekiel (1:4-28) and Isaiah (6:1-4), the image of Christ enthroned in glory surrounded by the four living beings was early discussed as a generalized theophany without attendant typological associations.[14] Attempts have also been made to suppress "...la denomination impropre et vague de 'Dieu de Majesté'..." in favor of specific (narrative) manifestations of God.[15] While the former approach largely avoids the problems, the latter clearly ignores the atemporal aspect of the theophany. Subsequently scholars have emphasized the generalized interpretation which carries diverse meanings according to its period and context. Thus, fifty years ago, van der Meer emphasized that the image of the Maiestas Domini based on Revelations, Ezekiel and Isaiah is a generalized theophany with clear

overtones of the Incarnate God.[16] Its evident early
Frankish expression and its continued use as a Gospels
frontispiece[17] as well as its use as a central motif for
altar decoration[18] affirm this interpretation. Moreover,
this orientation toward the Incarnation finds further confirmation in the early association of the four living
beings with the four evangelists and their homiletic interpretation as the sacramenta of Christ: the four principal natures of His temporal existence.[19]

More recently, in two brief but highly significant
studies addressing literary and visual interpretations
of Revelations 4 and 5, Christe has identified a diver-
gence between the interpretation more or less consistently given by medieval commentators and the intention
found in monumental images.[20] Briefly, for commentators
from Saint Augustine to Bruno of Segni (†1123) "...l'Apocalypse (4 and 5) est essentiellement une vision de l'état
présent et futur de l'Église céleste, des luttes de
l'Église terrestre pour sa réalisation eschatologique."[21]
Revelations 4 and 5 pertain not to the final judgement
but to the "...présent eschatologique, à des réalitiés
invisible, mais déjà réalisées, et on les justes ont accès
des leur mort."[22] Working from the surviving _tituli_ from
such destroyed images as the apsidal decorations of the
churches of Gorze (consecrated in 765) and Saint Peter
near Fulda (consecrated in 938), Christe argues that the

iconographic tradition differs from the commentary tradition:[23] "Dans le contexte christologique anti-arien
qui est celui de l'Occident des VIe-XIIe siècles...Le
Verbe en sa divinité étant placé rigoureusement sur le
même plan que le Père invisible, et ne peut être repré-
sente dans sa réalité eschatologique présente que par le
détour de la fin des temps."[24] At the risk of oversimpli-
fication, in Christe's view, the christological assertions
of the West necessitated representing Christ's present
(temporal) eschatologic reality in its "apocalyptic" form,
back from the end of time. Thus it would seem that Christe
would accept the view that the Maiestas of Revelations 4
and 5 with Christ on the throne represents (the Church of)
the present Eschaton in the form of the final Eschaton.[25]

It is, however, only with the recent and on-going
studies of van der Meulen that the essential creation
aspect of the Maiestas Domini has been "re-integrated"
into the modern understanding of the image.[26] Working
from the Johannine restatement of Genesis I and its
Augustinian exegesis, van der Meulen has demonstrated a
tradition of congruence between creation and eschaton
imagery.[27] Using Chartres WM as a focal point van der
Meulen has also shown that apart from an incarnational
aspect (the second person depicted in order to represent the Trinity)[28] the Maiestas necessarily carries
components of both creation (Alpha) and eschaton

(Omega) content[29] and with this also, strata related to
the Concordia Testamentorum.[30] In summary, the traditional
Western Maiestas Domini represents a supra-temporal theophany connoting the full extent of God's Providence
which, while eternal, may be said to commence with Creation, to be redirected at the Incarnation and to be ful-
filled at the Final Eschaton.[31]

The textual basis for, and the meaning of, the eight
enthroned apostles on the lintel go beyond the immediately
evident gospel passages in Matthew (19:28) and Luke (22:30)
in which Christ tells the apostles that they will sit on
thrones in Heaven judging the twelve tribes of Israel.[32]
The thrones on which the apostles at Saint-Loup sit,
together with the architectural motifs[33] which surmount
their star-bearing arches[34] do affirm both their celestial
location and their function as assessors; however, this is
not the only meaning with which enthroned apostles were
associated in the Middle Ages. It will be recalled that
the apostles, by biblical charter, have the right to be
heard[35] and that they are represented at Saint-Loup, in
disputatione,[36] as they so often are elsewhere. Saxl
has shown that apostolic dialogue developed as, and
remained during the Middle Ages, an image-type which
conveyed spiritual dialogue.[37] For the apostles, of
course, there can be no question of the process of
discerning truth from falsehood in which several would

argue for some particular point and several against it.
Rather, disputatious apostles must represent the fact of
truth already discerned from falsehood, specifically the
truth of the Gospels and the message of Christ of whom
they were the first divinely inspired heralds. In relationship to their role as witnesses, the apostles must
also be understood as an image of the Church, the basis
for which interpretation lies in their biblical commission (Acts 1:8).

Clearly these assembled strata of meaning are interrelated, but at this point only in a quasi-narrative way
and not entirely necessarily with the portal of Saint-
Loup-de-Naud. However, working from a Johannine and
Augustinian exegetical basis, van der Meulen has demonstrated that (ten and twelve) enthroned apostles possess
a creation component related to the Maiestas above.[38]
Biblically and exegetically associated with the material
creation,[39] the apostles must be seen as created by Christ
and as the pre-existant Church.[40] As such, and in relation to their assessor function, they are (in disputatione) supra-temporal witnesses to the Divine Providence
(Creation to Eschaton) encompassed in the Maiestas above.[41]
Moreover, in his study on Chartres West, van der Meulen
convincingly associates the ten enthroned apostles in
the northern, Creation portal with the creation of the
material world and with the Decalogue (era of Law).[42]

Further, he associates the twelve in the middle, Maiestas portal with the creation of the spiritual world and the Credo (era of Grace).[43]   Finally, in addition to the Concordia Testamentorum strata already evident in the relationship of ten apostles to twelve, van der Meulen also suggests intentional Concordia symbolism in the distribution of scrolls and books among the apostles of both lintels.[44]

The numerological requirements of ten and twelve implicit in this interpretation raise serious questions about the applicability of similar Concordia content to the only eight enthroned apostles at Saint-Loup, for which no theological basis has ever been found or postulated.   Indeed, only architectural exigency has been offered to account for their abbreviated number.[45] To accept this view, however, is to subject the representation of a supra-temporal truth to the vicissitudes of temporal process.[46]   On the contrary, we must assume that it was iconographically possible (i.e., theologically acceptable) to truncate four or two apostles from the original lintel block(s) and emplace only eight at Saint-Loup because those eight were understood to be "completed" as a group of ten by the images of Saint Peter and Saint Paul on the figured columns below.   In this respect, it is highly significant to note that the easily recognizable Princes of the Apostles are not

present on the lintel at Saint-Loup and that they are
placed beneath the angel archivolt (WM1) in immediate
association with the Maiestas "plane" of the portal's
composition (cf. figs. 23, 22 resp.).

In addition to their numerological relationship to
the lintel, the paired column figures of Saint Peter and
Saint Paul require further consideration. Such pairings
are not uncommon in "Early Gothic" portals, but an ade-
quate explanation for their meaning and placement has yet
to be put forward. Katzenellenbogen suggested a loose
"historical progression" in the arrangement of figured
columns which represented the transition from Old Testament to New.[47] While this system seemed to Katzenellenbogen to be applicable to Le Mans S, Paris WS and Saint-
Loup,[48] Saint-Bénigne WM could not be accommodated.[49]
In fact, it can be shown that each of these pairs of images
relates to the Maiestas in the tympanum[50] in a Traditio
Legis context. However, because of the physical distance between the Maiestas and the apostles and the
absence of inscriptions to identify the meaning, the
case may be argued on an analogical basis only.

Since Schumacher's important study nearly twenty
years ago[51] it has been understood that the Traditio
Legis is not a quasi-narrative event representing the
tradition of the law or the primacy of Peter but a theophanic vision of the resurrected Christ which marks the

commencement of a new epoch, that of the reign of Christ
and his Church. This ecclesial significance bears directly on our interpretation of the Maiestas cycle as a
whole.[52]

However, for all the appropriateness of the meaning,
the form of the image at Saint-Loup (and Le Mans or Paris
for that matter) hardly corresponds to the traditional
version of the Traditio Legis[53] in which Christ stands or
sits with Peter and Paul immediately flanking him.[54] At
Saint-Loup the apostles are separated from the Maiestas
not only by distance but also by intervening figures.
On the other hand, the same situation, relative to a
Maiestas tympanum and to intervening figures also obtains in the portal of Saint-Trophime at Arles where the
inscription on Saint Paul's banderole clearly refers to
a Traditio Legis context: "Lex Moisi celat quod Pauli
sermo revelat, Nunc data grana sina per eum sunt facta
farina,"[55] although no one seems to have made this association with respect to the tympanum.[56] Traditio Legis
content has been recognized in the twelfth-century
triumphal arch mosaic at San Clemente in Rome.[57] At
the center of the arch Christ appears blessing and
holding a book in a roundel. He is flanked laterally
by the four living beings below which, in the spandrels
are, on the left, Isaiah and above him Saint Lawrence
and Saint Paul, while on the right appears the prophet

Jeremiah and above him Saint Clement and Saint Peter.

The palm motifs beside Saint Peter and Saint Paul at San Clemente, a recurrent element of _Traditio Legis_ iconography, and the inscriptions which refer to their teaching roles within the Church assure a relationship to traditional _Traditio Legis_ imagery.[58] Clearly the figures at San Clemente are not part of a _Traditio Legis_ in the normal sense of the type but it would appear that as such, they constitute an essential part of a larger theophanic vision. _Traditio Legis_ iconography within a larger iconographic context also exists in the undated apse fresco in Berzé-la-Ville.[59] At Berzé, the Deity sits enthroned in a mandorla in the center of the semi-dome with his arms outstretched to the sides. The right hand of the Deity is extended in blessing toward Saint Paul who holds an unrolled scroll and stands at the front of a group of five other apostles. On the opposite side, He extends a scroll toward Saint Peter who holds the keys and, like Saint Paul, stands at the head of another group of five apostles. In the spandrel area beside the mandorla are two pairs of diminutive saints.

Ultimately, a separate investigation into the "Early Gothic" Peter and Paul figures must be undertaken.[60] For our purposes at Saint-Loup, it is sufficient to outline an association or context within which the figures of Saint Peter and Saint Paul may be understood in relation to the portal program as a whole.

In summary, the architectural circumstances at Saint-Loup-de-Naud may, indeed, have necessitated a truncation of iconographic elements, but not, evidently, in disregard for the portal's iconographic intention. The abbreviated apostolic college can be considered completed by the column-figures of Saint Peter and Saint Paul which together, by numbering ten, refer to the Decalogue (era of Law) and, by their own ecclesial significance, both groups are related to the reign of Christ and His Church (era of Grace).[61] These interwoven strata echo and confirm the providential significance of the Maiestas above.[62]

The angels represented in the inner archivolt continue the focus of the Maiestas cycle on the tripartite nature of Divine Providence. Their Early Christian and medieval interpretation as symbols of light relates them to the mandorla of the Deity and, with that, to both Creation and Eschaton.[63] At Saint-Loup, the cordon of angels also refers to the Incarnation and to Christ's redemptive act. They hold objects borne in the eucharistic procession: five hold censers, three hold candles and two, uniquely among portals of this type, hold humeral veils.[64]

This specific reference to the mass, which visually re-enacts Christ's redemptive sacrifice, is heightened

by the presence on the keystone of the same archivolt of
an Agnus Dei.[65] Accompanied by a cruciform nimbus and the
triumphant, pennoned cross-staff, the lamb represents the
salvific mystery of Christ and is present as an attribute
(not symbol) of the Maiestas.[66] It is worth remembering
that the Agnus Dei was chanted to accompany the breaking
of the Host during the mass.[67] Thus the first archivolt
consistently refers to the ritual re-enactment of the
sacrifice by which Christ took away the sins of the world
and, in so doing, refers to the Church as well.

III. The Nativity Cycle

The identification of the Virgin enthroned at the
center of the lintel and of the three Nativity cycle
scenes--Annunciation, Visitation and Magi before Herod--
represented on the bottom voussoirs of the outermost
pair of archivolts has been established since the very
beginning of scholarship on the portal (fig. 22).[68]
However, the iconographic details and the placement and
selection of scenes raise important questions relative to
any programmatic intention.

To begin, the unique accumulation of attributes
accorded to the Virgin on the lintel has never been fully
mentioned nor carefully investigated (figs. 24, 24a, 25,
26). Wearing a circlet crown and a veil, she sits on a
mandorla-backed throne beside which are tiny angels that

hold her nimbus and touch the throne-back.[69] Although
not a mandorla proper,[70] which would encompass the entire figure as does the mandorla of the tympanum, the
throne-back here extends well below the bench of the
throne thereby becoming more than a mere mandorla-like
backing (figs. 25, 26). Moreover, there are examples in
which Christ sits enthroned, surrounded by the four
living beings, in which He is enframed not by a complete
mandorla, but by a mandorla-like throne-back which
commences only at the bench of the throne on which he
sits: the apse fresco at Saint-Plancard and the chapter
house fresco at Lavaudieu.[71] Thus, an intentional association with a mandorla proper (and its meaning) seems
certain.

Further, the Virgin at Saint-Loup is positioned
axially below the Maiestas Domini in the tympanum and
associated directly with the abbreviated college of
apostles which fills out the lintel. This compositional
placement identifies the Virgin with the eschatological
realm described in Revelations 4 and 5 and Matthew 19:28
which together form the textual basis for representation
of the Maiestas and the apostles. Finally, and surprisingly, as Salet has pointed out, the Virgin does
not, nor did she ever, hold the Christ-Child on her
lap.[72] Instead she clasps (the remains of) a skein of
wool. This attribute derives from the text of the Proto-

evangelium of James which describes Mary as the maiden
selected to weave the true purple and the scarlet of the
new veil for the Temple.[73] In summary, the crown, the
mandorla-backed throne and the purple would seem to indicate an image of a glorified Maria Regina which requires
further consideration.

Several scholars have briefly addressed the problems
of this image. Mayeux suggested that the Virgin here
"...paraît (enthroned) pour la première fois au milieux
d'eux (apostles)" and goes on to say, "Celle qui deviendra
dans la suite la grande protectrice de l'humanité par son
intercession auprès de son Fils, prend place près de lui
pour le Judgement."[74] Aubert followed this idea somewhat differently stating, "The triumph of the Mother is
here associated with that of the Son, and this iconographic detail shows us new ideas, which point to a later
date in the 12th century."[75] Salet briefly compared the
Saint-Loup figure to representations of the Virgin in
similarly hieratic compositions at Charlieu (north side
of narthex, portal) and Lavaudieu, while making reference to the early roots of the type in frescoes of
Bawît.[76]

None of the authors who discuss the figure pursue
the "idea" which the attributes and placement connote.[77]
Moreover, none of the other images brought to bear is
strictly comparable in all significant details. Perhaps

the image at Lavaudieu comes closest.[78] There, too, the
Virgin sits enthroned beneath a _Maiestas_ and between
apostles. She wears a crown and a veil and has a nimbus.
She blesses with her right hand and holds a flower (lily?)
in her left. However, no mandorla-form enhances this
figure's throne and the context of the flanking apostles
is entirely different. At Lavaudieu they stand and turn
toward the Virgin. At Charlieu,[79] the heads are all destroyed so the presence of a crown cannot be established.
The Virgin sits similarly beneath a _Maiestas_ and is also
flanked by angels and apostles seated with her on a common
throne, so that, again, no mandorla-form enhances the
figure's throne.[80]

Devotional writers such as Haimo of Halberstadt in
the twelfth century applied texts like Ecclesiastes
24:14 (ab initio et ante saecula) to the Virgin Mary.[81]
Some of the motivation for ultimately theological associations like Haimo's may stem from the earlier identification of Mary with the Apocalyptic Woman (Revelations
12:1-12)[82] and the synchronous relationship Eschaton bears
with Creation.[83] However, while some particular devotional intention may in part be reflected in the central representation of the Virgin at Saint-Loup,[84] her
significance, both as a single image and as part of a
larger whole, can only be understood through consideration of the ancillary Nativity scenes which accompany

her. The Annunciation, Visitation and Magi before Herod

(fig. 22) constitute a remarkably short Nativity cycle,

even among portals with <u>Maiestas</u> tympana.[85] While the

extended capital cycles of Chartres West[86] and Étampes[87]

or the lengthy archivolt cycle of Le Mans[88] hardly offer

fair comparison, the lintel cycles of both Saint-Bénigne

in Dijon[89] and Notre-Dame-en-Vaux in Châlons-sur-Marne[90]

do, but even they are considerably longer.[91] Moreoever,

the selection of the Magi before Herod as single Epiphany

element in the cycle, and the exclusion of an image of

the Adoration of the Magi is curious to say the least.[92]

Indeed, in some large measure the significance of the

scene of the Magi before Herod lies in its type-anti-

type relationship with the scene of the Adoration (Magi

before Christ).[93] Isolated juxtaposition of these two

scenes communicates this message most clearly[94] but some

element of the same meaning probably obtains in at least

some of the larger cycles as well.[95] At Saint-Loup the

Magi before Herod episode does, however, share one im-

portant aspect in common with the Annunciation and

Visitation which transcends simple narrative for another

purpose: All three are announcements--indeed, the first

three biblical announcements--of the <u>truth</u> of the Incar-

nation of Christ. The angel tells Mary: "And, behold,

thou shalt conceive in thy womb, and bring forth a son,

and shalt call his name <u>Jesus</u>" (Luke 1:31). And Eliza-

beth greets Mary saying: "Blessed art thou among women
and blessed is the fruit of thy womb" (Luke 1:42).
Similarly the Magi do not ask whether or not Jesus is
born but ask instead: "Where is he that is born King of
the Jews?" (Matthew 2:2). In the words of Saint Augustine, "They announce and they question; they believe and
they seek, as it were, foreshadowing those who walk in
faith..."[96] Although spoliate in origin, the use of the
scene alone at Saint-Loup may have been subject to the
same theological developments which led to the increased
popularity of the Officium Stellae plays from the
eleventh century onward; they make much of the Magi's
meeting before Herod and also do not (usually) enact the
Adoration.[97]

Recognizing this incarnational significance in the
three scenes provides a context within which to understand the placement and attributes--i.e., the meaning--of
the Virgin on the lintel. Mary's role in the redemption
process at its redirection in the Incarnation is, of
course, biblical; whereas, her role at the end of the
process, at the Eschaton, is not. However, Mary's role
as intercessor on behalf of all mankind found rapid formulation in the earliest fathers: Justin, Irenaeus,
Tertullian[97a] and became a continuing concern of medieval devotional writers.[98] John of Salerno, who wrote
his life of Odo of Cluny (✝942) about 945, wrote that

Odo "...was in the habit of calling blessed Mary the Mother of Mercy."[99]   At least by the eleventh century Mary's active, dual role in Redemption (at the Incarnation and at the Eschaton) was being expressed. Thus, Peter Damian (✝1072) worte in a sermon:

> We ask you, most clement Mother of pity and mercy,
> that...we may deserve to have the help of your in-
> tercession in heaven; because, as the Son of God has
> deigned to descend to us through you, so we also
> must come to him through you.[100]

This same relationship was also expressed by Anselm of Canterbury (✝1109) in a prayer to the Virgin:

> Therefore, O Lady, Gate of Life, Door of Salvation,
> Way of Reconciliation, Entrance to Restoration, I
> beseech thee by thy saving fruitfulness, see that
> the pardon of my sins and the grace to live well are
> granted to me, and that this thy servant is guarded
> even to the end under thy protection.[101]

By the twelfth century, this juxtaposition of Mary's role at both the Incarnation and at the Eschaton becomes more frequent.[102]   To cite only one example, Arnaud, abbot of Bonneval near Chartres (✝ after 1156) emphasizes Mary's role in redemption at the Incarnation as Mother of Christ and at the Eschaton as an intercessor with an effective-ness common with Christ's by virtue of her affective participation in the Crucifixion and of His authority.[103]

        None of these texts, or others which might be cited, applies strictly to all of the details of the images of the Nativity and Virgin cycle at Saint-Loup. The texts do, however, provide the theological-devotional ambiance within which the images can have been selected and positioned, if not carved. Writers like Peter, Anselm and Bernard and others before them were concerned with Mary's role in the Divine Dispensation. In stressing her unique role in the Incarnation they were led to formulate a unique role for her as intercessor on man's behalf at the Judgement. In so doing they were led to speak of "the Maternal Majesty"[104] and to apply epithets such as Queen and Mediatrix to Mary.[105] The Virgin and the Nativity cycle at Saint-Loup seems to express precisely these ideas.

In the figure on the lintel, the Virgin is represented resplendent and associated with the divine realm where she was understood to play a special intercessory role on mankind's behalf.

Related to the image of the Virgin on the lintel is the figure of Saint John, beside her on the right[106] (fig. 23). Due to their biblical association at the Cross (John 19:25-27), an "O Intemerata" prayer of the eleventh (?) century (wrongly attributed to Saint Anselm) speaks of Mary and Saint John as intercessors in their roles as Mother of God and friend of the Saviour respectively.[107] We know that Benedictines held a special veneration for John and Mary (as virgins).[108] We know too, that the lateral lintel block on which John appears has been truncated on the inner end, thus allowing him to appear next to the Virgin. Given the physical interchangeability of the lateral blocks and the possibility of truncating each on either end, it is highly unlikely that the association of John and Mary at Saint-Loup was unintentional.

In summary, the Virgin in glory on the lintel takes her place logically beneath the Deity on the tympanum; her triumph and intercessory powers are analogous to, although less than, His. Her special role in the Incarnation is emphasized in the Nativity voussoirs. At Saint-Loup, Mary may be interpreted as both the "Gate of Life" and the "Door of Salvation."

Up to this point, the Virgin at the center of the lintel and the Nativity cycle voussoirs have been shown to reflect only one half (Incarnation to Eschaton) of the Divine Dispensation evident in the Maiestas cycle. In fact, these same images carry, at a second level, content related to the Concordia Testamentorum, and, hence, to the entirety of God's Providence.

The idea that the Virgin Mary is a type of the Church dates from the period of Fathers:[109] Saint Ambrose associated Mary with the Church in his exegis of both the Apocalyptic woman and the Nativity, stating for the former, "By the woman here we may also understand the Blessed Virgin Mary, because she is the Mother of the Church..."[110] and for the latter, "It is fitting

that Mary should be espoused, and at the same time a
Virgin; because she is the type of the Church, which is
spotless, and yet married."[111] Saint Augustine makes the
same association in several sermons on the Nativity.[112]
It is not, apparently, until the later eleventh and
twelfth centuries that Mary and the Church become virtually indistinguishable, both in commentary and devotional writing.[113] As Honorius of Autun writes in his
commentary on the Song of Songs: "Everything that is
said of the Church can also be understood as being said
of the Virgin herself, the bride and mother of the
bridegroom."[114] The same appears to be true for the
visual arts as well,[115] although the issue is somewhat
obscured by the lack of dating for monumental images.
Already in 1916, Clemen discussed in precisely these
terms the image of _Ecclesia_ in the late twelfth-century
Hortus _Deliciarum_ of Herrad of Landsberg,[116] which is
strikingly comparable to our image at Saint-Loup-de-
Naud. Ecclesia[117] is enthroned on a bench beneath a
tabernacle within an image of the Heavenly City. She
wears both crown and veil[118] and is surrounded by a
hierarchic arrangement of apostles and ecclesiastics.
Just outside the four corners of the city are evangelist
symbols accompanied by likewise bustate figures of
prophets. The inscription which explicates this scene
reads: "Hec regina est Ecclesia que dicitur Virgo Mater

et significat omnes prelatos."[119]

At Saint-Loup-de-Naud, the ecclesial context provided by the Maiestas cycle, particularly by the apostles on the lintel, encourages the identification of the Virgin at the center of the lintel as an image of the Church Triumphant. Consideration of the three Nativity scenes will confirm this association and provide a larger context in which to understand the image on the lintel.

That the Annunciation allegorizes the harmonious succession of the Old Law into the New, the Concordia Testamentorum, was determined in the Early Church.[120] The allegory, as it applies to the Annunciation, finds literary expression in an Eve-Mary juxtaposition in which the comparison between Eve and Mary "...is one both of likeness and contrast: of likeness, in original sanctity and virginal innocence; of contrast, in their actual conduct and its effects."[121] Articulation of the theme is consistent from early Fathers like Saint Augustine[122] through writers like Saint Bernard[123] and beyond. The entire, uninterrupted literary tradition assures us that one essential meaning of the Annunciation was precisely the harmonious passage from the Old Law to the New.

While art historians have long recognized that the Annunciation is a theological allegory of the Concordia Testamentorum, the fact that the Visitation also allegorizes that harmonious succession remains less well explored. Of the various lexica, Réau alone mentions this interpretation based on a Counter-Reformation treatise by Bossuet.[124] Guldan identifies as an image of the harmonious succession a Visitation from a Greek psalter dated mid-eleventh century (?)[125] in which Mary and Elizabeth meet before structures representing a church and a synagogue.[126] Working from Réau (Bossuet), Guldan and the context of his image, Adams suggests that the Visitation in the eastern portal of the north transept of Chartres Cathedral also represents, at an allegorical level, an image of Ecclesia and Synagoga.[127] There exists good reason to seek this meaning in images of the Visitation elsewhere.

This allegorical interpretation is implicit in Saint Ambrose's exegesis on Luke's description of the Visitation:[128]

> The superior comes to the inferior: Mary to Elizabeth, Christ to John the Baptist...[129]

The New Law comes to the Old. Grace contrasts with measure as Mary with Elizabeth.[130] This Old Law association with Elizabeth continues in the Glossa Ordinaria. Its author states that Elizabeth's prophecies (Luke 1:42) "conveniunt cum" the prophecy made to David in Psalm 132:11, Of the fruit of thy body will I set upon the throne.[131] Finally, Elizabeth's Old Covenant signification is also present in the Pseudo-Augustine sermon from which certain eleventh- and twelfth-century prophet plays derive.[132]

The Magi before Herod should also be understood to refer to the Concordia Testamentorum, although in a somewhat different way than the Annunciation and Visitation. As already discussed, the iconographic tradition of the Magi before Herod lies in its anti-typal relationship to the Magi before Christ (Adoration), beyond which typology, however, there lies a tradition of interpretation which links Herod to the "blindness" of the Jews to the coming of the New Law.

In both patristic and medieval exegesis this thesis finds expression. Saint Augustine tells us that "...we must not lose sight of the fact that the enlightenment of the Magi bears definite witness to the blindness of the Jews."[133] Saint Ambrose remarks that "The star is visible for them (the Magi) but invisible for Herod; it is newly visible and shows them the way to Christ. Thus this star is the way and the way is Christ."[134] The author of the Glossa Ordinaria, who was probably aware of Saint Ambrose's ideas concerning the Magi[135] tells us that, allegorically, "The star is the illumination of faith which leads toward Christ. As yet it is diverted from the Jews, it is lost to them."[136] From an exegetical point of view, then, the Magi before Herod refers to the fact that not all Jews accepted the child of Bethlehem as the Messiah.

However, the blindness of Jews to Christ is (from the Christian perspective) temporal and not in contradiction with the Divine Dispensation as such. As Augustine describes it, when Elijah comes, prior to the Final Eschaton, "...he will explain in a spiritual sense the Law which the Jews now take in a material sense, and by so doing he will 'turn the heart of the father toward the son'...that is, the Jews, will interpret the Law as their fathers--that is, the prophets, including Moses himself--interpreted it"[137] and, one might add, reconcile the temporal antagonism between the church and the synagogue in the supra-temporal Concordia Testamentorum. That this idea that Jews will, prior to the Last Judgement, recognize Christ remained current during the Middle Ages is attested to by the fact that both Lanfranc of Bec[138] and Saint Bernard of Clairvaux[139] appealed to it as reason to cease contemporary persecution of Jews.

Moreover, this same concept found visual formulation as well. In a twelfth-century sacramentary from Tours,[140] both Ecclesia and Synagoga turn toward a bustate, blessing Christ, while from above a Manus Dei lifts the veil from the eyes of Synagoga.[141] In the scene of the mystical wine press in the Hortus Deliciarum of Herrad of Landsberg, Jews are depicted among the audience which receives the eschatological message of Enoch and Elijah.[142]

Given the strata of Concordia Testamentorum symbolism evident in the Maiestas cycle and the certain associations between that concept and the Annunciation and the Visitation, it does not seem unreasonable to suggest that, in the context in which we find it at Saint-Loup-de Naud, the scene of the Magi before Herod, through its reference to the temporal blindness of the Jews, alludes to their future reconciliation with the Church within the Divine Dispensation. The image of Ecclesia at the center of the lintel may well represent, by placement and context, that Ecclesia Universalis which exists, reconciled as it were, supra-temporally in the heavenly realm.

In the absence of any assured interpretation of the king, queen and two prophets (?) on the two outermost figured columns in each embrasure,[143] it is difficult to relate them specifically to any part of the portal's program. Indeed, if only painted inscriptions originally identified the figures (each holds or, held, a rotulus and evidently no other, additional object),[144] then the very real possibility exists that inscriptions—and therefore identities—could be changed to suit the context; context thereby becomes the strongest criterion for identification.

In a general way the four figures probably connoted the concept of regnum et sacerdotium--the harmony between church and state in the Old Testament and in the French domain--which was so persuasively articulated by Katzen-ellenbogen for Saint-Denis and Chartres West.[145] Katzen-ellenbogen's thesis, apart from its "French connection," holds these Old Testament figures to be a general, typo-logical foundation for the New Testament themes which appear on the upper parts of the portals in question.[146] It goes without saying, of course, that this "way of thinking" is fundamental to Christian biblical exegesis and particularly to the concept of the Concordia Testa-mentorum.[146] It is also a fundamental part of religious drama in plays like the Ordo Prophetarum.[148]

The traditional question of the specific typological relationship between archivolts and their corresponding column-figures must, of course, be solved on a portal-by-portal basis. Recently, Adams has suggested a specific relationship between the archivolts and column-figures of Chartres NE:[149] Gerson has offered similar interpretations of several figures lost from Saint-Denis.[150] However, a typological relationship between the archivolt figures and the four-column-figures be-neath them has not yet been suggested for Saint-Loup-de-Naud. The axial alignment between column-figures and the archivolts above, together with the clear compositional distinctions between the several iconographies represented in the portal urges precisely this kind of association. Reasoning by analogy from the composition and the surrounding iconography suggests that these figures relate to the Nativity cycle and even permits tentative identification of the individual figures: Jeremiah (3-n); the Queen of Saba (2-n); Solomon (2-s) and Isaiah (3-s).

It must be assumed that the prophet at 3-n foretells the Incarnation through reference to the Annunciation; that the queen at 2-n can be associated with one or both of the women of the Visitation and that the king and prophet at 2-s and 3-s, respectively, can in some way be linked to the Magi. However, the identification is complicated by the multiple associations applicable throughout Christian exegesis. If, in addition, we assume that the column-figures are paired across the portal (taking our clue, as it were, from the figures of Saint Paul and Saint Peter at 1-n and 1-s) and that the typological relationships extend upward both vertically and diagonally (text fig. 13, p. 172), then the possibilities are narrowed down considerably.

The Queen of Saba was understood as a type of Ecclesia (and by extension, Mary) and her Journey to Solomon was recognized as an antetype of the Magi's journey to Christ.[151] With respect to the Visitation

Text Figure 13.
Tentative Identifications of the Four Outer
Column-Figures and Suggested Pattern of
Typological Relationships to the Nativity
Cycle Voussoirs

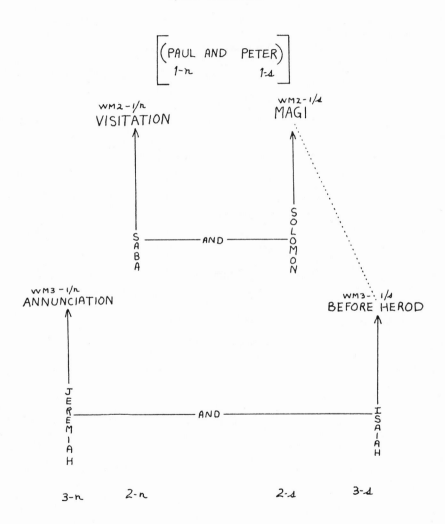

scene at Saint-Loup, the Queen of Saba can be associated with both figures: Elizabeth who recognizes Wisdom (in Mary) and Mary who journeys. Saba's reasonably certain identification assures the identification of the king opposite her as Solomon (2-s). Solomon stands as a type of Christ[152] whom the Magi seek and, we may suggest, as an anti-type of Herod, like Christ himself. Solomon alone cannot be linked to the Visitation, but, in the context of Saba's journey and wisdom recognized, he relates to it through her. As images of Solomon and Saba, this pair of column-figures together refer to that Old Testament journey and recognition of wisdom which can be said to prefigure the two New Testament journeys represented above which also result in the recognition of Wisdom, in the Incarnate Christ.

Turning to the liturgy as a basis for possible identifications of the prophet figures at 3-n and 3-s, we find that Isaiah is the prophet most commonly associated with both the Annunciation[153] and the Feast of the Epiphany.[154] It is unlikely that Isaiah would be represented twice and although Isaiah should probably be considered the prophet of the Annunciation par excellence;[155] the headpiece worn by the figure at 3-n sets him apart from the more traditional prophet-type at 3-s and suggests he might be an Old Testament priest and thus not Isaiah.[156] Of the two other so-called major

prophets, Jeremiah and Ezekiel, both were priests[157] and
both prophesied the Annunciation.[158] However, it is
Jeremiah whose prophesy most closely approximates
Isaiah's[159] and, indeed, was linked to it in the Middle
Ages. Hrabanus Maurus in his commentary on the Book of
Jeremiah links the two.[160] Again, Peter Comestor opens
a sermon on the Annunciation with the Jeremiahan
passage.[161] Jeremiah is paired with Isaiah in an axial
relationship to Gabriel and Mary at Ferrara Cathedral.[162]
In all respects, then, Jeremiah seems a reasonable sub-
stitute for Isaiah below the scene of the Annunciation.
Jeremiah cannot, however, be linked directly to the Magi
as Isaiah can be. However, his prophecy (Jeremiah 23:5)
that the Lord "will raise unto David a righteous Branch,
and a King shall reign and prosper and shall execute
judgement and justice in the earth" may be able to be
interpreted to refer anti-typally to the Magi before
Herod (the false king, or anti-type of Christ), at
least in the context in which we find the figures as
Saint-Loup-de-Naud.

None of these suggested identifications of the four
"Old Testament" figured columns can be considered
assured, but they provide a viable, unified iconography
in spite of the portal's at least partially spoliate
composition. By foretelling or pre-figuring the
Nativity cycle events represented above them, these

figures not only emphasize the Incarnation but stress it as part of a larger plan for mankind's Redemption, namely the Concordia Testamentorum.

In summary, the Nativity Cycle at Saint-Loup-de-Naud, which includes the Virgin/Church at the center of the lintel and the four "Old Testament" column-figures, thus reflects, like the Maiestas cycle, the completeness of God's Providence. It emphasizes the Incarnation—that transformational event between the Old Law and the New—and particularly stresses the role of the Virgin and the Church within the Divine Dispensation.

IV.   The Saint Loup Cycle

The descriptive catalogue shows that much of the present portal's sculpture centers on the life and miracles of the priory's patron saint, Lupus of Sens.[163]

For the medieval beholder, as for the modern one, the immediate visual focus of this extended saint's cycle rests on the monumental trumeau image (fig. 27). Saint Loup stands before the beholder resplendent in archiepiscopal costume and triumphant as a type (in the typology) of Christ treading on the beasts of Psalm 90:13. The association of this triumphal passage with Christ occurs in biblical exegesis at least as early as Saint Jerome;[164]   it has a long tradition in the visual arts as well, with examples dating at least as early as the late

eighth-century Genoels-Eldern ivory.[165] The association
of Saint Loup (or any saint) with this Psalm passage--
evidently chronologically prior to images of the 'Beau
Dieu' on portal trumeaux[166]--may in part have its explanation in Saint Augustine's differing interpretation of
the same passage: Saint Augustine states unequivocally
that the "thou" of the Psalm is to be understood as the
Church,[167] so that the saint may be considered to be both
a type of Christ and a type of Ecclesia. His (now-
damaged) crozier thus refers both to Christ in the role
of Good Shepherd (saviour, intercessor) and to the em-
bodiment of that role in perpetuity by the leaders of
Christ's Church.[168] The turning of his head and his
gesture of benediction lend a sense of immediacy and
power to this two-fold interpretation of the image.

Further evidence of Saint Loup's (and the Church's)
potency finds detailed witness in the surrounding cycle
of scenes taken from his life and miracles. Indeed, the
cycle is so extensive that there are no close analogies
among surviving "Early Gothic" portals:[169] although not
all figures and scenes can be conclusively identified
(cf. text fig. 14, p. 177),[170] seventeen episodes are
distributed in the two outermost archivolts and on the
trumeau capital (figs. 28-30, 48-60 and 63-73).[171] The
scenes appear to divide into two nearly equal groups:
miracles and wonders which occurred during the saint's

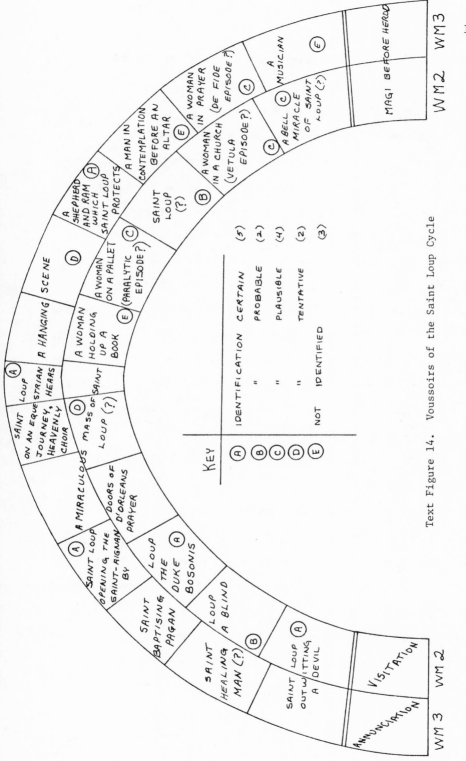

Text Figure 14. Voussoirs of the Saint Loup Cycle

lifetime and miracles effected through the saint's intervention after death.[172] This extensive _vita_ cycle,
particularly in view of its apparent _post_ _mortem_ emphasis, must be related to the historical context in which
it was carved:[173] The gift of the _partem_ _de_ _capite_ _et_
_de_ _reliquiis_ _corporis_ in 1161 was made in honor of
miracles already effected by the merits of the saint at
Saint-Loup-de-Naud, which, as the documents seem to
suggest, were based on a prior claim to possession of
some relics of the saint.[174] Thus, the sculptures representing the miracles of the saint can have been carved
at Saint-Loup-de-Naud either before 1161 to propagandize
the efficacy of relics claimed controversially to be in
possession of the church at Naud or, equally, after 1161
in response to having received further relics in that
year. Therefore, while we can relate the _vita_ cycle to
the context of the tradition of miracles wrought at
Saint-Loup-de-Naud in the name of the priory's patron
saint,[175] we cannot, as Pressouyre has recently done,
"date" the sculptures on the basis of the arrival of
relics in 1161.[176] Nevertheless, the extended vita cycle
and particularly the _post_ _mortem_ parts of it can be said
to refer directly to the power of the saint whose relics
were claimed to be physically present inside the church
and which manifested itself through the miracles wrought
there by invoking his name. The scenes are thus a kind

of propaganda both for the church in Naud and, ultimately,
for Sens as well.

In the broader context, quite apart from local
propaganda, the monumental figure of Saint Loup on the
trumeau and the vita cycle testify to the importance of
the (cult of the) saint in the Christian cosmology.[177]
As an image of Christ-like triumph, the trumeau figure
signals to the beholder the role of the saint both in,
and as proof of, redemption. The surrounding scenes from
the vita bear witness in explicit detail to the example
of a post-biblical imitatio Christi.[178] Moreover, the
vita scenes spell out the real and active intercessory
powers of the saint over the travails of the on-going
struggle of the temporal life, which is, of course, a
part of the redemptive process.[179] Finally, the individual miracles are witness to and confirmation of
the earthly Church's divine mission. Saint Paul tells
us (Ephesians 4:8, 11-12) that "...When He ascended up on
high, He led captivity captive, and gave gifts unto men...
And He gave some...pastors and teachers; for the per-
fecting of the saints (i.e., the faithful),[180] for the
work of the ministry, for the edifying of the body of
Christ..." These gifts (pastors and teachers or "saints"
in the restricted sense) are thus given to the Church for
its work of ministry.[181] Saint Augustine makes clear
that miracles are performed to make the world believe[182]

and, at the same time, bear witness to the faith in Christ of those who perform them.[183] Thus, the miracles represented in the archivolts of Saint-Loup-de-Naud, the living and after-life deeds of that local pastor Lupus, are the work of the Church's ministry and at the same time, proof of its divine mission because a miracle is ultimately an act of God.[184] To put the matter another way, the _vita_ cycle at Saint-Loup is part of the theophanic vision which unfolds hierarchically from the tympanum.

V.   Conclusion

The iconographic program of the western portal of Saint-Loup-de-Naud, as we encounter it today, is a complex theophanic statement primarily oriented toward expressing God's Providence.

Emanating from the timeless theophany in the tympanum, the portal program presents a hierarchically ordered sequence which emphasizes the intercessory roles/powers of holy personages within the Divine Dispensation, which itself is presented as extending harmoniously from Creation to Eschaton. Surrounded by liturgical symbols which refer to His sacrifice--through its ritual re-enactment in the Eucharist--the Deity manifests Himself to the beholder through the Attribute of the Agnus Dei as the ultimate proof of and hope for eternal salvation.

The Nativity cycle emphasizes the Incarnation and particularly the role of the Virgin. Her triumphant place within the celestial realm (at the center of the lintel) accords her, through ecclesiological typology (as a type, like the apostles, of the pre-existent Church) a status "just below" her Son and emphasizes her intercessory role at the present and final Eschaton equal to her role at the Incarnation. The Church, which the Virgin symbolizes, manifests its intercessory role in the present Eschaton in the daily offices. Likewise, the figure of Saint Loup, standing in Christ-like triumph on the trumeau, in immediate temporal proximity to the beholder, proclaims the saint as an active participant in, and proof of, the providential Design. The surrounding scenes from his _vita_, significantly elevated compositionally to the celestial realm, demonstrate in graphic detail Saint Loup's particular merits and the example of his post-biblical _imitatio Christi_. These scenes attest to Saint Loup's intercessory powers on behalf of the supplicant and, by their _continuing_, miraculous nature, describe the continuing theophany of God's redemptive plan.

These three cycles, of which the three central, axial figures can be read as epitomes, present a traditional idea in Christian thought. As early as Clement of Rome's authentic First Epistle to the Corinthians,

93-97 A.D., the notion of a hieratic descent from God

had been formulated:

> Now, the Gospel was given to the Apostles for us by
> the Lord Jesus Christ; and Jesus the Christ was sent
> from God...And as they (the Apostles) went through
> the territories and townships preaching, they ap-
> pointed their first converts--after testing them by
> the Spirit--to be bishops and deacons for the
> future.[185]

The "insertion" of the Virgin between Christ and the

apostles at Saint-Loup is merely a modification of the

Clementine schema. This same concept, seen as an as-

cending path of mediation, was later summarized by Saint

Bernard as the _Viae Domini_.[186]

At an allegorical level, the portal program also

presents, simultaneously with its statement of inter-

cession, a hierarchically ordered image of the reigning

Church, as the avenue of Christ's descent to man and man's

ascent to Christ. This concept also found early liter-

ary formulation. In his commentary of Revelations 4:4,

Beatus of Liebana (✝798) wrote:

> sic invenimus in descriptione civitatis Ierusalem
> de caelo descendentis, de Deo in homine Cristo,
> de Cristo in apostolos, de apostolis in episcopos,
> de episcopis in presbyteros, de episcopis et presby-
> teris in ceteros populos. Per hos grados civitas
> Ierusalem descendit ad terra, per ipsos cotidie
> ascendit ad caelos.[187]

We need only insert the Virgin-_Ecclesia_ into Beatus'

text to achieve the expression found at Saint-Loup.

Some of these same significances may well have

been present in such early hieratically arranged images

as the seventh-century (?) apse fresco from Bawît, now in the Coptic Museum in Cairo[188] or the seventh-century apse mosaic in the Chapel of Saint Venantius in the Lateran Baptistery in Rome.[189] The Saint-Loup composition (although certainly not its iconography) finds its closest lels, not surprisingly, in images of the Heavenly City from copies of Saint Augustine's de Civitate Dei.[190]

In summary, the portal of Saint-Loup-de-Naud presents a complex theological re-statement of God's Providence for mankind. Perhaps the most outstanding feature in its expression at Saint-Loup is the unequivocal optimism with which it has been put forward.

*   *   *

In Chapter III, it was demonstrated that the portal at Saint-Loup-de-Naud was assembled partly from sculpture designed for the architectural emplacement in which we now find it and partly from sculpture designed for (if not erected) elsewhere. The overriding programmatic intention of the portal as we now find it insists that the process of selection and assemblage was both intentional and subtle. Against the background of the iconographic program's complexity, we can better understand the care (not to say disguise) with which the assemblage took place.

All of this leads toward a different set of
questions: From whence came the re-used sculpture and
from whence came the atelier which carved the pieces made
for the site and which presumably assembled the portal?
What relationship do these two groups of sculpture have
with one another? To answer these questions we turn to
an analysis of the style of the sculpture of Saint-Loup-
de-Naud.

CHAPTER IV

FOOTNOTES

1. Not all the scenes can be identified from the texts which survive relating to Saint Loup. See Appendix C, pp. 445-458, 461-476 and below, pp. 175-180.

2. Introduction, p. xxi.

3. Introduction, p. xviii and n.5.

4. The general moralizing theme of the six embrasure capitals, which presents a contrast between salvation and perdition (suitably on the right and left with respect to the Deity on the tympanum), can be related to almost any larger Christian program. Although a part of the present portal, the capitals are treated separately in Appendix D where they are discussed in view of their possible original architectural setting.

5. Van der Meulen has stressed that the physical re-use of monumental sculpture must be understood in parallel with a reinterpretation (even if only contextually) of that sculpture. See 1975 (II), pp. 512 and 514 and 1978, pp. 81-86 and passim.

6. Sens does not appear to have been a center of theology or learning in any way comparable to, for example, the famous "school of Chartres." It had, however, a tradition of learning throughout the Middle Ages. See B.

Aspinwall, Les écoles épiscopales monastiques de l'ancienne province écclésiastique de Sens du VIe au XIIe siècle, Paris, 1904, esp. pp. 2-17.

7. For a recent overview of Maiestas imagery and literature see F. van der Meer, "Maiestas Domini" L.C.I., III, cols. 136-141. To this should be added, B. Brenk, Tradition und Neuerung in der Christlichen Kunst des ersten Jahrtausends. Studien zur Geschichte des Weltgerichtsbildes. (Wiener byzantinischen Studien, III) Vienna, 1966; Yves Christe, Les grands portails romans, études sur l'iconologie des théophanies romans, Geneva, 1969; J. Gaehde "The Turonian Sources of the San Paolo Bible," Frühmittelalterliche Studien, V (1971), pp. 359ff; van der Meulen, 1972, cols. 100-106, 1978, pp. 101f, 103-106 (especially), and passim and H. Kesseler, The Illustrated Bibles from Tours, Princeton, 1977 (Studies in Manuscript Illumination, 7), esp. pp. 36-42.

8. The placement and form of the attributes of the Maiestas itself are fairly consistent throughout the group of portals similar to Saint-Loup. All sit on bench-type thrones and have a cross-nimbus, except the destroyed figure of Avallon WM, which apparently had no nimbus. Only this figure and the destroyed figure from Saint-Bénigne WM had no mandorla. Only the figures at Saint-Thibault, Provins (now Saint-Quiriace), Saint-Loup and Vermenton(?) have, or had, thrones with a(n) implicitly curved seat. Only at

Chartres WM and Saint-Loup does the raised arm appear to significantly transgress the mandorla. All figures hold, or held books, of which about half are open. All footstools are either flat or sloping. Only those at Saint-Loup and the little Maiestas from Saint-Bénigne have an opening between the feet of the Deity. Only on the Maiestas fragment from Déols does the stool crush a basilisk and an adder according to the text of Psalm 90.

9. On the four living beings, see U. Nilgen, "Evangelisten Symbole," RDK, fasc. 64-65, Stuttgart, 1970, cols. 517-572, esp. I. Definition und Schriftquellen (cols. 514ff) and II. 2, Majestasdarstellungen (col. 551); F. van der Meer, Maiestas Domini, théophanies de l'Apolcaypse dans l'art chrétien, Rome and Paris, 1938 (Studi di Antichita Cristiana, XIII), pp. 223-228 and van der Meulen, 1972, cols. 105 and 117-118.

10. Within the group of portals with which we are concerned considerable variation occurs in the placement of the living beings. For example, only in the little Maiestas from Saint-Bénigne and, if the engravings are accurate, at Saint-Bénigne WM and in the portals of Château-Chalon and Vermenton does the eagle's body move away from the Maiestas. Again, based on an engraving, the winged man at Château-Chalon moves away from, but looks back toward the Maiestas. These changes probably should be considered charged with

symbolic intentions. What distinguishes all of them--with
the exception of the winged-man from Saint-Bénigne WM, which
may well be an engraver's error--is the Maiestas-directed
gaze, which, as van der Meer, 1938, pp. 315-351, has shown,
is an essential aspect of this particular type of Maiestas.

11. Among the portals with which we are concerned,
the presence or absence of the nimbi varies for no discernible reason. At Le Mans none of the creatures has a
nimbus. At Chartres WM, only the eagle is not nimbed, while
at Provins, Saint-Ayoul, the eagle is not nimbed, but the
winged man is (the other two destroyed creatures may or may
not have been nimbed. Bourges S, the little Maiestas from
Saint-Bénigne and probably Notre-Dame-en-Vaux in Châlons-sur-
Marne all have or had four nimbate living beings. If the
engravings are reliable in details such as these the creatures from Saint-Bénigne WM all had nimbi but none of those
from Vermenton did. One might suppose that the non-nimbate
figures had painted or attached metal nimbi, or that against
a gold ground nimbi were not necessary. Close-up physical
examination and refined scientific processes may one day
help unravel these problems. For the present, one must conclude that there exists no standard in the presence or
absence of nimbi among the living beings of this group of
portals.

12. Wing position also varies from tympanum to tym-

panum and creature to creature. More clearly than in any
of the other variables, the position of the wings can be
attributed to formal factors: the size and shape (and
empty space) of the block from which each figure was carved.

13. Like the nimbus, variation occurs in the specific
form given to the revealed word--either book or scroll--the
precise iconographic reason for which remains to be
determined. The usual arrangement (!) occurs at Saint-
Loup: a partially unrolled scroll for the eagle and three
closed books for the others. Chartres WM follows this
system. At Le Mans and Provins, Saint-Ayoul, the eagle
holds a closed book. At Le Mans, the winged-man's book is
open. If the engraving can be trusted, all four creatures
at Vermenton held open books. Presumably all open books
and scrolls once bore inscriptions. On the carolingian
significance of the eagle's unfurled scroll, see M.
Schapiro, "Two Romanesque Drawings in Auxerre," reprinted
in M. Schapiro, Selected Papers on Romanesque Art, New
York, 1977, pp. 306-310. On the book and scroll, see
also below, pp. 149-150.

14. Mâle, 1924, p. 378 speaks of the tympanum of Moissac (which also includes the twenty-four elders) as "...le
Christ de la vision apocalyptique..." This type he contrasts with the Ascension (Toulouse) and "...le Christ
apparaissant pour juger les hommes..." (Beaulieu). Later

(pp. 381-391) Mâle goes on to speak of this image type as "le Christ de l'Apolcalypse" and as "le Christ en majesté."

15. Mayeux, "Essai de classification méthodique des grands portails sculptés du XIIe siècle," Bulletin de la Société nationale des antiquaires de France, 1924, p. 295. Mayeux, who may have been reacting specifically to Mâle (1924), attempts to distinguish between "...l'Apocalypse, le retour du Fils de l'homme et le Jugement dernier" by differentiating their accompanying iconographic contexts. However, Mayeux insists on making his distinctions narratively rather than on the basis of theological concepts which, quite literally, transcend their original narrative setting. Mayeux speaks of the tympanum of Saint-Loup in terms of judgement, when according to his own schema, he should speak only of the return of the Son of Man (p. 293).

16. F. van der Meer, 1938, pp. 315-379. See also Y. Christe, "Les représentations médiévales d'Apocalypse IV (-V) en visions de seconde parousie; origines, textes et contexte," Cahiers archéologiques 23 (1974), esp. pp. 68-69.

17. Van der Meer, 1938, pp. 315-379, discusses Gospel Book frontispieces from the eighth-century Gundohinus Gospels through Ottonian manuscripts of the eleventh century. Later examples of French provenance can also be cited; a sacramentary of Reims usage dated ca. 1150, Walters Art Gallery ms. W 28, fol. 5^V (see W. Wixom, Treasures from

Medieval France, Cleveland, 1967, pp. 86-87) or the gold repousée evangeliary cover made by Hugues d'Oignies ca. 1228-1230 (see L'Europe gothique, XIIe-XIVe siècles, Paris, 1968, pp. 240-241 and pl. 98). While neither of the works in question is a Gospels frontispiece, both are from manuscripts used during the mass and serve to continue the same icono-graphic tradition.

18. Van der Meer, 1938, does not discuss altar fron-tals explicitly in terms of Maiestas symbolism and the mass (cf. pp. 378-379). However, the so-called Romanesque abounds in both murals on apse or sanctuary vaults and altar frontals with Maiestas images, to cite only two of the latter: the altar frontal from Santo-Domingo in Silos (see van der Meer, 1938, fig. 91) or the Eilbertus Altar, now in Berlin (see H. Swarzenski, Monuments of Romanesque Art, London, 2nd ed., 1967, pl. 106). A similar content to that proposed by van der Meer is suggested by their liturgical function.

19. See n. 9 above.

20. Christe, 1974 (I), pp. 61-72 and Y. Christe, "Apocalypse IV-VIII, 1:de Bède à Bruno de Segni," in Mélanges E. R. Labande, Poitiers, 1974, pp. 145-151.

21. Christe, 1974 (II), p. 146.

22. Christe, 1974 (I), p. 71.

23. Christe, 1974 (I), pp. 70-72.

24.   Ibid., p. 72.

25.   Christe, 1974 (I), p. 71, "...les Théophanies
eschatologiques et eschatiques de l'Occident médiéval sont
en effet ressenties comme un instant d'aveuglement, comme
une apparition de l'invisible où dans le style même de l'image
est signifiée cette distance infinie qui separe la divinité
un instant devoilée de l'incapacité humaine de comprendre
et de voir l'invisible."

26.   See n. 7 above.

27.   Van der Meulen, 1972, esp. cols. 108-119.

28.   Van der Meulen, 1978, pp. 103-104.

29.   Ibid., pp. 98-99, 104-106.

30.   Ibid., pp. 103-104.

31.   This will be expanded upon in the light of van
der Meulen's seminal work on the iconography of angels and
his work on the Apostolic College in a Maiestas context.
See below, pp. 154-155 and 149-150 respectively.

32.   The iconographic problem resulting from the
emplacement of only eight apostles on the lintel is discussed below, pp. 150-154.

33.   On this association see, J. Summerson, Heavenly
Mansions and Other Essays on Architecture, New York, 1963
(1st ed., 1948) pp. 1-28 and J. Baltrusaitis, "Villes sur
arcatures," in Urbanisme et Architecture, études écrites et
publiées en l'honneur de Pierre Lavedan, Paris, 1954, pp.

31-40.

34. Appendix C, p. 393 and n. 26.

35. M. L. Held, "Apostle: 1. in the Bible," N.C.E., I, pp. 679-691 esp. P. 687, stresses 2. Corinthians 5:20 and 1. Thessalonians 2:13.

36. On "dialogue" iconography, see F. Saxl, "Frühes Christentum und spätes Heidentum in ihren Künstlerischen Ausdruckformen. I: Der Dialog als Thema der Christlichen Kunst," Wiener Jahrbuch für Kunstgeschichte, n. 3., II (1923), pp. 64-77 and E. Rosenbaum, "Dialog," RDK, ed. O. Schmitt, Vol. III, Stuttgart, 1954, cc. 1400-1408. It should be pointed out that "dialogue" is used for discourse between two persons; disputation is used for more than two.

37. Saxl, 1923, pp. 67-77. Rosenbaum, 1954, c. 1401, disagreed with Saxl's interpretation of the literary type of Dialogue (Philosophical discourse) as discourse about spiritual things on the grounds that this was too narrow a view. Rosenbaum would include Terence scenes in this type as well. To argue thus, however, is to miss the thrust of Saxl's study which focuses on apostolic dialogue, but, as we will see, does not go far enough to fully explain dialogue in medieval monumental art. To the examples adduced by Saxl to demonstrate the continued currency of the meaning of the dialogue motif (which might otherwise be considered to have become merely formal convention in the case of the

Apostolic College), one can add the numerous instances of
its use to represent teaching and dispute between Chris-
tians and Jews discussed and illustrated by B. Blumenkranz, Le juif médiéval au miroir de l'art chrétien, Paris,
1966, pp. 17, 71 and passim. S.M. Crosby, The Apostle
Bas-Relief at Saint-Denis, New Haven, 1972, pp. 63-64,
briefly surveys Western Medieval apostle groups in disputatione. On the motif in prophet imagery see A. Watson,
The Early Iconography of the Tree of Jesse, London, 1934
pp. 54-57 and passim.

    38. Van der Meulen, 1978, pp. 108-112.

    39. Ibid., specifically the Gospel of John and
Augustine.

    40. Ibid.

    41. Ibid., pp. 110-112

    42. Ibid., pp. 110-113

    43. Ibid.

    44. Ibid., p. 110 and n. 13 above.

    45. Salet, 1933, p. 158, "L'étroitesse du portail
a imposé au sculpteur de n'en placer que huit." Had the
lintel been carved originally for emplacement at Saint-
Loup, this suggestion would be absurd at face value.
Given the spoliate nature of the apostle blocks, it contains an element of truth, but without the disregard for
iconography which Salet intended.

    46. See van der Meulen, 1978, p. 93, n. 29.

47.   A. Katzenellenbogen, "Iconographic Novelties
and Transformations in the Sculpture of French Church
Facades, ca. 1160-1190," in Romanesque and Gothic Art,
Studies in Western Art, Acts of the Twentieth Inter-
national Congress of the History of Art, I, Princeton,
1963, pp. 108-118, esp. pp. 108-110.

48.   Ibid., p. 108. Following Mâle, 1924, pp. 393f,
Katzenellenbogen argues that the portal at Le Mans is
earliest because of the formal differentiation between
jamb and column figures. One wonders, however, how
"loose" a progression can be and yet still hold meaning.
Even if the prophets are incorrectly identified at Saint-
Loup, all three major prophets and all four minor prophets lived after each of the possible king and queen
pairs which are represented between them and the apostles.
Would not the arrangement have been different if historical progression had been a primary intention? Adams,
1974, pp. 255-277 has taken issue with this same notion
for Chartres NM.

49.   Katzenellenbogen claims that the corresponding
figures at Saint-Bénigne refer to "...the idea of king-
ship and priesthood in relation to Christ in the tympanum
(Ibid., p. 109). For some reason he omits reference to
Chateau-Châlon, where both figures once appeared in the
right embrasure (see Sauerländer, 1972, p. 404 and ill.

24 after Dunod de Charnage's engraving). Perhaps it is because the figures are paired with at least one post-apostolic saint (the palliate abbot in the left embrasure) which would make the historical progression somewhat "looser" still. Likewise, the figures of Saint Peter and Saint Paul in the north embrasure of Provins, Saint-Ayoul have also been omitted (cf. Chapter III, pp. 92-96 and n. 38). Nesle-la-Repost (Sauerländer, 1972, pp. 391-392 and ill. 9 after Montfaucon's engraving) and Saint-Pierre in Nevers (Sauerländer, 1972, pp. 423-424 and ill. 45 after Morellet's lithograph) were probably left out because only Saint Peter appeared.

50. The _Maiestas_ on the tympanum in question at Paris is different from those at Saint-Loup and Le Mans. On Paris see, Cahn, 1969, pp. 55ff. This should not, however, affect the interpretation, particularly in view of the spoliate nature of that portal's composition.

51. W.N. Schuhmacher, "Dominus Legem Dat," _Römische Quartalschrift für christlichen Altertumskunde und Kirchengeschichte_, 54 (1959), pp. 1-39. See also now the author's "Traditio legis," _L.C.I._, 4, cols. 347-351. Recent significant literature is cited in Yves Christe, "Apocalypse et 'Traditio legis'," _Römische Quartalschrift für christlichen Altertumskunde und Kirchengeschichte_, 71 (1976), p. 42, n. 1.

52. Christe, 1976, pp. 42-55 discusses the relationship between the Traditio legis and the Present and
Final Eschaton in an approach which parallels his work
on the Maiestas.

53. Schuhmacher, L.C.I., 4, pp. 347-351. See also
C. Davis-Weyer, "Das Traditio-Legis-Bild und seine Nach-
folge," München Jahrbuch der Bildenden Kunst, ser. 3,
XII (1961), pp. 7-45.

54. Traditio legis imagery varies a good deal.
Either Peter or Paul may receive the law from Christ, but
neither needs to. Palm trees are a recurrent feature as
are lambs but neither is essential. The image can be
conflated and/or be part of a larger iconographic context. See n. 53 above.

55. On the iconography, see recently, V.M. Barsch,
RSCJ, The Church of Saint Trophîme, Arles: architectural
and iconographical problems, unpubl. diss. Northwestern
University, 1971, pp. 96-138. The inscription is quoted
on p. 99.

56. Each of the four apostles (Peter, Paul, John
and Andrew) in the straight embrasures of Arles carry
inscriptions which reflects their "mission in the Church
of Christ." That for Saint Peter reads "Criminibus
Demptis Reserat Petrvs Astra Redemptis" (Barsch, 1971,
p. 98). The increase by two figures hardly alters the

Traditio legis context, since numerous Roman apse mosaics representing the theme have more than the three primary figures. See Davis-Weyer, 1961, fig. 12 (p. 23) or fig. 13 (p. 24), e.g. Ultimately the Arles figures must also be re-interpreted in the light of van der Meulen, 1978, pp. 109-113.

57. On San Clemente, see E. Scaccia Scarafoni, "Il mosaico absidale di S. Clemente in Roma," Bolletino d'Arte, 29, II (1935), ser. III, sect. 1, pp. 44-68 and W. Oakeshott, The Mosaics of Rome, Greenwich, Ct., 1967, pp. 247-250 and fig. 159.

58. For a summary of the type, see Schuhmacher, L.C.I., 4, cols. 347-351.

59. Schuhmacher, L.C.I., 4, col. 351: "Die unter Clunys Einfluss stehenden Tympanon in Charlieu und im Elsass i.e. Andlau zeigen die nun kirchenpolitisch bedingte Abwandlung auf die Primatsidee und auf Donation hin: Petrus empfängt Schlüssel und Rolle und damit die hochste Gewalt: Berzé-la-Ville." See O. Demus, Romanesque Mural Painting, London, 1970, pl. 110 and 111.

60. The study should also include not only the Arles figures but the jamb and trumeau reliefs at Moissac and Beaulieu and other, obviously Traditio-Legis images like those at Andlau, Pavia, San Michele and Charlieu. Commentaries such as those on Paul's letter to the Gala-

tians and those on Zachariah 4 as well as sermons on the
feast of Saint Peter and Saint Paul must also be considered.

61. See above, p. 149f and nn. 38-44. Given the
placement of the column-figures with respect to the
Majesty in the tympanum and the biblical basis (Galatians
2:7-8) for interpreting Saint Peter and Saint Paul as
figures of the Church of the Circumcized and the Church
of the Uncircumcized (Concordia Testamentorum), it is
interesting to note that in the dedication liturgy the
prayer intoned by the bishop (celebrant) before the
second striking of the lintel (while the doors are closed,
prior to the processional entry into the church) speaks
of Christ as the cornerstone between Gentiles and Jews
[cf. M. Andrieu, Le Pontifical romain au moyen-âge, I
(Studi e Testi, 86) Vatican City, 1938, p. 179].

62. Van der Meulen's suggestions concerning the
Concordia symbolism implicit in the intermingled books
and scrolls held by the apostles (cf. fig. 23), and also
those found in the tympanum should be borne in mind here.
See above, pp. 149-150 and n. 44.

63. Van der Meulen, 1972, cols. 108-119, esp. cols.
113-114 and 1978, pp. 111 and 113.

64. On the attributes of the angels in the inner
archivolt, see Appendix C, pp. 430-438 and esp. p. 434.

and n. 98 on the humeral veil. A. Schoenberger, Über die Darstellung von Engeln als Liturgen in der mittelalterlichen Kunst (masch. Diss.), Munich, 1941, has been unavailable.

65. Perhaps more than any other single figure, the intention of the Lamb is thought to vary with its context. See the editors' article, "Lamm, Lamm Gottes," L.C.I., III, cols. 7-14, esp. cols. 10, 13 and, on the theology of the Lamb of God, F.X. Durwell, "Lamb of God," NCE, 8, pp. 338-340.

66. Van der Meulen, 1978, p. 104.

67. C. Kelly, "Agnus Dei," NCE, I, pp. 209-210.

68. Appendix C, pp. 444, 445 and 461.

69. Appendix C, pp. 381-382.

70. J. van der Meulen, in discussion with the author. See also, W. Messerer, "Mandorla," L.C.I., III, cols. 147-148.

71. Demus, 1970, pls. 122 and 187, respectively; pp. 418 and 432 for further literature. The former has been uncritically dated to the mid-twelfth century and the latter to the early thirteenth.

72. Salet, 1933, pp. 158-159.

73. M.R. James, The Apocryphal New Testament, Oxford, 1960, p. 43.

74. Mayeux, 1924, p. 293. It is clear that Mayeux

meant to say for the first time among portals of Saint-
Loup's type but it is not at all clear whether he intended that the Virgin be understood as a co-assessor
with the apostles or an intercessor.

75. Aubert, 1929, pp. 35-36; he also compared
Saint-Loup to Saint-Bénigne in Dijon because both possess
an enthroned Virgin at the center of the lintels below
a Maiestas tympanum (p. 53). However, at Saint-Bénigne,
the Virgin holds a Christ-child the absence of which at
Saint-Loup makes the two images incomparable.

76. Salet, 1933, p. 158, cites Mâle, 1924, pp.
32-37, where the position of the Virgin in the examples
cited is discussed and illustrated.

77. There are a number of studies on images of
the Virgin in Majesty which do not bear directly on the
Virgin at Saint-Loup: M. Lawrence, "Maria Regina," Art
Bulletin, 7 (1924/1925) pp. 15-161; A. Grabar, "The
Virgin in a Mandorla of Light," in Late Classical and
Medieval Studies in Honor of A.M. Friend, Jr., ed. K.
Weitzmann, Princeton, 1955, pp. 305-311; K. Wessel,
"Regina Coeli," Forschungen und Fortschnitte, 32 (1958),
pp. 11-16; J. de Borchgrave d'Altena, "Madones en
Majesté," Revue Belge d'archéologie et d'histoire de l'art,
30 (1961), pp. 3-114; F. Rademacher, Die Regina Angelorum
in der Kunst des frühen Mittelalters, Dusseldorf, 1972;

I. Forsyth, The Throne of Wisdom, Princeton, 1972 and
G. Francastel, Le Droit au trône, Paris, 1973. See also,
G. Wellen and W. Braunfels, "Maria, Marienbild, I. Das
Marienbild der frühchr. Kunst; IV. Das Marienbild in
der Kunst des Westens bis zum Konzil von Trient," L.C.I.,
III, cols. 156-161 and 181-198, esp. 181-184.

78. Demus, 1970, pls. 187-188. See also, n. 71
above.

79. See B. Rupprecht, Romanische Skulptur in
Frankreich, Munich, 1975, pp. 104-105, pp. 116-117 (includes bibliography) and pl. 195.

80. Neither the three-quarter length, orant Maria
Regina in a mandorla born by angels in the narthex of
Sant'Angelo in Formis nor the standing Maria Regina
flanked by angels and saints in the church of S. Maria
in Pallara in Rome is strictly comparable. At Sant'Angelo,
there is no throne and, more significantly, no comparable
surrounding iconographic context. At S. Maria, the Virgin
is flanked by angels and is set beneath a Maiestas and an
Agnus Dei, but she has no throne and no mandorla-form.
Cf. Lawrence, 1924/1925, p. 155 and fig. 5 and p. 154 and
fig. 2, respectively.

81. Migne, P.L. 118:765, Homilia V in Solemni-
tate Perpetuae Virginis Mariae. This and other analogous
phrases which were applied to the Virgin are discussed by

M. Levi d'Ancona, The Iconography of the Immaculate Conception in the Middle Ages and Early Renaissance, New
York, 1957 (CAA Monographs, VII), pp. 5-13 and passim.

82. Alcuin of York, Exegetica Commentarius in
Apocalypsim, lib. V, cap. xii (Migne, P.L. 100:1152).
See also n. 110 below.

83. See van der Meulen, 1978, fig. 3 (p. 96).

84. Nothing is known of the cult of the Virgin at
Saint-Loup-de-Naud beyond its existence before at least
the early thirteenth century. See Appendix B, Doc. X.

85. Nativity cycles are so frequent and widespread
in medieval art that we limit ourselves to those which
relate, either in style or iconography, to Saint-Loup.

86. The literature on the iconography of Chartres
West is enormous. Most recently on the tympana and
archivolts see, J. van der Meulen, 1978. See also
A. Katzenellenbogen, The Sculptural Programs of Chartres
Cathedral, New York, 1964 (1st ed., 1954); A. Lapeyre,
1960, pp. 19ff and, as always, M. Bulteau, Monographie
de la cathédrale de Chartres, 3 vols. Chartres, 1887-
1892, II, pp. 18ff. On the capital frieze specifically,
see A. Heimann, "The Capital Frieze and Pilasters of
the Portail Royal, Chartres," JWCI, 31 (1968), pp. 73-
102; R. Crozet, "A propos de chapiteaux de la façade
occidentale de Chartres," Cahiers de civilisation méd-

iévale, 14 (1971), pp. 159-165; the exchange of opinion by these authors in the same volume of the latter journal, pp. 349-353 and L. Pressouyre, "Contributions à l'iconographie du Portail Royal de Chartres," Bulletin Monumental, 127 (1969), pp. 242-245.

87. See L.-E. Lefèvre, Le Portail royal d'Étampes, 2nd. ed., Paris, 1908, pp. 41-48 and A. Lapeyre, 1960, pp. 53-66. The Infancy cycle extends across the capital zone of the left embrasure only.

88. See Lapeyre, 1960, pp. 90-100 and 281-285.

89. See P. Quarré, "La sculpture des anciens portails de Saint-Bénigne de Dijon," Gazette des Beaux-Arts, 6th ser., 50 (1957), pp. 177-194, esp. pp. 189-190; Lapeyre, 1960, pp. 101-108 and 286-287 and W. Schlink, Zwischen Cluny und Clairvaux, die Kathedrale von Langres und die burgundischen Architektur des 12. Jahrhunderts, Berlin, 1970, pp. 120-137. It is interesting to note that the bottom voussoirs of the archivolts appear to contain the same scenes as they do at Saint-Loup: Annunciation, Visitation and Magi before Herod (and his counsellors) although the placing of the scenes is reversed, the Annunciation and Visitation being on the right side of the portal at Saint-Bénigne. Cf. n. 91 below.

90. On the attempts to decipher the iconography of the severely damaged sculpture of Notre-Dame-en-Vaux,

see, Lapeyre, 1960, pp. 126-132, who reprises earlier attempts. To this should be added Schlink, 1970, pp. 130-131.

91. At Saint-Bénigne the Nativity and the Annunciation to the Shepherds plus three additional scenes of the Magi are included: the Journey, Adoration and Dream. Notre-Dame-en-Vaux appears to be similar to Saint-Bénigne but precisely which scenes appeared on the lintel has still to be resolved definitively.

92. On the Magi, see H. Kehrer, Die heiligen drei Könige in Literatur und Kunst, Leipzig, 1909; review, E. Mâle, Gazette des Beaux-Arts, 52 (1910), pp. 261-270; G. Vezin, L'Adoration et le cycle des Mages dans l'art chrétien primitif, étude des influences orientales et greques sur l'art chrétien, Paris, 1950; A. Wienand, ed. Die heiligen drei Könige, Cologne, 1974 and H. Hofmann, Die heilgen drei Könige, Bern 1975. In Vezin's treatment of Magi iconography in cyclic terms, the subordinate role of the Herod scene becomes clear. Even the seemingly comparable scene of the Magi before Herod on the lintel of the Sainte-Anne portal of Paris Cathedral (WS) conflates elements of Herod with his counsellors and the Magi's journey. The adorational aspects of the 'division of powers' also distinguishes this scene from the isolation of the Saint-Loup image. [See Sauerländer, 1972, pp. 404-406 (includes

bibliography), and pl. 40]. An extensive search has produced no other example in which the Magi before Herod
suffices as the sole Epiphany scene.

93. The type-anti-type concept occurs in exegetical
and homiletic literature. Saint Ambrose, in his commentary on the Gospel of Luke, sees two "ways" available
to the Magi: The way of Herod which is death and the
way of Christ which is life (see Sources chrétiennes, vol.
45 bis, p. 93).

94. The visual tradition of this juxtaposition is
at least as old as the Carolingian period where it occurs,
for example, on the predella of the Lorsch ivory in the
Vatican (see J. Hubert, J. Porcher and W. Volbach, The
Carolingian Renaissance, New York, 1970, pl. 210). W.
Cahn, The Romanesque Wooden Doors of Auvergne, N.Y., 1974
(CAA Monographs, vol. 30), pp. 40-41, briefly discusses
the iconography of this juxtaposition.

95. For example, the reliefs of the portal of Saint
Trophîme in Arles where the two scenes--part of a larger
sequence--are paired directly across the portal (see W.
Stoddard, The Facade of Saint-Gilles-du-Gard, Middletown,
Ct., 1973, pls. 392 and 393) or Chartres West where the
scenes, which are adjacent to one another in the capital
frieze of the right embrasure of the north portal, echo
one another in composition.

96. Saint Augustine, Sermo 199, "In Epiphania
Domini", P. L. 38:1027 [in English, M.S. Muldowney, Saint
Augustine: sermons on the liturgical seasons (the
Fathers of the Church, a new translation, 38) New York,
1959, p. 60]. The identical exegesis is already present
in Saint Bernard, "In Epiphania Dominini," sermo III,
Migne, P. L. 183:150 (in English, A Priest of Mount
Melleray, trans. Saint Bernard's Sermons for the Seasons
and the Principal Festivals of the Year, II, Westminster,
Md., 1950, p. 23).

97. See K. Young, The Drama of the Medieval Church,
2 vols., Oxford, 1962, (corrected edition), vol. I, pp.
50-101.

97a. Th. Livius, The Blessed Virgin in the Fathers
of the First Six Centuries, London, 1893, pp. 289-314.

98. See Sister M.V. Gripkey, The Blessed Virgin
Mary as Mediatrix in the Latin and Old French Legend prior
to the Fourteenth Century, Washington, 1938. See also,
D'Hubert du Manoir, s.j., ed., Maria, études sur la sainte
vierge, II, Paris, 1952; A. Wilmart, OSB, Auteurs spirituels et textes dévots du moyen age latin: études d'histoire litteraire, Paris, 1932 and W. Delius, Geschichte
der Marienverehung, Munich and Basel, 1963.

99. Migne, P.L. 133 : 72, quoted in translation
from H. Graef, Mary: A History of Doctrine and Devotion,

2 vols., New York, 1963 and 1965, I, p. 203.

100. Migne, P.L. 144:761, quoted in translation from Graef, I, p. 207.

101. E.R. Fairweather, ed. and trans., A Scholastic
Miscellany: Anselm to Ockham, Philadelphia, 1956, p. 202.
On the prayer, see H. Barré, Prières anciennes de l'occi-
dent à la Mère du Sauveur, des origines à saint Anselme,
Paris, 1963, pp. 196-197.

102. See Graef, I, p. 226 on Geoffrey of Vendôme
(†1132); p. 234 on Hermann of Tournai (†after 1147); p.
248 on Geoffrey of Admont (†1165). For a discussion of
Mary and benedictines in the twelfth century, see, particularly, J. Leclerq in du Manoir, II, 1952, pp. 557-559.

103. R. Laurentin, Maria, Ecclesia, Sacerdotium:
essai sur le developpement d'une idée religieuse, Paris,
1952, pp. 145-153.

104. In Saint Bernard's first sermon on the Assumption he speaks of Mary being received into Heaven by her
Son with an honor worthy of such a Mother, with a glory
in accord with such a Son (Migne, P. L. 183:415); so as
she was raised above others by grace that she received on
earth so a unique and incomparable glory was given to her
in heaven (Migne, P. L. 183:416-417) (italics mine).

105. Saint Bernard's disciple, Guerric of Igny
(†1153) refers to Jesus and Mary as Mediator and Mediatrix.

See Laurentin, 1952, pp. 154-156. Guibert of Nogent
(†1114) went so far as to call Mary salvatricem (quoted
from Graef, I, p. 225).

106. Appendix C., pp. 389-390.

107. See Wilmart, 1932, pp. 474-504 and J. Leclerq
in du Manoir, 1952, II, p. 557.

108. Leclerq in du Manoir, 1952, II, p. 557.

109. Livius, 1893, pp. 271-277 and passim. See
also, A. Müller, Ecclesia-Maria, Die Einheit Marias und
der Kirche (Paradosis: Beiträge zur Geschichte der alt-
christlichen Literatur und Theologie, V), Freiburg, 1951.

110. Migne, P. L. 17:959-960, quoted in translation from Livius, 1893, p. 271. On the authorship of
this Apocalypse commentary (Berengaudus?), see the ad-
monitio in Migne, cols. 841-844. The actual authorship
is not crucial to our discussion.

111. Sources chrétiennes, 45bis, In Luc. Lib. II:7,
quoted in translation from Livius, 1893, p. 271.

112. Livius, 1893, p. 271.

113. Laurentin, 1952, p. 128 and passim; J. Leclerq
in du Manoir, 1952, p. 560.

114. Migne, P. L. 172:494, quoted in translation
from S. Schwartz, "Symbolic Allusions in a Twelfth-Century
Ivory," Marsyas, 16 (1972-1973), p. 39, n. 25.

115. W. Seiferth, Synagogue and Church in the

Middle Ages: two symbols in art and literature, trans.
from the German by L. Chadeayne and P. Gottwald (original
ed., 1966), New York, 1970, pp. 136-140; further bibliography in Schwartz, 1972-1973, pp. 35-42.

116. P. Clemen, Die romanische monumental Malerei
in den Rheinlande, Dusseldorf, 1916, pp. 354-357. See
also H. Schrade, La Peinture romane, Paris (version française), 1966, pp. 120-192, "La Maiestas Mariae," esp.
pp. 172-174 on the image in question. Schrade does not
sufficiently attempt to distinguish between a Maiestas
Mariae and a Maiestas Ecclesiae and thus cannot discuss
their conflation.

117. Herrad von Landsberg, Hortus Deliciarum,
commentary and notes by A. Straub and G. Keller, ed. and
trans, A.D. Caratzas, n.d., New Rochelle, N.Y., pl. LIX
and p. 204.

118. W. Greisennegger, "Ecclesia," L.C.I., I, cols.
562-563 and "Ecclesia und Synagoge," L.C.I., I, cols. 571-
572, the primary attributes of the female Ecclesia are
the crown, the cross-staff and the chalice, of which both
the Herrad figure and the Saint-Loup Virgin have only the
crown, which, however, pertains equally to Maria Regina.

119. Clemen, 1916, pp. 354-357, also discusses
the heavily restored (but iconographically intact) image
of Ecclesia Triumphans frescoed on the sanctuary vault of

the monastery church in Prüfening (mid-twelfth century?).
The female figure is enthroned in a mandorla and holds
the cross-staff with pennon and an orb. She is both
crowned and vellate and has a nimbus. The four living
beings surround her glory in the vault spandrels. Christ
and the apostles appear in the apse while the lateral
walls below the figure are filled with a hieratic arrangement of saints and prophets. In general context, the
figure is comparable to both the Herrad figure (to which
Clemen compares it) and to Saint-Loup-de-Naud. The inscription around the mandorla: "Virtutum Gemmis Prelucens
Virgo Perennis Sponsi Iuncta Thoro Sponso Conregnat in Evo,"
is as suggestive as that of the Herrad miniature.

120.   Livius, 1893, pp. 51-55 and passim, discusses
Ambrose, Augustine, Jerome and others. See also E. Guldan,
Eva und Maria: eine Antithese als Bildmotiv, Cologne,
1966, esp. pp. 26-35 for the literary-theological basis.

121.   Livius, 1893, p. 39.

122.   Sermo 123: 2 De Natali Domini, "For Eve, who
was once cursed, has now, we believe, through Mary returned to the glory of benediction," quoted in translation from Livius, 1893, p. 53.

123.   See, for example, Saint Bernard's second
sermon on the Super missus est (Migne, P. L. 183:62).

124.   Réau, II, 2, p. 196. Réau, I, pp. 192-222

gives a rather extensive discussion of typological interpretation, but nowhere in this section does he treat the
Visitation.

125. The Barberini Psalter, Vatican Cod. Barb. gr.
372, fol. 146v.

126. E. Guldan, "Et verbum caro factum est--Die
Darstellung der Inkarnation Christi im Verkundigungsbild,"
Römische Quartalschrift für Christliche Altertumskunde und
für Kirchengeschichte, 63 (1968) p. 147.

127. Adams, 1974, pp. 197 and 314, nn. 288 and 289.

128. The Gospel of Luke was not often commented
upon by the Fathers or by medieval exegetes. From the
early period only the comments of Saint Ambrose have been
preserved; these were followed closely by Bede (Migne,
P. L., 92:307-634). The Glossa Ordinaria makes frequent
reference to both which attests to the importance of
Ambrose's original exegesis. A list of medieval commentators on each book of the Bible appears in C. Spicq,
Esquisse d'une histoire d'éxegese latin au moyen âge,
Paris, 1944 (Bibliothèque Thomiste, XXVI), pp. 395-401.

129. Sources chrétiennes, 45bis, II:22, "Contuen-
dum est enim quia superior uenit ad inferiorem, ut infer-
ior adiuuetur, Maria ad Elisabet, Christus ad Iohannem..."

130. In a previous passage (Ibid., II:9), Saint
Ambrose contrasted the modesty of Elizabeth and the modesty

of Mary in terms of measure and grace, which he associates with the Old Law and the New Law respectively.

131. Glossa Ordinaria, evangelium secundum Lucam, I, vers. 42. (Migne, P. L., 114:247). The author also writes for Luke I:5 a comment on Elizabeth's name: "Elisabeth, Dei mei saturitas, signat Mariam quae plena Deo fuit" (114:244), which continues to articulate Elizabeth's prophetic/symbolic role.

132. Young, 1962 (1st ed., 1933), pp. 126-131 and pp. 133-171, gives the text of (Pseudo-) Augustine's Contra Judaeos, Paganos, et Arianos Sermo de Symbolo and the texts of the Ordo plays, respectively. Elizabeth's lines, which are based on Luke I:43-44, are the same in the sermon and in the plays.

133. Quoted in translation from Muldowney, 1959, p. 64--from an Epiphany sermon entitled "They were the First Fruits of the Gentiles."

134. Sources chrétiennes, 45bis, II:45, "Stella ab his uidetur et ubi Herodes est non uidetur; ubi Christus est rursus uidetur et uiam monstrat. Ergo stella haec uia est et uia Christus,..."

135. The Glossa makes no reference to Ambrose directly in commenting on Matthew; however, Saint Ambrose commented on the Magi in his commentary to Luke to which the Glossa does make reference. See n. 128 above.

136. Migne, P. L. 114:73, "Allegorice. Stella est illuminatio fidei quae ad Christum ducit. Dum divertunt ad Judaeos, eam amittunt quia dum a malis consilium quaerunt veram illuminationem perdunt." The author also elaborates the Christ--Anti-Christ typology in his comment to Matthew II:3 (col. 74) "Nato rege coeli, rex terrae turbatus est..."

137. D. Knowles, ed., Augustine: City of God, trans. H. Bettenson, Baltimore, Md., 1972, Book XX:29.

138. Migne, P. L. 150:142 (in reference to Romans 11:8 and 13). The text is discussed by B. Blumenkranz, Les auteurs chrétiens latins du moyen âge sur les Juifs et le Judaïsme (Études juives, t. III), Paris, 1963, pp. 264-265; it was probably written between 1045-1070 at Bec.

139. "The Jews must not be persecuted and slaughtered--not even driven away...in the evening they will repent, and then their reward will not be wanting," quoted in translation from Seiferth, 1970, p. 74 from a letter of Bernard's in response to outbreaks of anti-Jewish terrorism along the Rhine which had been generated out of the frenzy surrounding the preaching of the Second Crusade.

140. Tours, Bibliothèque municipale, ms. 193, fol. 71.

141. Illustrated and discussed in Blumenkranz, 1966,

fig. 125 and p. 110.

142. Herrad von Landsberg (Straub and Keller),
n.d., pl. LXI.

143. Appendix C, pp. 409, 412, 419 and 423.

144. Appendix C, pp. 407, 410, 416 and 419-420.

145. Katzenellenbogen, (1959) 1964, pp. 27-36.

146. Katzenellenbogen, (1959) 1964, p. 36, to
which must be added van der Meulen, 1978, n. 15 (pp. 88-89).

147. See H. de Lubac, Exégèse mediévale, les quatre
sens de l'écriture, 2 vols., Paris, 1959-1964, I, pt. 1,
pp. 305-372 on "l'unité des deux testaments." See also,
M.D. Chenu, Nature, Man and Society in the Twelfth Century,
Essays on New Theological Perspectives in the Latin West,
selec., ed., and trans. by J. Taylor and L.K. Little,
Chicago, 1968, pp. 146-161.

148. See Young, 1962, II, pp. 125-171.

149. Adams, 1974, pp. 197-199, relates the Visitation column-figures to archivolts representing Justice
and Peace.

150. P.L. Gerson, The West Facade of Saint-Denis,
an Iconographic Study, unpubl. diss., Columbia University,
1970, pp. 140-161.

151. U. Mielke, "Königin von Saba," L.C.I., IV,
cols. 1-4, esp. cols. 1-2.

152. B. Kerber, "Salomo," L.C.I., IV, cols. 15-24, esp. cols. 22-23.

153. The Old Testament reading for the mass for the feast of the Annunciation is Isaiah 7:14: "Behold, a virgin shall conceive..." which parallels the angel Gabriel's words in Luke 1:31.

154. For the feast of the Epiphany, the reading is from Isaiah 60: (e.g. v.6) "All they from Sheba shall come: they shall bring gold and incense..." which makes reference to the entire Magi sequence in Matthew 2:1-12.

155. Isaiah 7:14 and 11:1-2 are the passages used in the Ordo Prophetarum (see Young, 1962, II, pp. 143-144). Moreover, often in medieval art a prophet is associated with the scene of the Annunciation. Where a single prophet can be identified with assurance as in the north transept wall at Conques or the southern lateral portal of Notre-Dame-du-Port, it is inevitably Isaiah.

156. On the headpiece see Appendix C, n. 65. Isaiah was traditionally held to be of royal lineage and, thus, not of the house of priests. See, H. Hollander, "Isaiah," L.C.I., II, cols. 357-358.

157. Jeremiah 1:1 and Ezekiel 1:3.

158. Jeremiah 31-22 and Ezekiel 44:1-3.

159. While Isaiah and Jeremiah express themselves in parallel to Gabriel's words in Luke 1:31, Ezekial only refers metaphorically to the virginal conception announced by Gabriel.

160. Migne, P. L. 3:1039. Saint Jerome (Migne, P. L., 24:914) clearly understood the passage in the reference to the Annunciation but did not refer to Isaiah. Strabo's commentary (Migne, P. L. 114:9-62) omits the Jeremiah verse in question.

161. Peter Comestor, In Annuntiatione B. Virginis (Migne, P. L., 198:1772).

162. Jeremiah appears below the Angel Gabriel on the left side of the portal; Isaiah appears below Mary on the right. Although figures of Daniel and Ezekial accompany Jeremiah and Isaiah, appearing to their left and right respectively, the axial alignment with the angel and Mary suggests a stronger connection between Jeremiah and Isaiah. Höllander (op. cit. n. 156, col. 356) discusses Jeremiah as Isaiah's "Partner."

163. Appendix C, pp. 394-402, 445-458 and 461-476.

164. Breviarum in Psalmos (Migne, P. L. 26:1162-1166, esp. 1166).

165. See P. Block, "Christus, Christusbild, III, Das Christusbild der Kunst der karolingischen, ottonischen und romanischen Epoche," L.C.I., I, col. 403. Ultimately,

the type has its origins in Roman imperial art; see

A. Grabar, L'Empereur dans l'art byzantin, Strasbourg,

1936, pp. 237ff.

166. A. Legner, "Christus, Christusbild, IV, 1:
Beau Dieu," L.C.I., I, cols. 414-415. The 'Beau Dieu'
type, which is (with the exception of the figure at Dax
in southwestern France, dated in the third quarter of
the thirteenth century) a limited phenomenon both in time
and area, itself merits a careful iconographic study.
The surviving examples are all located in the Ile-de-
France and dated in the High Gothic period. See, most
recently, M. Appellof, Gothic Sculpture: The Iconography
of the Beau Dieu, unpubl. Honors thesis, Wesleyan University, 1977.

167. Enarrationes in Psalmos (Migne, P. L. 37:1168).
In later exegesis, the two ideas--Christ and the Church--
are combined: see, for example, Saint Bernard, In Psalmum
XC, sermo 14 (Migne, P. L. 183:242).

168. The biblical basis for the Good Shepherd metaphor is John 10:1-18, specifically verse 11. The First
Epistle of Peter (2:25) extends the metaphor by calling
Christ "...the Shepherd and Bishop of your soul." Augustine, in his Tractates on the Gospel of Saint John, specifically Tractate 46 on John 10:11-13, also extended the
metaphor to include bishops, making reference to Saint

Timothy who was sent by Saint Paul to Ephesus to lead the
community there (see, Migne, P. L. 35:1727-1732, esp.
1730 and in English, P. Schaff, A Select Library of the
Nicene and Post-Nicene Fathers, New York, 1908, VII,
p. 257). On croziers and their symbolism, see A. Voretzch,
"Stab," L.C.I., IV, cols. 193-198.

169. Among the so-called Early Gothic portals
which include Saints' cycles, the limited Saint Nicholas
and Saint Stephen scenes in the archivolts at Notre-Dame
in Vermenton hardly compare with Saint-Loup. Perhaps
the closest comparison lies on the facade of the abbey
church of Saint-Denis where two lateral tympana and the
central trumeau represented events from the life of the
patron, Saint Denis. Later, extended Saints' cycles
become more common--for example, the Saint Stephen cycle,
now re-used, on the north transept of the Cathedral of
Saint Stephen in Meaux. Ultimately Saints' cycles take
over whole portals, as in the Calixtus Portal on the north
transept at Reims or in the Confessor's Portal on the
south transept at Chartres.

170. See Appendix C, n. 102.

171. Appendix C, pp. 399-402, 445-458 and 461-476.

172. Generally, scenes representing episodes which
occurred during the saints' lifetime appear in the left
half of the archivolts and the port mortem miracles on

the right. However, this distinction requires that the unidentifiable execution scene in WM3-s/6 and s/7 represents a <u>post mortem</u> miracle and not a reference to Saint-Loup freeing prisoners on his way through Paris. It also requires that the "Bell Miracle" in WM2-s/2 represents something more than a single or composite miracle related to bells in the vita episodes. In spite of these two irregularities, there nevertheless exists a further criterion for distinguishing the left (north) from the right. On the left half of the archivolts, Saint Loup repeats in each scene; whereas, on the right, he is represented only once in the center, thereby relating to all figures which surround him.

173. Chapter I, pp. 6-9.

174. Appendix B, Doc. VI.

175. The tradition of miracles wrought at Saint-Loup-de-Naud was so strong that Geoffrey of Courlon still made reference to it in 1293, after Innocent III had denied, about 1212 (Bourquelot, 1840/41, p. 256 and n. 1), the authenticity of the relics given in 1161 (see Julliot and Prou, 1887, p. 6 and Appendix B, Doc. VI and Sect. C: Comments and n. 6). More specific than Hugh of Toucy before him, who spoke only of <u>miraculis</u>, Geoffrey states, "...ob sancti Lupi merita, fiunt multorum infirmorum curationes..."

176. Pressouyre, 1970, p. 23.

177. P. Séjourné, "Culte des Saints," D.T.C., XIV, cols. 870-978, esp. cols. 950-958.

178. It is, of course, in this light that one must understand the scenes of demon trapping (as a variation of exorcism) in WM3-n/2 and WM2-n/2; healing a blind man (?) in WM3-n/3 and WM2-n/3 and baptism in WM3-n/4 and WM2-n/4.

179. This applies particularly to the post mortem scenes.

180. Saint Paul, as other Apostolic and other Early Church writers, uses the term sanctus to refer to the faithful who believe in Christ. In the Middle Ages, it came to refer only to those members of the community of the faithful who by their exemplary lives or deaths are already assimilated to Christ in Heaven and who, therefore, do not have to await the Final Judgement to achieve Paradise. For definitions and bibliography, see C. O'Neill, "Saint," N.C.E., 12, pp. 852-853. See also n. 177 above.

181. Saint Paul, 1 Corinthians 1:2, defined the Universal Church as being composed of various churches whose members were "saints" chosen by God. Saints in the later, restricted sense are clearly part, indeed, a special part, of that larger group of saints--the community of the faithful (see n. 180 above). In a way, we are arguing for a synecdochal substitution of Saint for saint (in terms of

Paul's definition) for this allegorical interpretation of the Saint-Loup cycle.

182. Saint Augustine, 1972, p. 1033ff (Book XXII:8).

183. Ibid., p. 1047ff (Book XXII:9). Saint Augustine speaks here of martyrs, but that is a function of his epoch and the discussion can be later extended to confessors as sainthood itself was.

184. On the nature and meaning of the miracle, see T.G. Pater, "Miracles, Theology of," N.C.E., 9, pp. 890-894. For a more extensive treatment, see A. Michel, "Miracle," D.T.C., X:2, 1798-1859.

185. Quoted in translation from M. Staniforth, Early Christian Writings: The Apostolic Fathers, Baltimore, 1968, p. 45. See also F. Klosterman, "Apostle: 2. in theology," N.C.E., 1, pp. 681-682.

186. P. Schmitz, Histoire de l'ordre de Saint Benoît, vol. 6, Liège, 1949, p. 225, "On ne tentera pas ici d'exposer en quelques lignes toute la théologie spirituelle de saint Bernard: ce serait une trahison. Ce qui importe, c'est de relever les quelques traits saillants de sa doctrine, ceux qui ont marqué davantage l'évolution de la piété médiévale. On peut les synthetiser d'un mot; celui-la meme que donnait le saint à ses directions: Viae Domini "les voies du Seigneur; ces médiations entre Dieu et l'homme: le Christ, la vierge Marie, les saints."

187. Quoted from Sanders, ed., <u>Beati in Apocalypsin</u> <u>librii XII</u> (Papers and Monographs of the American Academy in Rome, VII), Rome, 1930, p. 271.

188. Cf. P. du Bourguet, s.j., <u>The Art of the Copts</u>, trans. from the French by C. Hay-Shaw, New York, 1971 (1st ed., 1967), illus. on p. 53.

189. Cf. Oakeshott, 1967, pl. 99.

190. For example, in a <u>Civitas Dei</u> manuscript from Canterbury dated around 1120 [Florence, Bibl. Laurenziana, Cod. Plut. XII 17, fol. 2v, attributed to the Canterbury school and dated by C.M. Kauffman, <u>A Survey of Manuscripts</u> <u>Illuminated in the British Isles, III: Romanesque Manu-</u> <u>scripts, 1066-1190</u>, London and Boston, 1975, pp. 62-63 and pl. 50], Christ sits at the top of the composition in a mandorla flanked by angels with musical instruments. The next register contains palm-bearing apostles. Im- mediately below these, a figure of <u>Ecclesia</u> sits enthroned between two groups of saints. At the center of the lowest register a cherubim guards the heavenly gate between groups of saints and kings. The whole composition is en- framed by an architectural motif. On City of God manu- scripts in general see A. de Laborde, <u>Les manuscrits à</u> <u>peintures de la Cité de Dieu de Saint Augustine</u>, Paris, 1909.

CHAPTER V

CONSIDERATIONS ON THE STYLE OF THE PORTAL
SCULPTURE AT SAINT-LOUP-DE-NAUD

I. Introduction

Traditionally, the sculpture of Saint-Loup-de-Naud
has been described as stylistically homogeneous.[1] This
position must now be reexamined in view of the demonstra-
tion that nearly one half of the portal sculpture consists
of physically disparate elements, each of which may have
had a separate provenance. Following a reappraisal of the
state of literature on the internal style of Saint-Loup-de-
Naud, we will show that there exist limited stylistic differences which correspond to the physical disparities.

In relationship to the styles of other monuments,
Saint-Loup-de-Naud has been placed, invariably, among the
group of Maiestas portals associated with Chartres West.[2]
Recently, scholarship has placed Saint-Loup within a sub-
group of monuments located in Burgundy and the Champagne;[3]
its portal capitals have been linked to capitals of several
churches including the Cathedral of Sens.[4]

We have seen documentary evidence of strong, active
and continuing ties between the priory of Saint-Loup-de-
Naud and its parent abbey in the city of Sens, Saint-Pierre-

224

le-Vif.[5] We have seen, moreover, evidence of an even
wider involvement of the city of Sens in the region around
and beyond Saint-Loup.[6] Finally, we have presented evidence of formal connections (both general and specific) between the architecture of Saint-Loup-de-Naud and monuments
in the city of Sens.[7]

Much attention has been given to the artistic significance of the city of Sens following the execution of the
sculpture decorating the west facade of its cathedral.[8]
Conversely, little attention has been given to Senonais
sculptural activity preceding that time. In the light of
the historical and architectural ties between Saint-Loup
and Sens, as well as recent suggested sculptural relationships, a re-evaluation of the documentary evidence reflecting Senonais sculptural activity during the Middle Ages
is a necessary basis to any reconsideration of the relationships between Saint-Loup-de-Naud and other monuments.
We will show evidence of continuous sculptural activity in
Sens over the course of the Middle Ages and particularly
during the first three-quarters of the twelfth century.
(As a note of caution, it must be remarked that the greater
evidence for sculptural activity in the twelfth century
more likely reflects the greater number of records surviving from that period than any necessarily greater amount
of productivity.)

Following a reassessment of the state of literature
comparing Saint-Loup to other monuments, similarities be-

tween Saint-Loup and surviving Senonais sculpture will be shown to be sufficiently close to postulate a Senonais atelier evolving, over time, as the artistic origin for all Saint-Loup sculpture. With Saint-Loup-de-Naud as an exemplum of Senonais sculpture, the relationship of Sens to Chartres West, Burgundy and the Champagne will be briefly discussed.[8a]

II. The Sculpture of the Western Portal at Saint-Loup-de-Naud: Internal Stylistic Relationships

General similarities of sculptural form within the western portal at Saint-Loup-de-Naud[9] have produced the often implicitly but nevertheless uniformly held opinion that the sculptural cycle possesses a "...parfaite unité de son exécution..."[10] Indeed many significant features occur throughout the portal. The figures in general are disposed calmly and often express the limits of the block from which they were carved. Drapery is usually calm and folds which are rendered as blunted incisions appear in every figure. The arrangement of the garments pays a nominal respect to an ultimately inorganically conceived anatomy but seldom really reveals body structure. Areas of decorative handling of the drapery appear throughout the portal in a secondary role, often articulating joints, never dominating the conception of the figure. Physiognomically the figures also possess a combination of abstract and natural-

istic features. Doubly incised almond-shaped eyes set additively below symmetrically arching brows dominate more organic features such as the lips which swell quite naturalistically from the flesh of a usually heavy, curving jaw.

Yet in spite of these important similarities (and the
absence heretofore of any real reason to question the homogeneity of internal style) several scholars have pointed to
features which set various figures or groups of figures
apart.

In the embrasure zone, for example, both Stoddard and
Salet see the trumeau as being qualitatively distinct from
the six column-figures (cf. figs. 27, 31, 32). Stoddard
unequivocally calls the trumeau the "...finest sculpture
in the portal..."[11] Salet is less direct, stating that
"Les autres statues ne sont pas d'une qualité inférieure
à cet admirable morceau,"[12] but continuing on to describe
the queen (col. fig. 2-n) as "...banale, un peu empâ-
tée..."[13] and the two outermost figures (3-n and 3-s) as
being "...d'une exécution plus médiocre..."[14] These remarks do not, as we have seen,[15] reflect mere arbitrary distinctions of quality however much they may appear to do so.
There are, of course, important similarities between the
trumeau and the embrasure figures: the blunted incisions
which form the drapery folds, the general adherence to the
lateral block-contours, the calm hems and the sloping pose

of the feet and the facial features of the trumeau and
several of the column-figures, particularly those of the
queen.[16] However, significant differences also exist.
The eccentric placement of the trumeau relative to the
block behind it and the impression of movement given by
the turn of the head and the swing of the dalmatic sleeve
of the arm raised in blessing are most important. The
depth and spatial complexity of the undercutting of that
same sleeve are also greater than the handling of the
corresponding garments in any of the six column-figures
even though their attributes provide an even greater
opportunity for them. Moreover, we must mention that
visualizing the Saint-Loup column-figures in their intended compositional setting effectively eliminates one of
their "advanced features." Placement in wider embrasures
with short colonnettes below their ring consoles and
shafts projecting above their heads would radically alter
our visual impressions of their "proportions plus
justes."[17] Several of the column-figures, most particularly the king and queen (2-s and 2-n), are in fact quite
slender (cf. figs. 31, 32).[18] Finally, the handling of
the heads reveals two small but striking differences:
the eyes of the trumeau figure maintain themselves on
the frontal plane of the head unlike those of all six
column-figures whose eyes "bend" around onto the lateral

planes; the mouth of the trumeau figure is distinguished
by the absence of an idiosyncratic detail common to the
other (four) figures which it resembles, that is, the
absence of the asymmetrical extension (to the right) of
the line of intersection between the lips (cf. figs. 27a,
86, 95).[19]

For the upper zones of the portal, particularly the
lintel and tympanum, we find again that several scholars
have made observations which, although unpursued, implicitly call into question the stylistic homogeneity of the
sculpture of Saint-Loup-de-Naud. For example, Focillon
remarks:

> "...à Saint-Loup-de-Naud, nous avons le personnage
> sous arcade dans toute sa pureté, comme si l'art
> roman, à la veille de finir, revenait aux formules
> les plus anciennes, par une curieuse régression sur
> le style des ateliers acquitains."[20]

This remark contrasts with his interpretation of the
column-figures which he believes escape these features.[21]
Maillé also appears to have seen the apostles as being
stylistically distinct, but in what way is not entirely
clear.[22] Kerber comments on what he calls the Burgundian
quality of the "...schräggestellten Beinen des Christus"
on the tympanum by which he makes implicit reference to
the splayed legs of the Autun tympanum Christ and thereby
to an "older" style.[23]

These observations clearly respond to the relief

properties which are most obviously present in these two areas of the upper zone. On the lintel[24] (fig. 23) this mural quality evidences itself in the general adherence of the apostles to the limits of their architectural frame.[25] In apostle s/2 this relationship is most pronounced. The figure sits in profile from the hips downward and has his legs crossed. Above the waist the torso flattens back to parallel the ground, save for the right shoulder which is pulled slightly forward to suggest an unrealized three-quarter pose. Both the book held in the left hand and the left foot "transgress" the architectural frame and overlap the shaft and its base. But here, as in the overlapping elements of apostles s/3, s/4 and presumably also n/2,[26] the overlapping does not increase the plasticity of the figures. Instead, by pressing back onto the plane of the block (colonnettes), they reaffirm the dominant planar conception of the relief.

Kerber's assertion that the pose of the legs of the figure of Christ (in the tympanum) derives from an ultimately planar, mural style is surely also correct,[27] but far more compelling in its mural quality is the relationship of the winged man, or, Matthew symbol, to its block. Although similar in anatomical handling and drapery arrangement and even facial detail to several angels in the archivolts, for example, n/3, the winged man is remarkable for the rigorous control which the limits of the block seem to have imposed on the sculptor's conception of the figure.[28] His awkward, tilting pose results from the conformity of the figure's anatomy to the restrictive contours of the small triangular block.[29]

This relief property of the figures on the lintel and tympanum contrasts with a more plastic handling of the angels in the first archivolt (fig. 23).[30] While these figures all stand comfortably within the limits of their voussoir blocks, the movement present within the figures, for example, WM1-n/3 or WM1-s/2, occurs free of restraint from the block unlike, for example, apostle s/2 or the winged man. Moreover, seen from in front of the portal, the angels present a variety of poses from the nearly full profile of WM1-s/3 to the three-quarter profile of WM1-n/4 to the nearly frontal of WM1-s/5 and in so doing begin to "turn away" from the planar conception of sculptural form found on the lintel or tympanum. It must be pointed out that the differentiation between the angels and the figures of the tympanum and lintel is not solely a function of the inherently cubic form of a voussoir block. As Salet pointed out in discussing the movement and poses of the angels at Saint-Loup, the angels of the innermost archivolt at Saint-Ayoul in

Provins (WM) are, in comparison, "...figés dans des poses hiératiques" (i.e., frontal).[31]

Recognizing the existence of these formal differences within the general similarities of the sculpture of Saint-Loup-de-Naud poses fewer problems than assessing their significance. What factors account for the greater movement in the trumeau figure relative to the rigid frontality of the column-figures? Differences in movement, and in placement with respect to the block behind (eccentricity), can hardly reflect a difference in the architectonic function of trumeau and column-figure. At Chartres SM the column-figures turn their heads slightly while the trumeau remains rigidly frontal and symmetrically placed with respect to the lateral limits of its block.[32] The slight turn of the head of the Saint Anne trumeau at Chartres NM can be attributed to an element of narrative content imposed by a second figure--the infant Mary whom she holds.[33] The trumeau figures at Sens Cathedral (WM), Meaux (NM), Paris Cathedral, Sainte-Anne Portal (WS) and Bourges Cathedral (S) are also all frontal and symmetrically placed.[34] Moreover, no obvious iconographic motivation suggests itself for the movement and placement of the trumeau at Saint-Loup-de-Naud. In contrast, for the tympanum, lintel and innermost archivolt at Saint-Loup, one might argue that the different approach to the figures (relief as opposed to volume) is due to a kind of "iconographic inertia" in which theologically more important (tradition-bound) image-types respond more slowly to stylistic change than do less important types and thus account for formal differences, at least, in the upper zones.[35] Knowing that certain sculptures were not designed for their present emplacement at Saint-Loup suggests an alternative way to explain both the striking similarities and the curious differences within the portal sculpture. Both the similarities and the differences could be accounted for if the atelier which carved the trumeau (and the other sculptures designed for Saint-Loup) was also the same one which, at an earlier time, carved the column-figures, the tympanum and the lintel. This atelier could then have brought these latter sculptures with them from their place of origin at the time they came to erect the present ensemble. This hypothesis assumes that those sculptures carved for another location were carved first.[36] However likely, it must be stated that this is not necessarily true, since they can have been contemporary and designed for a different location or, in fact, even have been later although the evolving Gothic style as we now understand it makes the latter possibility unlikely.

Concerning the questions of relief area/sculptural volume and relative chronologies, the Virgin at the center

of the lintel and the Nativity voussoirs at the bottom
of the outer pair of archivolts raise interesting problems
(cf. figs. 23-26, 31, 32, 46, 47, 61, 62). Stylistically
homogeneous within themselves[37] and closely related both
to the column-figures below[38] and to the apostles on the
lintel,[39] they are at the same time, the most volumetri-
cally realized figures of the entire ensemble. In our
tentative relative chronology of the portal sculpture,
they correspond most closely to the "older" column
figures in facial type and drapery handling but are more
"advanced" in volumetric rendering than the "later" archivolts. Some of the difference in the three-dimensionality
of these figures could undoubtedly stem from differing
volumetric requirements of that other architectural setting for which these figures were originally designed.
Indeed, their volumetric properties may have been iconographically motivated to set them apart (presumably with
other scenes) in some way analogous to the "horizontal
register" which they occupy at Saint-Loup. Either or
both of these explanations would allow for a return to
the traditional opinion that the portal at Saint-Loup-de
Naud is a stylistic unity. To do so is tempting; however,
to do so is, by extension, to deny the validity of one
of the oldest, most consistently invoked assumptions
about the evolution of Early Gothic[39a] sculptural style:
namely, that it evolves from a relief conception toward

a volumetric conception of the figure.[40] Moreover, the
very factor of spolia further complicates the problem
by placing a practically insurmountable barrier between
the historian and the original formal and iconographic
context of the sculptures in question. Looked at in this
light, the combination of similarities and differences
in the Saint-Loup sculpture raises serious questions
about the viability of the concept of an ultimately
linear development of Early Gothic sculptural style.[41]

III. A Survey of the Evidence for Architectural and
Sculptural Activity in the City of Sens During the Middle
Ages to the Thirteenth Century

The sources for this preliminary survey are, for
the present, primarily literary, because much has been
destroyed, little has been excavated and, with the
exception of the church of Saint-Savinian which is now
(arbitrarily) dated in the eleventh century,[42] nothing
is thought to survive above ground from before the
twelfth century. Sens is, in comparison to many centers,
rich in literary records. Three chronicles written by
monks of Saint-Pierre-le-Vif survive from the Middle
Ages: the eleventh-century text of Odorannus,[43] the
twelfth-century text of Clarius[44] and the later thirteenth-
century text of Geoffrey of Courlon.[45] This same Geoffrey
has also left a "Book of Relics" which contains an
obituary list for the archbishops of Sens and the abbots

of Saint-Pierre-le-Vif.[46] Various charters and other
documents have been collected in a "pseudo-cartulary"
by Quantin, but no actual cartulary exists.[47] These
records can be supplemented by miscellaneous references
which appear in other medieval texts.[48] Finally, there
are several post-medieval texts which copy parts of other
lost medieval records, such as the two seventeenth-
century "monastic chronicles" of Dom Cottron.[49] This
wide range of materials provides considerable information
about architectural and sculptural activity in Sens
for the period in question.

Medieval tradition places the christianization of
the pagan Senones and the erection of the first Christian
church in Sens during the first century A.D.[50] Today,
nothing is known of the earliest structures. Monasticism
seems to have been established outside the city walls
during the Merovingian period. The oldest abbey, Saint-
Pierre-le-Vif, was founded by a daughter (?) of Clovis
in the early sixth century (509?).[51] The abbey of Sainte-
Colombe was founded under Clotaire II (†620) who had a
particular veneration for the patron saint.[52] How much
new construction or reuse of earlier materials was involved
in establishing these monasteries cannot be determined
from the documents.

Three periods before the thirteenth century set

themselves apart as periods of considerable activity (It is assumed that architectural campaigns involve at least some sculptural activity). The first of these is the archiepiscopacy of Wenilon (841-865); the second extends from the end of the tenth century to the early eleventh under, particularly, the archiepiscopacies of Anastasius (968-977) and Sewinus (978-999); the third extends over the middle of the twelfth century under the archiepiscopacies of Henri Sanglier (1122-1144) and Hugh of Toucy (1144-1168).

Wenilon appears to have at least partially rebuilt the cathedral: "aecclesiam vero Sancti-Stephani, quae erat vetustissima, renovavit idem Wenilo..." (Clarius).[53] He also celebrated consecrations in the abbeys of Saint-Pierre-le-Vif (847) and Sainte-Colombe (853).[54] These records, which reflect the discovery and translation of relics,[55] have been construed to indicate new buildings for these churches,[56] but the documents do not support this interpretation.[57] More certain is the statement that Wenilon finished (perfecit) the abbey and basilica of Saint-Rémi[58] which was begun (ceperat aedificare) before 829 (Clarius).[59] Shortly afterward began a period of Norman invasions and local internecine warfare which decimated the country side and appears to have damaged if not destroyed (destructa) a number of buildings.[60]

The second half of the tenth century was evidently a period of recovery during which the cathedral, which had been destroyed (damaged?) by fire in 968,[61] was rebuilt. That same year Archbishop Archambaldus began to rebuild the church (cepit restaurare); he completed the presbytery (perfitiens...presbyterium) together with a "cryptis retro" (Geoffrey).[62] Porée considered this last to be the apse, but it could refer to an eastern confessio as at Saint-Pierre-le-Vif.[63] This work was continued under Anastasius who completed the chancel and the middle part (?) of the church [perficiens cancellos et medietatem ipsius (basilice)][64] and Sewinus who completed (perfecit) the work and dedicated the church in 983 (Clarius).[65] During the abbacy of Sewinus' nephew Rainardus (†1015), Saint-Pierre-le-Vif was restored (renovavit) and the cloister together with surrounding buildings entirely rebuilt (monasterii claustra cum domibus ad se pertinentibus ex toto reedificavit) (Odorannus).[66] Although the text makes no mention of the fact, the work in the cloister probably involved some figurative sculpture, even if only on the capitals.

The eleventh century proper appears--from the documents--to have witnessed little building activity. The martyrial church of Saint-Savinian near the abbey of Saint-Pierre was rebuilt or restored from 1068[67] and

another martyrial church, Saint-Thibault, seems to have
been newly built: "Hoc anno (1076), Arnulfus, abbas
Sanctae-Columbae detulit de Italia reliquias de corpore
sancti Thebaudi, fratris sui, et posuit in eadem abbatia:
coepitque aedificare ecclesiam in honore ejus sancti
quae est euntibus de civitate ad eamdem abbatiam, juxta
viam, ad dexteram manum" (Clarius).[68] From the eleventh
century also comes the earliest reference to figural
sculpture: a tomb monument in Saint-Pierre-le-Vif
decorated with silver images (imagines argenteas).[69]

The twelfth century, like the late tenth, appears
to have been a major period of building activity. The
first decade witnessed the completion of the chevet
(perfecta est turris) and the vaulting of the choir
(coopertura super corum) of the abbey of Saint-Pierre-le-
Vif (Clarius).[70] Of course, the city's cathedral is
thought to have been under construction from either
c.1128 or c.1140--depending on which interpretation of
the vague documentary evidence is accepted--to about 1180
(?), except for the facade and western towers.[71] In
spite of the numerous studies on Sens Cathedral, there
has as yet been no comprehensive study of interior
sculpture, a fact which is partially accounted for by the
consequences of later building campaigns, Revolutionary
damage and nineteenth-century restoration.[72] The middle

of the century--1142 to perhaps 1165--saw the reconstruction of the church of the other major Benedictine abbey,
Sainte-Colombe.[73] From the twelfth century also survive
two records of monumental figural sculpture from before
the period now associated with the sculpture of the west
facade of the cathedral. The first is a tomb monument
for the archbishop Hugh of Toucy (†1168) which Geoffrey
describes in his obituary list: "Sepultus fuit in cenobio
Sancti Petri sub tumba lapidea, in qua ymago sue faciei est
elevata."[74] Equally interesting is the almost unique
record of an actual statue being executed for the cloister
of Saint-Pierre-le-Vif in or shortly after 1146. The
burghers of the city, being somewhat disaffected by the
dissolution of their commune, rioted within the abbey,
murdered the abbot and a nephew of the king and thereby
brought about royal intervention in the dispute. In
addition to throwing the leaders from the abbey tower,
Louis VII exacted an annual fine and caused a statue of
a cherub to be erected in the cloister to commemorate the
deceased abbot.[75] This statue was evidently of such
prominence that a century and a quarter later Geoffrey
could still use it to locate a tomb site: "Obitt Guido
de Fontanis, armiger; jacet juxta Cherubin, in prato
claustri."[76]

In summary, the fragmentary documentation by no
means reflects all artistic activity, but it clearly

suffices to demonstrate a continuous sculptural tradition
in Sens during the Middle Ages. It suggests three periods
of concentrated activity: the mid-ninth, late tenth and
twelfth centuries, and clearly indicates that some larger
position must be provided for Sens in our understanding
of the development of medieval sculpture.

IV. The Sculpture of the Western Portal at Saint-Loup-de-Naud: Stylistic Relationships with Other Monuments

Bourquelot first pointed out the formal similarity
between the tympana at Saint-Loup-de-Naud and Chartres
West (M) and it is now a commonplace of the history of
style to associate Saint-Loup with the larger circle of
monuments related to Chartres West.[77] Vöge, from whose
work most modern studies on style ultimately depend,
identified stylistic links between the column-figures[78]
at Saint-Loup and those at Chartres[79] and concluded that
"Das Portal von Saint-Loup-de-Naud ist ein Schulwerk des
Chartreser Hauptmeisters..."[80] Since Vöge, virtually
every author on the portal or on Early Gothic style
in general has pursued the connection to some degree,[81]
with Stoddard being more specific than most.[82] He claims
that the tympanum of Saint-Loup is closer to Chartres
than are Le Mans or Provins[83] and finds individual sources
for several Saint-Loup column-figures among those in the
Chartres central portal.[84] More recently, Sauerländer

has reconfirmed that Saint-Loup "...belongs to the same type and stylistic family..." as Chartres by comparing, among others, the head of Saint Paul (l-n) to a head by the so-called Saint-Denis Master (WS, col. fig. l-s).[85]

Ultimately the relationship between Chartres West and Saint-Loup[86] is made more complex by the question of the role of Burgundy in the formation of Early Gothic sculptural style. Specifically the issue hinges around the date assigned to the sculpture of the western portals of Saint-Bénigne in Dijon.[87] For certain scholars Saint-Bénigne dates around 1147[88] and thus exemplifies a Burgundian style thought to be reflected in Chartres West—which is, itself, undated[89]—and the Île-de-France.[90] For others, Saint-Bénigne is dated later than Chartres West and reflects the influence of Île-de-France forms in Burgundy.[91] While the current weight of opinion seems to favor a date around 1155-1160[92] (as it does for most Early Gothic sculpture, give or take ten years),[93] Quarré's proposed earlier date has not been entirely refuted and the sculptures remain undated in any absolute chronological sense. However because striking similarities have been pointed out between the sculpture at Saint-Loup-de-Naud and that from Saint-Bénigne, the relative chronological position of the latter is critical to any understanding of the former.[94]

Finally, Pressouyre, expanding upon Vöge and
Lapeyre,[95] suggested "un retard Champenois" which centers
(apparently) in Châlons-sur-Marne (in which group Saint-
Loup is included) and which absorbs influences from both
the Île-de-France (Chartres) and Burgundy (Saint-Bénigne).[96]

In the light of the foregoing, it is necessary to
reconsider the formal relationships between the sculpture
of Saint-Loup-de-Naud and other monuments. As a codicil,
we must consider both the origins of the spoliate
sculptures which now form a part of that portal and the
origins of the sculptors who carved those figures which
fit within their architectural setting and who presumably
assembled the entire portal complex.

Leaving aside for the moment those locations which
we have just discussed, the logical place to turn from
an historical point of view would be the city of Sens
upon which, as we know, Saint-Loup was administratively
dependent.[97] In this regard, Schlink has already
suggested that "...einige Kapitelle der Sockelarkatur
des Chorumgangs der Kathedrale von Sens, Kapitelle im
Chorneubau und am Westportal von Saint-Germain-des-Prés,
Kapitelle des Gewandes am Westportal von Saint-Loup-de-
Naud..." all belong together stylistically.[98] In view
of our previous discussion of lost but documented
medieval sculpture in the city of Sens we are in a
position to pursue the relationship between Saint-Loup-

de-Naud and Sens somewhat further and to return through
that investigation to the question of the relationship
between Burgundy, Chartres West and the Champagne.

When Schlink referred to capitals in the northern
choir aisle socle arcade at Sens, he was not at all specific about which capitals were intended. Presumably he
had in mind a beast capital like that at AIINI (fig. 141)
which can be successfully compared to the beast on
embrasure capital 2/s at Saint-Loup (fig. 142). He may
also have intended to compare the head of the female
ecclesiastic on the vintner's capital at Sens (AINI, fig.
148) with the veiled female head on the griffin capital
in the right embrasure at Saint-Loup (3/s, fig. 149).
This comparison can be successfully extended to the female
heads of the Nativity cycle voussoirs (fig. 147). Particularly compelling are the similarities of the swollen,
boneless flesh of the cheek, the heavy curve of the jaw
and the small, prominent chin. Similar also are the small,
pursed lips which swell organically from the face, the
arching of the brow--best seen on the left side of the
Sens head which is damaged at the right brow--and the
formation of the eyes as almond shapes enframed by now
barely visible, doubly incised lids extended by incisions
at the corners.[99] Given these similarities the differences
in the size of the pupils and the coarser handling of the
layered folds of the veils seem unimportant.[100] One can

also instructively compare the monk figure on the opposite
side of the same vintner's capital (fig. 150) with several
figures in the archivolts at Saint-Loup, for example,
the two figures from the lower voussoir of the execution
scene (WM3-s/6, fig. 151). In each case the standing,
short-waisted figures possess ox-bow folds to divide
torso from legs. The legs press through the drapery and
the cloth over them is articulated only by occasional,
incised folds which curve upward in defiance of gravity.
Between the legs of each male figure, thin, essentially
parallel incisions flare slightly at the bottom to terminate with little undercutting. Similar also is the relationship between the monk's extended arm and his torso
and those of the figure on the right side of the Saint-
Loup voussoir.[101] In view of the striking similarities
between the Sens capitals and the Saint-Loup sculpture,
it is surprising to find a gap of as much as forty years
(and never less than ten) between the dates assigned to
them and the arbitrarily chosen date of c.1160 or c.1170
for Saint-Loup.[102]

In 1960 Salet published a capital (?) plausibly
linked to Saint-Pierre-le-Vif which allows us to take
our comparisons still further (figs. 134-137).[103] This
narrow, nearly cylindrical stone contains four rather
severely damaged figures seated on a shallow moulding
beneath a continuous arcade borne on thin colonnettes.

All appear to be short-waisted, flat-chested and to have
thin tubular legs beneath drapery which varies from the
linear to a more fully modelled fold. The figure identified by inscription as Rex Robertus is of particular
concern for Saint-Loup.[104] This figure's nearly identical pose and costume affords an excellent basis for
comparison with the Herod figure at Saint-Loup (figs. 131
and 134). Given an allowance for a different degree of
plasticity which results from their differing architectural setting, the flatness of the chests and the only
semi-independent relationship between arms and torsos stand
out. Similar also is the organization and handling of
the thin, rope-like folds which sag rhythmically across
the chest in pairs. Reconstruction of the neckline and
damaged folds of the collar of the King Robert figure,
suggests an arrangement very similar to the overlapped
fold found on the collar of the Saint-Loup Herod. The
penchant for complicated hemlines, for thin, tubular,
flaring folds and for an elongated, cylindrical treatment
of the lower leg found on the Herod can also be seen on
the figure of Saint Paul (fig. 135) located on an adjacent face of the same Saint-Pierre-le-Vif capital.
Interesting also is the spirally-looped fold articulating
the waist of the Saint Paul figure (and the other two--
only the king does not have it) on the Saint-Pierre

capital.[105] This uncommon fold also appears on several voussoir figures in the portal at Saint-Loup.[106] Not present in any of the published sculptures from Châlons-sur-Marne, or in the portals at Le Mans or Bourges, for example, the fold appears almost as a "signature" of a particular artist or an atelier.[107] It appears, however, in several other, interesting places. It occurs on the tympanum from Issy-le-Moulineaux which can be linked historically through Saint-Germain-des-Prés to the Sens ambient.[108] The fold also occurs in several door-jamb figures and capital frieze on the West Facade of Chartres,[109] but it appears nowhere else on these portals.[110] Moreover, comparison of a jamb figure head from Chartres (WN, s jamb, 5, fig. 152) and an unpublished sculptural fragment from the Musée municipale in Sens (fig. 153)[111] reveals remarkably close similarities in general form and detail handling (facial structure, beard and hair form, e.g.). An assessment of the relationship between Saint-Loup and Chartres West must therefore begin with an inquiry into the nature of the artistic relationship between Sens and Chartres.[112]

V. Conclusions and New Directions

Several conclusions seem in order which point the way to new directions for research into the stylistic history of Early Gothic sculpture. Relatively consistent within itself, but not without its problems for an internal relative chronology, the sculpture of Saint-Loup-de-Naud shows strong stylistic links to surviving sculpture from the city of Sens. Given the historical connections between the priory and the city, it seems entirely reasonable to suggest that the spoliate sculptures as well as the atelier which carved the remainder of the sculptures for the portal came from the city of Sens and possibly even from the parent abbey of Saint-Pierre-le-Vif. It would not seem unreasonable to conclude that Saint-Loup-de-Naud is the product of one or more Senonais ateliers and, as such, representative of Senonais Early Gothic style. Moreover, lost but documented works, surviving sculpture and fragments and the portal at Saint-Loup itself indicate clearly that Sens has been alarmingly underevaluated in the literature on Early Gothic sculpture, particularly as it applies to the question of interrelationships between Chartres West and Burgundy. Entirely apart from any absolute or relative chronology, a potentially major sculptural center geographically and politically between Burgundy, Chartres and the Champagne must now be reckoned with. We cannot hope, nor will we attempt to address this issue here. To begin with, it requires the assembly and publication of a photographic archive not only of accessible monuments but also of unpublished collections like those now in the Musée municipale and the Palais synodale in Sens.[113] Such an investigation should be commenced, however, <u>before</u> the discussion of the development of Early Gothic sculpture proceeds much further. If this brief survey demonstrates nothing else, it shows that we have proceeded to conclusions without considering all of the evidence.

CHAPTER V

FOOTNOTES

1. See below, pp. 225-226.

2. See below, pp. 241-242.

3. See below, pp. 242-243.

4. See below, p. 243.

5. See above, Chapter I, pp. 4-6.

6. See above, Chapter I, p. 5 and Appendix B, Docs. VII, VIII.

7. See above, Chapter II, pp. 41-45.

8. W. Sauerländer, Von Sens bis Strassburg, ein Beitrag zur kunstgeschichtlichen Stellung der strassburger Querhausskulpturen, Berlin, 1966, pp. 19-33. See also, Sauerländer, 1972, pp. 416-419. Sauerländer dates the sculptures of the Baptist portal (WN), the earliest, shortly after 1184. This date derives in part from suggested stylistic connections with Mantes, dated "towards 1180" (Sauerländer, 1972, p. 409), in part from a fire in Sens in 1184 and in part from chapel consecrations in the western towers in 1210 (north) and 1221 (south). Although Sauerländer does not mention the dates, his portal chronology is also implicitly dependent upon a papal consecration, in 1164, of the "main altar" of the cathedral and a papal indulgence, in 1165, to continue work on the

church (see most recently, Severens, 1968, pp. 12-14).
However, Sauerländer, 1972, p. 408, himself acknowledges
that for Mantes, "...there is no documentary evidence
to determine the dates of the building operations." The
fire which had been thought to have substantially damaged
the cathedral is now considered to have done little,
if any, damage at all (see Severens, 1968, pp. 14-15).
Moreover, the chapel consecrations which provide termini
ante quem for the chapels in question, bear no necessary
relationship to the portal sculpture. Finally the "main
altar" consecration and the indulgence are themselves of
questionable value. Severens, 1968, pp. 12-14, uncritically accepts "...altare in honore beatorum apostolorum
Petri et Pauli..." as the main altar; this is unlikely
since the cathedral is dedicated to Saint Stephen.
[Earlier, C. Porée, "Les architectes et la construction
de la Cathédrale de Sens," Congrès archéologique, 74
(1908), p. 562, stated that this altar "...était adossé
aux deux piliers du fond du sanctuaire," but he gave no
source for this claim.] Ultimately, the indulgence and
the consecration of an altar to the two Roman apostles
more probably reflects papal presence in Sens in the early
1160's than any specific state of completion of the architectural work in progress (see also van der Meulen, 1967,
p. 154, n. 17e). With respect to our understanding of the
absolute architectural chronology of Sens Cathedral, which
was allegedly built de novo in a single campaign extending
over the middle of the twelfth century, it should be

pointed out that no study to date has even begun to address the curious fact that no two rectilinear bays of this supposedly homogeneous structure are equal in length. The actual chronology of the architecture and its sculpture remain to be thoroughly investigated. See also, Chapter II, n. 86.

8a. Many of the questions concerning relative and absolute chronologies of style raised in the following pages depend directly from discussions, seminars, and the published ideas of J. van der Meulen. See particularly, 1975 (I), pp. 14ff; 1977 (on Saint-Denis), and 1978, n. 9. Although van der Meulen's ideas have been formulated in direct relationship to specific monuments, notably the Cathedral of Chartres, the methodological implication of those ideas has always been articulated. In spite of that fact, it is to be hoped that van der Meulen will, in the future, write a more general methodological study aimed at bringing wider attention to what is one of the central issues of medieval art history at the present time.

9. Remarks on the style of the sculptures at Saint-Loup found in this chapter are based on the extended description in Appendix C.

10. Salet, 1933, p. 157. No scholar has ever questioned the stylistic "unity" of the portal. Although

not all go to the trouble to comment one way or the other,
the stylistic integrity of the portal underlies their
discussion of its sculpture. Recent important studies
on the style of Saint-Loup-de-Naud include: L. Pressouyre,
"Réflexions sur la sculpture du XIIème siècle en Champagne,"
Gesta, IX/2 (1970), esp. p. 23; W. Sauerländer, "Sculpture
on Early Gothic Churches: the State of Research and Open
Questions," Gesta, IX/2 (1970), esp. p. 40 (These opinions
were expressed in a more summary fashion in the original
1970 German edition of Sauerländer, 1972); W. Schlink,
Zwischen Cluny und Clairvaux, Die Kathedrale von Langres
und die burgundische Architektur des 12. Jahrhunderts,
Berlin, 1970 (Beiträge zur Kunstgeschichte, 4), Exkurs I:
Die Portalplastik von St. Bénigne zu Dijon, esp. p. 135
and B. Kerber, Burgund und die Entwicklung der französischen
Kathedralskulptur im zwölften Jahrhundert, Recklinghausen,
1966 (Münstersche Studien zur Kunstgeschichte, 4), esp.
p. 63. Other important studies include: Lapeyre, 1960,
pp. 132-138; L. Grodecki, "La 'première sculpture gothique':
Wilhelm Vöge et l'état actuel des problèmes," Bulletin
monumental, 117 (1959), esp. pp. 271-283; Stoddard, 1952,
pp. 35-38; Maillé, 1939, esp. pp. 89-90; L. Schürenberg,
"Spätromanische und frühgotische Plastik in Dijon und
ihre Bedeutung für die Skulpturen des Strassburger
Münsterquerschiffes," Jahrbuch der preussischen Kunstsammlungen, 58 (1937), esp. pp. 14-17; H. Focillon, L'art

des sculptures romans, Paris, 1964 (1st ed., 1931), passim.; Aubert, 1929, pp. 35-37 (his opinions reprised with modification in the dating only in his La sculpture française au moyen-âge, Paris, 1946, pp. 197-198); A. Mayeux, "Les grands portails du XIIe siècle et les bénédictines de Tiron, classement--dates--origines," Revue Mabillon, 1906, esp. pp. 111-112; and, W. Vöge, Die Anfänge des monumentalen Stiles im Mittelalter, Strassbourg, 1894, esp. pp. 187-191 and pp. 206-209. The monographic studies of Roblot-Delondre, 1913 and Bourquelot, 1840/41 should also be consulted.

11. Stoddard, 1952, p. 38. He goes on to say, "Neither the archaic directness of the Saint-Denis heads nor the classic repose of Chartres is seen here. This powerful image suggests a different age..."

12. Salet, 1933, p. 163. In a not entirely clear statement Maillé, 1939, p. 89, appears to echo the same sentiment: "Par ses personnages solidement construits et taillés en largeur,--exception faite de l'évêque Loup et des apôtres du trumeau, (?)..."

13. Salet, 1933, p. 165.

14. Ibid., pp. 165-166.

15. Appendix C. pp. 422-423.

16. In Appendix C, n. 56 it is pointed out that column figures 1-n and 3-n can be grouped together by

facial type; whereas, the other four form a group together which is more similar to the trumeau figure.

17. Lapeyre, 1960, p. 137; Salet, 1933, p. 163; Focillon, 1964 (1931) p. 264.

18. Sauerländer, 1970, p. 40, is almost certainly correct in dismissing the often observed difference in proportions between trumeau and column-figures, or more specifically, in dismissing the "more naturalistic" proportions of the column figures. He says, "This is, historically speaking, misleading. The proportions of these twelfth-century statues changes (sic) from case to case mostly according to the conditions of the architectural setting..." He might have mentioned, by way of comparison, the differences in size and proportion which apparently once existed at Saint-Bénigne and were recorded in Plancher's engraving (see Sauerländer, 1972, ill. 8).

19. It is tempting to see in the much greater emphasis on defining the lower lid of the eye and its less almondine shape, a certain stylistic distinction between the figures of the trumeau capital and those human-headed creatures on the capitals of the right embrasure column figures. It is, moreover, in several of the trumeau capital figures that we may speak of modelled folds rather than incised ones. Regrettably,

the linear handling of the veil of the nunnish sphinx on capital 3/s provides too slender a comparison to pursue this latter distinction.

20. Focillon, 1964 (1931), p. 266. Focillon also mentions the lintels of Bourges and Le Mans in this regard but he omits the lintels of Chartres WM and WN possibly because of the absence of colonnettes between the figures. Pressouyre, 1970, p. 23, speaks of "...un retard champenois..." to account for features such as this one. See below, n. 36 and n. 40.

21. Focillon, 1964 (1931), pp. 258 and 264.

22. See n. 12 above.

23. Kerber, 1966, p. 63. Kerber's observation leads one to wonder if the pose of the legs of the figure of Christ might not reflect the once broader (and higher) dimension of the tympanum (see above, Chapter III, pp. 78-79).

24. We will omit consideration of the image of the Virgin at the center of the lintel for the present and return to it together with the Nativity voussoirs below.

25. Appendix C, pp. 380 and 390.

26. The left hand which once probably overlapped the colonnette shaft is now broken off at the wrist within the frame.

27. See the remarks in n. 23 above.

28. Although not really germane to a discussion of the human form, similar remarks could be made for the other evangelist symbols (cf. Appendix C, pp. 377-380).

29. That this pose is a matter of conscious choice can be readily seen by comparing it to the less restricted pose of the winged man in the relatively more two-dimensional tympanum at Saint-Ayoul in Provins (see Sauerländer, 1972, ill. 22).

30. Because it is impossible to be certain when and how much movement and volumetric development is iconographically motivated and how much is not, the voussoirs representing the Saint Loup narrative will be omitted from this discussion. A glance at the scenes, particularly those on the right half of the archivolts, will show that their inclusion here could only support the argument which follows.

31. Salet, 1933, p. 159.

32. Sauerländer, 1972, pl. 107.

33. Ibid., pl. 77.

34. If the engravings can be trusted, so were those of Vermenton and Saint-Bénigne in Dijon.

35. One thinks automatically of the compelling treatment of the _Maiestas Domini_ of Chartres West, which nevertheless at the same time retains the decorative treatment of the blessing arm that ties the image to the

tradition of the Maiestas in the choir screen of Saint-
Sernin in Toulouse. On iconographic transmission and
change, see J. Bialostocki, "Iconography and Iconology"
in the Encyclopedia of World Art, VII (New York, 1963),
cols. 769-785, esp. cols. 778ff. See also, n. 36 below.

36. Generally negative adjectives used to describe
the column-figures, such as "provincial", "timid" or
"awkward" (cf. Sauerländer, 1972, p. 47; Aubert, 1929,
p. 36), may simply reflect the fact that those figures
are chronologically anterior to the trumeau. It should
also be pointed out that part of the reason for the
negative evaluation of the Saint-Loup sculpture, if not
all of it, lies not with the quality of the carving at
Saint-Loup but with the quality of the carving of the works
of the so-called Main-Master of Chartres West, which has
itself, recently been called into question (van der
Meulen, 1975 (II), p. 530f, n. 24; and more recently,
1978, n. 5). Because the sculptures at Saint-Loup have
been consistently dated after Chartres West--for which
we have no firm date at all (van der Meulen, 1978, pp.
81-83)--but nonetheless related to it, the degree to which
the Saint-Loup sculptors are unable to "reflect the
vision" of Chartres West (or are independent of it!) has
been the implicit criterion for judging the quality of
their work. Apart from the inherent lack of logic

within this often implicitly held position (which has
been applied to other portals of the so-called Chartres
West group as well) one wonders whether the negative
assessments of the column-figures at Saint-Loup would
continue if they were proven to have been executed before
the work at Chartres. On the "Grundfrage der Priorität,"
see J. van der Meulen, 1975 (I), pp. 14ff.

37. See Appendix C, pp. 383-384 and pp. 444-445.
A comparison of facial types among the female figures and
the handling of drapery in relation to the anatomy among
the standing figures reveals the similarities.

38. Compare, for example, the first or second
Magus with the king on the column below. Beyond the
similar handling of the nearly identical costume, the
shape, structure and detail forms of the faces assure
the relationship.

39. Compare, for example, the placement of the
arms and the organization of the folds in the pit of
the elbow of the left arms of the angel of the Annunciation and the apostle n/4. Compare also the position
and the relationship of legs to drapery in any of the
seated figures in the voussoirs and on the lintel. It
is somewhat surprising that closer parallels do not
appear between the faces of the kings in the voussoirs
and the apostles on the lintel. Perhaps it is a question
of models.

39a. The term "Early Gothic" is used as a convention herein, independently of any chronological implications.

40. The effect of constraints such as these on
the development of style is to make it unpredictable in
a narrow linear sense. Moreover, the concept of "un
retard", such as Pressouyre, 1970, p. 23, offers for
Saint-Loup, only varies the linear system and is ultimately
also unable to account for the factors discussed here.

41. These similarities and differences cannot be
dismissed as a simple matter of "archaisms" and "advances"
to be assigned to different hypothetical "masters" as
has been attempted for the West Facade of Chartres. At
Saint-Loup, the strong formal similarities between the
various figure groups makes distinctions of this type
unworkable. Moreover, van der Meulen has already cautioned,
regarding the various masters of Chartres West, that the
factor of re-used works of art must also be taken into
account before any conclusions can be drawn (cf. 1975
(II), p. 530f, n. 24).

42. See below, p. 238 and n. 67.

43. Rome, Vatican ms. Christina 577, published by
L.M. Duru, Bibliothèque historique de l'Yonne, II, Paris
and Auxerre, 1863, pp. 387-439.

44. Auxerre, Bibliothèque municipale, ms. 118 and
Paris, Bibliothèque nationale, ms. lat. 5002. The Auxerre

Clarius was published by Duru, op. cit., pp. 451-579.
The Paris Clarius, which Duru did not see, contains
references to architectural work on the cathedral in the
twelfth century which are not found in the other ms.
See Severens, 1968, p. 152, n. 3.

45. Sens, Bibliothèque municipale, ms. 59 (ancien
271) published by G. Julliot, Chronique de l'abbaye de
Saint-Pierre-le-Vif redigée vers la fin du XIIIe siècle
par Geoffroy de Courlon, Sens, 1876.

46. Paris, Bibliothèque nationale, ms. nouv. acq.
lat. 311, published by G. Julliot and M. Prou, Geoffroy
de Courlon, Le Livre des reliques de l'abbaye de Saint-
Pierre-le-Vif, Sens, 1887.

47. M. Quantin, Cartulaire générale de l'Yonne,
3 vols., Auxerre, 1854-1860.

48. See, e.g., R. Krautheimer, Studies in Early
Christian, Medieval and Renaissance Art, New York, 1969,
p. 224 and n. 124 on Archbishop Wilcharius of Sens who
directed restorations to Old Saint Peters at Charlemagne's
request.

49. Auxerre, Bibliothèque municipale, ms. 156,
Dom Cottron, Chronicon ecclesiae percelebris ac coenobii
regalis Sancti Petri Vivi Senonsis and Sens, Bibliothèque
municipale, ms. 116, Dom Cottron, Chronicon ecclesiae
Sanctae Colombae Senonsis.

50. H. Bouvier, 1906, I, pp. 1-45. See also
A.-C. Hénault, Recherches historiques sur la fondation
de l'église de Chartres et des églises de Sens, de Troyes
et d'Orléans, Paris and Chartres, 1884, and R. Fourrey,
Sens, ville d'art et d'histoire, Lyon, 1953, p. 9ff.

51. The materials are critically discussed by
Bouvier, 1891, pp. 185-203.

52. Brullée, 1852, pp. 39-42, "Ad ejus tumulum
et basilicam coenobium fondavit" (p. 40).

53. Duru, 1863, II, p. 473. This "rebuilding"
(?) has received little consideration in the literature
on the cathedral. E. Chartraire, La Cathédrale de Sens,
Paris, n.d. (1921), p. 11, n. 1, mentions it. Porée, 1908,
pp. 559-562, omits it from his treatment of the early
buildings. Severens, 1968, the most recent monograph on
the building, writes on the so-called "twelfth-century
cathedral" without considering the early structures.
See above Chapter II, n. 86.

54. Duru, 1863, II, p. 473.

55. Ibid.

56. Bouvier, 1891, pp. 50-60 for Saint-Pierre and
Brulée, 1852, pp. 70-76 for Sainte-Colombe.

57. On consecrations, see van der Meulen, 1967,
p. 154, n. 17e.

58. Duru, 1863, II, p. 472.

59. Ibid. In conversation with the author, van der Meulen has indicated that he believes _perficere_ to be a more definitive term than _reaedificare_ or _renovare_.

60. Duru, 1863, II, p. 477 (Clarius).

61. Ibid., pp. 487-488, "...incensae sunt basilicae Sancti-Stephani, et Sanctae-Mariae, Sancti-Johannis-Baptistae, et claustrum canonicorum crematum est igne. Periit autem im ipso coenobio librarium Sancti-Stephani, et ornamentum maximum, inmo etiam reliquae preciosissimae..." This extensive description indicates considerable damage. See also, Porée, 1908, p. 560 and n.1.

62. Julliot and Prou 1887, p. 350. Clarius (Duru, 1863, II, p. 488) states that Archambaldus "coepit renovare...presbyterium" and "perficiens criptas omnino."

63. Porée, 1908, p. 560. See Hubert, 1974 (1938), pp. 32-33 and 62-64 on the eastern complex at Saint-Pierre.

64. Duru, 1863, II, p. 490. Porée, 1908, p. 560, also suggests the "nef centrale" as an alternative reading for _medietatem_. The exact circumstances cannot hope to be resolved until excavations have determined when the cathedral complex of three buildings was unified. See J. Hubert, "Les 'cathédrales doubles' de la Gaule," _Genava_, nouv. sér. XI (1963), pp. 114-115.

65. Duru, 1863, II, p. 491.

66. Odorannus, who died only in 1046 (Duru, 1863,

II, p. 386), surely knew the extent of the work. He
appears to contrast <u>renovavit</u> with <u>ex toto reedificavit</u>.
See also p. 240 and n. 73 below.

67. Duru, 1863, II, p. 508, "Hoc anno, incepta est
renovari ecclesia sancti Saviniani..." (Clarius).
According to Clarius, Saint-Savinian was burned in 1093
(incensum est...sancti Saviniani, p. 512). Restoration
was apparently completed by 1108 when a ceremony was
held (p. 516). Saint-Savinian has been subject to some
controversy and merits further study; see the opposing
views of the building chronology in Hénault, 1884, pp.
440-448 and Chartraire, n.d. (1921), pp. 110-112.

68. Duru, 1863, II, p. 509.

69. Ibid., p. 401 (Odorannus).

70. Ibid., pp. 516-517. See van der Meulen, 1975
(I), p. 22f on <u>turris</u> as chevet.

71. See n. 8 above.

72. All scholars are agreed that the only original
"Early Gothic" capitals from the dado zone arcade which
remain in the cathedral are those in the northern choir
aisle and in the small chapel opening off the northern
arm of the transept. Of these, most are decorative
(vegetal), several are animal but only one is figural.
There are, in addition to these, a number of dado zone
arcade capitals preserved in the Palais Synodale and in
the Musée Municipale. They are damaged and sometimes

fragmentary or restored, but they considerably enhance our appreciation of Sens sculpture. There has been no systematic publication of these capitals; a catalogue raisonée of the surviving sculpture is, however, now underway for the Commission des Monuments Historiques. The best overview of later building campaigns is given by Porée, 1908, pp. 564-594 to which should be added R. Nelson, <u>Martin</u> <u>Chambiges</u> <u>and</u> <u>the</u> <u>Development</u> <u>of</u> <u>French</u> <u>Flamboyant</u> <u>Architecture</u>, unpubl. diss. The Johns Hopkins University, 1973, pp. 16-67. On the damage and restorations, see Chartraire, n.d. (1921), pp. 29-36.

    73. The original documents are lost but are known through the eighteenth-century "Chronicon Sanctae Columbae" of Dom Cottron (not seen; see above, n. 49). Brullée, 1852, p. 109, quotes Cottron: "En cette année 1142, Théobalde, abbé, jeta les fondements de cette église le jour de l'Annonciation..." The church was consecrated some twenty years later at the same time as the cathedral (see n. 8 above). Brullée takes this documentation to refer to a complete rebuilding of the abbey church. The documentation alone will not support so specific an interpretation. The most we can say is that it gives evidence of <u>some</u> building activity. Cf. van der Meulen, 1975 (I), p. 20 in regard to <u>in fundamento reedificare</u>. See also n. 66.

74. Julliot and Prou, 1887, p. 96. Geoffrey distinguishes other tomb monuments with the phrases sine litteris (p. 127), cum litteris and cum litteris sui nominis (p. 129). Hugh's tombstone is represented in a Gaignières drawing (Oxford, Bodleian Lib. MS Gough, Drawings Gaignières 11, fol. 79r). L. Pressouyre, "Un tombeau d'abbé provenant du cloître de Nesle-la-Reposte," Bulletin monumental, 125 (1967), p. 17, n. 3, discusses the monument briefly and calls it a "tombeau rétrospectif" on the basis of its similarity to the tomb of the abbot, Hélias (†1209-1210). Given the general similarity of tomb monuments of this type, there is no necessary reason for a dating "entre 1210 et 1220."

75. The original documents are again lost. The episode was described by Jacques Rousseau, Histoire de la ville de Sens, Sens (?), 1682 (not seen) and discussed by Bouvier, 1891, p. 112. Later Bouvier, 1906-1911, II, p. 52, identified the statue as that of an echevin. Perhaps there were two statues, one commemorating each of the deceased.

76. Julliot and Prou, 1887, p. 127. In another case Geoffrey states "...justa ymaginem lapideam Cherubin" (p. 124).

77. Bourquelot, 1840/41, p. 252. One wonders how consistently over time this formal relationship would have been stressed if the tympana did not both contain

Maiestas images.

78. It should be remarked that considerations of the Saint-Loup style--and the style of other portals for that matter--have always focused on the larger, more accessible statuary. Quite apart from any errors which may result from the "missing links", no history of style can hope to be satisfactorily realized until all surviving objects are inventorized and made accessible for study. See also below, n. 110.

79. Vöge, 1894, pp. 206-209. Vöge also discussed the iconographic ties between the two groups of column-figures (p. 181) wherein a stylistic nexus is implicit.

80. Ibid., p. 209. In a previous passage (pp. 190-191) Vöge grouped the portals of Le Mans, Saint-Germain-des-Prés, Provins and the cloister of Saint-Denis together with Saint-Loup as "Atelierwerke." He also compares (p. 208, n. 1) the embrasure capitals of Saint-Loup with those of Notre-Dame-en-Vaux in Châlons-sur-Marne.

81. See, for example, Aubert, 1929, pp. 35-36; Salet, 1933, p. 156; Maillé, 1939, p. 90; or, Lapeyre, 1960, p. 137.

82. Stoddard, 1952, pp. 37-38.

83. Ibid., p. 38. Stoddard cites the pose--which Kerber interpreted differently (see above, p. 9)--and the arrangement of drapery (cf. fig. 23 and Sauerländer, 1972, pls. 5 and 16 and ill. 22). Often the relationship

to Chartres is characterized negatively: for example,
Salet, 1933, p. 157 (in reference to the tympanum) "Ce
Christ n'a pas la beauté de celui de Chartres..." In
this regard, see the remarks on 'timidity' and 'awkwardness' above, n. 36.

84. Stoddard, 1952, p. 37, identifies as the model
for the body of the Saint-Loup column-figure l-s: the
Chartres column-figure WM 2-n; for the head of l-s:
WM l-s; for 2-s: WM 4-s and so on. Stoddard (p. 38)
also claims to find specific models at Chartres for
four of the Saint-Loup lintel apostles. In making his
comparisons so precise, Stoddard faces easy rebuttal.
To take only one example, it is clearly the similarities
of pose and costume which underlie his remarks on l-s
(fig. 32; Sauerländer, 1972, pl. 11). However, one
must also consider the more varied lateral contours,
the suggestion of contrapposto given by the differentiation in the knees and the greater depth of undercutting
which we see in the Chartres figure but do not find in
the figure at Saint-Loup. One wonders how the Saint-
Loup sculptor could have managed to carve the figure
as well as he did (from a technical point of view) and
still have been so artistically regressive. While one
can easily fault Stoddard's comparisons, one realizes
the difficulties of making precise the relationship

between Saint-Loup and Chartres West, a difficulty which most studies skirt by keeping their references to that relationship less specific.

85. Sauerländer, 1970, p. 40 and figs. 13 and 14. The block-like quality of the head together with details like the formation of the eyes and the arrangement of the beard make this comparison "striking" as Sauerländer calls it. A consideration of the entire figures, however, produces stronger differences than similarities (see fig. 31 and Sauerländer, 1972, pl. 13). The curvilinear emphasis of the anatomy and the drapery together with the varied contour found at Chartres are missing at Saint-Loup.

86. We will return to this relationship below, pp. 246-247.

87. For a critical overview of the Saint-Bénigne literature, see Schlink, 1970, pp. 120-137, esp. the summary on pp. 136-137. To this should be added Sauerländer, 1970, pp. 36-39 and Pressouyre, 1970, pp. 19-25.

88. This thesis was most forcefully put forward by P. Quarré, "La sculpture des anciens portails de St. Bénigne de Dijon," Gazette des Beaux-Arts, 50 (1957), pp. 177-194. Reasoning by analogy from documentary and paleographic evidence Quarré argued that the sculpture

was commenced after a fire in 1137 and probably completed before a dedication of the next church in 1147. Reaction was swift to Quarré's study, coming later in the same year from M. Beaulieu in the "Chronique" of the Bulletin monumental, 115 (1957), pp. 293-295. The arguments given by Beaulieu are sufficient to weaken Quarré's "proof" but are insufficient to a full refutation of it. As an hypothesis, Quarré's ideas remain entirely reasonable, whether sufficiently proven or not.

89. On the inability of stylistic and documentary criteria to date the sculpture of the West Facade of Chartres, see van der Meulen, 1975 (II), p. 530, n. 24 and, more recently, 1978, pp. 81-85.

90. Grodecki, 1959, p. 281. See also Kerber, 1966, pp. 41-44.

91. Sauerländer, 1970, pp. 34-35 reviews the other side of the question and suggests an indirect relationship between the Eve lintel at Autun and column-figure WM3-s at Chartres West. See also n. 87 above. Ultimately, the postulate of wandering masters, whose contributions can be refuted by the postulate of other wandering masters, will bring us, not a better under-standing of the nature of these formal interrelationships, but only a more complex one.

92. See Schlink, 1970, pp. 136-137. This date is based on stylistic and compositional comparisons to

monuments such as Chartres West, Le Mans, and Notre-Dame-en-Vaux whose 'given' dates are themselves open to question. Professor Thomas Polk of the University of Georgia, Athens is preparing a study of portal composition which argues compellingly for a relative date for Le Mans between Saint-Denis and Chartres West. The same argument could be extended to Notre-Dame-en-Vaux. It is hoped that Professor Polk will soon publish the results of his work.

93. See n. 88 above.

94. Lapeyre, 1960, pp. 130-131 and p. 130, n. 1 reviews the iconographic and compositional parallels between Saint-Loup and Saint-Bénigne (and Le Mans). Maillé, 1939, p. 89, n. 2, while aware of the general dissimilarities, drew parallels between the winged ox on the little Maiestas tympanum from Saint-Bénigne and the corresponding beast at Saint-Loup (Lapeyre, 1960, p. 138, n. 2, erroneously states that Maillé compared the winged ox from the destroyed Maiestas tympanum of Saint-Bénigne.). Sauerländer, 1970, p. 40, compared the head of the king at Saint-Loup (2-s) to the head of Saint-Bénigne from the portal trumeau (on the identification, compare the 'fleuron' at the center of the mitre to the two mitres in Plancher's engraving). To these, several other striking comparisons can be added. Apart from the iconographic link between the two mustachioed

figures of Saint Jean (see Appendix C, pp.389-390) a
close comparison between the handling of the linear
drapery folds and their relationship to the underlying
leg structure can be made between several apostles on
the Saint-Loup lintel and the Saint-Bénigne Last Supper
tympanum (see figs. 128 and 129). More compelling
still is the identity of conception and detail treatment
of individual forms between the heads of the Magi before
Herod group and those of the Last Supper tympanum (see
figs. 130-133). Recently, Pressouyre, 1970, p. 23 and
figs. 16-17, compared the Magi group to a cloister
column figure from Châlons-sur-Marne, which complicates
the issue further.

95. Vöge, see above, n. 80. Lapeyre, 1960, pp.
126-138, groups Saint-Loup-de-Naud among a series of
"portails franco-bourguignon."

96. Pressouyre, 1970, pp. 19-24.

97. See Chapter I, pp.4-6.

98. Schlink, 1970, p. 135, also includes the
Reims tomb fragment, the western capitals from Til
Châtel and sculpture from the cathedral of Geneva in the
group. "Alle hier herangezogenen Vergleichsbeispiele
gehören aber einer Gruppe an, deren Zentrum und Ausgang
hypothetisch in St. Denis angenommen wird." This
orientation toward Saint-Denis depends substantially on

Kerber's (1966, p. 45) association of the king's head
in Liebieghaus with the cloister at Saint-Denis. However, Pressouyre, "Quelques vestiges sculptés de l'abbaye
de Nesle-la-Reposte (Marne), Bulletin de la Société
nationale des Antiquaires de France, 1967, p. 109, n.1,
has shown convincingly that the head is from Nesle-la-
Reposte. He uses it (1970, p. 23) in support of his
"retard champenois."

99. Several damaged dado zone arcade capitals
now in the Palais Synodale in Sens were taken from the
cathedral (presumably in the nineteenth century) and
replaced by copies. Two of these unpublished capitals
compare closely with the embrasure capitals at Saint-
Loup. Both of the Sens capitals combine human heads
and animal bodies. One, which is an end capital, combines
the "human intimacy" of the touching heads of embrasure
capital 1/s and the relationship of body to entwining
foliation of embrasure capital 1/n at Saint-Loup (see
figs. 138, 139 and 140). Another, from an intermediate
colonnette, echoes the raised, touching legs of both
embrasure capitals 1/s and 3/s at Saint-Loup (see figs.
139, 143 and 144). Moreover, the head of the creature
on the right side of this second Sens capital corresponds
so closely in shape and volume, in the linear articulation of the layered locks of hair, the handling of the

brow and formation of the eyes to the male head on embrasure capital 1/s as to suggest the same atelier (see figs. 145 and 146).

100. Perhaps the difference in location--inside the building as opposed to outside--contributes to the "broader" handling of the Sens capital.

101. The head of the monk, while maintaining some similarities in the shape and arrangement of the beard and in the general volume to the heads in the voussoir, is not as close as are the bodies. The cheek is fleshier and the eyes larger as is the case with the female figures just compared. The circular fold articulating the shoulder of the monk has numerous parallels at Saint-Loup also. Compare, for example, the fold on the right shoulder of the figure of Saint-Loup on the trumeau capital (fig. 30).

102. Sauerländer, 1970, p. 40 (c. 1160); Salet, 1933, p. 166 (c. 1170-1175--after 1167). Kerber, 1966, pp. 28-29 follows E. Alp, Die Kapitelle des 12 Jahrhundert im Entstehungsgebiete der Gotik, Freiburg, 1926, and places the capitals in relationship to both the Île-de-France and Burgundy. He dates them "um 1150." Maillé, 1939, p. 89, n. 1, links, from the north choir aisle dado zone arcade, "...un masque qui rejette des rinceaux de la même façon que ceux de Saint-Loup-de-Naud et de

Vermenton et qui leur est certainement anterieur"
(Lapeyre, 1960, p. 138, n. 2, adheres to Maillé's
comparison). Most literature on the capitals is contained within the literature on the architecture (see,
Chapter II, n. 66). Architectural chronologies such as
F. Salet, "La cathédrale de Sens et sa place dans
l'architecture médiévale, Comptes rendus de l'Académie
des Inscriptions et Belles-Lettres, 1955, pp. 182-187,
could presumably date these capitals as early as the
late 1130's and certainly in the early 1140's. In sum,
their date remains as open to question as does the
dating of the sculpture at Saint-Loup-de-Naud.

103. F. Salet, "Un chapiteau venant de Saint-
Pierre-le-Vif de Sens, Bulletin de la Société nationale
des Antiquaires de France, 1960, pp. 143-146. The
object was found, immured, "...non loin de l'emplacement
de l'antique et célèbre abbaye de Saint-Pierre-le-Vif..."
(p. 143). Salet gives the dimensions of the object as
44cm in height with a diameter of 25cm (p. 145). It is
several centimeters wider (in diameter) at the top,
which is damaged and difficult to measure, than at the
bottom. It must once have been wider still but so
nearly cylindrical as to question whether or not it was
ever a capital. Salet himself questioned this (p. 146)
as did several respondents at his presentation (p. 146).

While the provenance is reasonably secure, the function
of the object remains unknown. Salet dates the object
to "vers 1180" on the basis of tenuous comparisons to
the Baptist portal of the cathedral (WN) which is
itself undated (see above n. 8).

104. Ibid., p. 143. Salet identified two other
figures as Saint Peter (key fragment, costume and bare
feet) and Saint Paul (costume, bare feet) to whom the
abbey was dedicated. The fourth figure, Salet suggests
is Robert's queen, Constance. P. Parruzot, in a communication to the Société archéologique de Sens, on 6 March
1962 correctly argued on the basis of costume (see the
pontifical lappets beside the left shoulder of fig. 137)
that the remaining figure is an ecclesiastic. (This
information was kindly communicated to me by Mlle.
Lydwine Saulnier.)

105. One can recognize this fold as a stylization
of the "blousing" of the classical chiton. The fold also
appears on one of the cloister figures from the Senonais
abbey of Sainte-Colombe (?) (see Sauerländer, 1972, p. 413,
ill. 29, second figure from the left) to which Salet
also compared the capital in assigning it a date of
c. 1180 (Salet, 1960, pp. 145-146). See n. 103 above.

106. These figures include: voussoirs WM1-s/1;
WM2-s/3 and s/5; WM3-s/3 and the rightmost figure (a

deacon?) on the trumeau capital. See figs. 41, 65, 69, 66 and 30 respectively.

107. The two apostles on the Saint Pierre capital (figs. 126 and 127) have another curious fold--a sort of concave rectangle--which articulates their chests. This fold also appears on several figures at Saint-Loup: on the lintel, apostle s/3; in voussoir WM1-n/2 and s/2. See figs. 36, 42 and 23 respectively.

108. See Sauerländer, 1972, pl. 21 and p. 388. Issy belonged to Saint-Germain-des-Prés from the sixth century until the Revolution. Comparisons between Saint-Loup, Sens and Saint-Germain have already been identified by Schlink (see above, p. 243 and n. 98). Sauerländer suggests that the Issy fragment "...reflects something of the manifold stylistic possibilities opening up in Parisian sculpture after the middle of the century." Without entering into the question of dating, one wonders if a history of style based not on geography but on dip-lomatic might prove to be more useful. Given the rarity of this fold form and its use in Sens, it is interesting to note how close are the ties between Saint-Germain and its archdiocesan see in Sens. In 1126 the archbishop Henri Sanglier gave two churches to the abbey (see J. Bouillart, Histoire de l'abbaye de Saint-Germain-des-Préz, Paris, 1794, p. 83 and the recueil des pièces justicatives,

p. xxxvj). According to Bouillart, p. 93, Abbot Hugh of Saint-Germain presided over the election of the new abbot of Sainte-Colombe in 1165. By 1177 the same Abbot Hugh was embroiled in a controversy with the archbishop, Guy de Noyers, over the latter's alleged misuses of his rights of visitation in the abbey's dependencies (ibid., p. 97). It should not surprise us that Vöge, 1894, p. 99, n. 1, on the basis of the Montfaucon engraving, claimed that "...der Paulus (in the lost west portal) steht genau entsprechend am Portal von Saint-Loup-de-Naud..."

109. In the middle portal, the north jamb, the third figure from the bottom; in the north portal, the second figure from the bottom on both jambs; in the south portal, the north jamb, the third figure from the bottom. On the capital frieze of the middle portal, the figure of the Virgin Annunciate in the north embrasure; in the south portal, the figure to the right of Christ in the Arrest scene in the north embrasure. The Arrest scene is published in E. Houvet, Cathédrale de Chartres, portail occidental ou royal, Chartres, n.d., pl. 91.

110. A suggestion of this fold also appears on the waist of the Christ of the little Maiestas tympanum from Saint-Bénigne (see Sauerländer, 1972, pl. 23) but I have not been able to locate any other examples.

In reviewing these figures I have had the invaluable

aid of access to the photo collection of Professor Jan van der Meulen of Cleveland State University which was begun at The Pennsylvania State University as the basis for a computerized archive of all surviving medieval monumental sculpture. On the current status of the archive, see Adams, 1974, pp. xvi-xvii and the Mediaeval Academy of America Newsletter, No. 63 (11/75), p. 5. The author's collection of some 500 photographs of the portal at Saint-Loup-de-Naud is intended as a contribution to the future archive.

111. The head is small, about 6cm in height. It appears to have been part of a scene involving at least one other figure because there are traces of another head on the right. The block itself, which appears to be a capital fragment, is 21.5cm wide and 10cm high.

112. As Sauerländer, 1970, p. 35, has pointed out, "The problem of the style of the Chartres frieze (and, one might add, the doorjambs) is entirely open and has never been truly investigated."

113. I am indebted to the Commission des Monuments Historiques and to the staffs of the Musée Municipale and the Palais Synodale for permission to view and photograph unpublished sculptures in those collections.

CHAPTER VI

CONCLUSION: RESULTS AND IMPLICATIONS

Through a detailed monographic investigation our
understanding of the complex history and meaning of
the western portal at Saint-Loup-de-Naud has increased
considerably. That "most homogeneous" of Early Gothic
portals has been shown to be the composite result of
combining subtly altered sculptures designed to be
emplaced at another location with sculptures carved to
be emplaced where they are today. This subtle physical
(re-) assemblage produces the complexity of a theophanic
presentation of God's Providence which, however unique
in its detail formulation at Saint-Loup-de-Naud, is
entirely traditional in its hieratic conception of
Intercessorship and the Church within the Divine Dispensation. The relative stylistic unity of the compositionally disparate sculptures stems from a common
stylistic origin in the metropolitan city of Sens, the
artistic standing of which within the so-called "Early
Gothic" period must, as a consequence, be re-evaluated.

These results are important for any meaningful
appreciation of the history and art-history of the priory
of Saint-Loup-de-Naud. Still more important are the

implications of these results for the study of medieval monumental art in general. That the "homogeneity" of the portal at Saint-Loup-de-Naud can be shown to be but an empathetic fantasy confirms the warnings of van der Meulen, Deichmann and others that every medieval building and portal must be considered from the point of view of spolia. The existence of spoils should not, however, be considered "destructive" in our larger understanding of medieval monumental art. In the light of the richness of the iconographic program at Saint-Loup-de-Naud, spoils should rather be seen as a basis for establishing a true measure of the complexity of the medieval creative genius. Finally, as van der Meulen has repeatedly cautioned, the factor of spoils seriously calls into question the validity of our traditional approach to the history of style. Spoils provide a new challenge to the search for stylistic relationships. These relationships, as this study demonstrates, must be explored along the paths of ecclesio-political connections independently of any absolute chronology. It would indeed be interesting to overlay the results of a large-scale re-investigation of stylistic relationships among so-called Early Gothic monuments on an independently constructed grid of diplomatic ties. Conceivably such a study could provide a firmer chronological foundation for the re-writing of a now arbitrary history of style.

APPENDIX A

THE STATE OF PRESERVATION OF THE PRIORY
CHURCH OF SAINT-LOUP-DE-NAUD WITH SPECIAL
ATTENTION TO THE WESTERN PORTAL

"Respecté des protestants et des révolutionnaires,
préservé par son porche des injures du temps, il (the
portal) se propose aujourd'hui presque intact à l'admira-
tion du visiteur."[1] Indeed, the portal sculpture is
"exceptionally well preserved;"[2] perhaps one might even
go as far as Aufauvre and say that it is difficult to
imagine "...en France quelque chose de plus complet, de
plus remarquable et de mieux conservé."[3]

Nevertheless, the general zeal of the nineteenth
century toward restoration projects and the questions
concerning the intended original emplacement of some of
the Saint-Loup sculpture which have to be raised in
regard to structural analysis (see Chapter III) necessitate
a systematic reappraisal of the sculpture, the portal
complex and the church itself. Moreover, several scholars
have informally expressed skepticism over the integrity
of the Saint-Loup sculpture.[4] However, the material,
both visual and written, which is investigated in this
appendix leaves little doubt that the portal complex
of Saint-Loup-de-Naud is a work of the Middle Ages, free
from the hand of the restorer. In the process of delineat-
ing the integrity of the portal, attention will also be
given to the restorative work undertaken elsewhere in
the fabric of the church.

I. Recent Documented Work

The repair in 1967 of a dangerous fracture which

passed diagonally through figure s/1 (Saint John) on the lintel thereby causing an opening along the mortar joint between the central and bottom-right blocks of the tympanum is evident in a comparison of photographs of the tympanum and lintel taken before 1960 with those taken after 1970 (cf. figs. 23, 26). A photograph dated by the Archives des Monuments historiques to 1872[5] reveals that the fracture was already visible in the nineteenth century. Presumably this was the same "...fissure...dans le beau tympan de la porte principale..." referred to in a report on Saint-Loup made in 1900 by Selmarsheim.[6] Records maintained by the Archives des Monuments historiques in Paris indicate both private and official concern about the crack, which was worsening, in the early sixties.[7] Payment records indicate that the repair was finally carried out by Entreprise Maimbonte in 1967.[8]

On-site inspection made in October 1977 reveals that the visible repair work comprised:

1. Sealing the crack within the tympanum and lintel in a material which approximates the color and texture of the stone itself;

2. Harmonizing the seam with the architectual and drapery forms which had been damaged;

3. Reconstruction, in the same material, of parts of the footstools of apostles s/1 and s/2, the base of the colonnette between them and the

soffit and lower fillet of the lintel;[9]

4. Insertion of metal rods (into drilled channels)
   in the lower fillet of the lintel to help sta-
   bilize it.[10]

This repair clearly required little attention to
the surface of the sculpture itself.

No documents exist in the Archives des Monuments
historiques which indicate any other twentieth-century
work on the portal sculpture.

II. The Work of the Nineteenth Century

The possibility that restoration work was undertaken at Saint-Loup-de-Naud earlier, in the course of the
nineteenth century, remains of greatest concern to
scholarship. The former priory church was designated
an historic monument in 1843.[11] This date may reasonably
serve as a _terminus_ _post_ _quem_ for any work which might
have been undertaken on the sculpture. The anonymous
photograph dated 1872, which shows a view of the entire
sculptural program from just outside the porch, provides
a _terminus_ _ante_ _quem_ since there are no noticeable des-
crepancies between it and the portal as we find it today.[12]
This twenty-eight year period--between 1844 and 1872--
rightly becomes the focus for our search.[13] During this
period of time two architects were in charge of the work:
M. Buval, the first, held responsibility from 1844 to

1867; M. Mimey, the second, for the remaining years.

A. The Pictorial Evidence

Between 1844 and 1872 three pictorial documents
testify to the integrity of the sculpture at Saint-Loup-
de-Naud. The most recent of these is the large etching
by Charles Fichot (fig. 110) which accompanied Aufauvre's
descriptive text in Les Monuments de Seine-et-Marne which
appeared in Paris and Melun between 1854 and 1858. The
fasicule which included Saint-Loup was published in 1856[14]
so that the original etching was probably made in or
shortly before 1855. Comparison of the print with photographs (cf. figs. 22, 110) reveals such surprising faith-
fulness that we must conclude that it was made with the
aid of a prism device like a camera lucida: the arrangement of drapery in the print, the poses and the attributes--
even the repetitive candles and censers of the angels in
the first voussoir--are consistently accurate. Fichot
resisted temptation to "repair" damage: the three headless figures in the bottom voussoirs remain headless; the
right shoulder of the trumeau figure remains broken.
Furthermore, Fichot reveals his concern for literalness
and a sharp eye for observation: he represents the
interruption of the continuous undulating cloud band
where we see it interrupted, beneath the symbol of Saint
John; he distinguishes between the "half-capitals" on the
inner ends of the lintel and the "three-quarter capitals"

on the outer ends.[15] In summary, one can almost agree
with Grésy that "...est un chef-d'oeuvre d'exactitude si
consciencieuse que l'on peut y étudier tous les détails
de la sculpture avec autant de confiance que sur le monument même."[16] The etching may be considered to reduce
our chronological parameters to about eleven years--from
1844 to 1855.

The second pictorial document is a photograph taken
in 1851 by Henri le Secq.[17] It shows the column figures
of the right embrasure only and not the entire portal.
Because the photograph by le Secq corresponds exactly to
the present condition of the sculptures,[18] the terminus
ante quem for any restoration to at least these three
figures may be moved back to 1851. Indirectly, the
photograph helps to confirm the accuracy of Fichot's
etching.

The third pictorial document is a "coupe sur le
milieu du porche faisant voir l'élévation du portail"
signed by the architect Buval and dated by him, 10 January, 1844 (fig. 111).[19] While one might hope for the
kind of accuracy found in the Fichot etching, Buval's
drawing does not provide it. Unfortunately, the architect produced a curious mélange of the purely fanciful
and the remarkably accurate: archivolt figures, which
are reasonably accurate in themselves (cf. fig. 22,
archivolt 3, s/2 and fig. 111, archivolt 2, s/3), are

often misplaced and sometimes duplicated (fig. 111, archivolt 2, n/3 and s/5) by Buval so that the archivolt
cycle makes no sense at all; conversely, archivolt 2,
s/1 and archivolt 3, n/1 are correctly represented without their heads.[20] The accuracy of some of the individual motifs together with the misplacement and duplication of others suggests the conclusion that the drawing
reflects haste or lack of concern for literal accuracy--
at least of sculptural details which are difficult to
see--rather than that it reflects an earlier and different arrangement of the portal sculpture. What can be
said with certainty is that the drawing indicates the
existence of a complete sculptural program in 1844.
Written documents, including Buval's own, will confirm
this interpretation.

B. The Written Evidence

Three groups of written documents provide additional information concerning the physical integrity of
the sculpture at Saint-Loup-de-Naud. These are: publications by early scholars before 1872; reports and
records of the work planned and executed by the architects Buval and Mimey; and a group of lesser documents,
mostly letters, which help to confirm information contained in the first two.

1. Publications Before 1872

The first major written document of the nineteenth century is perhaps the most important. This is the "Notice..." published by Felix Bourquelot in the Bibliothèque de l'école des chartes in 1840/41,[21] three years before the priory was designated an historic monument. As such, Bourquelot's text predates the most likely period of possible restoration (1844-1872) and assumes increased importance for that fact. Bourquelot sees the portal as "...la partie la plus intéressante du monument...,"[22] calling it "...un grand tableau de pierre..."[23] He describes the sculptures individually and makes a genuine contribution to our understanding of the portal iconography.[24] Moreover, Bourquelot comments on the general state of preservation, stating that the sculptures are "admirablement conservées."[25] But most importantly, during the course of his description, Bourquelot remarks on the state of preservation of individual figures: thus he tells us that the heads of one figure in archivolt 2, s/1 and one in archivolt 3, n/1 are missing.[26] Since these figures remain today in the state in which Bourquelot saw them, the likelihood increases that none of the figures has been restored.

Some fifteen years after Bourquelot wrote, Aufauvre published the text which accompanies Fichot's etching and which nearly equals the latter's descriptive prowess.[27] Aufauvre describes, and often correctly identifies, each figure in the portal. No indication whatsoever in his text suggests that Aufauvre felt any of the sculpture to have been restored.

Neither Grésy,[28] nor Leroy,[29] who also published before 1872, provide additional information on the state of preservation of the portal, although Leroy does describe the condition of the church in some detail.[30]

2. Architectural Reports and Records

Buval left two documents which attest to the physical integrity of the Saint-Loup portal sculpture. The first of these is a formal "notice" (signed and dated, Melun, 15 January 1844), which deals with the condition of the monument.[31] Buval claims that the portal is "la plus intéressante partie de l'édifice..."[32] He goes on to identify several elements of the iconography[33] and to praise the "...grande richesse d'éxecution et (le) fini parfait..."[34] stating that "...par un bonheur exceptionel très peu de parties en ont été avariées."[35] Interestingly, he also states that "ces sculptures sont recouverts d'un grossier badigeon à la chaux..."[36] Traces of this gesso layer can still be seen in the angles of folds on the column-figures. A similar coating is known to have existed on the column-figures of Chartres.[37] There is no indication in any records concerning Saint-Loup that an entire layer (if Buval is to be believed literally) was systematically removed, but it must have been because, protected as the portal is from the weather, it can hardly have worn off in the interim.[38]

Buval also wrote a "Devis de Travaux"[39] which is a report of the work to be undertaken for "...la conservation et la consolidation..." of the church.[40] In it Buval indicates a primary concern with the roofing structures.[41] The "devis" also contains no mention of any intended or necessary work on the portal sculpture, although it does include a projected reconstruction of the second storey of the tower porch.[42]

When he took over as architect in 1867, Mimey submitted a report of work accomplished (by Buval) and of work yet to be done.[43] Mimey wrote that "Toute la partie intérieur primitive est...encore intact..."[44] Except for repairs to one transept pier, which had been begun but not finished,[45] "...les travaux entrepris... (ont) consisté principalement en travaux extérieurs."[46]

He goes on to say that Buval's exterior work included new timber work and roofing for the entire church (except the crossing tower) and repointing the masonry in the exterior walls "en mortier noirci."[47] No mention is made of any work done by Buval on the portal or its sculpture.

Neither is the portal mentioned among the repairs which Mimey himself intended to execute in the structural fabric of the interior of the eastern part of the building.[48] The architect does, however, refer twice to the portal and its condition in the course of his report: "Ce portail est...un des spécimins le plus remarquables et les mieux conservés d'architecture byzantine."[49] And later: "Le portail dont les sculptures sont d'une exécution si remarquable est un bon état également, les murs et les soubassements du porche ont seule soufferts."[50]

A report by (Mimey's successor?) Eugene Millet to the Ministre de Instruction Publique des Cultes et des Beaux-Arts dated 14 July 1874[51] provides specific information about what had been accomplished during the tenure of the architect Mimey. Millet states that the work executed "...ont été fort bien faits..."[52] and "...concernent le choeur et le transept..."[53] Millet goes on to detail, among other things, repairs to the footings of piers en and es and various vaults and arches in the sanctuary and transept areas.[54] At no point is there any reference to work undertaken on the portal sculpture.

Millet also goes on to list work which was still being undertaken, including the complete reconstruction of pier es, repairs to the south transept wall, the

north transept door, repaving the interior, and repairs
to the south side-aisle exterior buttresses.[55] This
section of the report contains two references to the
portal. Millet speaks of necessary "...reprises dans le
trumeau..."[56] without being more specific. Presumably,
this refers to consolidating the fracture still present
in the lower right side of the trumeau. In any case,
the photograph of 1872 assures that the sculpture itself
was not the object of the work referred to in 1874--work
which, in the end, may never have been executed.[57] In
his second reference to the portal Millet writes:

> "Au dessus du porche est une salle...toute cette
> construction est en assez mauvais état; les piles
> isolées vers l'ouest sont lezardées; les materiaux
> sont décomposées et disjoints et les soubassements
> sont déchaussés par suite de la déclivité du ter-
> rain. Il serait vraiment indispensable de remedie
> à ses desordres, qui intéressent la conservation
> de la porte..."[58]

Millet seems to be suggesting that the importance (excellent preservation!) of the portal justifies repair-
ing the porch.[59] Millet's remarks in this regard are
even more interesting because, as we will see, they
reprise a Leitmotif of other records written between
the years 1844 and 1872.

3. Other Documents

A group of lesser documents, mostly letters, also
make reference to the sculpted portal. The earliest

of these is the report submitted by Garrez to the Ministre Secrétaire d'État et d'Intérieur on 10 April
1845.[60] After praising the sculpture as being "admirablement conservés" and of "un travail extrêmement remarquable" he states, "...c'est principalement pour
cette moitié de l'édifice...qu'il y a importance majeure
a l'occuper de la consolidation de partie du fond de la
nef, du choeur..."[61] In short, the church should be
saved because of the portal. In a letter addressed to
the same ministry and dated 10 September, 1851, the
bishop of Meaux suggests that the church "...menace de
tomber avec son intéressant portail, si l'on n'y fait
promptement les reparations nécessaires." Nine months
later the ministry was addressed to the same effect by
the Prefect of the Seine-et-Marne.[62]

4. Conclusion

The written evidence thus confirms the visual
evidence: that of a portal so well preserved that it
was not in need of any restoration or repair. In
retrospect, it appears that those concerned with the
fate of the former priory of Saint-Loup-de-Naud around
the middle of the nineteenth century sometimes appealed to the quality and state of preservation of the
portal as levers to hasten the restoration of the
church which, in contrast, was in need of repairs.

C. Summary

In evaluating the import of the information concerning restoration work at Saint-Loup-de-Naud, it
should be kept in mind that the primary motivation for
restoration resides in the need for it.[63] The documents for Saint-Loup, both visual and written, all indicate that in the nineteenth century no such need existed. In a general sense, reservations concerning the
physical integrity of the Saint-Loup sculpture should
be put aside for the modern period.

Yet, reservations remain. The keystone of the
third archivolt appears to have been repaired in stone
at the lower left corner (fig. 60).[63a] Various repairs to the lintel have been executed in stone: (1)
to the architecture, above figure n/3; (2) to the lower
portion of the colonnette on the left end; and, (3) to
the lower fillet beneath figure n/4. All these repairs
can be seen in photographs taken before the repairs to
the other end of the lintel were effected in 1967.[64]
The location and nature of these repairs--filler blocks
along the edges matching the original stonework--ren-
ders it unlikely that they would have been caused or
have been executed after placement of the lintel.[65]
Indeed the documentation already cited might be appealed to as indirect confirmation of the fact. But
still, in view of the range of types of restoration

work known to have been done at Saint-Denis in the last century,[66] reservations must remain. The state of preservation of no portal can be considered certainly known until a thorough study has been carried out from a scaffold. For the purposes of this study, however, the weight of evidence allows us to assume that the sculpture at Saint-Loup-de-Naud was not restored in modern times, although an extended physical examination of the stone could require a reassessment of some of the conclusions herein.

III. The Period Before the Nineteenth Century

The often quoted caution that what survives is not necessarily representative of what once existed applies to restoration more categorically than has been assumed. The fact that the monks of Nesle-le-Reposte dismantled, transported and re-erected their sculpted portal when they moved to Villenauxe in the seventeenth century[67] should expand our horizons when considering the physical integrity of any monument. The probable post-medieval reconstructions on the foreportals of the northern transept of the cathedral of Chartres should inform us that (outside of Paris at least) the currency of medieval forms lived on and that later artists could be frighteningly subtle in their modifications to medieval structures.[68] Two post-medieval periods: the period of the Huguenot Wars and the period of the Hundred Years War are areas of concern for

Saint-Loup-de-Naud.

A. The Period of the Huguenot Wars

Since Bourquelot's early study of the priory it has
been known that the Huguenot Wars brought damage to Saint-
Loup-de-Naud.[69] Our best source for the events which
transpired there remains the chronicle of a local church-
man, Claude Haton, which Bourquelot also published in
1857.[70] For the year 1567, Haton informs us that an ad-
vance unit of Huguenots was sent to Saint-Loup to pillage
the priory, but that the monks, being forewarned, hid
their valuables with the result that "...n'y trouverent
les barbares voleurs que les ymages qu'ils rompirent en
plusieurs pièces, excepté celle dudit Saint-Loup, a
laquelle ils ne toucherent..."[71] When Salet, who first
brought the Haton material to bear directly on a study of
the priory, quoted this passage, he wrote, "Si le mot
'image' est synonyme de statue, il ne peut s'agir évidem-
ment que de statues décorant l'interieur de l'édifice et
non de la statuaire du portail."[72] Although Salet's
supposition is probably correct, the fact that certain of
the sculptures at Saint-Loup were not originally designed
for their present emplacement,[73] together with Haton's text
obliges us to ask whether the assemblage as we find it today could perhaps be the result of a post-1567 reconstruction. The possibility of a post-medieval assemblage of
some of the portal sculpture becomes heightened when we re-

call that the large, easily accessible and essentially undamaged trumeau representing Saint Loup is not among the
sculptures which can be considered spolia.[74]

In fact, the question--as also Salet's implicit ques-
tion--resolves itself in the remainder of the passage given
by Haton: "C'est ymage demours en son entier et en sa
place jusques après la St. Martin d'hiver et au retour de
la grande trouppe desditz hugenotz revenant de St. Denys
en ce pays icy, au retour desquels eut la test rompue seule-
ment et avec grande difficulte."[75] Since the head of the
trumeau has never been broken, neither Haton nor the Huguenots were concerned with the portal structure. Moreover,
the presence inside the church today of a now headless
statue representing a prelate whose costume includes the
pallium suggests that Salet's surmise about damage to interior sculpture was correct.[76] In this additional light,
it seems improbable that repairs to the portal were necessary in the sixteenth century.

B. The Period at the Close of the Hundred Years War

The period of the Hundred Years War was an impover-
ishing one for the priory of Saint-Loup-de-Naud.[77] Four
documents are known which bear on the question of the physical condition of the priory at this time. A letter of
Charles VII of France makes clear by implication that the
English armies, which occupied the Brie region, wrought

havoc upon the physical structure of the priory complex:
among the "benefactors" of funds were to be "...les maisons,
heritages, édifices et labourages appartenant audit prioré..."[78] What damage the English did is not described in
detail in the King's letter, although it many have been so
described in the "supplice" made to the king by Guillaume
Quatrain which, regrettably, does not appear to have sur-
vived. None of the three other documents, which are accords between the abbeys of Sainte-Colombe and Saint-Pierre and the priory of Saint-Loup for relic quests to obtain funds for the work of repair, provides any specific
information about the nature of the damage or the repairs.[79]
While it is probably significant that the church is not
mentioned, there is no evidence to suggest, one way or the
other, what the fate of the sculpted portal may have been
at this time.

IV. Conclusions

    In summary, none of the surviving documentation for
any period indicates that the assemblage of sculpture at
Saint-Loup-de-Naud, in all its details, is anything other
than medieval in date. For the modern period,--that is,
the nineteenth century and the twentieth century--the evidence reveals a portal so well preserved that it could even
be appealed to as a raison d'être for effecting repairs
elsewhere on the fabric of the church. For the earlier

period, the evidence is less clear; it suggests that the
only damage to works of art at Saint-Loup-de-Naud probably
was done to objects inside the church. In the absence of
any indication of damage, either physical or documentary,
there is little cause to suppose subsequent restoration
or repair. Moreover, as Chapter IV demonstrates, the iconographic program reflects medieval concerns.

Although the evidence assembled here relating to the
state of preservation is not sufficient to categorically
assert that the portal's physical integrity has remained
intact from the time of its erection,[80] this study has come
nearer than any other to justifying the assumption that the
portal is authentic in all its details.

In some ways, perhaps more important than the state
of preservation in the past will be the state of preservation in the future. The sculpture at Saint-Loup-de-Naud
is besieged on two fronts:[81] a gold-colored lichen, common in the region, now covers much of the surface of the
sculpture and slowly deteriorates it; as photographs clearly show, atmospheric pollution has in the last fifty years
abraded features that were recently still visible. As Al-
bert Elsen has recently pointed out, the very presence of
these photographic records may lessen our concern for pre-
serving the monument itself.[82] One obvious remark remains:
Unless governments and individuals make an immediate and
substantial commitment to the issue of preservation on all

levels, we will become in the foreseeable future not art historians, but photo historians and chapters on the states of preservation will read like the office for the dead.

APPENDIX A

FOOTNOTES

1. Salet, 1933, p. 157.

2. Sauerländer, 1972, p. 393.

3. Aufauvre and Fichot, 1854-1858, p. 140.

4. Dr. Pamela Z. Blum, in a conversation with the author during May 1975, expressed the opinion that the pattern of staining on the figures of archivolt 2, n/1 and the handling of some of the drapery of several apostles on the lintel suggested the possibility of a restorer's hand. More recently, in October of 1977, M. Alain Erlande-Brandenburg, Directeur du Bulletin monumental, shared our concern about some of the compositional disparities (e.g., the bottom voussoirs in the two outer archivolts). He also felt these disparities might indicate the need to reconsider the integrity of the portal sculpture.

5. Archives des Monuments historiques, cliché #3181. No negative is available for this apparently anonymous photograph.

6. Archives des Monuments historiques, series H, Saint-Loup-de-Naud, (all subsequent references to archival documents pertain to this series unless otherwise speci-

fied): M. Selmersheim, Inspecteur Général, "Rapport à la Commission," 15 novembre 1900. Payment records for work carried out at that time by Entreprise Delorme of Provins make no mention of repairs to the tympanum and lintel in any of the sixty-eight items listed. Continued presence of the crack in photographs taken over the course of the century assures that Delorme was not asked to repair it. Salet refers to four iron bars being set in the soffit of the lintel in 1900 (1933, p. 136). While no reference to this work could be found, 1900 is a likely date for it and helps to explain why nothing else was done to the crack at this time. It should also be noted that the term "tympan" is often used in the documents--as it appears to be here--to refer to the entire tympanum and lintel zone.

7. A letter dated 6 May 1963 from one Pierre Dalloy calls attention to the problem. A letter dated 10 June of the same year from M.J. Verney, Conservateur régionale des bâtiments de France, indicates that the government was already aware of the problem. A "rapport détaillé" had been submitted just seven days after Dalloy's original letter.

8. Payment sheet #57, "remise en état du tympan de l'église". Presumably a description of the actual work carried out (and hopefully photographs as well) can be found in the office of M. de Bergevin, Architect des Bâtiments de France, Fontainebleau.

9. Presumably the repair to the toe of the left foot of the angel immediately adjacent to the lintel on the right (archivolt 1, s/1) was also done at this time.

10. The iron bars visible in the soffit before this repair (see above, n. 6 and fig. 22) must have been left in place and covered with the repair material.

11. Roblot-Delondre, 1913, p. 128. Restoration work under Buval commenced in January of 1844 (see below). It is unlikely that any work had been undertaken before Buval arrived because of the documented poverty of the rural community. A letter from the bishop of Meaux dated 3 August 1866 to the Ministère de la Maison de l'Empereur et des Beaux-Arts indicates that the portal was classified earlier than the church itself: "Ce portail...a été classé au nombre des monuments historiques; mais l'église entière mériterait la meme faveur." In an article written about the same time, G. Leroy, "Une visite à Saint-Loup-de-Naud," Bulletin de la Société d'archéologie, sciences et arts du département de Seine-et-Marne, 1867, p. 126, echoes the desire of the bishop's letter. We will return to the relationship between the restoration of the portal and of the church in discussing the written evidence.

12. See above n. 5.

13. There are no records of restoration of the sculpture for the period between 1872 and 1900. In a

"Rapport à la Commission" dated 16 May 1884, M.R. de Lasteyrie responds to a request by the curé of Saint-Loup and the bishop of Meaux by charging the architect M.P. Boeswillwald with responsibility to replace the large wooden doors. A letter from the latter dated 12 December 1889 indicates that this had been accomplished.

14. Roblot-Delondre, 1913, p. 112, n. 1.

15. In view of this detailed accuracy, it is to be expected that the head of the tiny angel to the left of the Virgin on the lintel has been lost in the interim and today probably forms part of some collection. See also, n. 20.

16. E. Grésy, "Iconographie de Saint Loup empruntée principalement aux monuments de l'art local," Bulletin de la Société d'archéologie sciences et arts du département de Seine-et-Marne, 1867, p. 69.

17. Archives des Monuments historiques, cliché #147.

18. In 1851 column figure 3-s still held a cylindrical object (presumbaly part of a rotulus) in his upraised left hand. Today the hand is damaged and the object is missing.

19. Archives des Monuments historiques #2710. The drawing is reproduced by A. Raguenet, Petits édifices historiques, Paris, n.d. (before 1933), 143e numero, Saint-Loup-de-Naud, p. 1706, although Buval's original author-

ship is not acknowledged. The drawing has also been published photographically in a magazine article entitled
"Trois églises briardes" by Marguerite David-Rey (after
1933, because Salet's study is cited). An offprint of
the article is on file in the offices of the Archives
départementales de la Seine-et-Marne in Melun, but the
publication in which it originally appeared is unknown.

20. Among the portal elements which can be called
remarkably accurate are: the trumeau (including the
figure's damaged right shoulder and its capital), the column-figures, the lintel, the tympanum, the bottom voussoirs on the right side and several other voussoirs as
well. In contrast to these are some obvious errors: the
seated Virgin Annunciate (archivolt 3, n/l), correctly
represented with her gesture of surprise, has been given
the head of a king. Archivolt 3, n/6 in Buval's drawing
appears nowhere in the voussoirs of the portal. Interestingly, the headless angel in archivolt 1, n/l is shown
with its head intact. Perhaps at this time the head was
still there (cf. n. 15).

21. Bourquelot, 1840/41, pp. 244-271.

22. Bourquelot, 1840/41, p. 251.

23. Ibid., p. 250.

24. Ibid., pp. 251-255.

25. Ibid., p. 255.

26. Ibid., pp. 253 and 255 respectively.

27. Aufauvre and Fichot, 1854-1858, pp. 140-141.

28. Grésy, 1867, pp. 67-69, is largely dependent on Bourquelot and on Aufauvre (see above, p. 286) for his discussion of the iconography.

29. Leroy, 1867, pp. 125-128, is occasioned by a visit to Saint-Loup made by the Société during the "séance générale" of 1865.

30. Ibid., p. 126, "Une humidité constante et un défaut presque absolu de réparations, mettent en péril la partie orientale de la construction. Les voûtes et les arcades sont étayées, en prévision d'une chute prochaine; le culte n'est plus exercé que dans les travées voisines du porche. Le bon aspect des murs exterieurs et du portail, la solidité du clocher roman et des absides trinitaires font naître des espérances qui s'évanouissent en franchissant le seuil." We will return to the condition of the building with the discussion of the architect's records and reports.

31. "Notice abrégée sur l'église de Saint-Loup... sur besoins à l'état actuel du monument" (four pages, unpaginated). Like most of the documents on file it bears no identifying number. This report is included with three others in the special "Dossier de Protection" for Saint-Loup. The others comprise: an essay by the bishop of Meaux entitled "Église de Saint-Loup-de-Naud" (largely

derived from Bourquelot, 1840/41); a letter by the architect P. Boeswillwald (16 September 1868) concerning the
lost frescoes and the report on the frescoes by Laurière
cited in n. 48 below.

32. Page one of the report.

33. Interestingly, Buval's text appears to be independent of the earlier article by Bourquelot (1840/41).

34. Page two of the report.

35. Ibid. Presumably those très peu de parties are
the several headless voussoirs (and other minor areas of
damage) which remain unrepaired today. Buval cites as one
reason for the good state of preservation the probably
true story that the local populace forcibly repelled revo-
lutionaries bent on destroying the portal.

36. Ibid.

37. On-site inspection at Saint-Loup is needed to
see the traces; b/w photographs are inadequate to the
task. On Chartres, see the dossier actuel on Chartres
West. Work there is now under the direction of M. Jean
Feray, Inspecteur de la Commission des Monuments historiques, to whom I am indebted for facilitating my research
while in Paris in October, 1977. The slick of gesso at
Chartres is described as being "jaune-ochre" in color.

38. A complete layer of gesso would have protected
the surface of the sculpture and is probably a major

reason for its good state of preservation. Careful re-
moval of such a layer would certainly not in itself have
occasioned reworking of the surface of the sculpture.
On the other hand, it may be the case that when Buval
said the sculptures "sont recouverts" with a layer of
gesso, he meant that it was once entirely covered and
that traces were still visible. Except in the event of
the discovery of further documentation, we will probably
never know what Buval saw.

39. This written report was also submitted 15
January 1844 (sixteen pages, unpaginated).

40. Page one of the report.

41. The report also mentions projected work:
(1) on the tower walls (consolidation with the metal
bars still visible on the exterior); (2) on pier en;
(3) on the north wall (construction of the two buttresses
on the north transept arm and the buttress on the west
end of the northern absidiole); (4) on the crossing tower
carpentry and (5) "reparations diverses" (which included
repointing the exterior masonry).

42. Drawing #2711 submitted by Buval, 10 January
1844, as part of the "Projet de restauration et de consolidation."

43. "Rapport sur l'église de St.-Loup-de-Naud, à
le Ministre de la Maison de l'Empereur et des Beaux-Arts"

(23 April 1867, seven pages, unpaginated).

44. Page three of the report. Particularly the
western parts of which he later states, "Les constructions
postérieures à celles del'abside et des deux premières
travées de la nef et des bas-côtes, soit les deux der-
nières travées en entrer de la nef, sont en bon état,
comme piliers, murs et voutes" (p. 4f). Earlier, one
M. Garrez submitted a "Rapport à le Ministre d'État et
d'Interieur sur les travaux les plus urgents à exécuter
à l'Église de Saint-Loup" (Paris, 10 April 1845, four
pages, unpaginated) which indicates the same condition
twenty-two years earlier: "Les deux travées de la nef
en entrant de la même epoque que la porche, tout dans un
état parfait de conservation à l'intérieur..." (p. 1).
In the total absence of any opinion to the contrary and
of any record of repair, we may consider these bays
(WIII-WVI) to be unrestored.

45. Page three of the report.

46. See the report by M. Selmarsheim, 15 November
1900 (op. cit., n. 6) and records for work undertaken in
1910-1912 by Louzier, who restored the tower roof at
that time.

47. Pages three and four of Mimey's report.

48. Pages 5-6 of the report. These included:
demolition and rebuilding of the vaults in travée EI, of

the three semi-domes plus part of the walls which support them and of part of the transept vaults (These were in imminent danger of collapse.); total reworking of pier en and the arches which abut it; various "reprises" in the other crossing arches, in the cupola vault and construction of the exterior buttresses projected but never built by Buval (see above, n. 41).

In carrying out this work, Mimey was forced to destroy the frescoes which covered the vaults of the choir and apse. Of what was once an extensive sanctuary cycle, only fragments of a zodiac on the intrados of the arch at the head of the choir and an over-life-sized, palliate abbot-saint on the southern sanctuary wall remain today. Minute traces of paint on the piers in the transept and eastern nave bays indicate a decorative program even larger than that which was visible in the nineteenth century. Copies of the paintings which were sacrificed to the necessary vault reconstructions were undertaken in 1868 by M. Denuelle (letter of 27 October accepting commission to make the copies). The water-color copies, which are preserved in the Palais de Chaillot were exhibited at the Salon of 1876. They were reviewed by A. de Montaiglon, "L'architecture au salon de 1876, Gazette des Beaux-Arts, 1876, 1, ser. 2, vol. 13, pp. 744-746 wherein they are wrongly identified as having

been made by M. Lameire. Subsequently, chromolithographs
were made of the copies, indeed, by one Ch. Lameire;
these were published by Roblot-Delondre, 1913, pls. X-XIII.
Other important discussions of the murals at Saint-Loup
include: E. Mâle, "La peinture murale en France" in
André Michel, ed., Histoire de l'art, I, p. 779; P. Deschamps and M. Thibout, La Peinture murale en France, le
haut moyen age et l'époque romane, Paris, 1951, pp. 130-
131 and the unpublished note by Ch. Laurière, "Rapport
sur les peintures murales de l'église Saint-Loup-de-Naud
près Provins" (19 March 1877, 8 pages, unpaginated) now
part of the "Dossier de Protection" for Saint-Loup (see
above, n. 31).

The loss of the vault paintings probably is respon-
sible for the negligible role given Saint-Loup in his-
tories of medieval wall painting (e.g., Demus, 1970 makes
no mention of the paintings at all). However, as Mâle
justly observed (loc. cit.), few important Romanesque
churches in France "preserve" such an extensive fresco
cycle. The existence of the copies, which provide iconographic if not stylistic evidence, together with the
zodiac fragments and the sainted abbot, which provide
substantial original stylistic and technical information
and a (limited) style control on the copies, combine to
produce sufficient data of all kinds to warrant a major

reassessment of the Saint-Loup cycle and its place in the general history of medieval wall painting. Moreover, the sanctuary cycle provides an almost unique opportunity to effect an iconological analysis of the Gesamtkunstwerk-relationship between portal and sanctuary programs.

49. Page two of the report.

50. Page five of the report.

51. Six pages long, unpaginated.

52. Page one of the report. In a sadly humorous presage of cost overruns on government contracts in this century, Millet says that because "...au mauvais état de la construction il avait été impossible à M. Mimey de se renfermer dans les limites des crédits."

53. Ibid.

54. Page two of the report. More specifically the work included: new semi-domes for the three apses; re-building the apse windows and surrounding masonry; re-working of the "têtes de murs" at the entrance to the apse; restoring the blind arcade of the apse; construction of the (exterior) transept buttresses on the north (and presumably the buttress on the northern absidiole); re-working of the crossing bay arches and restoration of the cupola vault "...aussi bien que la plupart des voûtes du choeur et du transept..." The vaulting campaign also in-cluded replacing the original barrel-vault in bay WI with

a groin-vault. From an on-site inspection it would appear
that pier en was entirely rebuilt and not just refooted,
although this work was begun by Buval. Detailed payment
records for work accomplished by Mimey (année 1870 and
année 1871) confirm Millet's summary of the former's tenure
as architect.

55. Ibid.

56. Page five of the report.

57. No subsequent record on file indicates that it
was. The iron bar holding the broken piece in place
today is already visible in the photograph of 1872.

58. Page three of the report. The 1872 photograph
partially reveals the condition (on the exterior) to
which Millet here refers. Payment records for the mid-
1890's indicate that the repairs to the porch and south
side exterior buttresses--essentially a task of consolida-
tion--was being carried out at that time. This project
evidently dragged on long enough to include re-roofing the
crossing tower by the architect Louzier between 1910 and
1912.

59. Millet does not seem to see the need for re-
pairing the porch as self-justifying.

60. Cited in n. 44 above.

61. Page one of Garrez's report.

62. In a variation on this theme, de Lasteyrie

wrote in a report (cited in n. 13 above) concerning the need to replace the doors: "Ses ais disjoints et à demi-disloquer donnent à ce beau portail une apparence de misère et d'abandon."

63. For years it has been as fashionable to criticize the nineteenth century for its restorations as the Revolution for its destruction. Recently, however, there have been steps to restore the integrity of the latter's intention (see, e.g., D. Reiff, "Viollet-le-Duc and Historic Restoration: the West Portals of Notre-Dame," Journal of the Society of Architectural Historians, 30 (1971), pp. 17-30). Indirectly, this reappraisal must bear upon how we approach all restorative work.

63a. See Chapter III, p. 114.

64. See figs. 112 and 113.

65. We will see this confirmed by the circumstances surrounding the (re-) use of the lintel itself (see Chapter III, pp. 82-85.

66. S.M. Crosby and P.Z. Blum, "Le portail central de la facade occidentale de Saint-Denis," Bulletin monumental 131 (1973), pp. 209-266.

67. See, L. Pressouyre, "Quelques vestiques sculptés de l'abbaye de Nesle-la-Reposte," Bulletin de la Société national des Antiquaires de France, 1967, p. 105 and n. 1.

68. Although he has not yet published a full study of the foreportals, J. van der Meulen, "Die Bauge-schichte der Kathedrale Notre-Dame de Chartres, nach 1194," Bulletin de la Société archéologique d'Eure-et-Loir, 1965, pp. 114-115, has already indicated the likelihood of post-medieval reconstructions. The "accepted" dating (ca. 1220-1230, cf. Sauerländer, 1972, p. 438) of at least one figure in the northern foreportal ensemble has also been challenged, on iconographic grounds, by R. Adams, "The Column Figures of the Chartres Northern Foreportal and a Monumental Representation of Saint Louis," Zeitschrift für Kunstgeschichte, 36 (1973), pp. 153-162.

69. Bourquelot, 1840/41, p. 260.

70. F. Bourquelot, ed., Mémoires de Claude Haton (1553-1582), 2 vols., Paris, 1857 (Documents inédits sur l'histoire de France, ser. 1, vol. 32, pties 1 and 2).

71. Ibid., p. 442.

72. Salet, 1933, p. 135, n. 4.

73. See Chapter III. The tympanum, the lintel, the column figures, the four lowest voussoirs on the two outer archivolts and, probably, the keystone of the middle archivolt fall into this group.

74. See Chapter III, pp. 86-87.

75. Bourquelot, 1857, p. 442f.

76. The assumption here is that this is the damaged

statue of Saint Loup referred to by Haton. Of course a
mitred head is necessary to distinguish an archbishop
from a palliate abbot, like the figure in fresco on the
south-side choir wall, but the association of the statue
with the northern absidiole--by tradition associated with
Saint Loup--encourages the assumption. Curiously, this
statue, which can perhaps be dated to the third quarter
of the thirteenth century on stylistic grounds, does not
seem to have found its way into any of the literature on
the church. While this fact makes its provenance potentially suspect, one might also remark that it is not an
exceptional piece and, like the wooden crucifix in the
northern side aisle and the several large paintings in
the church, may have been omitted for that reason alone.
Unless evidence is found to the contrary, it seems reasonable to assume the statue has not been brought from
another local church and, in fact, belongs at Saint-Loup.

77. See above, Chapter I, p. 10.

78. Bourquelot, 1840/41, p. 271. See Appendix B,
Doc. XI, where the full text is included.

79. All three have been published as appendices
in Geoffroy de Courlon, Le Livre des reliques de l'abbaye
de Saint-Pierre-le-Vif de Sens, ed. G. Julliot and M.
Prou, Sens, 1887, pp. 249-268.

80. The assumption continues to be that the repairs

to the left end of the lintel are medieval.

81. The church itself continues to suffer, as it probably always has, from the high moisture content in the heavy clay-laden soil, the level of which continues to be too high against the church walls on the north.

82. A. Elsen, "Bomb the Church? What we don't tell our students in Art I," Art Journal, 37 (1977), p. 33, n. 4.

APPENDIX B

THE DOCUMENTATION FOR THE PRIORY OF

SAINT-LOUP-DE-NAUD

TO 1438

CHRONOLOGICAL OUTLINE FOR THE PRIORY OF

SAINT-LOUP-DE-NAUD

DOC. #	DATE		
I	980 A.D.	--	Foundation of the first monastic community
II	999	--	Confirmation of original charter
III	1063	--	Archbishop of Sens confirms parent abbey in original grant
IV	1120	--	Visit by Abbot of Saint-Pierre-le-Vif
V	1124-30	--	Pope Honorius II confirms priory in possession of parent abbey
VI	1160	--	Gift of relics of Saint Loup by Hugh of Toucy, archbishop of Sens
VII	1167	--	Exchange between Henry-the-Libéral and Saint-Pierre-le-Vif
	(1170)	--	(see doc. V)
	(1178)	--	(see doc. VII)
	(1179)	--	(see doc. V)
VIII	1188	--	Transaction between Saint-Quiriace in Provins and parent abbey concerning a well in Naud
IX	1202	--	Gift of Milo Brebannus to Saint-Pierre-le-Vif
X	1212	--	Accord between monks and village curé
	(1214)	--	(see doc. VI)
	(1239)	--	(see doc. IX)

DOC. #	DATE		
	(1253)	--	(see doc. IX)
	(1367)	--	(see doc. VI)
	(1375)	--	(see doc. VI)
	(1432)	--	(see doc. VI)
XI	1438	--	Priory falls _in commendam_

DOCUMENT I.

980 A.D.   Charter of Sewinus, archbishop of Sens, granting
a chapel (?) ad supplementum victus et vestitus in the
town of Naud to the abbot and monks of Saint-Pierre-le-Vif
in Sens, in return for which the abbey was to establish a
priory.

A.   Sources

    1.   Original: lost

    2.   Copies:

        a.   Chronicon sancti Petri Vivi Senonensis,
             auctore Clario (12th C), Bibliothèque
             d'Auxerre, ms. 212, fol. 125 v.
             Published by: 1.   D. Luc d'Achery,
                                  Spicilège, II, p. 472.
                             1a. Bourquelot, 1840/41,
                                  pp. 246-247.
                             2.   L.-M. Duru, Bibliothèque
                                  historique de L'Yonne, II,
                                  Auxerre and Paris, 1863,
                                  p. 570.
             Excerpted by: Salet, 1933, p. 131, n.1.
             Another copy of the chronicle, the so-called
             "Paris Clarius," Bib. nat. ms. lat. 5002,
             remains unpublished.

b. Archives de L'Yonne, H. 250 copy of charter (ms. 18th c).

Published by: M. Quantin, Cartulaire générale de l'Yonne, I, Auxerre, 1860, p. 148.

c. Michel Caillot, Cartulaire de Provins (ms. 18th c), Bibliothèque de Provins, ms. 92, fol. 204r and v.

Published by: Bourquelot, 1840/41, pp. 246-247.

d. N.-P. Ythier, Histoire ecclésiastique de Provins, 15 vols ms., Supplement à l'abbaye de Jouy (ms. 18th c), Bibliothèque de Provins, ms. 116, pp. 408 and 434.

Published by: Bourquelot, 1840/41, pp. 246-247.

B. Text (Caillot version)

Anno ab incarnatione Christi DCCCCLXXX, indictione VIII, eam sederem ego. Sewinus, archiepiscopus senonensis, et circumsederent quidam de coepiscopis nostris, cum personis ecclesie sancte Marie Virginis sanctique Stephani protomartyris, quorum consilio et actu vigor ecclesiasticus vigere debet, venerunt ante nostram presentiam abbas monasterii sancti Petri vivi et sancti Saviniani martyris, cum turma monachorum ejusdem ecclesie, petentes a nobis, ad supplementum victus et vestitus sui et successorum suorum, aliquod augmentum largiri a nobis sibi clementer. Quorum petitionibus et precibus predictarum vel prenominendarum personarum consentientes, aurem accommodavimus, et quod petebant, quia suum esse vidimus, concessimus: scilicet, altare quod est in pago senonico, in

villa que dicitur Athonus, in honore sancti Petri
dicatum, quod olim dominus Egidius bone memorie,
hujus sedis archiepiscopus, eidem ecclesie dedit et
literis firmavit; item in villa que dicitur Sancezas,
altare quod est in honore sancti Sanctiani martyris
consecratum; item tertium, quod distat a crypta
predicti monasterii dextras, in honore sancti
Saviniani martyris et protopresulis nostri; quartum
quoque, in pago pruvinensi, in villa que dicitur
Naudus, in honore sancti Lupi consecratum, ad petitionem magistri Raynardi, ejusdem monasterii abbatis,
et monachorum ejus, dedimus hec quatuor altaria,
ut ipsi et successores eorum ea omni tempore posside-
ant, absque alicujus servicii administratione, et in
eis fideles sacerdotes ad serviendum Deo omnipotenti
digne constituant. Postulo autem serenitatem successorum meorum archiepiscoporum, ut, sicut cupimus
scripta voluntatum suarum cuncto tempore tieri rata,
ita orthographiam desiderii mei fideliumque meorum
perenniter servent, stabiliter unde et propria manu
firmo, roborandum que coepiscopis nostris et fideli-
bus sancte Dei ecclesie humiliter deprecor et trado.
Preterea, violatores hujus privilegii et diminutores,
gladio spiritus sancti, nisi resipuerint et satis-
fecerint, quibus datum est ferimus. Actum in ecclesia Sancte-Marie et Sancti-Stephani senonice urbis,
feliciter alque synodatim.
    SEVINUS peccator, archiepiscopus, firmo et sigillo
meo munio.
    ODO, Carnotensis , episopus.
    RAINOTEUS, parisiensis episcopus.
    EGO MANASSES, aurelianensis episcopus.
    MILO, Trecarum episcopus.
    THEODORICUS, hujus sedis archidiaconus.
    GREGORIUS, archiclavis hujus ecclesie.
    ALBERICUS, Gastinensis archidiaconus.
    LEOTHERICUS, archidiaconus melodunensis.
    Data anno quinto regnante HUGONE rege, mense
Martio.--GARNERIUS, cancellarius scripsit.

C. Comments

    The Caillot version is the most complete. Bourque-
lot also gives textual variations from the Clarius and
Ythier versions. Salet publishes the Clarius versions
with omissions.

Precisely what, in terms of church architecture, is intended by altare cannot be established with certainty. Possible readings range from a simple Christian altar, to the (liturgical)·choir of a church, to the parish revenues deriving from the sacerdotal ministry: oblations, baptism and burial dues, etc.[1] Regardless of which reading one chooses, the text implies the existence of an ecclesiastical structure of some sort, perhaps a parish church.[2] This interpretation is confirmed by the phrase ad supplementum victus et vestitus.[3] The term victus seems to imply a prebend or "...the landed property affected to the sustenance of a community of canons or monks,..."[4] Vestitus refers to possession or tenure of a "furnished" estate.[5] From this is would appear that the grant of a chapel (?) or part of a parish church (?) was accompanied by sufficient lands, revenues (and buildings) to support a monastic community. We may conclude that Saint-Loup-de-Naud was, at the outset, an establishment of some economic strength and one which would have been considered important by its parent abbey.[6]

D. Notes

1. J.F. Niermeyer, Mediae Latinitas Lexicon Minus, Leiden, 1976, p. 38. Other readings include a lateral chapel and the portion of the total parish revenue assigned to the priest (as a rule one-third, the rest being re-

served for the lord of the church).

2. A controversy recorded in the early thirteenth century (see Doc. X) between the parish priest and the monastic community raises the question of how far back in time the pastoral duties were so divided. This interpretation of altare might suggest that the church was served by two clergies since the tenth century.

3. This phrase refers to each of the "altars" named in the grant. It would seem to apply to all of them equally; no reason exists to lessen its import because it applies to more than one foundation.

4. Niermeyer, 1976, p. 1097.

5. Niermeyer, 1976, p. 1084.

6. There is no reason to assume at this time that Saint-Loup-de-Naud was more important than the other foundations, but its proximity to Provins clearly increased its importance over time.

DOCUMENT II.

999 A.D. Obituary notice of Archbishop Sewinus of Sens

which confirms the original grant of the chapel in Naud,

with perpetua privilegia, to the monastery of Saint-

Pierre-le-Vif.

A. Sources

    1. Original: lost

    2. Copies: Odoranni monachi opuscula (chronicle of

                   Saint-Pierre-le-Vif, 11th c), Rome,

                   Vatican Library, Coll. of the Queen of

                   Sweden, Cristina, ms. 577.

                   Published by: 1. Migne, P. L. CXLII,

                                     cols. 772-773,

                           2. Duru, 1863, pp. 395-

                                     396.

                   Excerpted by: Salet, 1933, p. 131, n.2.

    3. Variants: Cronica fratis Gaufridi (ms. lt. 13th

                   c/early 14th c), Bibliothèque munici-

                   pale de Sens, ms. 59.

                   Published and translated by: G. Julliot,

                   Chronique de l'abbaye de Saint-Pierre-

                   le-Vif . . . redigée vers la fin du

                   XIIIe siècle par Geoffroy de Courlon

                   (sér. Soc. arch. de Sens, Docs. T. 1)

                   Sens, 1876, pp. 366-367.

B. Text (Odorannus version)

ANNO DCCCCXCIX; obiit Sewinus   archiepiscopus,
qui jacturam monasterii Sancti-Petri, quam Anastasius,
archiepiscopus, antecessor ejus, relevare caeperat,
in pristinum resituit statum: ibique sub districtione
regulari ordinavit abbatem, Rainardum, cujus etiam
corpus in codem monasterio est sepultum. Hic ab urbe
Roma, per manum Joannis, papae, archiepiscopale
pallium, quo antecessores ejus infulati sunt, et
primatum Galliae suscepit. Hic etiam monasterium
Sancti-Petri Milidunensis ab imo relevavit, et monachos in illo mittens, abbatem Walterium eis prae-
fecit. Hic matrem ecclesiam Sancti-Stephani, quae
igne cremata fuerat, ab epistiliis erigens, et ex
integro perficiens, signis et ornamentis ecclesias-
ticis decoravit, et adjunctis sibi Milone, episcopo
Trecassensium, et Eriberto Autissiodorensium, Rocleno
quoque Nivernensium, cum maximo honore dedicavit.
Eadem quoque die ad stipendia clericorum ibidem Deo
famulantium, tria altaria sub privilegii testamento
delegavit. Deinde brachium sancti Leonis, papae,
cum digitis sancti Ebonis ab abbate Rainardo, et a
fratribus monasterii Santi-Petri multa prece obtinens,
auro et gemmis ornavit et eidem Casae-Dei contulit.
Pro quibus mutua vicissitudine, et pro remedio ani-
mae suae, de altario Sancti-Saviniani,   quod XXX
passus a crypta monasterii abest, et de altario Sancti-
Sanctiani, quod est in villa Sanceias, et de altario
Sancti-Petri, quod est in villa quae Alsonus vocatur,
et de altario Sancti-Lupi, quod est in villa quae
Naudus dicitur, perpetua privilegia una cum consensu
et voluntate papae romani et coepiscoporum suorum,
Sancto-Petro ejusque monachis fecit. Decrevit etiam
ut abba ejusdem monasterii in conventu abbatum vel
clericorum post episcopum primus sedeat, et inter
ceteros ejusdem episcopatus abbates primatum teneat.
Ipse autem talem se exhibeat, ut dignus sit tali
honore. Tabulam quoque ex auro et argento ante altare Sancti-Stephani construxit, de qua postmodum
ante monasterium facta est turris.

B. Text (Variant)   (Julliot translation)

Dominus Seuinus rest-   Le seigneur Sévin res-
aurauit cenobium Sancti-   taura le monastère de
Petri-Uiui ponens in   Saint-Pierre-le-Vif et
illo abbatem nepotem   lui donna pour abbé son
suum nomine Rainnardum,   neveu nommé Rainard,

monachum Sancte-Co-
lumbe, uirum reli-
giosum. Retinuit dic-
tus archiepiscopus
quasdam possessiones
Sancti-Petri non
cupiditate sed neces-
sitate, quia Arch-
ambaudus obligauerat
laicis possessiones
Sancti-Stephani.
Propter quod fecit
etiam idem Seuinus
maiorem ecclesiam
et dedicauit sexto
anno ordinationis
sue, tertio nonas
octobris. Ipsa die,
dedit quasdem uillas
et ecclesias ad
stipendia canoni-
corum quas iure here-
ditario possidebat.
Ab illo die quo
sacerdotium sumpsit
usque ad transitum,
carnes non comedit,
nec lino usus fuit
desubter. Istam vero
dedicationem maioris
ecclesie celebrauit
dominus Seuinus,
presentibus Emberto
Autissiodorensi, et
Rocleno Niuernensi
episcopis cum
honore maximo.
Signis et orna-
mentis ecclesias-
ticis ipsam maioram
ecclesiam decorauit;
brachiumque sancti
Leonis, pape doc-
toris, cum reliquiis
de digitis sancti
Ebbonis ab abbate
Rainnardo Sancti-
Petri obtinuit, et
maiori ecclesie con-
donauit; priuilegia-

moine de Sainte-
Columbe, d'une grande
piété. Ledit arche-
vêque retint quel-
ques biens de Saint-
Pierre, non par
cupidité mais par
nécessité, car Arch-
ambaud avait engagé
à des laics les biens
de Saint-Etienne.
C'est par ce moyen
que le même Sévin ache-
va la cathédrale, et
en fit la dédicace la
sixième année de son
ordination, trois
jours avant les nones
d'octobre. Le même
jour, il donna pour
les prébendes des
chanoines, certaines
terres et certaines
églises qu'il avait
reçues en patrimoine.
Depuis le jour qu'il
reçut le sacerdoce
jusqu'à sa mort, il ne
mangea point de viande,
et ne se servit point
de vêtements intimes
en lin. Or il célébra
cette dédicace de la
cathédrale en présence
de Embert, évêque
d'Auxerre, et de
Roclenus, évêque de
Nevers, avec la plus
grande pompe, et il
enrichit cette même
église de cloches et
d'ornements ecclé-
siastiques. Il obtint
de Rainard, abbé de
Saint-Pierre-le-Vif,
le bras de saint Léon,
pape et docteur, avec
des reliques des
doigts de saint Ebbon,
et en fit présent à la

que fecit monasterio
Sancti-Petri de altaris
Sancti-Sauiniani-in-burgo,
Sancti-Sanctiani-in-
uineis, Sancti-Petri-
de-Alxonno et Sancti-
Petri-de-Naudo de con-
silio coepiscoporum et
consentiente domino papa
Iohanne XVI. Decreuit-
que dominus Seuinus ut
abbas Sancti-Petri post
episcopos primus sedeat.
Tabulam argenteam et
auream ante altare Sancti-
Stephani construxit, de
qua postea ante maiorem
ecclesiam facta est turris
mire et famose altitudinis.

cathédrale. Il donna
au monastère de Saint-
Pierre des privilèges
touchant l'autel de
Saint-Savinien-
du-Bourg, de Saint-
Sanctien-des-Vignes,
de Saint-Pierre d'Aul-
xon et de Saint-Pierre-
de-Naud d'après l'avis
des évêques et du
consentement du seig-
neur pape Jean XVI.
Le seigneur Sévin
décréta aussi que l'abbé
de Saint-Pierre siéger-
ait le premier après
les évêques. Il fit
placer devant l'autel
de Saint-Etienne un
rétable d'argent et
d'or, qui plus tard fut
vendu pour élever de-
vant la grande église
une tour d'une hauteur
étonnante et devenue
fameuse.

C. Comments

Confirmation of the original grant in Sewinus' will
suggests that the terms of the grant had been carried out
prior to the archbishop's death.

Roblot-Delondre, 1913, p. 111 and n. 2 misinterprets
the variant as representing an original grant of a chapel (?) dedicated to "Saint-Pierre" in Naud and assigns
it a date of 978. The reference to "Saint-Pierre" is
more likely a scribal error by Geoffrey or his copyist,
particularly since the preceding church named was also dedicated to Saint Peter (correctly, in comparison with the
Odorannus version).

DOCUMENT III

1063 A.D. Charter of Richerius, archbishop of Sens, confirming (among other items) the rights of synod and
visitation held for the priory of Saint-Loup-de-Naud by
the abbot and monks of Saint-Pierre-le-Vif.

A. Sources

    1. Original: Auxerre, Archives de l'Yonne, Fond
                     de l'abbaye Saint-Pierre-le-Vif.

                     Published by: Quantin, 1860, I,

                                pp. 184-186, esp.

                                p. 185.

                     Excerpted by: Salet, 1933, p. 131,

                                n. 3.

    2. Copies: D. Cottron, Chronique de Saint-
                  Pierre-le-Vif, Bibliothèque d'Auxerre,
                  ms. 157, p. 487.

B. Text (original from Quantin)

Postulavit item exorans praenominatus abbas cum monachis ut canonica auctoritate confirmarem ante-
cessoris mei donni Sewini bonae memoriae +, quoddam
adnotatum litteris optabile praeceptum, quod fecit
firmans Deo et Sancto Petro sanctoque Saviniano,
de sinodis et circadiis duarum aecclesiarum, scilicet
Ausonis et Naudi, et de ipsarum altaribus;...

C. Comments

    This document attests to close ties between parent
abbey and priory from the very beginning of the priory's

history. The absence of one of the four chapels (?)
named in the original grant (i.e., Sancezas, because
Saint-Savinian lay in immediate physical proximity to
the parent abbey and is here named with it) attests to
the continued importance of the two dependencies mentioned.[1] This document also reveals the parent abbey's
rights of synod and visitation. Presumably they were
among the privileges confirmed in Sewinus' will (Doc. II)
and were held from the foundation of the priory.

D. Notes

1. Comparison of "Ausonis" here with the Alsonus
in the Odorannus version of Doc. II and the Athonus in
the Caillot version of the original grant (Doc. I) suggests all three variants refer to the same foundation.

DOCUMENT IV

1120 A.D. Presumably a charter (or charters) confirming
the gifts of Alexander, a capellanus at Saint-Loup-de-
Naud, to the abbey of Saint-Pierre-le-Vif which is known
through the narrative of a contemporary chronicler.

A. Sources

    1. Original(s): lost

    2. Copies: none known

    3. Variants: none known

    4. Versions: a. The episode is related in con-
                    siderable detail in the Clarius
                    chronicle, fol. 89v.

                    Published by: Luc d'Achery, II,
                                p. 483, Duru, 1863,
                                II, pp. 535-537.

                    Excerpted and translated by:
                                Bourquelot, 1840/
                                41, pp. 248-249.

                b. The episode is related in much
                    shorter form in the Geoffrey
                    chronicle.

                    Published and translated by:
                              Juillot, 1876,
                                pp. 462-463.

B. Text (Clarius version)

Celebratum est concilium, XV Kal. Novembris a
domno Conone, Prenestino episcopo, qui tunc legatus
dicebatur trium provinciarum Rothomagensium et
Senonensium, atque Remensium. Ad quod consilium cum
archiepiscopi cum suffragancis suis, tam episcopis,
quam abbatibus, Belvaco harum invitarentur provinciarum, domnus Daingbertus, Senonensis archiepiscopus invitatus, molestia corporis detentus, venire
non potuit. Contigit itaque quod Arnaldum, abbatem
Sancti-Petri-Vivi, invitaret cum universis episcopis
et abbatibus sibi subditis. Arnaldus itaque abbas,
monitus, libenter se ad tantum iter praeparavit,
et, quam cicius potuit, iter aggressus est. Primo
autem die, cum ad aecclesiam Sancti-Lupi, videlicet
Naudo, pervenisset, defessus itinere, et detentus
pluviali tempore, corporali infirmitate ingraves-
cente, et prae senectute corpore adeficiente virtute,
in propria domo sua inibi remansit. Mox quemdam
suorum monarchorum, nomine Clarium, ut se excusaret
ad concilum transmisit. Monachus vero ille ad
concilium veniens, abbatem A. [Arnaldum] dominum
suum veris racionibus excusavit, et totum concilium
audivit, et reversus illic ubi eum dimiserat,
repperit. Ibique cum per aliquot dies demorarentur
expectantes ut convalesceret, tandem convaluit, et
ad proprium monasterium, cooperante divina clementia,
redire disposuit.
    Cum autem inde exire vellet, accessit ad eum
vir venerabilis, Alexander vocatus, ipsium aecclesie
capellanus, omni laude dignus, multisque virtutibus
honestissime condecoratus, IIII philacteria argenti
deaurata, unum de ligno sanctae crucis Domini,
alterum de dente sancti Nicholai, tertium de sepulchro Domini, quartum de sancto Georgio praesenta-
vit, et, ut domnus abbas secum deferret, obtinuit.
Referens quia cum esset capellanus comitis Stephani
ultra mare secum ivit, sed antequam transirent,
a summo pontifice Romanae aecclesiae inter se et
Dominum Arnulfum, qui nunc patriarcha videtur, li-
centiam ligandi atque solvendi accepit. Postquam
mare transierunt populum convocabat, exhortabatur,
poenitentias injungebat, et ita populum magis
virtutibus quam telis instructum in praeliis mitte-
bat. Sicque faciendo ad sepulchrum Domini, sicut
idem Alexander referebat, pervenerunt, celebrataque
oratione pro qua venerant, conspectibus regis se
praesentaverunt. Rex igitur Balduinus, audiens

tantum virum venisse, videlicet comitem Stephanum,
virum in rebus bellicis strenuum, omni religione
praeditum ad se accersiri praecepit, et apertis
thesauris, optionem dedit, ut quicquid sibi
placeret de thesauro regio acciperet. Tunc comes
Stephanus respondit se divitem possessione auri et
argenti, et omnium rerum terrenarum, tantum se
indigere thesauro sanctarum reliquiarum. Audiens
hoc, rex vocavit Arnulfum scriniarium suum, et ait
ei ut quicquid sanctuarii in capella sua eligeret,
totum absque mora sibi tribueret. Comes igitur
Stephanus accepit de sepulchro Domini, et de cruce
ejus, et de corpore sancti Georgii. Effecit autem
idem Alexander cum summa sagacitate, sicut ipse
referebat, per societatem quam cum Arnulfo habuerat,
ut sibi de hisdem reliquiis clam portiunculas daret,
qui non negavit, quoniam antiqua societas cum hoc
facere coegit. Has porciunculas decenter auro
argentoque conditas et dimidium dentem sancti
Nicholai, pro quo asserebat se dedisse marcam et
dimidiam argenti, et integram unxiam auri, domino
abbati apportavit, et in archivo Sancti-Petri
apportare memorans sic obsecravit:

"Summe et venerande pater, lacrymans memoro cum
quanto labore has reliquias habui, de Jherusalem
apportavi, et cum quanto amore servavi. Ast ego,
indignus et peccator, non ita cum digno honore
servavi, nec tractavi sicut tractare debui. Nunc,
summe pater, quoniam thuribulum argenteum vobis
dedi, et duos argenteos calices, alterum horum optime
deauratum, et casula sacerdotis, cum vestibus reli-
quis usque etiam ad subdiaconum, missae necesariis,
vobis quoque dedo ista philacteria, videlicet
cor meum et animam meam. Et ut has honorifice
tractetis, domum meam, quam in castro Pruvini habeo,
cum omnibus utensilibus suis, et uno lecto vestito,
post obitum meum suscipiatis. Accersitoque dicta-
tore et notario, cartam vobis scribere faciatis,
et obsecro, ut illum qui vobis amodo auferre voluerit, excommunicetis. Pro hac mercede mihi recom-
pensate anniversarium meum v solidis de eadem domo
eadem die in refectione Fratrum, et honorem (sic),
harum reliquiarum: ut honorifice condiantur et in
archivo Sancti-Petri sollempniter ab omnibus cele-
brentur, ad laudem et ad gloriam nominis Christi,
beneficio cujus dantur bona omnia, per omnia secula,
Amen."

Elevans itaque dominus abbas tanta et tam magna
munera, reversus est ad propria. Receptae sunt
autem capsellae sanctarum reliquiarum a clero

et a populo, monstrata sollempniter et deoscu-
lata, II Kal. Novembris, regnante domino nostro
Jhesu Christo, cujus regnum et imperium sine fine
permanet in secula seculorum. Amen.

(Geoffrey version)

Eodem anno, Calixtus papa
celebrauit concilium Re-
mis; fuit ibi dominus
Daimbertus, senex, et
secum adduxit dominum
papam. Quo papa Rome
reuerso, Conon tenuit concilium Beluaco, anno
Domini millesimo cen-
tesimo uigesimo.
Dominus Daimbertus ex-
cusabat se per Arnaldum,
abbatem Sancti-Petri-
Uiui, litteratorie.
Abbas iter arripuit; sed
in itinere infirmatus
remansit. Et sic pro
domino Senonense et pro
se misit monachum nomine
Clarium ualde bene
litteratum, qui monachos
illos bene excusauit, ex-
cusatione condigna sus-
cepto concilio aportata.
Qui a concilio reueniens,
abbatem apud Naudum-
Sancti-Lupi inuenit,
et reduxit Senonis, et
domino Senonensi omne
concilium enarrauit.

(Julliot translation)

La même année, le pape
Calixte présida un con-
cile à Reims. Le seig-
neur Daimbert déjà
vieux y assista, et il
amena avec lui le
seigneur pape. Lorsque
le pape fut de retour à
Rome, Conon réunit un
concile à Beauvais,
l'an du Seigneur 1120.
Le seigneur Daimbert
se fit excuser par Ar-
naud, abbé de Saint-
Pierre-le-Vif, porteur
de sa lettre. L'abbé
se mit en route; mais
il resta malade en
chemin. Et alors il
envoya, pour le seig-
neur de Sens et pour
lui un moine d'un grand
savoir nommé Clarius,
qui présenta leur ex-
cuse en très-bons
termes. A son retour
du concile, il retrouva
l'abbé à Saint-Loup-
de-Naud, et le ramena
à Sens, et il fit au
seigneur de Sens un
récit de tout le
concile.

C. Comments

This passage contains the oldest surviving reference
describing Saint-Loup-de-Naud as a church (aecclesiam).

The circumstances surrounding Arnaldus' visit--his

ill health--suggest that the chronicle does not record a canonical visitation, a right the abbots presumably exercised,[1] but rather the exercise of the simple feudal prerogative of an overlord being hosted by his dependents.[2] Precisely what is intended by the words propria domo is not clear. They may refer to the priory as a whole in the sense of being the abbot's dependency; they may refer to a house held by the abbots of Saint-Pierre-le-Vif.[3]

The reason for recording the event at all must center in some large measure on the gift of relics and other items from Alexander, capellanus, or presbiter, as Geoffrey later calls him,[4] to the parent abbey.[5] The gift of the relics reflects two facts of interest here: obtained in the East by the priest himself, they reveal priory-personnel to be actively involved in the affairs of the time;[6] being given to the parent abbey, they reflect the orientation of the priory to Sens. Finally, it is important to mention that the house in Provins, which is among the other items given by Alexander to Saint-Pierre-le-Vif, reveals interest in that wealthy town by both the priory and its parent abbey.

D. Notes

1. Canonical visitation is an official juridical act exercised by bishops and abbots to maintain the faith and discipline and to correct abuses. See, A.B.

Meehan, "Visitation, canonical," Catholic Encyclopedia,
15 (New York, 1912), pp. 479-480. According to Bouvier,
"Histoire de Saint-Pierre-le-Vif," SSHNY-B, XLV (1891)
p. 132, the abbey exercised its rights of assembly, at
least by the thirteenth century, holding regular annual
meetings attended by its dependencies. We may reasonably
assume the practice was established considerably earlier.

2. It may not have been an entirely onerous task.
In terms of local prestige in a rural hamlet like Saint-
Loup, the extended presence of the abbot of Saint-Pierre
should probably be seen as analogous to a temporary residence or a visit by the pope in one of the cathedral
towns. (I am indebted to Professor Stephen White of the
History Department at Wesleyan University for this suggestion.)

3. See Niermeyer, 1976, pp. 863-864 and 354-355
respectively. Proprius references ownership or possession; domus can refer to either a residence or an entire
monastery.

4. Gaufridi de Collone, Libellus editus super
reliquiis et fundatione Monasterii Sancti Petri Vivi
Senonensis, Paris, Bibliothèque nationale, published by
G. Julliot and M. Prou, Geoffroy de Courlon, Le Livre des
reliques de l'abbaye de Saint-Pierre-le-Vif de Sens (ser.
Société archéologique de Sens, Doc. 5, T.2), Sens, 1887,
p. 7, e.g. It is entirely possible that Alexander be-

longed to the secular clergy attached to the priory church. See Doc. X below.

5. Another possible reason for the episode's inclusion is the name of the monk sent to the council in place of the abbot: Clarius. Reading the Geoffrey version, where Clarius is styled <u>ualde bene litteratum</u>, one might think him to be the same Clarius who wrote the chronicle (Salet, 1933, p. 132 thought so). If he was, and at the time a monk at Saint-Loup (<u>suorum monachorum</u>) who subsequently moved to the parent abbey, this would indicate further close ties between priory and parent abbey.

6. Whether Alexander was presbiter at Naud only after he served Count Stephan as chaplain does not matter.

DOCUMENT V.

1124-1130 A.D. A Bull issued by Pope Honorius II con-

firming the priory Saint-Loup-de-Naud (and the other

churches of Sewinus' original grant) in the possession

of Saint-Pierre-le-Vif.

A. Sources

    1. Original: lost (?)

    2. Copies: a copy, presumably of the original, is

                    included in the Clarius chronicle,

                    fol. 105v.

                    Published by: Duru, 1863, II, pp. 564-

                    565.

                    Excerpted by: Salet, 1933,

                    p. 132 and n. 2.

B. Text (Clarius copy)

Honorius, episcopus, servus servorum Dei, dilecto in
Christo filio Erberto, abbati Senonensis monasterii,
quod, in honore apostolorum Petri et Pauli, situm est
in vico qui Vivus dicitur, ejusque successoribus
regulariter promovendis in perpetuum.

Ad hoc nos, disponente Domino, in Apostolicae
Sedis servitium permotos agnoscimus, ut ejus filiis
auxilium implorantibus efficaciter subvenire, et ei
obedientes tueri ac protegere, prout Dominus dederit,
debeamus. Unde oportet nos venerabilibus locis manum
protexionis extendere, et servorum Dei quieti atten-
tius providere. Proinde, karissime in Christo fili,
Erberte, abbas, supplicationibus tuis clementer
annuimus, et Beati-Petri monasterium cui, Domino
ductore, praesides, cum omnibus ad ipsum pertinentibus, ad instar domni praedecessoris nostri beatae
memoriae, Paschalis, papae, sub tutela Apostolicae
Sedis excipimus, sicut venerabilis fratris Damberti,

Senonensis archiepiscopi, devotio ab eodem domino
postulavit. Quod videlicet monasterium sanctae
memoriae Teodechildis, Clodovaei regis filia, fun-
dasse et rerum suarum muneribus ditasse cognoscitur,
per praesentis igitur privilegii paginam, apostolica
auctoritate statuimus, ut quaecumque praedia, quas-
cumque possessiones eadem sancta femina Teochildis
eidem monasterio contulit, et quaecumque ad ipsum
aliorum fidelium legitimis videntur donationibus
pertinere, quecumque etiam in futuro concessione
pontificum, liberalitate principum, vel oblatione
fidelium, juste atque canonice poterit adipisci, firma
vobis vestrisque successoribus et illibata permaneant.
In quibus, haec propriis visa sunt nominibus expri-
menda: scilicet, altare quod est in pago Senonico,
in villa quae vocatur Alsonus, in honore sancti Petri
dedicatum, quod olim domnus Egil, bonae memoriae
Senonensis archiepiscopus, eidem monasterio dedit;
tria quoque altaria quae Sewinus, archiepiscopus,
vestrae aecclesiae contulit et suis litteris confirma-
vit; videlicet, in villa quae vocatur Sanceias, altare sancti Sanctiani, martyris; item altare quod
distat a crypta praedicti monasterii quinquaginta
dextris, in honore sancti Saviniani, martyris atque
pontificis, consecratum: in pago Pruvinensi, in villa
quae   vocatur Naudus, altare Sancti-Lupi, et
quatuor altaria, sicut a praedictis praesulibus concessa sunt, monasterium vestrum, omni tempore possi-
deat absque alicujus servitii administratione, et in
eis fideles sacerdotes ad serviendum Deo omnipotenti
digne constituantur. Sane Mauriacensem cellam, in
Arvernico pago constitutam, sub jure semper et ditione
monasterii vestri permanere sancimus, cum omnibus
rebus et possessionibus suis. Decernimus ergo ut
mulli omnino hominum liceat idem monasterium temere
perturbare, aut ejus possessiones offerre (sic), vel
ablatas retinere, minuere, vel temerariis vexationibus
fatigare; sed omnia integra conserventur, eorum pro
quorum sustentatione et gubernatione concessa sunt,
usibus omnimodis profutura, salva in omnibus Senonensis metropolitani canonica reverentia. Obeunte te,
nunc ejusdem loci abbate, vel tuorum quolibet successorum nullus ibi quilibet subreptionis astutia, seu
violentia proponatur, nisi quem fratres communi consensu, vel fratrum pars sanioris consilii, secundum
Domini timorem et beati Benedicti regulam, providerint
eligendum. Quicquid praeterea inmunitatis, quicquid
liberalitatis seu donationis a Senonensis aecclesiae
archiepiscopis, vel catholicis regibus, monasterium
vestrum juste hactenus obtinuisse cognoscitur, ratum

firmumque manere sancimus. Si qua igitur in futurum
aecclesiastica saecularisve persona hanc nostrae
constitutionis paginam, sciens, contra eam temere
venire temptaverit, secundo tertiove commonita, si
non satisfactione congrua emendaverit, potestatis
honorisque sui dignitate careat, reumque se divino
judicio existere de perpetrata iniquitate cognoscat,
et a sacratissimo corpore et sanguine Domini nostri
Jhesu-Christi aliena fiat, atque in extremo examine
districte ultioni subjaceat. Cunctis aut eidem loco
justa servantibus sit pax Domini nostri Jhesu-Christi,
quatenus et hic fructum bonae actionis percipiant, et
apud districtum judicem praemia aeternae pacis in-
veniant.
     AMEN. AMEN. AMEN.
     Ego, HONORIUS, Catholicae Ecclesiae episcopus SS.

C. Comments

Whether this charter represents merely the process
of keeping records "up to date" or whether it responds
to an attempt (by the priory itself? or by the archbishop?) to sever the original bond cannot be ascertained
on the basis of surviving data. The process repeated
itself several times over the course of the twelfth century: a bull of Innocent II dated 1137 confirms the bull
of Honorius;[1] a bull of Lucius II from 1144[2] and two of
Alexander III dated 1170[3] and 1179[4] respectively do the
same thing.

The period in question, the middle years of the
twelfth century, is a period of growth and importance
for the priory, if liturgical (see Doc. VI) and artistic
evidence are any indication. Perhaps the parent abbey
is simply assuring its continued dominant influence.

D. Notes

1. The original, which has been lost, is copied by
D. Cottron, <u>Histoire de l'abbaye Saint-Pierre-le-Vif de
Sens</u>, Bibliothèque d'Auxerre, Ms. 156, p. 592. The ms.
is unpublished but is cited by Quantin, 1860, II, p. 216.

2. The original of this bull was also copied by
Cottron, <u>op. cit.</u>, p. 602. See Quantin, 1860, II, p. 216.

3. Quoted by Quantin, 1860, II, pp. 214-216 from
Cottron, <u>op. cit.</u>, p. 631f.

4. Quoted by Quantin, 1860, II, p. 303 from Cottron,
<u>op. cit.</u>, p. 646. This confirmation calls the church in
Naud "Sancti-Petri," although the other churches in the
original grant are named correctly. Whether this scribal
error (?) belongs to Alexander III's court or to Cottron
is insignificant. See also Doc. II above. This confirmation makes reference to another, otherwise unknown one by
Willelmus, archbishop of Reims, who was earlier archbishop of Sens.

DOCUMENT VI.

c. 1161 A.D. A charter of Hugh of Toucy, archbishop of Sens, attesting that he witnessed relics of Saint-Loup at the request of the abbot and monks of Sainte-Colombe de Sens and that he obtained and gave portions of those relics to the church of Saint-Loup-de-Naud in honor of miracles worked there in the saint's name.

A. Sources

    1. Original: with (broken) seal of the archbishop in the Archives de l'Yonne, séries H, 172 (formerly séries F, Saint-Pierre-le-Vif).

              Published by: Quantin, 1860, II, p. 128; Bourquelot, 1840/41, p. 255, n.3; AASS, 1 September, p. 254.

    2. Copies: D. Cottron, op. cit., p. 608. (According to Salet, 1933, p. 134, n.1, Cottron dated the charter to 1144.)

B. Text (from Quantin)

Hugo, Dei gratia archiepiscopus Senonensis, omnibus ad quos presentes littere pervenerint, in Domino salutem. Noverit universitas vestra quod cum, ad peticionem et instantiam abbatis et monachorum Sancte-Columbe, reliquias beati Lupi, archiepiscopi Senonensis, populo qui ad hoc videndum devote venerat, osten-

dissemus, humiliter ab eodem abbate postulavimus
quatinus aliquam portionem de reliquiis sanctissimi
confessoris nobis concederet. Quod nobis benigne
concedens, donavit quamdam partem de capite et de reliquiis corporis ipsius, involutam in quadam particula
capsule sue.
        Nos vero moti plurimum pro evidentissimis miracu-
lis, que per merita dicti confessoris frequentius
fiebant in ecclesia ejusdem confessoris Lupi de No, et
fere omnes illuc confluebant, jam dictas reliquias cum
multa devotione donavimus et in quadam capsa reposui-
mus.

C. Comments

        This document provides two important pieces of in-

formation: It dates the arrival of specific relics of

Saint Loup at the priory in Naud; it renders evidence of

an effective cult at the church prior to the arrival of

relics in the early 1160's.

        The full import of this information cannot, however,

be understood without reference to another, slightly

earlier charter of this same Hugh of Toucy.[1] This docu-

ment records that Hugh went on two occasions, once during

the reign of Abbot Girardus (1148-1149) and once during

that of a successor, Odo (1150-1164)[2] to view, witness

and attest to the integrity of the corpus of Saint Loup

which was interred in the other major abbey in Sens, that

of Sainte-Colombe. This charter is hazy about whatever

events precipitated the viewing stating only that with

this action "...tota ulterius cessaret ambiguitas, omnis-

que ex inde aborta sopiretus contentio."[3] Little imagi-

nation is needed, however, to see the relationship between the two documents and to suppose that the source of the "rumors" about the relics at Sainte-Colombe stemmed from the priory of Saint-Loup-de-Naud which possessed an efficacious cult and presumably also claimed possession of some relics of their patron.[4] The vigorous response by the abbey of Sainte-Colombe attests to the importance of the cult of Saint Loup both for them and for the priory at this time.

The controversy over who possessed which relics continued throughout the Middle Ages.[5] Around 1212, Innocent III ruled in favor of the relics at Sainte-Colombe.[6] According to the Bollandists the monks of the priory continued to claim some relics (although not the capse et quaedam membra).[7] The archbishops of Sens and Reims allowed these relics to be circulated in their dioceses and this was later confirmed by Urban V in 1367.[8] In the interim, Alexander IV (1254-1261) forbade the abbot and monks of Saint-Pierre-le-Vif from pretending that their priory at Naud possessed relics which in fact were at Sainte-Colombe.[9] However, in 1375, the monks of Saint-Loup (and Saint-Pierre) again claimed to circulate the "reliquiae de corpore, capite et vestimentis" over which the controversy had originally begun.[10] By the fifteenth century, a quid pro quo seems to have been agreed upon. Both monasteries and the priory entered into agreements which allowed both sides to claim their relics.[11]

D. Notes

1. The original charter exists in the Archives de l'Yonne, Fonds H. 4, no. 1 (Bibliothèque de Sens) and has been published by Quantin, 1860, II, p. 120 and by Julliot and Prou, 1887, pp. 288-289.

2. According to the charter the second visit was prompted by the insistence of Pope Hadrian IV. Evidently the first visit did not quash the rumors. The pope's intervention helps to measure the importance of the controversy.

3. Julliot and Prou, 1887, p. 288.

4. H. Bouvier, Histoire de l'église et de l'ancien archdiocèse de Sens, 3 vols., Paris, 1906-1911, II, p. 60 made this connection.

5. Summaries of the controversy and references to the document can be found in Bourquelot, 1840/41, pp. 255-257 and Salet, 1933, pp. 133-134, and will be used for the following discussion.

6. Bourquelot, 1840/41, p. 256 and n.1 and Salet, 1933, p. 134 and n.2.

7. AASS, 1 September, p. 254 and Bourquelot, 1840/41, p. 256.

8. Bourquelot, 1840/41, p. 256 and n.3, where he cites Ythier, Supplément à l'abbaye de Jouy, p. 379.

9. Salet, 1933, p. 134 and n.3.

10. Bourquelot, p. 356, n.2 citing <u>Gallia Chris-</u>
<u>tiana</u>, t. XII, col. 49. Bourquelot says that the relics
"...sont transportées dans une nouvelle chasse."

11. Bourquelot, pp. 256-257 and (p. 257) n.1, cites
an accord dated 1432. Julliot and Prou, 1887, pp. 249f
and 256, publish the text of two: the 1432 agreement and
a second dated 1453.

DOCUMENT VII.

1167 A.D. Henry-the-Liberal, Count of Troyes, cedes to the abbey of Saint-Pierre-le-Vif and its priory at Naud all that he possesses in Naud, except for fiefs, and two houses in Provins in recognition of a gift of relics made to him by the abbot and monks of Saint-Pierre-le-Vif.

A. Sources

    1. Original: with a comital seal (broken) in the Archives de l'Yonne, H. 172.

            Published by: Quantin, 1860, II, pp. 193-194; d'Arbois de Jubainville, His-toire des ducs et des comtes de Champagne, 7 vols., Paris, 1859-1866, III, p. 353.

            Excerpted by: Salet, 1933, p. 132, n.3.[1]

    2. Copies: none known

B. Text (from Quantin)

Ego Henricus, Trecensium comes palatinus, univer-sis tam presentibus quam futuris, notum fieri volo quod, cum, orationum causa, Senonis, aecclesiam Sancti-Petri-Vivi et beatos martires Savinianum, Potencianum et Altinum adiissem, placuit domino Odoni, tunc ejusdem loci abbati, et fratribus ejus, quod mihi de sacrosanctis reliquiis predictorum martyrum Potenciani scilicet et Altini darent; quas

Trecis, in ecclesia beati prothomartiris Stephani, cum
summa veneratione et debita reverentia, collocavi.
Hujus itaque rei gratia, et propter amorem quem erga
prefatam ecclesiam ego et antecessores mei ab antiquo
habueramus, eidem aecclesiae Sancti-Petri-Vivi Senonensis et aecclesiae de Naudo, pro animabus patris et
matris meae, et antecessorum meorum, et pro remissione
peccatorum meorum, quicquid apud Naudum, et in par-
rochia ejusdem villae, tam in hominibus et censibus
quam in justicia et rebus aliis, exceptis casamentis,
habebam, in perpetuam elemosinam libere possidendum
donavi. Hoc etiam de prefata donatione mihi et here-
dibus meis retinui, quod predictarum rerum custodia
et advocatio in aliam quam in meam et heredum meorum
manum transferri non poterit.
     Concessi etiam prefatae aecclesiae, apud Pruvinum,
domos duas liberas a justicia et ab omni exactione et
consuetudine ad me pertinenti: domum videlicet quae
fuit Johannis filii Almanni, sitam in vico Sancti-
Johannis, et domum Hugonis Bridelli, que sita est
juxta Sanctum-Teobaldum.
     Que ut nota permaneant et in statu suo rata perse-
verent, litteris annotata sigilli mei impressione
firmavi, sub testibus istis quorum hec sunt nomina:
magister Stephanus, Pruvinensis aecclesiae prepositus;
dominus Nicholaus, capellanus meus; Ansellus de Triag-
nello; Odo, constabularius; Hugo de Planceio; Robertus de Milliaco; Drogo de Pruvino; Petrus, frater
ejus: Deymbertus de Braio; Girardus Eventatus; Guil-
lelmus, marescallus et Artaldus, camerarius.
     Aeta sunt hec, anno incarnati Verbi M° C° LX°
VII°; data Trecis, per manum Guillelmi, cancellarii.

C.   Comments

     This document records a pious transaction between

the count and the abbey of Saint-Pierre-le-Vif. Presum-

ably the priory was to act in the capacity of administra-

tor for the parent abbey and is included in the document

for that reason. The primary position of the parent

abbey is affirmed in the bull of Alexander III, dated

1170, which confirms only Saint-Pierre-le-Vif in the

possession of Henry's gift.[2]

A similar relationship with respect to the parent abbey appears to have obtained eleven years later, in 1178, when Count Henry ceded to the priory of Saint-Loup rights which he held in the adjacent hamlet of Courton in exchange for a rentless tenure held by the monks.[3] In effecting this transaction, Henry obtained the consent (assensu) of the abbot and all the monks of Saint-Pierre-le-Vif.[4]

These two documents thus shed further light on the close and continuing ties between priory and parent abbey.[5] How much, if any, of the revenues involved in these arrangements returned directly to the priory is difficult if not impossible to know.

D. Notes

1. Salet omits, in his excerpt, the opening portions of the document. In so doing he minimizes the role of Saint-Pierre-le-Vif and completely eliminates the "exchange," making the record appear to be a one-sided donation.

2. This document is referred to in Doc. V, n.3 above. The passage can be found in Quantin, 1860, II, p. 216.

3. The original is lost and is known only through the copy in the so-called Cartulary of Michel Caillot,

in the Bibliothèque de Provins, ms. 92, fol. 205. The
text is discussed and published by Bourquelot, 1840/41,
pp. 257 and 264 respectively.

4. Bourquelot, 1840/41, p. 264.

5. This bond was noted by Bourquelot, 1840/41,
p. 258, but, it has received insufficient emphasis in
the interim.

DOCUMENT VIII.

1188 A.D. A transaction between the chapter of the collegiate church of Saint-Quiriace in Provins and the abbey of Saint-Pierre-le-Vif concerning the terms under which the priory at Naud was to operate a mill in that village, use of which had been given by the chapter to the monks of Saint-Loup.

A. Sources

　　1. Original: lost

　　2. Copies: The transaction is known only through:

Ythier, Histoire ecclésiastique de Provins, 15 vols. ms., supplément à l'abbaye de Jouy, pp. 398 and 401, which is ms. 116 located in the Bibliothèque municipale de Provins. Published by: Bourquelot, 1840/41, pp. 264-265.

B. Text

　　Ego GUIDO, Dei gratia beati Quiriaci decanus, totumque ejusdem ecclesiae capitulum, notum facimus universis tam praesentibus quam futuris, quod super omnibus querelis quae inter ecclesiam nostram et ecclesiam b. Petri Vivi versabantur, inter praedictas ecclesias ita compositum est: siquidem controversia erat inter praedictas ecclesias, super tenemento deffuncti Theobaldi, decani, quod est apud Naudum, vivario scilicet ejusdem Theobaldi, molendino, vinea juxta molendinum sita, terra arabili et censu, quae omnia quittavit ecclesia nostra ecclesiae b. Petri Vivi, libere et quiete possidenda. Nos vero in

praefato molendino, singulis annis, viginti et unum
sextaria frumenti et tres minellos et totidem avenae,
sine omni diminutione et contradictione, medietatem
in Natali Domini et medietatem ad festum sancti
Johannis, quittos habebimus, neque ad reparandum vel
renovandum molendinum, vel ad aliquid circa ea, vel
propter ea faciendum, aliquid de nostro expendemus.
Se autem infra praedictos terminos annonam praefatam
de numero ejusdem molendini habere non potuerimus, ad
priorem Naudi, vel ad eum qui ejus vices aget, recur-
remus, ipsumque, ut nobis super hoc satisfaciat, com-
monebimus. Quod si prior vel ejus vicarius super hoc
nobis non satisfecerit, nec annonam praefatam post
commonitionem infra octo dies nobis reddere voluerit,
praedictum molendinum sine contradictione ad opus
nostri faciemus, donec nobis inde satisfactum fuerit.
Quod ut ratum in posterum conservetur, litteris istis
commendari et sigillo nostro muniri praecepimus. Actum anno ab Incarnatione MCLXXXVII.

C. Comments

As Bourquelot implies, this transaction between

Saint-Quiriace and Saint-Loup-de-Naud is enacted on be-

half of the latter by the parent abbey.[1]

Bourquelot lists several other documents which make

reference to the mill.[2] The most interesting of these is

a charter from the end of the twelfth century wherein

the following testators are named: "Ex parte ecclesiae

b. Petri Vivi, Galterius, prior de Naudo, Ansellus, capel-

lanus abbatis, Salo et Hugo, milites de Naudo..."[3] This

same Galterius (†1202) also served as abbot of Saint-

Pierre-le-Vif[4] and, apparently held both offices simulta-

neously for a time.

It would be very interesting to know more of the

names of priors of Saint-Loup. Galterius is the first

known to us; the second, a Brother Hélias (†1209), also succeeded to the abbacy of Saint-Pierre-le-Vif.[5] Was this a normal practice? Did the abbot concurrently claim title of prior (at least in the early centuries of the priory's foundation) as a way to maintain control? Or, are the surviving records merely coincidences?

D. Notes

1. Bourquelot, 1840/41, p. 258.

2. Bourquelot, 1840/41, p. 258, n.1. The first of these is a charter of Hugh of Toucy, archbishop of Sens, dated 1160. It confirms the goods and privileges of the abbey of Saint-Jacques-de-Provins following the establishment there of regular canons from Saint-Quiriace. The mill in Naud appears among the items listed. The document, which again is known only from the copy of Ythier (op. cit., III, p. 12) was published by Bourquelot, Histoire de Provins, 2 vols., Provins and Paris, 1839 and 1840, II (1840), pp. 382-385. Another reference to the mill occurs in the Necrology of the Hôtel-Dieu in Provins, p. 86r. Identified by Bourquelot, it has never been published. Another unpublished transaction dated 1414 may have been between Saint-Quiriace and Saint-Loup directly without the involvement of Saint-Pierre-le-Vif. Bourquelot's description implies this but does not make it clear.

3.   Bourquelot, 1840/41, pp. 265-266 publishes this document which is known only through the copy of Ythier (op. cit., Supplément à l'abbaye de Jouy, p. 399).

4.   See the reference by Geoffrey of Courlon: Julliot et Prou, 1887, p. 82.   Bourquelot, 1840/41, pp. 261-263 publishes a list of priors which he takes over largely from Ythier, op. cit., Livre D, le prieuré de St. Loup de Nô les Provins, pp. 359-372.   According to Ythier, Galterius was prior from 1176.   By 1182 he was abbot of Saint-Pierre-le-Vif.   Roblot-Delondre, 1913, p. 139, states that this Galterius gave relics from the Holy Land to the priory.   Presumably her source for this is the Geoffrey reference cited which, however, states only that he brought relics back; no destination is named for them.

5.   Bourquelot, 1840/41, p. 261.

DOCUMENT IX.

1202 A.D. The record of an exchange between one Milo Brebannus and Saint-Pierre-le-Vif in which shares of the produce from the former's mill in Glatigny were assigned to Saint-Loup-de-Naud in return for masses said in Saint-Pierre-le-Vif and in Saint-Loup-de-Naud on the anniversary of the former's death.

A. Sources

    1. Original: lost

    2. Copies: The document is known only through three copies made by Ythier, op. cit., Miscellanea, p. 31 and Supplément à l'abbaye de Jouy, pp. 410 and 411.

                Published by: Bourquelot, 1840/41, pp. 266-267.[1]

B. Text (Bourquelot version)

    Ego GALTERUS, Dei gratia abbas Sancti Petri Vivi senonensis, et totus ejusdem ecclesiae conventus, notum facimus universis tam praesentibus quam futuris, quod usuarium quod ecclesia beati Lupi de Naudo clamabat in nemore de Corberon, scilicet in nemore quod dominus Milo Brebannus habebat ex parte fratris sui defuncti Johannis, et in illo nemore quod idem Milo habebat ad Corberon, ex domino Hugone, filio defuncti Manasseri de Villagruis, eidem Miloni et haeredibus ejus, communi assensu, in perpetuum quittavimus; ipse vero Milo, pro recompensatione hujus quittationis, in molendino suo de Glatigny dimidium modium bladi, medietatem frumenti et medietatem tremesii, praefatae ecclesiae Sancti Lupi assignavit. Pro qua eleemosina, nos, ad preces ipsius Milonis, singulis annis, unam missam de Sancto Spiritu, in ecclesia Sancti Petri

Vivi et etiam in praefata ecclesia Sancti Lupi, quamdiu vixerit, pro eo concessimus celebrandas, audito vero ejus obitu, ipsius Milonis anniversarium, in utraque praedictarum ecclesiarum, singulis annis, concessimus celebrandum. In cujus rei testimonium praesentem cartam sigilli nostri munimine fecimus roborari, anno ab Incarnatione Domini MCII.

C. Comments

This document, which clearly survives by chance alone, must represent a much larger number of similar documents in which the parent abbey and its priory profited materially in return for spiritual services rendered.

Salet notes that in 1239 Anseau, lord of Trainel, gave 20 sous de Provins "...pour l'entretien d'une lampe dans l'église de Saint-Loup-de-Naud..."[2] Presumably some spiritual service was rendered in return. Salet also mentions the sale in 1253 of the rights of low justice in the parish of Saint-Loup-de-Naud to the priory by Henri Bouchard, a "chevalier de Nô."[3]

Bourquelot refers to a series of late-thirteenth-century transactions of a more purely secular nature.[4] These are of a different order than the document under discussion here and need not concern us further.

D. Notes

1. Bourquelot, 1840/41, p. 267, n.1 states "Les trois copies sont défectueuses et fort différentes entre elles, et M. Ythier leur donne des intitules différents."

Presumably the version published by Bourquelot is edited.

2. Salet, 1933, p. 134, n.6 does not quote the document which is an eighteenth-century copy of the original (lost). The copy remains unpublished in the Archives de l'Yonne, H. 250.

3. Ibid. This contract is located in Paris, Bibliothèque nationale, Collection Champagne, T. XXXVIII, fol. 120.

4. Bourquelot, 1840/41, p. 259 and nn.1-5.

DOCUMENT X.

1212 A.D. An accord concerning rights, privileges, etc.
between the curé of Naud and the abbey of Saint-Pierre-
le-Vif (representing the monastic community in Naud)
finalized in the presence of the archbishop of Sens,
Pierre de Corbeil.

A. Sources

    1. Original: lost

    2. Copies: The document is known only through
            the copy by Ythier, op. cit., Sup-
            plément à l'abbaye de Jouy, p. 393.
            Published by: Bourquelot, 1840/41,
                    pp. 267-270.

B. Text

     PETRUS, Dei gratia senonensis archiepiscopus,
omnibus ad quos litterae praesentes pervenerint, in
domino salutem. Noverint universi, quod controversia
quae vertebatur inter Hulderium abbatem et conventum
Sancti Petri Vivi senonensis ex una parte, et Hugo-
nem presbyterum de Naudo ex alia, coram nobis paci-
ficata est in hunc modum: videlicet quod terra de
Cortaon juxta viam sita, cujus medietatem Garnerus,
miles, ecclesiae legavit, et Houdrezel li pelee aliam
medietatem, remanet penitus quitta presbytero. --Di-
midium arpentum terrae defuncti Gaufridi molendinarii
similiter remanet presbytero. --Donatio scholarum de
Naudo remanet similiter presbytero. --Presbyter nun-
quam comedet cum monachis, nisi fuerit vocatus ab
ipsis. --In rogationibus, presbyter habet sex denarios tantum. --Chevagia fient de caetero per manum
presbyteri; si tamen presbyter absens fuerit, fient
per manum alicujus de monachis, salvo jure presbyteri,
qui habet tantum quartam partem in omnibus chevagiis
quatuor denariorum, tantummodo quando primo facta

fuerint chevagia ab omnibus illis qui b. Lupo homagium
facere voluerint. --Presbyter habet....candelae tantum singulis hebdomadis, ad usum hospitii sui. --Prima
missa celebranda est a praesbytero, praeter in Natali
Domini; ad primam missam presbyteri poterunt licite
offere ad manum ipsius quaecumque voluerint, sine aliqua interruptione, in qua missa presbyter habet medietatem tantum; ad secundam missam ipsius vel capellani
sui, possunt monachi interrumpere oblationes. Si tamen oblati fuerint decem solidi, et de illis decem solidis habent monachi medietatem, quidquid, inquam, su-
perfuerit quantum ad secundam missam, est monachorum,
totum aurum, tota cera, omnes candelae, totum oleum,
et omnia animalia sunt monachorum, excepta candela
quae remanet de obsequio mortuorum parochiae; si forte
aliqua ornamenta ecclesiastica ibi fuerint oblata, omnia sunt monachorum. --Monachi ad matutinas, ad missam presbyteri necessaria, quantum pertinet ad cande-
lam et ornamenta, ministrabunt; nichilominus tenetur
presbyter inducere parochianos suos ad calicem, crucem,
libros et alia necessaria ornamenta, si necesse fuerit, emenda, quorum usus erit communis inter presbyterum
et monachos, in festis annualibus. --Non poterunt
monachi rumpere oblationes in festo Omnium Sanctorum
et in festo sancti Lupi, quod est in septembri, et in
Natali Domini; antequam dividantur oblationes inter
monachos et presbyterum, prior capit in oblationibus
XII denarios, thesaurarius ejusdem loci XII, cellarius
XII, et alii duo vel tres monachi ibi commorantes,
unusquisque VI denarios: famuli monachorum percipiunt
V panes et V den. in residuo oblationum, quae fiunt;
in omnibus missis tantum dictarum festivitatum, dictus
prior capit medietatem et abbas et presbyter Sancti
Lupi, aliam medietatem monachi et presbyter dividunt,
et panem et vinum ibi oblatum per medietatem similiter;
et argentum erit in pixide repositum, exceptis tribus
dictis festivitatibus, in quibus presbyter habet tantummodo quartam partem; totum residuum erit monachorum.
Si vero ab aliquo peregrino vel ab aliqua peregrina
duo denarii vel plures offerantur, unus denarius
tantum n pixide reponetur. --Matricularius dicti
prioratus hostias, vinum et aquam presbytero ministra-
bit, in diebus dominicis salem et aquam benedicendam.
--Idem matricularius habet singulis diebus dominicis
unum denarium in oblationibus, antequam dividantur--
In festis, coadjutor erit matricularius ad pulsandas
campanas, quando omnes campanae similiter pulsantur.
--In decima vellerum habet presbyter IV sol. tantum;
in decima agnorum habet presbyter unum agnum tantum,
qualemcumque elegerit. --Monachi licite vendunt

candelas ab eis requisitas in tricenariis, in carita-
tibus, in benedictionibus perarum, in nuptiis. --In
omnibus legatis presbytero vel presbyterio factis,
habent monachi medietatem; in denariis ecclesiae vel
monachis legatis a parochianis de Naudo, tantum habet
presbyter medietatem; omnia alia legata sunt monachorum
quitta, et illa similiter quae sunt facta ab illis qui
in caemeterio monachorum sunt sepulti, sive de denariis
sive de aliis rebus facta fuerint. --Presbyter habet
gallinam nuptiarum quittam. --In festo Innocentium,
unica missa celebranda erit in ecclesia beati Lupi,
quae a monachis celebrabitur, et si quas oblationes in
praedicta missa offerri contigerit, presbyter, salva
praedicta exceptione, medietatem habebit; si tamen
ipsa die Innocentium, pro praesente defuncto missas
celebrari opportuerit, presbyter in missa monachorum
illa die celebrata nihil habebit. --Ad pascha flori-
dum de communi oblatione emetur buxum. --De cruce
presbyter habet adorata sex denarios tantum. --In
ovibus paschae presbyter habet medietatem tantum.
--De omnibus confessionibus reddit presbyter monachis
annuatim, in die Paschae, decem solidos tantum.
--Visitationes infirmorum sunt quittae presbytero.
--Residuum cerei benedicti remanet monachis. --In
baptismo habent monachi medietatem. --In die Paschae,
in die Pentecostes, in die festivitatis parochiae,
habet presbyter medietatem oblationum in omnibus missis, retenta dicta exceptione. --In festo Sancti
Lupi, quod est in septembri, pro parte omnium oblationum illius diei, habet presbyter in oblationibus
decem solidos tantum, salvis chevagiis quatuor denariorum, tantum primo factis. --In decima segetum
percipiet presbyter annuatim tres sextarios frumenti
et tres hordei, et quartus sextarius frumenti adjunc-
tus est ei in ipsa decima, pro sextario frumenti et
duabus gallinis quas presbyter solebat habere in
legato defuncti Hugonis de Comble quod quittavit
monachis. --In decima vini habet presbyter annuatim
unum modium et dimidium tantum, quod recipiet in
ipsa decima, ut voluerit. --De tortellis beati
Stephani habet six frumenti, si ibi fuerint; residuum
est monachorum. --Ad hostias Paschae, reddunt monachi
presbytero unum minellum frumenti. --In omnibus
festis beatae Mariae, beati Joannis et beati Nicolai,
si presbyter voluerit, ad corum altaria celebrabit.
--In octava b. Lupi, dabit prior presbytero unum
verrem, qualem prior voluerit, et unam logaliam,
qualem similiter prior voluerit. Quod ut ratum et
inconcussum in perpetuum permaneat, ad petitionem
utriusque partis, sigilli nostri munimine roboravimus.
Actum anno gratiae MCCXII°, mense maio.

C.   Comments

This document reveals a great deal about the sharing
of goods and responsibilities which existed between the
secular curé and the monastic community at Saint-Loup-de-
Naud.   In his discussion of the document Bourquelot already raised the important questions.[1]   Was there always
a village priest who used Saint-Loup as a parish church
concurrent with its use as a monastic church?[2]   Or were
the monks themselves, at the beginning, also fulfilling
curial duties?   For Bourquelot "C'est ce qu'il est dif-
ficile de décider."[3]   The episode related by Clarius
concerning the "presbiter" Alexander would seem to
indicate that shared duties existed at least as far
back as 1122.[4]

Regrettably the document tells us little about the
liturgical layout of the church of Saint-Loup, little
about altar or chapel dedications.   We may assume that
the feasts singled out for mention in the transaction
are those of greatest local importance; but, most of
these are the major feasts of the liturgical year.   One
particularly interesting passage tells us that "In
omnibus festis beatae Mariae, beati Joannis et beati
Nicolai, si presbyter voluerit, ad corum altaria celebrabit."   We may construe that these feasts are major
feasts in the parish and that the curé was not normally

allowed access to the altar in the (liturgical) choir.
We may speculate that it (the choir) may well have been
closed off and that the curé normally had access only to
the western parts of the church.[5]

D. Notes

1. Bourquelot, 1840/41, pp. 258-259.

2. See above, Doc. I, Comments, and n.6.

3. Bourquelot, 1840/41, p. 258.

4. See above, Doc. IV, Comments, and n.4.

5. Bourquelot, 1840/41, p. 259, n.1, states "Le
curé avait à Saint-Loup un autel particulier, celui de
Saint-Sébastien." It would be helpful to know the
location of this altar; exceptionally, Bourquelot does
not reveal his source. Since he refers (p. 259 and n.3)
to other similar transactions (1675, 1685, 1717, 1727,
e.g.) between curé and monks (again without sources),
we may assume that the altar is mentioned in one of these.
Presumably his source lies in the unpublished manuscripts
of one or more of the early historians of Provins.

DOCUMENT XI.

1438 A.D. This charter of Charles the VII commits the
priory of Saint-Loup-de-Naud to temporal administration,
following a request for intervention by the prior.[1]

A. Sources

    1. Original: lost

    2. Copies: The text is known only through Ythier,

              op. cit., Supplément à l'abbaye de

              Jouy, p. 393.

              Published by: Bourquelot, 1840/41,

                      pp. 270-271

B. Text

      Charles par la grâce de Dieu Roi de France, au
bailly de Meaux ou à son lieutenant à Provins, salut:
Reçue avons l'umble supplication de frére Guillaume
Quatrain, prieur du prioré de Saint-Loup de No, lés
le dit Provins, contenant que le dit prioré est telle-
ment dommagé et desolé par les guerres et gens d'armes
qui ont esté et sont encore en notre royaume, et
mesmement ou payis et environ ledit prioré et autre-
ment, et à l'occasion des choses desusdites, les
droits, cens, rentes, revenus et autres avoirs dimin-
ués et apeticés, et aussy les maisons, terres molins
et autres heritages diceluy tant gastés et desolés et
le dit suppliant apauvry, que à peine ait de quoy
vivre, et qui plus est, pour raison des dites guerres,
pertes, dommages et autres molestes, est tenu et
obligé iceluy suppliant envers plusieurs personnes,
à grand somme de deniers, de grains, arrerages de
rente et autres choses qu'il doit à cause du dit
prioré, auxquelles il ne pourroit bonnement fair
satisfaction, ne payement, sans faire vile et miser-
able distraction de ses biens, dont le service divin
qui se fait oudit prioré pourroit estre retardé et
cessé, et ledit suppliant, s'il estoit à ce contraint,
en admettant qu'il ne luy convenoit delaisser ledit

service et luy et les relligieux qui font avec luy
ledit service oudit prioré en aller et departir
d'iceluy, se par nous ne luy estoit sur ce pourvu de
notre grâce, ainsy qu'il dit, en nous humblement
requerant icelle; pourquoy nous, ces choses conside-
rées, et afin que le service divin puisse estre fait
et continué en iceluy prioré, vous mandons, et pour
ce que ledit suppliant et aussy sesdits creanciers ou
la plus grande partie d'iceux sont demeurants en
votre bailliage, commettons, se mestier est, que se
par information il vous appert de ce que dit est,
vous commettiés et deputiés de par nous, aux moindres
frais que faire se pourra, par le consentement dudit
suppliant, aucunes bonnes personnes souffisant et
convenables, une ou plusieurs, au gouvernement du
temporel et des rentes et revenues de son dit prioré,
lesquels commis seront tenus de gouverner et recevoir,
par et sous nostre nom, ses rentes et revenues,
jusques à trois ans prochainement venant, à compter
de la date de ces presentes, dont ils feront trois
parties, et les employeront et distribueront par
nostre main de la manière qui s'ensuit: c'est à
scavoir, la premiére partie pour faire et celebrer
le service divin ou dit prioré et pour le vivre et
autres necessités du dit suppliant et des autres relligieux qui feront avec luy ledit service, et leur
famille; la second partie pour les maisons, heritages,
edifices et labourages appartenant audit prioré faire,
soutenir et retenir, et aussy pour soutenir, pour-
suivre et defendre les procès qui sont et seroient
avenus et pendant à cause des droits d'icelluy prioré;
et la tierce partie au payement et solution desdites
dettes par luy dues à sesdits creanciers et à chacun
d'eux, par proportion au sol la livre et selon la
qualité de la dette qui leur sera due, parmy ce que
lesdits commis en seront tenus rendre compte et
reliqua là et ou il appartiendra, toutefois que mestier sera, et assurer auxdits creanciers autre solution que dessus est dit, ne contraigner, ne souffrir
estre contraint ledit suppliant, ses pleiges ne
autres pour luy obligés en quelque manière que ce
soit; mais se aucuns de ses biens ou de sesdits
pleiges estoient pour ce pris, saisis, arrestés ou
empechés ou aucune chose faite ou attemptée au con-
traire, luy faire rendre et restituer et mettre sans
delay à pleine délivrance, et au premier estat; car
ainsy nous plaist estre fait de grace especiale,
nonobstant quelconques lettres subreptices à ce con-
traires. Donné à Paris le XIIIe jour de janvier, l'an
de grace MCCCCXXXVIII, et de nostre regne le XVIIe;
ainsy signé, Par le Roy, à la relation du conseil,
MOREL.

C. Comments

This document, which marks the end of the "medieval"
priory as it had been known, reveals the impact and socio-
economic disruption wrought by the Hundred Years War upon
it and upon the lands and revenues it held.

It is interesting to note that, in this transaction,
no reference is made to the parent abbey of Saint-Pierre-
le-Vif, particularly because the abbey was involved with
the priory after the time of this charter.[2]

D. Notes

1. Salet, 1933, p. 135 and n.3, states that the
priory finally fell into commendatory status in 1515,
citing a document in the Archives de l'Yonne, H. 252.
See also Bourquelot, 1840/41, p. 260 and n.1. An indivi-
dual--often a layman--holds an ecclesiastical benefice
in commendam when its revenues were granted to him
during a vacancy (see E. Livingstone and F. Cross, eds.
The Oxford Dictionary of the Christian Church, 2nd. ed.,
London, 1974, p. 319).

2. See, e.g., above, Doc. VI, Comments, and n.11.

APPENDIX C

DESCRIPTIVE CATALOGUE OF THE SCULPTURE
OF THE WEST PORTAL OF SAINT-LOUP-DE-NAUD

APPENDIX C

TABLE OF CONTENTS

Text Figure 15. Saint-Loup-de-Naud
Western Portal (WM) with Sculpture Designations
(Hamann-MacLean system) (corresponds to fig. 22)

TYMPANUM: MAIESTAS DOMINI (fig. 23)

The tympanum consists of five large figured blocks
of which the largest, in the center, depicts the cross-
nimbed Deity enthroned in glory. Each of the four other
blocks contains a Living Being or, "Evangelist Symbol":
in the upper left, the winged man (for Saint Matthew);
in the upper right, the eagle (for Saint John); in the
lower left, the winged lion (for Saint Mark) and in the
lower right, the winged ox (for Saint Luke). All four
creatures are nimbate and carry a book, except for the
eagle which clasps a scroll. All face or turn their
heads toward the central Maiestas. The handling of the
drapery of the human figures is essentially linear, little
undercut and, in a restrained fashion, decorative. All of
the figures exhibit a strong sense of the block. Undulating masses representing cloud-like matter border the
entire tympanum except above the head of the figure of
God. Similar bands border the lower edges of the upper
lateral stones. Apparently once continuous, the inter-
ruptions of this border and their implications are discussed in depth in Chapter III, pp. 75-79.

CENTRAL BLOCK: Christ in Majesty (fig. 23)

The figure of Christ sits frontally on a curved
arcuated bench-type throne within a wide, oval mandorla.

With his left hand, which is broken off at the knuckles, he rests a closed book on his knee.[1] His right hand, which is broken off below the wrist, certainly once gestured in blessing. Like the head and its cruciform nimbus, this arm extends beyond the frame of the mandorla. Both the head and the gesture are thereby emphasized. Below, his bare feet rest on a flat, arcuated footstool, the curve of which echoes the mandorla. Uniquely among surviving Maiestas portal tympana, this footstool has an arched opening on the upper surface between the feet.[2]

The figure wears two garments: a loose-fitting tunic with a decorated collar is visible across the torso, on the arms and at the ankles. An outer mantle covers his chest behind the book and appears just at the edge of his right shoulder. This same garment is evidently drawn across the waist and draped over the knees, nearly masking the figure's entire right leg.

Except for the damage mentioned, a small section of the halo and several toes which have broken off and some general abrasion of the surface, the figure is in remarkably good condition. Sheltered as it is by the fore-porch to the west, it comes as no surprise to find substantial traces of pigmentation remaining, particularly on the hair and beard.[3]

A myriad of incisions masks the body of the figure; however, the generally naturalistic directionality of the fold-lines restrains the sense of movement and decoration.

Intensely decorative areas such as the elaborate swirl
of folds around his right arm, the tendency to isolate
joints within drapery patterns (as it appears on his
right shoulder and knee) and the little wind-blown puff
of drapery at the feet, are relegated to the periphery.
More restrained, but still decorative, are the centrally
placed parallel folds between the knees and the regularly
spaced, interlocking zigzag folds across the chest. While
the figure is generally convincing anatomically, the in-
articulate handling of the elbow of the blessing arm,
the wide splay of the knees[4] and the absence of any planar
distinction between upper arms, shoulders and torso all
reflect a conception of the figure more closely related
to the form of the block than at first appears.

The head, too, reflects this awareness of the block
(figs. 40, 74). While the features relate organically to
the head, the expanse of the forehead and even the cheeks
reveal a planar conception which terminates abruptly at
the sides of the head and leaves almost no area for
transition to the sides. This results in a head of curious, and within the portal, unique, proportions; one in
which the distance from the forward edge of the ear to
the forward plane of the cheek is extremely short.[5]

A long, thick nose separates the eyes and dominates
the face. The eyes themselves open wide and are enframed

by pointed oval lids. Their importance for the face was further enhanced by once sharply defined, high-arching, symmetrical brows (similar to other figures in the portal). The "dark" hair and beard, arranged symmetrically in undulating locks, enframe and thereby emphasize the other features.

UPPER LEFT BLOCK: The Winged Man (for Saint Matthew) (fig. 23)

The constricting, spherically triangular shape of this small block, which is long and narrow at the top, conditions the pose. The figure strides toward the central <u>Maiestas</u> in a three-quarter position. His right leg, side and both wings parallel the long, outer side of the block. The lower half of the bent, or striding, leg thus nearly parallels the horizontal edge of the bottom of the stone. The resulting "inclination" of the figure further animates the pose.

The book which the winged man clasps in both hands is held "in front of" his body but sideways to the viewer. It cannot have been intended, therefore, for display in the way that every other book and scroll in the tympanum and lintel are displayed.

The winged man wears two garments. A loose-fitting tunic is visible at the left side of the torso, along the right shin at the ankles. An outer mantle can be seen

across the right side of the torso. It covers his left
hand (?) and is pulled across the waist covering both legs
except for the shin on the right.

The state of preservation of the figure is good.
Minor breakage has occurred on the wing tips,[6] the chin,
the nose, the hair on the left side of the head, the nimbus
rim on the same side, and both hands, but none of this is
substantial. Damage in the lower left corner of the block,
although small, makes it possible to determine what the
original relationships were between the damaged left foot,
the drapery and the undulating cloud band. Traces of
pigmentation remain in the hair, on the nimbus and on the
background along the inside near the top.

The handling of the drapery is linear. Long, uninterrupted parallel lines run the length of the right shin.
Incised parallel grooves also form deep "v"-shaped lines
in the gap between the legs. The rectilinearity of these
folds contrasts with the rather more curving folds elsewhere in the figure. Concentric elliptical folds isolate
thigh, knee-cap and shin from each other and from the
folds elsewhere on the lower half of the figure. This
latter, curving fold is also found in the torso area;
over the left arm it isolates the forearm.

To the left of the figure, the mantle swings out
stiffly behind the body in response to the movement
toward the center of the tympanum. Although the hemlines

are relatively calm, the outer edge of this drapery nearly parallels the lines of the right leg that, together with the intervening "v"-folds, creates an angular rhythm which animates the figure and makes it among the most active in the portal.

The comparatively busy, decorative handling of the drapery parallels the additive handling of the anatomy. The figure is very short-waisted and "hipless," so that the upper thighs simply disappear into the torso. The legs themselves are disproportionately long and unequal in length. In spite of the implied three-quarter view of the pose, the left hip nevertheless is pressed back frontally into the plane of the block. As remarked above, elements of the anatomy (for example, the left thigh) are isolated from the rest of the body.

The face of the winged man is more difficult to analyze because of damage to the stone in the area of the nose, mouth and chin. Pointed almond-shaped lids enframe round, slightly projecting pupils. Above, the broadly arched symmetrical brows provide an echo for the eyes while below an almost planar handling of the cheek areas helps to "bend" them around to the sides of the head. The hair is rendered by undulating tufts which terminate in tight curls arranged symmetrically.

UPPER RIGHT BLOCK: The Eagle (for Saint John) (fig. 23)

Smallest of the four symbols, the sculptor had no difficulty adjusting the figure to the narrow-necked shape of the block. The eagle is nimbed and clasps a partially unrolled scroll in both claws. Like the winged-man opposite, the eagle faces inward toward the center with its back, neck and extended wings roughly parallel to the outer edge of the tympanum. The figure is remarkably well preserved for one with so much undercutting.

The body of the bird takes the shape of a modulated cylindrical solid. Only the near leg is truly treated as a separate mass and even that is handled additively. The narrow shoulder of the right wing simply "attaches" at the base of the neck. Like the winged-man, the three-quarter pose of the bird has been distorted to reflect the plane of the block.[7]

Feathers are rendered as squares set diagonally and covered with incised, parallel lines separated by an incised central ridge. Long, thin feathers cover the extended parts of the wings and the blunt tail. Overlapping circular patterns distinguish the wings at the shoulders.

Living birds have so frequented this symbolic one that details of the head are difficult to discuss. Short incised strokes, rather than any anatomical distinction separate the head from the neck. The hawk-like beak curves both down and, curiously, outward. The eyes, which appear not to have been particularly emphasized, have a highly arched upper lid but are more nearly flat along the bottom. They are outlined both above and below.

LOWER LEFT BLOCK: The Winged Lion (for Saint Mark) (fig. 23)

The winged lion moves laterally outward from the Maiestas and twists its nimbate head back and up to gaze at the Deity. The hind paws stand on the undulating cloud border while the raised forepaws clutch a closed book. Both wings open above the beast's back.[8] The long tail is held between the legs.

Except for some surface abrasion and the tail which is broken in three places and has been repaired,[9] the figure is in an excellent state of preservation.

As in the eagle concern for the block dominates the conception of the figure. While the body is once again handled as an essentially cylindrical solid, the flat, additively applied near wing and the nearly straight diagonal of the near haunch reflect that forward surface.

Long, parallel incised feathers cover the wings. On the near wing a feather covered ring or band separates the wing proper from the foreleg at the "elbow." The head, neck, chest, upper back and haunches are covered with undulating tufts of fur which are articulated by incised lines terminating in points.

The head takes the shape of that of a short-snouted
dog. Its mouth is held open to reveal a set of triangular
teeth. The ears are small and held flat against the head.
The eyes have been conceived additively. Thick lids,
separated by a narrow empty band enframe round, bulging
pupils.

LOWER RIGHT BLOCK: The Winged Ox (for Saint Luke) (fig. 23)

Like the pendant winged lion, the winged ox moves
laterally outward from the Maiestas at the center and
twists its nimbate head around to gaze toward the Deity.
Here, too, the hind hoofs stand on the undulating border
while the forehoofs display a closed book. Again both
wings open over the creature's back[10] but here the tail
curls forward over the near haunch onto the animal's side.

Except for a small piece broken out of the tail near
its base and the ears which are broken off at the skull,
the figure is excellently preserved.

In this figure also, a concern for the shape of the
block predominates. While the body of this creature is
the largest of the tympanum, its volume is essentially
flattened by the handling of the near haunch and wing.
This sense of the unmodelled slab is further heightened
by rendering only the tail in relief and by treating the
twisting musculature of the neck as curving, parallel tubes

which extend deep into the chest.

Except for undulating tufts of hair along the back
of each leg, on the tassle and at the end of the tail,
this creature is smooth skinned. Again, long parallel
feathers cover the wings which are separated from the
forelegs by an almost crown-like "bracelet."

The head of this beast resembles that of an ox
except for a bloated, boneless quality. Large cow-like
pupils, rounder on the upper side than on the lower, project out of a concavity in the skull. Although enframed
by single lids and set into the skull, their protuberance
renders them as additively conceived as the lion's.

LINTEL: THE VIRGIN AND APOSTLES ENTHRONED
(fig. 23)

The lintel zone is composed of three blocks. The
central, smaller block bears the largest figure: an image
of the Virgin enthroned. The other two, larger blocks are
nearly identical. Each contains four enthroned, nimbate
apostles seated within an arcade surmounted by architectural forms. Whereas the Virgin is realized in front of
the block from which she was carved, the apostles all
adhere strictly to the limits of the blocks into which
they have been sculpted. Whereas she is the least well-
preserved figure in the portal ensemble, they are all,
apart from minor damage, in a good state of preservation.

The block which contains the figure of the Virgin shows evidence of having been adjusted to accommodate it to its narrow setting. Likewise, the architectural frames surrounding the apostles have been demonstrably altered indicating that both blocks are now shorter than they were originally. These adjustments and their implications are discussed at length in Chapter III, pp. 81-85.

CENTRAL BLOCK (M): The Virgin (figs. 24-26)

Crowned, vellate and nimbed, the Virgin is seated frontally[11] and takes up virtually the full width and height of the relatively narrow block from which she was carved. In her left hand, which rests on her lap, she must once have held the end of a now missing skein of wool. Part of this skein, which no scholar has remarked, still survives above her right arm which is bent at the elbow and held diagonally across her chest. The skein appears much like a rotulus or banderole; however, the thin narrow band of stone bears closely spaced parallel incisions which preclude that possibility (fig. 24a).[12] The Virgin sits on a simple bench-type throne, the capitals of which are visible beside each knee. Attached to this throne is a mandorla-like back which enframes the Virgin on both sides, passes behind her halo and (apparently) terminates below the throne at the block from which protrudes the acanthus console on which she

rests her sandaled feet.[13] Although clearly not a mandorla proper--which would have encompassed her entirely--the
throne back is clearly associated with that attribute.[14]
Two tiny angels in the upper spandrels of the block reach
down with one arm to touch the mandorla-like throne back
beside her shoulders and reach up with the other arm which
rests on the rim of the nimbus. The Virgin appears to
wear two garments: a simple undergarment, visible at the
ankles and the wrist, and a more elaborate outer garment
which has decorated borders and a decorated strip down the
center of the torso. Areas of significant surface damage
to the central block include both hands, both knees and
the tips of both feet of the Virgin as well as portions
of her face, particularly the nose and lips.[15] Missing
entirely are the head of the tiny angel to the left of
the Virgin, a large piece of the throne back on its upper
left side and the large section of the still partially
preserved skein of wool which extended between the Virgin's hands. Perhaps most importantly, it has never been
remarked that the crowned and veiled head has been "replaced." The substantial amount of light-colored mortar
added at the base of the neck attests to this fact (fig.
78). When viewed from either side the inserted mortar
produces a curious sharp angle in the profile of the neck.
Originally this head must have been placed slightly
to the right which would have permitted the head to fall

more clearly within the perimeter of the halo as is
the case with the Godhead above (fig. 23). This would
also eliminate the slight tilt to the left out of the
vertical axis of the body which the head now possesses.
The question immediately arises: is this the original
head replaced or a replacement head? If the head were
also to be repositioned slightly higher, fold lines on
the veil would align, across the break, with those on
the shoulders, making it reasonably certain that this is
the original head. The lack of any attempt to conceal
the repair argues for a medieval rather than a modern
date for the repositioning.[16]

The "lines" of the Virgin's drapery are rendered by
blunted incisions and function to mask anatomy rather
than to reveal it (fig. 24). Where the body is revealed,
for example, the right breast or the left knee-cap, it is
achieved by concentric folds which, by their decorative-
ness, reduce any naturalistic effect. There is little
undercutting (except in the area of the attribute) and in
general the handling of the drapery is calm, although the
parallelity and the pairing of fold-lines, particularly
in the lower half of the body, results in a decorative,
if restrained effect.

The Virgin is unconvincing anatomically. This is
particularly clear in the hip area where the abdomen[17]
swells and no attempt is made to deal with the awkward

juncture of the legs and torso. Moreover, the body is widest at the knees, precisely where the mandorla-like throne back also reaches its widest point.

The jaw of the Virgin's nearly spherical head appears softly modelled and the cheeks slightly swollen. The eyes, which appear to have been enframed by flat-arched brows, are placed on the frontal plane of the head. Damage to the Virgin's face and abrasion to its surface make more precise observations impossible. In comparison, the handling of the little angels appears more coarse.

LATERAL BLOCKS: Apostles Enthroned

Each of the eight apostles[18] holds either a book or a scroll and places his bare feet on a small footstool. The three outer figures on each block enter into dialogue with a neighboring figure, either by pose, or gesture, or both. The inner two, which flank the Virgin, are isolated from the others by comparison.

Each of the figures wears two garments: a tunic with a decorated collar that is visible on the torso and arms and at the ankles; an outer mantle which is draped over one or both shoulders and is pulled across the waist. Blunted incisions establish linear patterns in the drapery which, by their multiplicity, make these among the most line-dominated figures in the portal ensemble. The generally restrained, frontal poses and the absence of much undercutting (except in the areas of the attributes)

results in a relatively calm impression. A lesser emphasis on a more overtly decorative handling can be seen in
each figure in the tendency to separate anatomical forms
(e.g., knee-caps, shoulders) into ovoid compartments. By
being relatively long-waisted and by giving the appearance
of foreshortened thighs (at least for the frontal figures)
the apostles seem more anatomically convincing than they
actually are. In each figure some part of the anatomy has
been altered for compositional purposes. With the exception of the innermost figure on the right block, all the
apostles are bearded and have long hair. Almondine eyes
applied additively to slightly swollen cheeks are enframed
above by broadly arching symmetrical brows. They dominate
each of the faces. In comparison to the eyes, the areas
around the mouths and noses are more organically handled.

n/1: apostle (fig. 23)

This apostle sits absolutely frontally. He bends
his right forearm, palm inward, diagonally across the
chest and holds a small, nearly square book on his left
knee. Apart from the missing tip of his right index
finger and some surface abrasion (the knee-caps) there
has been no damage to this figure. His tunic hangs vertically from the knees to terminate in a semi-circular
hemline. Although the mantle hangs convincingly between
the knees (the folds expand as they move downward) the hem

of this garment presses to the legs in long, decorative zig-zag folds. Only along the upper arms an even more decorative handling is evident: on the left side folds curve upward in nearly parallel rows.

n/2: apostle (fig. 23)

Unlike his neighbor, this apostle turns his head slightly out of axis to his left and dips his rather un-naturally extended left shoulder accordingly. In his left hand he holds an oblong book which he rests on his left knee. He extends his right arm in front of the colonette on that side. This arm is broken at the wrist and damaged; traces of where it overlapped the colonette appear below the capital. Except for surface abrasion this is the only real damage to the figure.

One area of drapery received a pronounced decorative emphasis. The great rhythmic sweep of the mantle as it curves inward toward the chest before looping down and over to the left wrist establishes a pattern of visual activity in defiance of natural form. Moreover, the inner folds of this sweep of drapery are so arranged that they create a blank, circular area at the pit of the elbow. This feature, together with the decorative continuity of the line of the mantle's curving hem above the left ankle, and the parallel folds along the upper right arm, create a movement in opposition to the figure's static pose.

This apostle's face is the broadest in the group.

n/3:   apostle (fig. 23)

This apostle sits with his legs crossed and his head
turned in three-quarter profile to "communicate" with
apostle n/4. Although the torso is essentially parallel
with the ground of the lintel, his right shoulder extends
forward slightly to suggest a three-quarter pose in opposition to that parallelity. His right forearm bends upward across the torso while in his left hand (which alone
is damaged) he holds a slightly rhomboid book in front of
his chest.

In keeping with the movemented pose, the drapery of
this figure receives an agitated, decorative treatment.
The hemline at the ankles is active, particularly between
the feet where a trumpet-shaped fold takes on its own
life. The folds of the tunic follow the direction of the
diagonally placed legs. More than the handling of the
drapery, however, the angular rhythms set up by the
crossed legs, the position of his right arm and the shape
of the book make this apostle the most animated of any on
this side of the lintel.

n/4:   apostle (fig. 23)

This apostle reveals traces of a seated contrapposto
while still adhering to the planar limitations imposed by
the frame. His lower body is placed frontally while the

torso and head turn slightly to the right. His right shoulder is dropped and pulled slightly forward as that arm is bent across the torso to his left shoulder to respond to apostle n/3. Commensurately his left shoulder is pushed back slightly and his right knee is dropped slightly to imply an axial shift in the hips. Beyond a certain awkwardness the result is an unequal length of the arms. His left, which holds a small, square book on his right knee, is noticeably longer. A break at the bottom of an evidently once long beard and minor chipping on the nose, the two fingers extending across the face of the book and the cuff of the right sleeve represent the only damage to the figure. The linear folds are comparatively calm, although rather more numerous across the left side. Like figure n/3, this apostle yields a greater sense of rhythmic movement than either n/2 or n/1 because of the point-counterpoint positioning of the arms, a movement which is echoed in the arrangement of the folds on the right forearm.

s/1: Saint John (fig. 23)

The first apostle to the right of the Virgin also sits frontally. A ramped and arcaded footstool distinguishes this figure from all the other apostles. The sloping stool raises his right leg and accommodates the contemplative pose of the figure who rests that elbow on the knee and places his hand beside his cheek. He

holds his left arm, which is damaged around the hand, in
a position nearly identical to figure n/3. The object
once held in his hand has been destroyed. It may have
been either a small codex or a small scroll like the one
held by figure s/4. Additional, minor damage is also
present on the left forearm and the right knee. The
severe crack in this block which ran through this figure
was repaired in 1967 (see Appendix A).

The relatively calm, linear drapery of this figure
is distinguished from the other seven apostles by the
"crinkle-fold" of the cuff at the left wrist. Also unlike the other seven figures, this figure has short hair
and no beard. Instead he wears a full mustache and a thin,
incised "goatee" immediately below his lower lip (fig. 117).

This "beardless" face first led Aufauvre to suggest
that this apostle represents Saint John.[19] It was
apparently the contemplative quality of the figure's pose
which led Salet to follow Aufauvre's interpreation nearly
eighty years later.[20]   Indeed, the comparative isolation
of the figure together with the contemplative pose and
the relatively beardless face all do suggest identification
of the figure as Saint John.[21] However, it is the mustache
which confirms the identity of the apostle. In the West,
Saint John is ordinarily represented as a youthful, beardless type.[22] Yet on the Last Supper tympanum from

Saint Bénigne in Dijon the figure asleep on Christ's arm--

therefore indubitably Saint John--also has a mustache

(cf. figs. 117, 118)![23] Comparable, contemporary Île-

de-France sculpture reveals no other similar example.[24]

Thus this detail would seem to confirm not only the identi-

fication of the figure but also the stylistic link between

Saint-Loup-de-Naud and Burgundy so often advanced in

recent scholarship.[25]

s/2: apostle (fig. 23)

In pose this figure is the most complex of any of

the eight apostles. He sits in profile from the hips

downward with his legs crossed. Above the waist, the

torso parallels the ground save for his left shoulder

which is pulled slightly forward suggesting an unrealized

three-quarter view. Correspondingly, the head is turned

at a three-quarter angle toward the figure of Saint John.

Unlike the four apostles who hold closed books, this figure

holds an open book in his right hand and extends it out in

front of the column to the viewer. His right foot also

"transgresses" the frame, as it overlaps the lower torus

and plinth of the colonette to the left. But rather than

increasing the plasticity of the figure, these violations

of the architectural boundary, press, distorted, into the

plane of the block thereby forcefully reaffirming it.

The apostle's left hand is broken off at the wrist. Traces visible on the book and on the mantle indicate that the hand originally pointed at the open book, presumably to a text painted on it.

Like figure n/3 the drapery of this figure takes on an agitation which parallels the pose. The folds between the feet again receive a trumpet shape which billows slightly, as does the hem of the outer mantle just below the thigh. Indeed, nearly the entire length of the mantle zigzags sometimes angularly (as below the waist), sometimes in loops (as around the hip). This animated drapery together with the ovoid forms at the left shoulder and right forearm and the very awkward anatomy of especially the left forearm yield the most pronounced decorative effect of the entire lintel.

s/3: apostle (fig. 23)

This figure sits frontally on his throne with his head turned out of axis toward his left. His right arm bends across the torso toward his left shoulder while his left arm rests on the lap. There is a small spur on his left shoulder just beyond his right hand. Evidently the broken index finger--the only significant damage--pointed toward the adjacent figure. In an attempt to reflect the shift in axis toward apostle s/4 and still maintain the figure's adherence to the frame, the sculptor has shortened and raised the left shoulder while dropping and extending

the right one. In his left hand the apostle holds a
rotulus which extends leftward to the colonette where it
makes a ninety-degree turn and runs up the shaft to a
point several inches below the capital.

While most of the drapery folds of this figure
appear relatively calm, there is one area where a decorative impulse is allowed free rein. Along the figure's
right leg the hem of the outer garment loops up and then
undulates downward toward the foot as if activated by a
puff of wind. The folds here are far more decorative
than the drapery outlined against the background of
figures s/2, n/1 or n/2. Something of the same sense of
animation may be at work just above his right ankle where
the hem inexplicably folds back.

s/4: apostle (fig. 23)

The remaining apostle sits in an essentialy frontal
position with his head turned out of axis to our left.
His right arm rests across the lap with the hand clasping
part of the outer garment at the hip. His left arm, its
shoulder pulled accordingly forward, extends down and
across the torso to the neighboring colonette where the
hand pinions a diminutive banderole to the shaft. In pose
this apostle approximates and echoes figure n/4 as each
turns visual movement inward toward the middle of the
lintel. Damage has occurred only to several of the
fingers on the hand at the colonette.

Great sweeping curves of drapery (analogous to the left arm of figure n/2) dominate one's visual impression of this figure. Long uninterrupted fold lines run from the right shoulder to the cuff. These find a foil in the folds of the left arm and an echo in both cuffs and in the repeated sweeps of drapery running from the right calf up to the waist area. The resultant visual animation leaves this figure surpassed only by the two apostles (n/3 and s/2)who have crossed legs.

LATERAL BLOCKS: The Architectural Frame (fig. 23)

The frames in which the eight apostles sit consist of a highly decorated arcade surmounted by a variety of architectural motifs. On the left block, single colonettes alternate with paired colonettes while on the right block only single colonettes are used. The bases rest on low plinths. Each shaft is spirally fluted and each capital is surmounted by an architectural motif which, together with the building above the neighboring colonettes, enframes the three structures which surmount each arch. The floral motifs which cover the intrados of each of the arches should probably be seen as stars representing the heavenly realm,[26] to which the architecture above also refers. The buildings take a variety of forms. Some are single storied; others have two stories. Some are clearly centrally planned; others are longitudinal, arcuated buildings perhaps intended to represent basilicas. These buildings may have possessed specific content (Old Law, New Law: centrally planned, basilica) but no discernible pattern can now be recognized.

The architectural frame on the left block has been repaired with a stone filler in the architectural motifs above figure n/3. There are also repairs in stone on the lower left end and to the soffit of the same block. These are discussed in Appendix A.

TRUMEAU FIGURE: Saint Loup (fig. 27)

The trumeau of the priory's western portal represents an over-life-sized figure of a sainted ecclesiastic. Dressed in archiepiscopal garb, the nimbed saint stands precariously above two badly weathered, fantastic creatures. Save for his head, which is turned out of axis to our left, the figure is disposed like the comparable trumeau figure of Saint Marcel in Paris [27]: that is, frontally, with one hand raised in blessing in front of the chest and the other extending across his left hip to support a crozier as a symbol of pastoral rank and duties. Apart from the damage to the hands and the crozier, the mitre, and a large fragment broken out of his left shoulder, the figure survives in a remarkably good state of preservation.

The highly organized arrangement of ecclesiastical costume does not readily lend itself to a visually exciting

handling, either in a decorative mode or in a naturalistic one. In spite of this, the saint's full archiepiscopal
costume receives a varied and elaborate carving. The alb
(or tunicelle?), visible at the ankles, hangs in thin,
vertically arranged, tubular folds.[28] A broad, lightly
carved pattern embroiders its hem. The dalmatic, visible
at mid-calf, is covered with a deeply incised diamond
pattern bordered at the bottom by a beaded chevron motif.
Presumably the dalmatic is the richly decorated, loose-
sleeved garment visible at his right wrist and the alb,
the tight-fitting one. A stole, which is visible only
above each foot, and a maniple which hangs stiffly from
his left wrist, each bear a star pattern at their broad
decorated tips. The chasuble, which covers nearly the
entire figure, varies the dalmatic's diamond motif on the
upper chest. The pallium--a 'Y'-shaped garment which
hangs from the shoulders--is carved only with incised
crosses. A flattened, lightly patterned amice at the neck
and a mitre with lappets extending down the back complete
the saint's dress.[29]

Only the chasuble and the alb permit a real discussion of the handling of drapery folds. Wide, deep incisions, which suggest modelling but which ultimately
maintain a linear conception, characterize the folds of
the former. While in general these folds follow the
limited movement of the upper body (the lower body is

entirely masked by the garments) gathering at the inside
of the right elbow and across the left forearm,[30] their
regular, undiminishing spacing across the front, together
with regular repetition of sharply angled folds along the
right side, produce the dominance of a calmed, but nevertheless decorative effect. This interpretation finds
reinforcement in the insistence on maintaining the parallel
pattern across the upper arms and torso where the chasuble
might be expected to hang flat.

The thin, tubular folds at the base of the alb
terminate in a gently undulating, regularized pattern.
The horizontal line of the hem is virtually uninterrupted
by the bishop's sandals across which it hangs.

The decorated borders of the chasuble, which fold
thinly back upon themselves, typify the dearth of undercutting of the figure as a whole. The organization of
ecclesiastical garb and the restrained contour of the
figure, which reveals only slight 'breaks' in the vertical
at the elbows, contribute to this end. But the dominant
factor remains a desire to retain the figure within the
strict architectonic of the trumeau.[31] In direct
contrast, almost in contradiction, are both the deeply
undercut, weighted swing of the dalmatic at his right
wrist as it responds to the gesture of blessing and the
twist of the head out of axis to our left. Particularly

the latter motif increases the sense of the momentary and provides some element of humanity in an otherwise relatively abstract figure. Quite possibly the turn of the head and the dalmatic drapery are related and iconographically motivated, although we can probably never hope to be certain of this.

Apart from the animation of the leftward twist, the head follows what might be termed a "tetrarchan" mode. Arranged around the symmetry of a large, straight nose and arching brows which emphasize the slightly bulging, almond-shaped eyes, the head is characterized by a cubic quality caused by the flatness of the brow and the sharp planar transitions to the side of the skull. The beard and hair are arranged in a stylized pattern of short incised tufts.[32] To these stylised features can be added the heavy-lobed, over-large, fleshy ears and the almost semi-circular curve of the massive jaw. In contrast to these abstractions, the lips swell organically out of the beard area and, one might add, the edges of the eyebrows are softened, although this latter may be partially due to time and weathering.

Seen frontally the curiously convex halo behind the head is alarmingly eccentric: the right half has a notice-ably shorter radius. Artistic incompetence is not the reason, however, because if viewed axially from the left, face and halo read concentrically. The eccentricity is then a subtle visual adjustment and speaks compellingly to the iconographic relationship between head and halo.

Since the middle of the nineteenth century, this monumental trumeau figure has been identified as Saint Loup, seventh-century archbishop of Sens and patron of the priory of Saint-Loup-de-Naud.[33]

The trumeau figure stands on the shoulders of two fantastic winged beasts. These apparently identical creatures[34] are placed back to back and turn their heads upward along the sides of the saint's legs. Their feet rest on a small shaft ring which their tails overlap.

Although very badly eroded, enough of the two beasts remains to assert that they are winged, composite creatures made up of a lion-like chest, bird's feet and a serpent's tail. The traces of the neck, mouth and eye of the beast on the right and the otherwise identical form on two column-figure capitals suggests that these paired creatures should be understood as either dragons or asps.[35] Past identifications of the creatures have ranged from birds[36] to dragons[37] to "animaux fantastiques."[38] However, in spite of this lack of agreement, virtually all scholarship accords them an evil symbolism[39] and their association with Psalm 91 goes back to the early literature of the portal.[40]

TRUMEAU BASE: (fig. 22)

The socle block is composed of a badly weathered,
cavettoed sill register surmounted by a low plinth and
the base proper. The curving edge of the base is offset
establishing a distinction between half-column and pilaster. The modified attic base consists of a large torus
bound to the plinth by spurs, a scotia set off sharply
above and below, and a small upper torus nearly indistinguishable from the upper offset.

TRUMEAU CAPITAL: Miraculous Mass of Saint Loup (figs.
28-30)

The capital zone atop the main block is divided into
two sections. The forward historiated section, corresponding to the half-column of the main stone, contains the
narrative. The rear section, which corresponds to the
pilaster below, has been left 'en bosse,' unlike the
corresponding section of the base below which we saw to
be carved.

On the capital, which is capped above by an arcade
supporting tiny architectural forms, the actors in the
drama are symmetrically arranged around the locus of the
event. On the forward face, at the center of the composition, a chalice stands on a draped altar. Above this,
against the blank ground of the capital core, we see a
smoothly ovoid object. From the right, a saint,[41]

dressed in full episcopal regalia,[42] advances toward the altar bearing a now damaged object--probably a paten-- in front of his waist. At the left of the altar, a figure, probably a sub-deacon,[43] kneels with over-large hands up- raised to signal witness to the event depicted. Two figures, one on each side, fill out the remaining space. The figure on the right follows in three-quarter profile behind the bishop and holds up a closed book to which he points. His costume suggests that he is to be understood as a deacon who, together with the kneeling sub-deacon, would assist the officiant at the mass.[44] The remaining figure, perhaps a priest,[45] is posed frontally on the left side of the capital. He, too, holds a book to which he also points with a damaged finger. In comparison to the other figures he is isolated from the narrative.

In formal terms all the figures on the capital serve a visual, tectonic function. Their poses follow the expanding curve of the core, which makes their large heads more visible from below, so that they aid in the visual transition from bearing member to load borne. Moreover, the poses of the kneeling witness and the saint are distorted from the naturalistic to accommodate the corners of the capital. Seen from the front, particularly the witness appears awkwardly formed. However, facing the capital diagonally on either side, both of these poses become much more comprehensible.

Modelling rather than incised lines characterize the drapery of the figures which nevertheless remains stylised in its fold patterns and which reveals an only additively conceived anatomy.[46]

Modelled folds are particularly clear on the right side of the saint's chasuble, across the waist and down the right leg of the attendant figure behind him, and on the altar cloth itself. On the other hand, the frontal figure on the left side of the capital wears drapery which is "thinner" and somewhat more incised, particularly in the folds gathered across his legs.[47] The tendency to reveal anatomy through stylized drapery folds occurs in the legs of all four figures and also on the right shoulder of the saint.

The softly contoured heads of the four figures are large in relation to their bodies (approximately 1:4). Slightly bulging, ovoid eyes, enframed by incised lids, are set within a socket structure defined above by symmetrically arching brows which like the cheeks below are softly modelled.[48] The lips of the figures swell organically from the flesh between the chins and the broad, straight noses. The hair of all four figures is organized in stylized tufts established by incised lines as is the "tetrarchan" beard of the saint.

The scene represents a miraculous mass of Saint Loup.[49] According to the text of the _vita_, one Sunday when the saint was saying mass a precious stone fell from heaven into the chalice. This radiant and sweet-smelling stone was placed by the king among the relics of Sens and later worked many miracles. The smooth ovoid object-- i.e., the precious stone[50]--suspended above the chalice on the forward face of the capital fixes the moment of the scene. None of the three figures present on the capital with Saint Loup is mentioned in the text, but the deacon and sub-deacon relate formally to the narrative and can be explained as assisting the saint at the mass. The other (priest?) figure is unrelated to the scene and is subject to no similar explanation of his presence. However, his isolation and his significant pointing gesture suggest an interpretation of his role. Pointing toward books (or scrolls) calls attention to the written word and, by extension, to the truth of the word.[51] The compositional parallel between the deacon on the right side of the capital, who points to his (liturgical) book and the figure in question on the left, who also points to his book, is surely meaning-laden. The detachment from the narrative of the figure on the left suggests that he is a witness; his gesture alludes to the truth of the record contained within the book (vita).[52]

TRUMEAU IMPOST: (fig. 27)

The impost block which is undamaged is a large trapezoidal solid. Its offset fillet is carried on an enormous

champfer decorated with a foliate pattern. The arrangement of the foliation vertically emphasizes the corners
of the block and maintains a centrally symmetrical
arrangement on each of the three flat faces. The leaves
themselves are relatively thick and fleshy and are
applied additively to the champfer core with little
undercutting. Here and there clusters of fruit appear
among them.

JAMBS AND EMBRASURES   (figs. 22, 31, 32)

Each of the two strongly projecting jambs rises
baseless to foliate capitals. Each of the stepped
embrasures contains three frontally disposed, monumental
column-figures which stand on sloping consoles[53] set
between modified attic bases and inhabited capitals with
no visible intervening shaft. A continuous foliate
impost extends over each jamb and embrasure.

Each of the five male and one female column-figures
wears one or more undergarments partially masked by an
outer mantle. Each displays an attribute in front of
the body while the three in the right embrasure also gesture in blessing. The column-figures each reveal a rigid
adherence to the lateral contours of their blocks and
manifest little undercutting save for the areas around
the attributes, which are also the only areas of
significant damage to the generally well-preserved
figures.

The drapery of the figures is formed by blunted linear incisions and does little to reveal the anatomy beneath it. The plenitude of folds results in a decorative effect which is muted somewhat by a generally convincing arrangement. Minor areas, such as the knee-caps, receive a more overtly decorative treatment. As the handling of the hips and the relationship between arms and torsoes reveals, there is little concern for anatomical structure in spite of the appearance of correct proportions. The faces are also abstractly handled. Large, straight noses and additively applied, doubly incised, almondine eyes enframed by symmetrically arching brows dominate the more organic handling of the mouths. The handling of the eyes, ears and mouths permits the innermost and outermost figures in the left embrasure to be grouped together, separate from the other four.

The innermost pair of column-figures represent apostles. The outer four figures represent Old Testament personnages.[54]

Each of the six column-figures shows evidences of adjustments in order to emplace it in the present setting: shaft axes (relative to the bases and capitals) are deflected; haloes are cropped and figures overlap. In contrast, the bases and capitals appear to have been

carved for their present emplacement. These circumstances and their implications are discussed in detail
in Chapter III, pp. 90-103.

WM1-n: Saint Paul (figs. 31, 83, 84)

This large-headed, slim-waisted, male figure bends
his right arm sharply up across his chest and extends his
left one downward across his hip to grasp, respectively,
the top and bottom of a large book held thereby in front
of his torso. He is bald, bearded and barefooted and
wears a loose fitting tunic which sags with its own
weight from the shoulders and his right wrist. It hangs
nearly vertically at the ankles and rises up over the
remaining traces of the damaged feet. An outer mantle
has been draped over the shoulders, gathered at the waist
and pulled over the right forearm to hang diagonally
across the legs. In addition to the feet, the nose,
the left ear, the tips of his beard and fingers of his
right hand are slightly damaged.

In general, the blunted incisions which form the
drapery folds do not affect the linear contour of the
figure which shows only slight deviations from the
vertical, for instance along the figure's left arm or,
particularly, along the left side of the waist. Even an
exceptional area, such as the left shin, where the folds
are allowed to create an uneven contour, still remains

contained within the strict line of the outer garment.
Generally convincing in its arrangement, the drapery
receives a clearly decorative handling in the isolation
of the left knee, the repetition of the gently exaggerated
curve of the mantle over the left shoulder and the evenly-
spaced repetitive folds on the upper right arm. The
folds of the mantle press flat across the legs and along
the lower hem of the tunic where the slightly flared
ends of the thin tubular folds have not been hollowed out
at all.

The figure's large head is characterized by a block-
like quality defined by the sharp angle between the forehead and the sides of the head at the crown. The high
forehead, incised with softened, horizontal "worry" lines
between the brows and abstract concentric patterns of
symmetrical creases in the skin at the upper corners[55]
and large slightly bulging eyes dominate the face.[56] The
lids, nearly flat below the eye, arch up above it in
wide semi-circles which are then echoed by the oxbow of
the brow. The lips swell organically from the strictly,
incised, undulating clumps of beard and mustache which
surround them. They are slightly parted at the center
which further animates the already expressive face.
Finally, the ears, which are shaped like inverted '8's
and which are carved with teardrop shapes at the centers,
can really be said to be modelled. But they are additively

applied, low, on the sides of the head.

The book, together with the bare feet, the bald head
and beard assure the identification of this figure as
the apostle Saint Paul.[57]

WM2-n: the Queen of Sheba (?) (figs. 31, 86)

The crown, the hip-length braids and the stylised
circular area of the drapery on the left of the torso (a
schematic rendering of a breast) assure that the second
figure in the left embrasure represents a queen. Her
right arm extends in front of her thigh where she holds
the remnant of a rotulus which must once have extended
upward to be held by her now missing left hand. The
queen wears two, or perhaps, three garments. The most
prominent is a close-fitting, delicately incised, full-
length tunic, the deeply cut neckline of which is clasped
together by a rhomboid fibula so that the heavily embroidered border forms a broad-stemmed 'Y.' Whether the incised
lines above the 'Y' form part of this garment or an
undergarment is not clear. The tunic is belted twice
at the waist and then tied loosely with a knotted sash,
the ends of which extend nearly to the ankles. An outer
mantle is draped over the right shoulder and arm and hangs
vertically to mid-calf. On the left, it passes over the
shoulder and then tucks underneath the arm to hang, on
this side also, to mid-calf. Minor damage occurs on the

garment hems. The fleurons of the crown are also missing.

The multiplicity of linear folds creates a sense of decoration which remains, however, highly controlled, as the expanse of vertically parallel folds covering the legs reveals.[58] The disposition of the drapery does almost nothing to define the anatomy which is further masked by the sheer number of folds. No knees interrupt the thin incisions of the skirt. The slight swelling of the abdomen disrupts nothing in the pattern of incisions which flow across it. The blank, circular area on the chest "reveals" the breast only in a conventionalized, abstract way. The linear handling of the drapery and the "flat-slab" treatment of the body correspond to the strict vertical contours at the sides of the figure. Indeed, the contour on the left is so rigidly adhered to that the left arm appears only three-quarters round, fused, as it were, to the side of the figure. The condition of the contours is paralleled by the almost complete absence of undercutting. The right side of the drilled mantle border folds back flat on the chest. The braids nowhere fall free of the body. The bottom hem undulates gently around the feet, but is never opened up deeply underneath.

The long, thin nose and heavy, curving jaw dominate the queen's face. The physiognomy is organized around an axial symmetry once more obvious in the presence of the missing central fleuron of the crown.[59] Although the

brows appear almost modelled,[60] and the parts of the face
seem organically related--especially the lips and their
surrounding area--the prevailing sense is one of swelling
surface rather than of bone-supported flesh.[61] The eyes
yield revealing information. Almond-shaped and enframed
by doubly incised lids, they appear set beneath the projection of the brow but upon the plane of the cheek. Moreover, they do not remain entirely on the forward plane of
the face, "bending" slightly around at the sides. The ears
are set low on the sides of the head. They are elliptical
and fleshy. Significantly, the incised line between the
lips extends asymmetrically further to the right with
respect to the axis defined by the nose.

Accepting the conventional theory that crowned column
figures represent Old Testament and not French or Frankish
kings and queens,[62] most scholars have tentatively suggested that this figure may represent the Queen of Sheba.[63]
Presumably the basis for the suggestion lies in a pairing
with the king opposite her in the right embrasure and in
the limited number of Old Testament possibilities. A probable typological relationship with the voussoir immediately
above will add further weight to an identification of the
figure as the Queen of Sheba.[64]

WM3-n: Jeremiah (?) (figs. 31, 85)

Again a large-headed figure, which wears a type of

Jewish mitre[65] and bends his left arm sharply across the
chest holding the end of a rotulus in his hand (fig. 31).
Today the rotulus is broken off behind the wrist; it must
once have been connected to the remaining piece which
undulates from his left forearm down almost to the knee,
where it is again broken off. His right arm, which is brok-
en off at the wrist, bends slightly at the elbow and extends
in front of the abdomen; it must once have held an attribute. It may well be that the rotulus, which begins to
curve forward and upward where it is broken off at the
bottom, may once have curved upward to be clasped in the
figure's right hand.[66]

The figure wears two garments: a loose fitting tunic
with embroidered neck and cuffs underneath a mantle with
a decorated border. The mantle is draped over both
shoulders and arms and is gathered at the waist to hang
diagonally across the legs.[67] Minor damage has occurred
to the hems of the garments.

In general, the folds are arranged in directions
which suggest a naturalistic intention as attested by
the vertical folds on the chest and the long diagonal
sweep from the right hip. Within this general concept,
however, there are areas of clear decorative emphasis.
Most obvious in this regard are the compartmentalizations
of folds on the left thigh and on the upper arms. Moreover,
the parallel regularity of the more naturalistically

arranged folds, for example across the chest, gives them a certain decorative quality as well.

The naturalistic relationship between body and drapery in this figure is limited; overall, little has been done to reveal the form of the body through the drapery. Precisely where the body-drapery relationship should be most pronounced the drapery is most decorative (for example, the left thigh). While it might be argued that the thin, tubular folds of the tunic bend slightly at the foot, they never break the stark, descending line of the folds above. Instead, primacy belongs to the contours of the block. The cubic quality is evidenced in the lateral contours which are almost vertical and in the sense of a flat forward plane which is produced by the flat chest and the undifferentiated hip and thigh area. Those folds of drapery which might have hung free, like the mantle hem, lie flat against the figure. Even the ends of the thin, slightly flared tubular folds at the hem of the alb are not deeply undercut.

The large, bearded head is characterized by a cubic quality given by the sharp orthogonal transitions of the forehead and cheeks. Here, too, the large, slightly bulging eyes, identical to Saint Paul's in the arching semi-circular lids and symmetrical ox-bow brow, dominate the face. The brow and the flesh beside the nose have softened creases but those of the former are underplayed because of the headgear. High, prominent cheek bones and the organically swelling, parted lips animate a face which is as expressive as that of Saint Paul.

Based only on the "coiffre juive et une ruban à la main" Aufauvre ventured to identify the figure as Jeremiah.[68] These two attributes alone are insufficient to distinguish Jeremiah from other Old Testament possibilities. However, reasoning analogically in Chapter IV, we find further confirmation of this identification.[69]

WM1-s: Saint Peter (fig. 32)

This short-bearded, bare-footed figure bends his right arm sharply at the elbow to hold the hand, palm outward, in a gesture of benediction. His left arm bends slightly across the waist to clasp a large key by its slightly damaged handle. The figure has a circular bald spot, like a monastic tonsure.

The figure wears several garments which are difficult to distinguish clearly. One undergarment is revealed by the tight-fitting sleeve visible at the figure's right wrist. A loose fitting tunic covers the torso and the blessing arm and is also visible as a triangular area from his left knee to the ankles. An outer mantle is draped over both shoulders and across the figure's upper left side and arm. Presumably it is this outer mantle which is pulled across the figure's right leg and gathered at the waist. However, no legible continuity occurs between the mantle proper where it falls from the figure's right shoulder to his right ankle and the supposed continuation of the mantle diagonally upward from that ankle to the figure's left knee. Indeed, the opposite is suggested. The mantle, where it falls from the shoulder, bears a chevron pattern on its border. Its supposed diagonal continuation bears the same diamond pattern found on the tunic at the neck and the figure's right wrist. Moreover, no clear distinction is made between the loose-fitting tunic which covers the torso and the supposed continuation of the mantle at the waist. Since a tunic cannot be gathered up as this "continuation garment" is one can only conclude confusion on the part of the sculptor or his model.

Probably the best preserved of the six embrasure figures, minor damage has occurred only to the fingers of each hand and to the toes of especially the left foot.

In general the drapery of this figure manifests the same blunted blend between incised and modelled folds found in the other figures. This is particularly evident in the handling of the alb and outer mantle. Exceptionally, sharp, more linear incisions characterize the handling of the ambiguous garment draped across the figure's waist.

The arrangement of the folds nowhere violates the contour of the block defined by the outer mantle which plummets vertically to the ankles (save for where the elbow presses outward ever so slightly on the right). Within the mantle's contour, a suggestion of a narrowed waist appears on the left, but the real contour variation occurs in the ambiguous garment where the folds along the outer side of the figure's right leg reveal a low-key irregularity. One might expect variation to occur here, because it is only in this area that any real attempt to present the body beneath the cloth occurs. While the left knee is identified by a (an abraded) circular incision it does press forward just enough to relax the lower half of the leg with a resulting faint suggestion of a contrapposto pose. While none of this movement is evident in the pose of the feet, the small narrow area, which is devoid of folds, on the inside of the figure's right shin can be understood to reveal the leg also. The remainder of the folds follow a generally rational system. The thin, slightly flared tubes of the alb drop vertically down the right shin, although they flare slightly to the left to fill the gap between the legs. The folds across the chest and upper arms descend with the direction of the body and the zigzagging hems of the various garments press back with the weight of their decorated edges against the body which is, however, little revealed. Only in the area around the arms at the waist is the drapery given a looping rhythmic arrangement which echoes

the decorative handling of the left knee. The folds
here are not deeply undercut, although there is a little
more depth under the outer mantle beside the calf on the
right than is to be found in any comparable instance in
the left embrasure.

One area can be strikingly compared with the trumeau.
In both figures the left arms (their right) are raised in
benediction so that the covering sleeve should swing
free. Whereas on the trumeau the cutting within the sleeve
and behind it is quite deep, no attempt is made in the
column figure either to free the sleeve from the waist or
to hollow the space between the arm and the sleeve.

Heavy, symmetrical, gently arching brows, a straight,
prominent nose and an aggressive, animating tilt of the
chin characterize the figure's face. The face is enframed
by a symmetrically arranged cap of hair and a beard, both
of which are formed by incised locks which terminate in
stylized swirls. The almondine eyes bend slightly around
the sides of the head. Together these elements stress the
abstract aspect of the face. In contrast, the lips swell
organically out of the surrounding area.

The presence of the key identifies this column-figure
as Saint Peter.[70] Although the longish, wavy curls do not
correspond precisely to the traditional physiognomical
type, the circular bald spot corroborates his identity as
do the bare feet and the pairing with the figure of Saint
Paul opposite him in the left embrasure.

WM2-s: <u>Solomon</u> (?) (fig. 32)

This remarkably slender, crowned and bearded figure
bends his right arm sharply upward to hold the palm of
his damaged hand outward in a gesture of benediction. He
extends his draped left arm downward across his waist
where the covered hand held the cylindrical end of a
rotulus which is today almost entirely destroyed. A portion
of the other end of the scroll extends upward and terminates in a coil on the upper arm.   The absence of folds
at the elbow of the figure's right arm and the linear
chip just above on the wrist suggest that the scroll may
have originally extended from the covered hand laterally
to that elbow before extending, free of the chest as the
folds there indicate that it was, to connect with the
remaining fragment at the figure's left shoulder.

The king wears two garments. Revealed along the
figure's right side and at the ankles is a loose-fitting,
tight-sleeved, alb-like undergarment which is gathered at
his slim waist. An outer cloak covers his body down to
mid-calf except along his right side where it is clasped
at the shoulder and parted by the gesturing arm. The
king wears decorated slippers.

Aside from the damage already mentioned, damage to
the fleurons of his crown and breakage on both sides of his
halo, the figure is well-preserved.

The drapery is again largely rendered by blunted
incisions, but there are also considerable areas of the
most crisply linear folds of any of the column figures
save for the queen opposite. While the repetitious sagging folds across the chest exemplify the former, the
repeated looping incisions on the left thigh and the thin
'V'-shaped folds falling to the right from the draped
hand represent the latter.

The contour of the figure adheres strictly to the
lateral limits of the block as defined by the outer
cloak. Even the king's left elbow does not project
laterally to interrupt the contour.[71] The resultant
vertical rigidity and the slenderness of the figure
distinguish it somewhat from its neighbors.

In spite of a general appearance of correct proportions[72] and drapery which responds in ways that one might
expect, there is little real concern for body structure.
The interior contour is varied at the waist but there is
no attempt to articulate the hip joint.[73] As one might
expect in an image which relates strongly to the archi-
tectonics of its emplacement, neither arm is freed from
the body; instead, they "disappear" partially into the block
of the torso. Similarly, while drapery "falls" toward
the feet, its fall is conceived in terms of rhythmically
repeated pattern. The evenly spaced, incised scallops

on his right thigh, the multiple 'V'-shaped incisions
falling from his left wrist, the concentric interlocking
pattern across the torso and, more importantly, the symmetrical zigzag hemline extending outward from the off-
vertical flaring trumpet of drapery descending from covered
hand at the center, all emphasize decoration through
patterned repetition.

The hems of the king's garments are calm and little
undercut. The exception--and it is unique among these
six figures--is at the open end of the trumpet fold at
the knees. Here the deep undercutting creates a shadowy
pocket which, as the focal point of the most significant
drapery arrangement, serves a rather more decorative intention than that of any naturalistic aim of gradually
freeing itself from the confines of the architectonic
block.

In many respects the head of this king closely
resembles that of its neighbor to the left. Both faces
are animated by the aggressive tilt of their chins and
the "questioning" look one reads into the gently arching,
symmetrical brows. Yet like the head of Saint Peter,
this king's head is also enframed by decoratively arranged,
rigidly symmetrical hair and beard. An axial symmetry,
once more strongly emphasized by the crown fleuron
directly above the central part in the hair,[74] still
remains clear in the hair, beard, brow and strong vertical

nose. Like Saint Peter and the queen, the eyes, which are almond-shaped, slightly bulging and doubly incised, sit "behind" the heavy brow but "upon" the plane of cheeks which read as slightly swollen. Here, too, the eyes tend to curve off the forward plane of the face. As with the other figures, these abstract, hieratic elements are subtly balanced by the naturalistic handling of the nose-brow juncture and the entire area around the mouth.

The crown and the pairing with the queen directly opposite in the left embrasure have led scholars to assume this royal figure to be either Solomon or David.[75] Of those who chose between the two kings, an implicit preference for the Queen of Sheba over Bathsheba has resulted in a loose consensus for Solomon.[76] Presumably the rotulus once bore a painted text or inscription. Typological relationships with the archivolt scene of the Magi before Herod lends support to the claim for Solomon by reason of analogy.[77]

WM3-s: Isaiah (?) (fig. 32)

This long-bearded, long-haired male figure raises his right arm sharply across the torso. He extends his left arm downward at a sloping angle across the waist. Although his right hand is badly damaged (his left is broken off at the wrist), enough remains to be certain that the palm was turned at right angles to the chest and therefore once held an object. In very early images of the portal the figure can be seen to have held the cylindrical end of what must have been a rotulus (fig. 110).[78] The scroll must have been a rather long one because there is a connecting node still visible on the outer garment between the knees, a fact which indicates that the figure's left hand probably once held the scroll in a way similar to the queen in the opposite embrasure.

This figure wears three garments. One undergarment is revealed only as a tight-fitting sleeve at his right wrist. A second undergarment, a loose-sleeved tunic with a decorated neckline, appears at the left half of the upper body and in the area of the lower legs. An outer mantle with a richly decorated border is draped over the figure's left shoulder and arm. It passes behind him and is gathered at the waist to hang diagonally across the lower half of the body on the left.

Minor areas of damage to the figure include the halo, the ears, beard-tips and garment hems.

Most of the drapery folds of this figure are rendered as blunted incisions, e.g., the vertically parallel folds across the chest, those on the upper right arm or in the undergarment visible at the calves. The thinner, more linear incisions appear in the repeated scallops which descend down the left thigh.

On the right side of the figure the uninterrupted vertical line of the outer cloak defines both the contour of the block and the figure. On the left both contours are again defined by the outer cloak, but only to the waist. At that point the latter terminates and the former is defined by the leg itself and, to a lesser extent, by the folds which play over it. As was the case with the Saint Peter figure, the contour of the leg curves slightly inward from the knee downward.

It would be going too far to suggest, however, that the lower left leg reveals a real concern for a naturalistic handling of the drapery or an interest in anatomy. The conception of human form and its attendant drapery here, as elsewhere in the embrasure, reflects a restrained decorative approach with a generalized, surface adherence to naturalistic form. Thus the folds of cloth across the torso hang vertically but repeat at regular intervals to mask the body. The same is true elsewhere in the figure, as at the bottom of the tunic where the folds hang vertically but in near perfect parallelity. Neither is there any interruption in the forward plane to indicate the existence of a leg structure. Precisely where the leg is supposed to be revealed on the left thigh, the scallops repeat rhythmically at regular intervals to the stylized decorative swirl which equals knee-joint.

There is also little undercutting, except for the area around the lost attribute. The zigzagging hem of the cloak lies nearly flat against the body; the sleeves of the tunic are shallow below the wrists[79] and the arms are never really freed from the torso. As with the lateral contours, the sculptor's primary concern is to realize the form within the limits of its block. This architectonic subjection obviously lends itself more easily to a decorative handling, however restrained, than to any supposed impulse toward the naturalism of a nascent Gothic style.

Encircled by the overlapping flame-like tufts of hair and the long, full, undulating beard, the eyes become the dominant element of the face. Slightly bulging almonds, they are surrounded by double incisions[80] and are placed "behind" the symmetrically arching brows[81] and upon the plane of the cheeks. Again, the eyes "bend" around onto the sides of the head rather than remaining on the forward plane. Although less obvious than on the neighboring figures, the hair here (and the beard) is also arranged symmetrically.

In contrast to these abstract features the handling of the lips relates organically to the surrounding area. Damage to the right side of the lower lip gives the appearance of a more linear, schematic handling, but this appearance is inaccurate.

Some writers have suggested that this figure represents the prophet Isaiah, but they (can) offer no criteria
to support their hypothesis.[82]   Indeed, without the critical (presumably inscribed) rotulus, the figure himself
can offer no attribute for specific identification.
However, iconographic features, which here more than any
other column figure seem to condition the style, do confirm
the general type. The large size of the head and its
relationship to the body proportionally are apparently
the result of a requirement for a long, full beard and
visibly full head of hair. Too, the animation of the
flame-like hair and undulating beard together with the
angular cheeks suggest a "coarser" handling[83] but are
probably intended to represent the less-serene, visionary
physiognomical type related to prophecy. Indeed, the
quality of the drapery handling speaks against any
coarseness resulting from lack of ability and increases
the likelihood of iconographic intention. Assuming the
figure to represent a prophet, we can, on the basis of
analogy with the voussoir scene of the Magi before Herod
immediately above, suggest that this figure does indeed
represent the prophet Isaiah.[84]

EMBRASURE BASES: 1/n-3/n and 1/s-3/s (figs. 31, 32)

Although the bases of the south embrasure have
weathered almost beyond recognition, enough remains to
assert that all embrasure base units consist of a modified

attic base set on a plinth or die-block which surmounts
a moulding course. The bases themselves consist of a
large torus, a deep scotia boldly set off above and below
and an upper torus so small that it appears to duplicate
the upper offset.[85] Spurs connect the lower tori to the
otherwise undecorated plinths.

The profiles of all the bases are nearly the same
but the lower torus of 3/n is considerably higher and
thicker than its neighbors. The same condition may also
have obtained in the south embrasure. The first and
second plinths in each embrasure form rectangles rather
than squares (and their bases ellipses rather than circles).
The third plinth in each embrasure is slightly larger and
more nearly square (and each base is more nearly circular).
The configuration of the plinths and bases reflect the
configuration of the upper zone of the "intermediate" portal at Saint-Loup. These circumstances are discussed in
detail in Chapter III, pp. 103-109.

The moulding course immediately below the bases and
plinths is separate from them. It consists of a projecting
torus flanked above and below by offset cavettoes.

JAMB CAPITALS: n and s (fig. 33, 34)

Each of the well-preserved jamb capitals consists of
two blocks. The larger covers the reveal of the jamb and
extends over about one-third of the forward face (figs. 33,
34). A narrow "filler" block is interposed between the

larger one and each embrasure capital which also extends onto the face of its adjacent jamb. Both "filler" blocks continue the foliate patterns of the larger portions of the capitals.

Both jamb capitals derive their organization from the classical corinthian capital--the north capital more clearly so than the south. The foliation of the north capital is arranged in two tiers around projecting acanthus leaves from behind which rise spiral volutes at the corners. Across the reveal, three large leaves form a lower tier. Smaller leaves fill the spaces between them and are continuous with the stems of the larger leaves which rise behind them to form the second tier of foliation. Spiral helixes rise above the two tiers of foliation at the center of each face and support, like the volutes, the projections of the abacus above. The south jamb capital follows a more decorative pattern. Again arranged in two tiers, large leaves occupy the corners and "bend" around the corners, curling outward slightly to provide limited vertical to horizontal transition. On the reveal, a large mass of foliation rises at the center, from the astragal, to spread outward across the upper surface of the capital. The volutes and helixes, although still present, have been reduced to small undulating incisions which actually transgress the abacus boundary in several places.

Despite the similar style of the foliation and their common debt to the classical corinthian capital, the salient aspect of the jamb capitals is their strikingly different organization: architectonically ordered on the north; decoratively arranged on the south. In and of itself insignificant this distinction appears to be part of a larger contrast between the north and south sides within the capital zone.

Embrasure Capital 1/n (fig. 33)

This well-preserved capital contains two affronted, composite beasts intertwined with a curving palmette motif which begins behind the creatures at the astragal. The beasts have the head of a lion, the body and wings of a bird and the tail of a serpent.[86] They place their inner legs upon the plant stem which separates them and turn their heads up and away from the projecting angle of the capital.

The relatively thick leaves and beaded stalks undulate over the empty areas of the capital core and across the necks of the beasts. The stalks branch to support the abacus bosses and combine at the projecting angle to form a vertical emphasis at that point. While the foliation continues onto the face of the jamb, its pattern remains independent of the jamb capital's corinthian arrangement.

The pair of beasts on this capital may represent asps or, perhaps, dragons.[87]

Embrasure Capital 2/n (fig. 33)

This capital contains two affronted birds with damaged beaks which are intertwined with a foliate motif that springs up between them from the astragal. They rest their raised inner legs on this plant and turn their heads up and away from the capital's projecting angle.

The foliation branches above a collar between the bird's breasts. One stalk rises to support the projecting angle of the abacus. The other two pass around in front of the bird's necks and branches again to support each of the abacus bosses and to fill the empty space behind the birds.

While these birds may perhaps represent eagles or phoenixes, no assurance can be had in their identification.[88]

Embrasure Capital 3/n (fig. 33)

This capital contains well-preserved winged quadrupeds with the body of a lion and the head of an eagle which are disposed on the lateral faces. Both beasts move outward, away from the portal, but the outer one twists its head backwards thereby arresting the movement somewhat. Each holds its wings and inner foreleg upraised and each raises its head upward.[89] Palmette leaves occupy the empty space against the core.

These creatures represent griffins.[90]

Embrasure Capital 1/s (fig. 34)

This well-preserved capital contains two affronted composite creatures which have the body of a bird, the tail of a serpent and a human head: on the left a short-haired male and on the right a long-tressed female. Rather than dispose each creature on a separate face of the capital, the male has been drawn outward so that its head occupies a volute's position immediately below the projecting angle of the abacus.[91] The female creature inclines her head toward her partner so that they almost touch. The male, which alone has upraised wings, rests one cloven hoof on the palmette leaf between them while the female raises her inner leg and points toward him.

Fleshy palmette forms fill the interstices around the figures. As with the corresponding capital in the opposite embrasure, the foliation continues onto the face of the jamb. Again it bears no relation to the foliation of the jamb capital.

These creatures represent sirens.[92]

Embrasure Capital 2/s (fig. 34)

This undamaged capital contains two affronted, composite creatures which have the body and upraised wings of a bird and the tail of a serpent. The male head of the beast on the left is short-haired, tonsured and is placed beneath the projecting angle of the abacus. The beast on the right is lion-headed. The human-headed creature rests one upraised cloven hoof on the palmette leaf (This is the only foliation of the capital.); the other raises its inner leg to touch its partner on the neck. These creatures probably represent a siren and an asp or dragon respectively.[93]

Embrasure Capital 3/s (fig. 34)

This well-preserved capital contains two affronted, winged quadrupeds which have human heads. The head on the left is male, tonsured and is enframed by a monk's hood or cowl. The female head on the right is covered by a nunnish veil. The creatures clasp raised forelegs[94] and incline their heads to touch just beneath the projecting angle of the abacus. A single palmette frond rises behind the hind-quarters of each creature. These beasts represent sphinxes.[95]

JAMB AND EMBRASURE IMPOSTS: (figs. 33, 34)

The impost course on each side of the portal is a massive champfer set off beneath a fillet. The foliate patterns in each embrasure fall into two groups corresponding to each of their two large blocks. On the innermost block of the north embrasure, a fruited vine forms spiral patterns on the inner faces and less regular, undulating patterns on the outer faces. On the outer block, the spiral clusters of vine and foliage originate from the

mouths of monstrous heads on the projecting angles. The
innermost block of the south embrasure contains an upright
palmette acanthus frieze in the classical tradition.
The outer block repeats the basic pattern, but it is
enriched by leaf tips which curl forward at the projecting angles and by tiny volutes above the foliation. As
in the jamb and embrasure capitals below there is a clear
distinction between the two sides of the portal. The
imposts are undamaged.

ARCHIVOLT I (WM1): (fig. 22)

This archivolt contains ten standing angels arranged
in a variety of static and animated poses and an Agnus Dei
on the keystone. Each holds a liturgical object and turns
inward toward the tympanum and lintel. All are winged,
nimbed and barefoot. The lowest angel on each side of the
archivolt stands on a small convex console. The other
eight each stand on a small undulant mass which represents
clouds of the heavenly realm. All of the sculptures of
this archivolt survive in a very good state of preservation.

Each angel wears a long-sleeved, ankle-length tunic
with a decorated collar and a richly bordered mantle which
is draped over one or both shoulders and gathered at the
waist to hang downward across the legs. The drapery is
arranged in a generally convincing way throughout the
archivolt, but it is formed by blunt incisions which
produce a linear effect (more strong in some figures than

in others). The resultant, muted decorative impression
is heightened by a still more abstract handling of lesser
areas such as the shoulders or knees. Nearly all the
angels are short-waisted and flat-chested. Little concern
is given to exact anatomical relationships--as the
conventionalized handling of the hips indicates--or to
revealing body structure through drapery. Although the
shapes of the angels' heads vary from the nearly spherical
to the almost cubic, all the faces are dominated by
doubly-incised, almondine eyes set additively on the
cheeks beneath symmetrical, low-arching brows. In each
angel, a heavily curving jaw leads to a small prominent
chin below a mouth with small, thick lips which swell,
by comparison, more organically from the surrounding
area.

All of the figures in this archivolt fit comfortably within the limits of their individual blocks, none
of which show any evidence of cropping or adjustment.
All appear to have been carved for their present emplacement.

WM1-n/1: Angel (fig. 35)

This recently headless figure,[96] who holds a censer
beside him in his left hand, stands frontally with the
wings spread out symmetrically against the ground behind
him. His right arm, which is bent at the elbow and

extended across the waist, is broken off at the wrist.
Probably the hand once held an incense boat as do the
angels of voussoirs s/1 and s/2 which also hold censers.

Two areas demonstrate the lack of relationship
between body and drapery: the "oxbow" of drapery which
conventionalizes the hip area and the evenly spaced
symmetrical 'v' patterns on the chest. While it is true
that the contour of each leg projects forward, the mantle,
even in the left leg,[97] does not respond to the body
beneath it. Though not deeply undercut, the hemlines
maintain a certain activity, along the sides of the
figure in particular.

WM1-n/2: Angel (fig. 36)

This angel stands also frontally with wings outstretched against the ground. He holds a large candle
upright in his left hand while his partially broken right
hand extends across the waist to clasp the hem of the
mantle which sweeps in a great arc across the right side
of the torso. On this figure, the drapery takes on a
rhythmic animation which makes its surface come alive.
Sweeping curves isolate expanses of anatomy--for example,
his right thigh and forearm--establishing patterns which
stand in stark contrast to the repeated, sharp hairpin
folds of the outer mantle between the thighs.

Wml-n/3:   Angel (fig. 37)

This more animated angel lifts his left leg to
"stride" toward the tympanum. He swings a censer across
his chest with his right arm and extends his left underneath in the opposite direction thereby creating a counter-
rhythm which animates the figure still more. The movemented quality of the figure is heightened further by the
tendency toward sweeping folds which isolate areas of
anatomy--for example, the legs and arms--and by the insistence on an active hemline. The awkward juncture of
the two legs and the torso, which is masked by an oxbow
fold convention, typifies the relationship between
anatomy and drapery.

WMl-n/4:   Angel (fig. 38)

Although the torso of this angel is held parallel
to the plane of the voussoir block, both legs are bent at
the knees and "turned" toward the tympanum in a conventionalized walking pose. Both arms bend at the elbows:
his left to hold a candle, his right to clasp the hem of
the mantle. Together they repeat the directed movement of
the legs. The drapery responds to the animation of the
figure's pose through a decorative animation of its own.
Portions of the arms and legs are isolated from one
another and ringed with concentric linear folds. Similar
also are the swings and swirls of drapery around the

the ankles which, although at first appearing to be motivated by the movement of the figure itself, in the end
remain mere adjuncts to indicate movement.

WM1-n/5: Angel (fig. 39)

     In contrast to the animation of the figures below
him, this angel stand calmly and with both hands presents
a long, narrow cloth incised with parallel striations
which is draped over his right shoulder. Presumably
this cloth is the humeral veil worn by acolytes in liturgical processions since at least the eighth century.[98]
If so, then the object held by this angel is at one with
the liturgical nature of the objects (candles and censers)
held by the other angels in this archivolt.[99]

     The post of this angel reverses that of the angel
immediately beneath him. Here the legs are held to the
ground and the torso turned toward the tympanum. In keeping with this bodily torsion, there is a hint of contrapposto in the position of the feet which also carries over
into the legs. The figure's right leg is rigid; his
left bends slightly at the knee. Save for the burst of
folds beside the figure's right hip, the drapery and its
hems are fairly calm. Moreover, the drapery responds
quite convincingly, sagging downward slightly in concentric
ridges on the chest and hanging vertically below the
waist. However the knees reveal the same tendency toward

isolation and stylization found in the other figures,
the vertical folds are rigidly parallel, and, although it
is masked by the humeral veil and the figure's right arm,
the same conventional ox-bow of folds can be found at
the waist.

WM1-s/1: Angel (fig. 41)

Like the pendant figure opposite, this angel is
calmly posed and positioned frontally. He bends his
left arm across his waist to grasp the incense boat
once probably connected to the censer which sways gently
from his right arm beside the knee.[100] The movement implicit in the curving cords of the censer must originally
have found a dramatic echo in the sweep of fold which
once articulated the drapery beside and behind the figure's
right arm. Because the fold has been broken the figure
appears more calmly disposed than must originally have
been the case.

In general the drapery is arranged quietly. The
hemlines undulate rhythmically but not wildly and the
direction of the folds generally follows their weight.
This is particularly evident across the chest where the
individual folds curve irregularly and unevenly downward.
In contrast areas of the body, such as the left thigh and
knee, are isolated with enframing loops of folds.

WM1-s/2:   Angel (fig. 42)

Alone in the archivolt, this angel stands frontally with his legs crossed and wears a mantle with an un- decorated border. Both arms bend slightly at the elbows and extend across the waist thereby continuing the line of the legs and animating the figure. The head of the angel also turns inward slightly, in keeping with the direction of the movement given by the legs. In his right hand, the figure holds an incense boat in front of the abdomen, while a censer swings outward on the end of a cord held in his left.

The folds are thick, and appear almost modelled but they do not reveal the body beneath them. Instead their tubular regularity masks it, as happens on the thighs, or they unnaturalistically isolate an area of anatomy, as happens on the chest.

WM1-s/3:   Angel (fig. 43)

This angel stands frontally with his right arm bent at the elbow to grasp a large candle and his left arm bent and extended across the chest. The palm of the left hand is raised as if to shield the candle.

The drapery, which largely masks the body, consists of looping rhythmic patterns such as those created by mantle and sleeves over the arms which contrast with sharper, more angular patterns such as can be found on the outer mantle along the right side. The tendency to render the leg pressing through drapery finds itself offset by the insistence on isolation of anatomical areas like the knee or the hip.

The spherically formed head is probably the least satisfying qualitatively. The forehead is extremely low (more so even than n/3) and the nose accordingly enlarged. The result is a head of curious proportions and appearance. There is, however, no reason in the handling of the rest of the figure to separate it from the group.

WM1-s/4: Angel (fig. 44)

Like figure n/3, this angel strides inward toward the tympanum. Both arms bend slightly at the elbow. The figure's right holds a spherical object once evidently attached to the censer which swings upside down in front of his right wing. His left hand is broken off at the wrist.[101]

In spite of the movement of the figure's pose, the handling of the drapery remains relatively calm and approaches a naturalistic arrangement. The vast majority of fold lines run vertically with few sharp angles or rhythmic loops. The figure's raised right leg pushes through the drapery of the undergarment, obliterating fold lines as it does so. Visible folds in this area hang from the point of the knee or along the inside of the thigh. Accordingly, the tendency to isolate anatomical areas is held to a minimum, for example, his left knee

and the pit of his right elbow. The articulation of the
hip area, however, adheres to a conventionalized horizontal fold.

The head of the figure is essentially spherical
and noteworthy only in the inorganic handling of the
mouth. The lips, which seem to project, are tucked up
at the corners to produce a kind of "archaic smile."
Only this angel possesses this feature.

WM1-s/5: Angel (fig. 45)

This angel stand frontally with his feet splayed
outward toward the sides. He raises both arms, bending
them forward at the elbows to present, like the pendant
angel n/5, a humerale veil. Here, however, the cloth
is much longer; it passes around the neck and hangs
from both hands to the knees.

Incised, linear folds dominate the handling of the
drapery of this angel more so than any other. Composed
of close, parallel striations which run largely in a
vertical direction, there is almost no indication of underlying anatomical structure. There is also little of
the sense of movement produced in other figures by looping folds of garment. Such folds, where they do exist
as in the space between the arms, and the sharp angular
folds along the figure's left side are simply outweighed
by the plethora of vertical incisions. Thus, in spite of
the linear handling of the drapery, this angel yields

the most static impression of any figure in the archivolt.

WM1-keystone: Agnus-Dei (fig. 40)

The Lamb of God has been placed laterally on the block with its cross-nimbed head to the right. The head twists around over the back in the direction of the cross-staffed penon balanced behind the animal on the hoof of the upraised near foreleg. The snout of the Lamb has broken off but otherwise the sculpture remains in an excellent state of preservation.

Little attention has been given to the Lamb's anatomical structure. There are thickenings above the legs which correspond to haunch and shoulder, but the thin parallel strips of diamond patterned incisions (a convention for the wool) serve to effectively mask any concern for anatomy. The eye which is set in a shallow depression on the skull is almond in shape, enframed by doubly incised lids and echoed by a gently curved brow.

ARCHIVOLTS II AND III (WM2 & WM3): (fig. 22)

The middle and outermost archivolts must be described together because of the distribution of their iconographic elements (see text fig. 16, p. 440). These two archivolts contain two separate narrative cycles: The bottom four voussoirs contain three scenes of an abbreviated Nativity cycle; the remaining voussoirs, including the

Text Figure 16.
Schematic Showing the Order of Description of Archivolts WM2 and WM3
and the Physical Relationships Between Iconographically Related Voussoirs

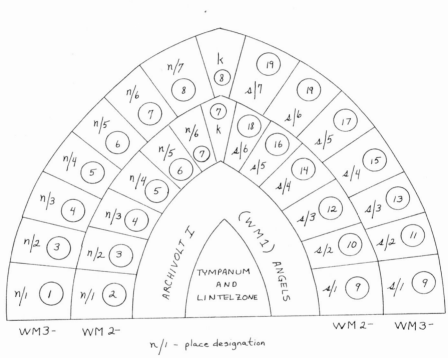

n/1 - place designation

(1) - order of description and
iconographic relationship

keystones, appear to contain images which derive from the vita of the priory's patron, Saint Loup. This latter cycle can be shown to divide into two groups: one, narrative scenes which spread across two or more adjacent voussoirs (Because of their relatively equal size and the different radii of the two archivolts, "iconographically adjacent" voussoirs become less and less physically adjacent as they mount toward the apex of the arch.) and two, isolated, individual images which relate as a group to episodes of the vita in a different, more symbolic way. However, of the seventeen scenes and individual figures, only seven can be said to be certainly identified, with two more being probable but not certain; four can be plausibly linked to the vita and four remain thoroughly unidentified.[102]

In spite of the iconographic variety, the figures in these voussoirs share many elements in common. They exhibit little concern for anatomical structure. Most figures are short-waisted, flat-chested and have an additively handled hip area. In some cases, limbs are exaggerated in the service of meaning. The drapery is linear and largely formed by blunted incisions. Usually relatively calm, the folds mask the body rather than reveal it; where the body breaks through, for example, at a forearm or a thigh, the drapery tends to become more overtly decorative. Although there is a range of facial types, almond-shaped, doubly-incised eyes, which are set additively upon often swollen cheeks beneath symmetrically arching brows, dominate the faces. In contrast, the area of the small, prominent chins and the mouths is always more organically handled.

There are also differences between the two iconographic groups. The Nativity Cycle scenes distinguish themselves from the other voussoirs in the scale, the degree of plasticity and, to a lesser extent, the more static poses of their figures. Moreover, the Nativity voussoirs are too large for the emplacements which they now occupy. In contrast the Saint Loup voussoirs--with the exception of one, and possibly both keystones--fit in their emplacements with no evidence of manipulation or adjustment. These circumstances and their implications are discussed in Chapter III, pp. 112-113.

WM3-n/1: The Annunciation (fig. 46)

An angel, with his wings held upward to the right against the ground, stands at the left of this scene and once gestured with his right hand which, like his head, is now broken off, toward the female figure enthroned[103] beside him. The female figure who is seated with her back to the angel responds to him by turning her head slightly in his direction and by raising both hands (her right has broken off at the wrist), palm outward, against her chest in a conventionalized gesture of surprise. Both of these figures have weathered badly. Additional breakage occurs in the garment hems of each figure and to the nose, lips, eyebrows and the right side of the skull of the female.

The angel wears two garments: a loose-sleeved ankle-length tunic and mantle which is draped over his left shoulder and held across his right hip by his left hand which acts as a foil to his gesturing right arm.

The figure is anatomically awkward as the area at the hips reveals. The curving contour along especially the left side gives an impression of greater naturalism than the figure actually possesses. The drapery is essentially linear in handling although it must once have been sharper than it now appears. In spite of the linearism, however, the arrangement is calm: the hemline undulates gently at the ankles and the decorated borders fold back upon themselves. Here and there segments of anatomy are isolated by loops of cloth, for example, the right forearm.

The seated female wears three or perhaps four garments. One undergarment is visible only at the tight-fitting sleeves of the wrist. A long, loose-sleeved undergarment with a decorated band down the center of the torso is visible above the waist and at the ankles. An outer mantle appears to be draped over the shoulders (?) and pulled across the legs. The female's head is covered with an elaborate veil[104] which apparently also forms the collar and hangs down the back. However, the absence of any clear distinction between these garments (for example, at the waist) makes an absolute assessment of costume difficult.

The female "sits" awkwardly on her throne with the legs spread slightly and the thighs foreshortened in the extreme. The arms, of which her right is remarkably short from shoulder to elbow, are nowhere free of the chest; in fact, the forearms appear to protrude from the rib-cage.

As in the adjacent figure, the linearity of the drapery must once have been more pronounced. In general the folds follow the lines of the body but they do not reveal it except in isolated areas like the left knee which are stylized by concentric rings of folds.

The scene represents the Archangel Gabriel announcing the birth of Christ to the seated figure of Mary.[105]

WM2-n/1: The Visitation (fig. 47)

Two stained and weathered female figures stand in three-quarter profile with their outer arms lifted to embrace: the left figure to the shoulder, the right figure to the waist. The women are identically dressed. Each wears a long veil with a decorated border and an ankle-length dress which appears to be separated at the waist. Except for parts of the sleeves and hands of the raised outer arms which are broken, these figures are well-preserved.

The two figures are remarkably calm given the narrative moment. This stasis results not only from the symmetrical composition but also from the handling of the drapery which, in both figures, hangs from the waist in regularly spaced parallel incisions arranged on a near perfect vertical. The hems are calm and hardly undercut at all. The faint undulation in drapery surface below the waist (visible only from the side) corresponds to but cannot be said to reveal the legs underneath. The heads of the figures are both spheroid in form. Characterized by swollen, boneless cheeks, broad, flat brows and a heavy curving jaw, the two faces are indistinguishable.

These figures represent Mary and Elizabeth at the Visitation.[106] Without their presumed original layer of paint, there is no longer any way to distinguish between them.[107]

WM2-n/2 and WM3-n/2: Saint Loup outwitting a devil (fig. 48, 49)

On the left (WM3-n/2) a nimbed male figure lies on his back on a pallet. He wears a shirt of indeterminate type and a bull-horned mitre,[108] while his body is covered from the waist to his bare toes by a bedsheet. Both arms are extended to his left: his right extends across his body with the damaged hand held in a gesture of blessing;[109] his left is raised to display a pillow beside his head. The gesturing arms, the slight turn of the head and even the bedsheet, the folds of which flow toward the right, all lead to the adjacent voussoir (WM2-n/2) where a bearded figure who is dressed in an ankle-length, flowing garment girt at the waist,[110] kneels in a conventionalized pose and holds up a large two-handled vase with the demon's head protruding from its top. The figure is positioned in three-quarter profile facing to the left so that the action is effective across the voussoirs.

In both these short-waisted, rubber-limbed figures the drapery functions to direct visual movement (for example, the bedsheet) or to animate the image (for example, the hem of the servant). Where the body occasionally pushes through the drapery (the legs of each figure, e.g.), the areas revealed are decoratively enframed by swirls of folds so that even the blank areas function with a concern for rhythm and movement.

The head of the saint is cubic with a heavy curving jaw covered by a "tetrarchan-type" beard and a short crop of hair visible below the mitre. The head of the demon appearing atop the vase has expressively distorted features: the almondine eyes are set within deep depressions beneath exaggeratedly projecting brows. The mouth opens wide to reveal a set of triangular teeth.

This scene shows Saint Loup about to trap a devil in a vase with his pillow. Partially identified by Bourquelot in 1840/41,[111] the entire scene, and the principle that the narrative extends across two archivolts, was not recognized until about fifteen years later when Aufauvre wrote the text to accompany Fichot's engraving of the portal.[112]

According to the text of the vita,[113] a devil aroused a terrific thirst in the saint during an evening vigil. When water was brought to quench Saint Loup's thirst, he perceived the devil's wiles and trapped the demon in the drinking vessel by putting his pillow tightly over it.

WM2-n/3 and WM3-n/3: Saint Loup healing a blind man (?) (figs. 50, 51)

On the left voussoir, a bearded nimbate saint sits frontally on an architectural throne. He turns his head slightly to his left and raises his right arm in front of his chest with the fingers extended and the palm held outward in gesture of greeting or communication. His left arm extends across the waist to rest on the left knee, thereby creating a counter-rhythm to the movement of the figure. The saint wears a bull-horned mitre, an alb-like undergarment and outer mantle held by a clasp at his right shoulder. This mantle spills across the lap to the right creating a movement toward the neighboring voussoir. There, a bearded, balding man in a pilgrim's costume kneels in a contorted three-quarter pose facing the saint. He raises both arms across his chest; his right hand turns palm inward while his left is upraised in response to the gesture of the saint. He wears a loose, flowing undergarment, boots and a knee-length, hooded cloak. A small satchel hangs from a strap over the left shoulder and is partially visible on the figure's right side. Beside the figure, to the right stands a long knobbed walking staff.

In each figure the drapery folds are handled in a decorative way. The sweep of fold between the legs of the saint moves upward in a curve which continues in the folds hanging on the right beside him thereby drawing attention to that side and to the neighboring voussoir. The folds of both figures tend to fall into regular patterns, for example, across the chests of both figures. Little attention has been paid to naturalistic relationships between drapery and anatomy or to anatomy alone. Instead expressive emphasis on narrative content is stressed. Thus the saint's left arm and torso are used

as a frame to emphasize his gesturing right arm, which
is made short and rubbery to allow emphasis on the hand.
Thus, also, the kneeling figure is twisted to reveal his
torso almost frontally while his legs are bent into a
nearly profile view.

This scene represents Saint Loup seated before a
kneeling pilgrim. Three explanations have been offered
for the figure in WM2-n/3. Bourquelot questioned whether
or not this "vieillard" might be "...un convertisseur
priant pour le renversement des temples paiens," an
interpretation which he based on a misreading of the
figure's staff as a column from a pagan temple.[115]
Aufauvre suggested "un viellard dans l'attitude de
l'invocation ou de la reconnaisance."[116] Recently,
Lapeyre argued that the figure "...représente vraisem-
blablement l'aveugle..." whom Saint Loup healed.[117]

Although none of the authors to whom we have
referred make reference to the text of Saint Loup's
vita, all the episodes suggested come from the same
period in the saint's career, namely, during his exile
from Sens.[118] It is during this period that Saint Loup
instructed and converted an unbelieving population, and
healed a blind man.[119] However, none of the brief,
relatively unspecific text passages can be conclusively
applied to the scene as we find it represented.

Are we to regard the staff as abandoned by a man who has just received his sight (but who reveals nothing of blindness in the handling of the eyes or in his expression), or as an attribute of class status? In support of the former, it might be pointed out that the shepherd on WM3-s/5 holds his staff. However, unless we are prepared to accept the walking staff as cast aside we have no internal evidence to associate this figure with the blind man. Thus Aufauvre's identification of the man's pose as one of "invocation or recognition" is probably the safest interpretation and one which conveys the obvious meaning of the scene even if its textual basis remains uncertain. However, reasoning by analogy from the presence of the baptism scene in the succeeding voussoir pair and the proximity of the healing and the baptism in the text Lapeyre's identification of the scene as the healing of the blind man remains entirely plausible and may well be correct.[120]

WM2-n/4 and WM3-n/4: Saint Loup baptising the pagan duke Bosonis (figs. 52, 53)

In the left voussoir we see a nimbate, bearded saint dressed in episcopal garb. He stands frontally and holds both arms in front of his torso. His right hand is raised in a gesture of blessing directed, like his gaze, toward the adjacent voussoir. His left hand holds a spherical object with a small circular base (an anointment vial?).

The saint is assisted, to his right, by a cowled monk who presents an open book in front of his chest. The adjacent voussoir bears a nude, bearded and crowned figure protruding from a barrel-like form. This figure is assisted by a second cleric, who wears a loose fitting, ankle-length garment. These two figures are presented in three-quarter view with respect to the frontal plane of the voussoir block. Thus their action is directed back toward the saint.

Compared with the relative animation of the two previous scenes, the four figures here represented are remarkably static. The drapery reflects this stasis (not the bodies beneath it). The linear folds flow uninterrupted in a predominantly vertical direction and terminate in gently undulating hems. More interesting is the handling of the nude torso of the duke. The sculptor has rendered anatomy through a system of incisions to delineate ribs, nipples and navel. The flesh exists without the underlying tectonic of a bone structure. Indeed the flesh almost sags, an impression given by direction of the incisions as much as by the absence of bone, or else it bends as it does in the rubbery, withered arms held in front of the body.

This scene represents Saint Loup officiating at the baptism of the pagan duke, Bosonis.[121] First paired together by Aufauvre,[122] the scene was not identified precisely until Lapeyre who first connected it, albeit indirectly, with the saint's vita.[123] According to the text,[124] the duke was converted to Christianity and baptised after having witnessed the saint's power in restoring sight to a blind man.

WM2-n/5 and WM3-n/5: Saint Loup miraculously opening the doors of Saint-Aignan d'Orléans by prayer (figs. 54, 55)

On the left we see a nimbate, beardless saint, hands clasped in prayer, represented in a conventionalized kneeling pose. The saint is dressed in an alb-like undergarment visible at the lower legs, a hooded mantle, bull-horned mitre and boots. Positioned in three-quarter profile facing to the right, the saint's pose and gesture lead the eye toward the adjacent voussoir which contains a synecdochal image of a church façade with its wooden doors partially opened. The façade consists of a large arch framed by colonnettes which in turn support two small towers between which is a small projecting gable. The entire architecture rests on a series of steps.

This image corresponds to the more animated, expressive imagery of the initial vita scenes. In fact the entire organization of the pose is built around oppositional relationships: the shape and direction of the legs are echoed in the drapery gatherings just above them; at a different angle, the hands also relate to this formal device; the swirl of foldless drapery which represents

buttock is reprised by the similar form on the left forearm. The agitated hem-line of the alb also contributes to
the resultant sense of animation.

This voussoir pair represents an episode in which
Saint Loup's prayers caused the doors of Saint-Aignan
d'Orléans to open miraculously. Partially understood by
Bourquelot in 1840/41,[125] the voussoirs were first related
and correctly identified by Aufauvre.[126]

According to the text of the vita,[127] one night the
saint found the doors of the church locked by the guardian,
making it impossible to enter. Saint Loup prostrated himself in prayer before the doors which miraculously opened.
We can consider the steps beneath the façade to represent
the threshold (limini) mentioned in the text.

WM2-n/6, WM3-n/6 and WM2-keystone: A Miraculous Mass (?)
(figs. 56, 57, 58)

On WM2-n/6 we see a nimbate saint, attired in somewhat misunderstood archiepiscopal costume[128] standing
behind an altar to celebrate mass. At the center of the
draped cushion which surmounts the single-arched architecture of the altar rest the base and stem fragment of
what must have been a chalice.[129] The saint raises both
hands in front of his chest, palms turned outward. Both
the thumbs and index fingers have been broken off, but
enough remains of their stubs to be able to say that each

thumb and index finger must have touched at the tips and
formed a circle. This gesture was one made by the celebrant after the host had been consecrated. Although he
stands in an essentially frontal position, the saint
"tilts" his upper body slightly to the left and turns his
head slightly to the right to gaze in the direction of two
anomalous forms suspended against the ground beside his
head. The first of these takes the shape of a hand, but
it carries no articulation apart from the fingers[130] and
is hollow at the wrist, like a glove. The second consists
of a flat, circular shape where it intersects the nimbus
and a long, tail-like appendage which extends behind the
hand/glove to the inner edge of the voussoir and which
appears to be articulated by parallel grooves that seem to
separate as they re-emerge beside the hand/glove on the
right.

On the adjacent voussoir we see two assistants to
the celebrant who stand frontally and gesture or gaze toward the saint. On the left side is a tonsured subdeacon
who extends his left arm downward to clasp his tunicelle
at the waist as he extends his right arm in front of the
deacon to point toward the saint.[131] The deacon holds a
book (Gospels?) in front of his chest with both hands and
turns his head slightly to the right to gaze toward the
saint in the neighboring voussoir.[132]

On the keystone of the second archivolt, a large right hand held in a gesture of blessing is set against a cruciform nimbus. The hand issues forth from a stylised undulant cloud mass which fills the upper right corner of the block and extends downward along the right side nearly to the bottom. The cuff of a garment is visible at the wrist. Although it can be shown that this block was designed for a different emplacement (see Chapter III, pp. 113-114) its re-use and diagonal placement clearly relate it to the scene of the mass immediately below.

Like the scene of the baptism, the iconographic moment here presented induces a stasis in the composition which is reflected in the style. With limited exception, such as the sweep of folds at the subdeacon's hip, the folds and hems are carved calmly in either verticals or long, gradual curves for the former or gently, rhythmically repeated undulations for the latter. Little attention is given to the isolating swirls which animate other figures,[133] or to revealing anatomical structure beneath the drapery.[134]

Since Aufauvre, it has been traditional to identify this scene as the mass of the miraculous stone which is (also) represented on the trumeau capital.[135] Not until Lapeyre did the two assistants on the outer voussoir become specifically associated with the scene of the mass shown on the inner one.[136] The keystone has never been associated with the scene as its diagonality requires it to be.

Entirely apart from the question of iconographic duplication, it will become clear that there are problems in
the accepted identification of the scene relative to the
mass of the miraculous stone described in the vita.[137]

The hand/glove on the background of WM2-n/6 has always been interpreted, when discussed at all, to be a
Manus dei representing the divine origin of the miraculous
stone which is, of course, the central element of the
episode which this scene is thought to represent.[138] Only
one author has discussed the other form: Lapeyre believes
that it represents the stone as it descends toward the
chalice.[139] These two forms are clearly both central to
the interpretation of the scene and problematic within
themselves.

It has already been remarked that the diagonal placement of the Manus dei keystone visually relates it to the
mass scene where the saint officiates. If the hand/glove
form on the latter is to be read as a Manus dei also, then
the motif is needlessly and alarmingly duplicated. Considering that the blessing gesture and the cloud motif are
integral parts of Manus dei iconography,[140] it is virtually
impossible that the hand/glove form to the right of Saint
Loup's head is also a Manus dei. Thus in all likelihood
this mass scene in which Saint Loup (?) officiates does
not represent the episode of the mass of the miraculous
stone at least not in any known version. Regrettably, no

other episode from the saint's vita can be suggested
as the source for this scene, which must for now remain
"de-identified".[141]

WM3-n/7 and WM3-keystone: Saint Loup on an equestrian
journey listening to a heavenly choir (figs. 59, 60)

On the voussoir we see a nimbate saint astride a now
headless horse. The form of the voussoir block has resulted in the compositional exigency of having the saint
lean forward over the horse's neck. The saint's costume
is difficult to discern because of the pose. He appears
to wear a tight-sleeved, loose-fitting undergarment and an
outer mantle which is clasped at the shoulder. On the
keystone above appear two bustate angels who symmetrically
clasp the cloaks which cover their tunics with their inner
hands and, simultaneously, display an unfurled banderole
in front of their waists with their outer ones. A stylised
undulant cloud band enframes the angels at the sides and
the bottom of the block. The keystone has been damaged
in several places and repaired once. The face of the angel
on the left, his right hand and part of the banderole
have been broken. The right wing of the same angel, which
once stood free of the ground in front of the left wing--
cf. the angel on the right--has also been broken and now
remains only as a "strut" projecting off his right shoulder.
Given the size and shape of the three surviving wings, it

is not clear whether this wing could have been carved
within the present limits of the block. The undulating
cloud band, which tapers gradually to its terminus beside
the angel on the right, has been broken and an asymmetrical filler inserted on the lower left edge of the block.
Possibly this repair was related to the breakage of the
wing. It is not clear from the evidence whether the keystone was carved, like the voussoir, for this emplacement
or for another. This problem is discussed in Chapter III,
p. 114.

Given the composition of the scene it is rather
more difficult to discuss matters of style. The drapery
can hardly relate naturalistically to a body already distorted for compositional reasons. The saint and the angels
again appear short-waisted and drapery folds continue to
be realized with blunted incisions although the treatment
of the folds is somewhat coarser and more schematic in
the angels. The anatomy of the horse reveals a greater
concern for individuation--in the tautened muscles of the
legs and neck, for example. The scene was first correctly
identified by Grésy in general study on the iconography of
Saint Loup.[142] According to the text of the vita, which
Grésy cites, Saint Loup was journeying on horseback when
he "...orationem dominicam ab angelis decantari audit."[143]

WM2-s/1 and WM3-s/1: The Magi before Herod (figs. 61, 62)

On the left block, two figures stand in three-quarter profile looking toward the adjacent block. The figure to the left is today headless and both his hands have broken off at the wrists which are held in front of his torso. The figure to the right is crowned, bearded, and holds the remains of a walking staff between his hands which are also extended in front of his body. Both figures wear a loose-fitting, tight-sleeved undergarment girt at the waist which is masked by a mantle draped over one shoulder and arm to hang in front of each figure. In spite of the damage and weathering to these figures, we can conclude, given their nearly identical poses and attire, that both originally wore crowns and held a chest-high walking stick in front.[144] On the right voussoir, a third, identically posed, crowned and bearded figure stands beside a fourth crowned and bearded figure who sits cross-legged on a small bench-type throne. Both hands of the third king are also broken off at the wrists. Thus, we cannot be certain whether he, too, held a walking stick or whether he gestured toward the seated figure.[145] The fourth king sits frontally and does not acknowledge the standing figure to whom he is equal in height. His right arm is broken at the wrist and his left damaged about the hand. Traces of a cylindrical form in that hand and a knob of stone on his left shoulder indicate the figure once held a scepter.

These two kings are garbed identically to the others.[146]
All four stand on convex consoles like the figures of the
Nativity scenes on the opposite end of the same archivolts.

All three standing kings, short-waisted and "hipless"
as we would expect, reveal a contrapposto arrangement in
their feet. There is, however, no corresponding contrapposto in the legs or torso. Thus their out-turned left
feet probably conventionalize movement toward the seated
figure. This latter is more animated than are the three
standing kings, largely because of the movement given by
the crossed position of his legs, which is echoed by that
of his arms.

The general abrasion and chipping of the surface of
the stone makes an appreciation of the carving difficult.
The blunted incisions as they now appear are softened, almost modelled. However, the better preserved folds across
the torso of the second standing king reveal a sharp upper
edge which indicates an originally harsher, more linear
handling. The drapery is generally calm and the arrangement vertical whenever possible, for example, in the undergarments of the Magi. The paired folds of the mantles
curve downward gradually. Here and there an area of anatomy
is revealed by stylized swirls of fold as happens on the
left legs of the figures on the left voussoir and as
probably once happened at the knees of the seated figure.
With the exception of the seated figure, hemlines undulate

rhythmically or fold back upon themselves. In the former, the thin, slightly flaring trumpets of fold begin to project sideways of their own accord. Before the weathering, a greater sense of movement must also have been obvious in the loops of the outer mantle as it falls across the waist. But even this (limited) animation occurs within the context of a general stasis, both in pose and in overall handling of the drapery. In contrast to the heavy curving line of the jaw which is typical in these two archivolts the jaw structure of the three surviving heads tends to curve further downward and forward more sharply. This scene represents the three Magi before Herod.[147]

WM2-s/2: A Man pinioned inside a bell (fig. 63)

We see a man in a kneeling position pinioned inside a bell. His head protrudes from the top of the bell while his hands rest on his thighs. The man's costume is evidently secular: He wears leggings articulated by numerous parallel blunted incisions and boots. His face shows no expressive distortion or exaggerated emotion. Indeed, the face displays the same balance of symmetrically arranged, idealized features and more naturalistic ones seen throughout the portal. Immediately above his head one sees the top of the bell (apparently separated to allow for the man's head) suspended from a three-cusped, architectural form which presumably represents the tower in which the bell hangs. Prominently displayed against the background to the left of the man is the bell-rope.

In 1840/41, Bourquelot outlined the known possible interpretations for this scene.[148] The three episodes include: one in which Saint Loup saved Sens from invasion by ringing the cathedral bell to strike fear in the men of Clotaire's army and cause them to flee;[149] one in which Saint Loup miraculously silenced the cathedral bell when Clotaire had it sent to Paris so that he might hear its sweet sounds (The king returned it when he discovered the miracle; naturally, it regained its former sound.);[150] one in which Saint Loup removed licentious thoughts from the minds of two clerics by praying for their souls and by touching the cathedral bell.[151] Bourquelot himself did not choose between the episodes, although he seems to have expressed a preference for the second by discussing it alone in the text.[152]

Since Bourquelot scholars have either adopted his preference[153] or, more recently, have followed a more cautious route, saying that no episode in the text corresponds precisely to the image represented in the voussoir.[154] In fact, a case could probably be made for all three episodes, or for the ambiguity as a result of combining all three miracles into one image; each episode recounts men being controlled through the miraculous medium of a bell. Of course, the possibility exists that the episode which this voussoir represents has been lost to us.

WM3-s/2: A Musician (?) (fig. 64)

This voussoir contains a single male figure, dressed
in secular garb. With his left arm, he holds aloft a
slightly damaged stringed instrument toward which he turns
his head and his body.[155] His right arm extends downward
to the waist where the hand clasps an unidentified cylindrical object.[156] A pouch (?) of some sort is suspended
at his waist. The man wears two garments: a loose
fitting, ankle-length undergarment which has tight sleeves
and is girt at the waist, and a huge cloak which hangs
across the torso and over his left arm. It is clasped
at the figure's right shoulder and stands out beside the
figure on the left. The bearded man is bareheaded and
has long flowing hair.

Although the figure "turns" in space, his body has
not been formed with a naturalism attendant to the movement. The supporting leg presses through the calm vertical incisions of the undergarment on the left simply as
a long, thin cylinder. His right arm is withered while
the proportions of his left, which are equally awkward,
are masked within the drapery. The drapery itself is
not active. It is arranged in concentric loops across
the chest or hangs vertically save for the sweep of
parallel folds on the ground below the instrument.

No plausible interpretation of this figure has ever been offered. With one exception,[157] scholars have been content to follow Bourquelot and describe him as a man holding a violin.[158] The text of Saint Loup's vita appears to offer no episode with which this figure can be linked.

WM2-s/3: A woman inside a church (fig. 65)

This voussoir shows a single female figure who kneels in a conventionalized three-quarter pose in front of a draped architectural form and beneath an architectural baldachino. The woman is veiled, barefoot and wears an ankle-length gown with a decorated collar that extends down the front. Her left arm has broken off at the elbow, but enough remains to state that it once held the now-broken end of a small sack or purse which she also grasps with her right hand. The form before which she kneels consists of a small arch at the base surmounted by a large rectangular block covered with a cloth.[159] The arch of the balachine, which pilasters support, bears three distinct architectural forms: two two-story towers flank a triple-arcuated, gabled structure at the center.

The pose and the stiff curving folds about the ankles give this figure a certain animation. The rendering of the drapery over the legs as undulating parallel lines and the curious, tightly undulant band of fold which articulates the waist produces an abstract effect. Typically, the knees, shoulders and breasts become articulated by the isolating drapery surrounding them.

This figure has never been linked with an episode from the vita of the saint, nor has an identification of the personage represented ever been ventured. Those who describe the figure usually follow Aufauvre's description: "Une femme à genoux devant un temple; elle offre une bourse."[160] We can, with reasonable certainty, say that the figure kneels <u>within</u> the building and that the building is a church.[161]

A possible interpretation of the scene can be offered on the basis of one of a series of miracles wrought by the saint at his tomb. According to the vita a woman named Vetula suffered in pain without food or sleep for a week from a terrible toothache. When she went to the tomb of the saint and mixed dust from it with sputum and applied that to the spot, she was healed. The text further states that whoever goes to the tomb and venerates the saint there in faith, as Vetula did, shall also receive medicine from the dust.[162] While the woman neither rubs dust from a tomb nor applies dust to a sore tooth, we do see an act of veneration before an object which may represent the saint's tomb. Clearly this interpretation cannot be considered certain, but, by reason of analogy, it takes strength from the context of the imagery on this half of the archivolts.

WM3-s/3:   A female (ecclesiastic?) with her hands
clasped in prayer (fig. 66)

This voussoir contains a single female who stands
turned slightly to the right with her hands pressed together
in front of her breast in an attitude of prayer. She apparently wears two garments: An undergarment appears, covered with crinkle folds, only at the wrists; an outer dress
(?) with a collar and incredibly wide sleeves covers her
body from neck to ankles.[163] The same, curious spiral fold
seen on the previous figure appears to girt the waist. A
long veil, which lies flat over the shoulder, covers the
head and flutters out beside the figure on the right. Her
feet appear to be covered with slippers of some sort.

Although the figure's feet are differentiated (the
right is turned out) and the legs press through the skirt,
there is no organic approach to anatomy. The figure stands
short-waisted, short-armed and hipless. The legs press
through simply as isolated ovals of fold and at least the
right knee is treated as a circular abstraction. Except
for the fluttering veil on the right side, the drapery hangs
almost entirely vertically to terminate in gently undulating
hems.

At first glance the low-browed head appears to have
a rectangular shape and to be among the more awkwardly
handled heads in the portal. However, closer scrutiny reveals that the left cheek and jaw have broken away. Orig-

inally the head must have been much rounder.

Bourquelot described the figure accurately, if briefly.[164] The figure has never been associated with an episode from the saint's vita; however, a possible interpretation can be offered based on another of the sequence of miracles effected by the saint after his death. According to the text of the vita a woman who had been without sight for thirty years visited the saint('s tomb) in faith (or, more correctly from a position of faith) and was healed.[165] The prayerful or supplicating gesture of the female on this voussoir suggests that this figure may refer to the episode described. This interpretation must be qualified by the fact that nothing in the figure indicates blindness, or the immediate loss of it.[166]

WM2-s/4: Saint Loup (?) (fig. 67)

This voussoir contains an image of a nimbate bishop who stands frontally but who turns his mitred head to the right. Precise episcopal costume has not been followed in this figure. He wears a long, loose undergarment (alb?), a chasuble and slippers. No dalmatic, maniple, stole or amice appear to be present.[167] Both arms extend across the waist (his right above his left) to grasp the stem of a crozier of which the curled upper end is still visible against the ground to the left of the saint's head.[168]

Apart from the turning head, the figure impresses

with its stasis. Largely this impression results from
the regularly parallel vertical and 'v'-shaped folds which
predominate. Although the undergarment is arranged to indicate the placement of the legs, the drapery successfully
conceals anatomy, save for the stylised fold in the pit of
the right elbow. Only the mitre lappet which flares out
to the left of the figure reveals any sense of agitation.

The face bears the short, stylised incisions across
the jaw which create the tetrarchan-type beard. the essentially rectangular head contains features which are formulaic at Saint Loup; exceptionally, the forehead is furrowed.

Since Bourquelot, this figure has been traditionally
identified as Saint Loup.[169] Given the dedication of the
church and the identifiable figures and scenes elsewhere
in the portal, that is probably correct. However, given
the absence of internal criteria (e.g. full archiepiscopal
costume) it is perhaps necessary to include a note of
caution.[170]

Compared to the voussoirs on the left side of the
archivolts where an image of the saint repeats once within
each changing narrative context, the presence of a single
image of the saint without any obvious "adjacent" narrative
context raises questions about how the voussoirs on the
right relate to one another.

The independent nature of each voussoir on the right,[171]
their compositional isolation one from another, strongly

suggests that these images do not function in the same way as do those on the left side and that the figure, if indeed it is Saint Loup, may in fact be applicable, in a different, more general way, to all of the images on this side of the two archivolts.

WM3/s-4: A male figure seated in contemplation before an altar (fig. 68)

This voussoir carries a figure of a layman seated in three-quarter profile before a draped altar.[172] He rests his head in his left hand and extends his right to grasp the slightly splayed cylindrical shaft of a now destroyed object which rests on the left knee.[173] Bareheaded and barefoot the man wears two garments: a loose-fitting, tight-sleeved undergarment extends to the ankles; a cloak drapes over the left arm and masks the torso. It is clasped at the right shoulder. The altar closely resembles the one on the voussoir diagonally below it (WM2-s/3) save that it has a base. The chair or throne is articulated with a large arch at the bottom and two tiers of rectangular openings.

Although the back relates at nearly a ninety-degree angle to the upper legs; the juncture with the hip remains awkward. In several places the body presses through the drapery, as it does at the knees and at his left shoulder. However, the body is "revealed," is rendered as an isolated area rather than organically understood anatomy.

This figure has never been identified nor has it ever been related to an episode of Saint Loup's vita. Without the attribute of contemplation, it appears impossible to go beyond Bourquelot's original description.[174]

WM2-s/5: A woman lying on a pallet (fig. 69)

This voussoir shows a long-haired female figure lying, with her knees drawn up, on a pallet or bed. The figure lies with her legs pushed over into a profile position. Her head, resting on the small pillow, lolls to the right also. Her right arm bends at a right angle across the waist; her left, bent slightly, rests on her left thigh. The position of the arms suggests something was once held between the hands; however, both hands are balled into fists and, on close inspection, can be seen never to have held anything. Short-waisted and small in the arms, the woman wears a single ankle-length garment which has a decorated collar and is bound at the waist by the same, curious spiral fold seen in several other female figures.

As with other figures presented in an animated pose, there is little concern for anatomical correctness here. The placement of the arms and legs creates a series of sharp angles which contrasts with the looping rhythms of the fold patterns on the pallet. In spite of the impression of an "all-over" carving, the handling of the drapery, including the hems, remains calm. Visual movement comes through the plentitude of folds rather than through agitation.

Without any suggested textual basis, Bourquelot hypothesized that this figure represented someone who was sick and was kneeling to implore the saint's aid.[175] Aufauvre corrected his predecessor on the matter of the pose but kept the same iconographic purpose.[176] Since these two early writers, those scholars who deal with this figure merely describe her pose.[177] The vita of Saint Loup does, however, describe an episode which can be tentatively related to the figure in question. Yet a third of the miracles worked at the tomb of the saint involves a woman paralyzed from birth who is brought "ad locum sepulchri" where, upon inspection, it is discovered that her "neglected limbs" have begun to revivify.[178]

It may be an overinterpretation to suggest that the sprawling pose of the woman and her curiously balled fists are intended to represent a paralytic, but it is useful to recollect that the paralytic healed by Christ according to Gospel narrative is presented on a bed.[179] If this interpretation of the image is correct, then the paralytic also relates to the image of the saint immediately beneath it.

WM3-s/5: A shepherd leading a ram (fig. 70)

This voussoir bears two figures. A shepherd stands in the center of the block. He extends his right arm outward at a ninety-degree angle to grasp a long crozier or staff[180] and rests his left hand on the head of a ram which appears out of the ground beside him on the right.

Although the feet are differentiated and the head turns inward slightly, the body of the shepherd is presented frontally. He is clothed in boots, a mid-calf-length, tight-sleeved undergarment girt at the waist and a hooded outer mantle clasped at his right shoulder. The hood, which covers his left shoulder and upper arm, and the mantle essentially mask any articulation of the body. A differentiation in drapery folds in the undergarment indicates rather than reveals his right leg. His right arm relates so additively to the torso that it can almost be read as appearing from the back. The drapery is rendered calmly in keeping with the static pose.

Undulant tufts of fur are arranged over the chest and back of the ram which show no other articulation. The head has the same almondine eye forms as the human figures and the spiralled horns of a ram.

The identification of this figure as a shepherd poses no problem.[181] However, the reason for its inclusion in the cycle has never been explained. It is likely that the image is based on a play on words for which the inspiration lies in the vita itself. During the period of Saint Loup's exile from Sens, the vita speaks of the people of Sens falling victim to the jaws of wolves in the absence of their shepherd.[182] Thus we can understand Saint Loup, or wolf, as a patron saint of shepherds and their flocks.[183] The inclusion of a shepherd and a ram in the archivolts thus probably represents this group of individuals over whom the saint watches, rather than any narrative episode for which no text today survives.

WM2-s/6: A woman holding up a book (fig. 72)

This female figure stands frontally with her head turned slightly to the right. She raises her left arm sharply upward to display a thick square object identified by Bourquelot as a book.[184] Her right arm, which is broken off at mid-fore-arm, once extended downward in front of her waist to gather up her skirt in which she carries (at least) two large, rounded objects said by Aufauvre to be bread.[185]

The woman wears a close-fitting undergarment visible at the neck, wrists and below the knees and an incredibly wide-sleeved outer dress with a decorated collar. She is bareheaded and wears her hair in long braids, one of which is visible against the background to her right. Little attention has been given to articulating the anatomy except in a stylized way, as is clear in the handling of the breasts. The sweeping loops of the narrow oval cuffs of the outergarment and the repetition of the 'v'-shaped folds create an animation which finds an echo in the gathered skirt and which contrasts with both the static pose and the calmer vertical or horizontal arrangement of the rest of the drapery. Her head is curiously proportioned: the forehead is exceptionally low.

This figure has never been identified nor has it been linked to the legend of Saint Loup. No episode or personnage from the vita suggests a correspondence to the image.

WM3-s/6 and s/7: A hanging (figs. 71, 73)

The last scene spreads across the two remaining voussoirs in the third archivolt. On the lower voussoir two bearded, short-haired laymen stand side by side. The figure on the left is blindfolded and has his hands bound behind his back. A hangman's noose passes around his neck. The figure beside him extends his left arm in front of his body to grasp the prisoner by the arm. His right arm extends behind the figure to grasp the rope just above the knot. The rope itself continues onto the upper voussoir where a third layman, this one with distorted facial features, grasps it in his left hand. The pose of this figure is also expressively distorted and from the point of view of all other voussoirs, he is upside-down. A stylised vegetal form passes with the hangman's rope, behind the figure to appear again at his feet. The rope itself is intertwined with the figure.

The three figures are identically dressed. They each wear what appears to be a single tight-sleeved, mid-calf-length alb-like garment. The figure on the upper block alone wears a belt and only the left figure on the lower block is barefoot.

Little attention is given to anatomical structure, particularly in the expressively twisted pose of the upper figure. Even in the leg area of the other two figures, where the thighs press through as long tubes articulated with occasional incisions and flank a thin, flaring trumpet of folds which indicates the void between them, one cannot speak of true anatomical concern or interest. The faces of the two standing figures fall within the formulaic approach seen in other figures. The features of the upper figure fall within these limits also, save that the lips have been thickened and the mouth opened, tongue extended, to reveal a large set of triangular teeth.

We may with reasonable caution interpret the scene: it represents a hanging; the hangman is, quite literally, in a tree (stylised vegetal form) above the victim. The only problem remains in the identification of the figure beside the victim. The facts that his features are <u>not</u> distorted and that he grasps the rope suggest that he aids or comforts the victim. The fact that the features of the hangman are distorted suggests that he, not the prisoner, is the villain here. Whether the problematic figure accompanies the victim (as a comforter) or whether he <u>saves</u> the victim cannot, unfortunately, be determined from the image.

Described accurately by Bourquelot,[186] the scene was first linked to the vita of Saint Loup by Aufauvre,[187] who saw in it the release of prisoners miraculously effected by the saint as he passed through Paris.[188] On the basis of the vita as we know it, this remains the most plausible interpretation; however, it is not without its problems. The text speaks of incarcerated prisoners whose chains are broken, of doors opening and of their release.[189] Only a generous interpretation of the hanging scene can relate it to this episode. More over, we can scarcely interpret the halo-less layman beside the victim as the saint effecting his release.

It may be that there once existed a different episode about the release of a prisoner or condemned man for which the text is now lost and to which this scene corresponded directly. It may also be that on the basis of the episode which does survive, Saint Loup was regarded as a patron of prisoners/condemned men and that this scene--like the figure of the shepherd below--represents only a general reference to that fact.

APPENDIX C

FOOTNOTES

1. Right and left refer to the viewer's right and left except when modified by a possessive, e.g. the figure's right hand.

2. There is one parallel, the smaller Maiestas tympanum from Saint Bénigne now in the Musee archéologique in Dijon. There the opening is rectangular, as are the openings on the forward face of the footstool. Although the actual form of the footstool at Saint-Loup most closely parallels those at Le Mans and Chartres, this idiosyncratic detail appears to lend credence to the arguments for a "Burgundian connection" for Saint-Loup. The question is discussed at length in Chapter V. See also, pp. 389-390.

3. Other traces of pigmentation can be seen on the ground of the mandorla, on the footstool, on the upper edge of the throne and, here and there on the drapery itself.

4. This splay relates the figure more closely to the shape of the enframing mandorla. The throne sides parallel the angle of the lower legs.

5. This foreshortening of the head may serve an iconographic function since it emphasizes the austerity and frontality of the Godhead.

6. This breakage is in addition to the apparent truncation of the upper wing which is discussed in

Chapter III, pp. 76-79.

7. The placement of the legs and their scroll as well as the head indicate that a three-quarter pose was intended. But the right wing is "bent" back to parallel the forward plane of the body thereby reflecting a conceptual awareness of the block similar to the other figures described thus far.

8. The forward wing is free of the ground except for a thick stone strut at the tip near the mandorla. The rearward wing is carved in relief and is visible just above the tip of the forward one.

9. In view of the fact that there is no evidence of sculptural restoration in the nineteenth century (See Appendix A) and that the tail appears complete in early images of the portal (figs. 110, 111), the repair may well have occurred in the medieval period.

10. As in the winged lion, a thick, cylindrical stone strut supports the near wing which is otherwise completely free of the ground. The rearward wing is again in relief and nearly invisible from in front of the image.

11. Bourquelot, 1840/1841, p. 252, first recognized the figure as the Virgin enthroned.

12. The textual basis for this attribute lies in the Protoevangelium of James. It appears elsewhere among Virgins annunciate (e.g., in the scene on the lower lintel of the southern portal of Chartres West) and among Virgins of the Visitation (e.g., the adjacent at Chartres West). However, in neither the scene of the Annunciation nor the scene

of the Visitation at Saint-Loup does the Virgin hold a skein
of wool (cf. figs. 46, 47).

13. Aubert, 1929, p. 35, first noticed the form which
he called "a great glory." Lapeyre, 1960, p. 132, repeated
Aubert's identification of the form ("une gloire"). Neither
noticed that the form is not a mandorla proper.

14. I am indebted to Professor Jan van der Meulen for
this suggestion.

15. Comparison between photographs taken earlier in
the century and the present condition makes clear that most
of the surface abrasion is very recent. Considering Saint-
Loup's rural location, the deterioration of the sculpture
is alarming.

16. On the repositioning of this head relative to the
figure's emplacement below the tympanum, see Chapter III,
pp. 80-82.

17. The blank area across the abdomen resulted from
the presence of the skein of wool. The spur to which it was
attached is still visible.

18. Aufauvre and Fichot, 1854-1858, p. 141, first
identified these figures as apostles.

19. Aufauvre and Fichot, 1854-1858, p. 141. The
identification is repeated uncritically by Lefevre-Pontalis
[(?) see Roblot-Delondre, 1913, p. 122)] in Le Clert,
Lefevre-Pontalis and Ditsch, 1903, p. 84.

20. Salet, 1933, p. 158, "... Saint Jean, imberbe,
paraît rêver, le menton dans la main et le conde appuyé sur

le genou relevé par l'inclinaison du tabouret où posent
ses pieds."

21. Isolation of Saint John within the college of
apostles also occurs in the "Crosby relief," where the
other eleven each communicate in groups of two or three.
See Crosby, 1972, p. 50 and the frontispiece. On the
other hand, at Saint-Loup, n/1 is as isolated as is Saint
John.

22. L. Réau, III, pt. 2 p. 711f and M. Lechner,
"Johannes der Evangelist", L.C.I., 7, cols. 111-112.
Cf. n. 21.

23. When coupled with the other iconographic factors
listed above, the faint "goatee" of the Saint-Loup Saint
John would not appear to override the identification.

24. On the apostle lintels of the central portal of
Chartres West and the southern lateral portal of Le Mans
Cathedral as well as on the apostle bas-relief from Saint-
Denis, one figure only (Saint John) is beardless. On the
southern lateral portal lintel of Bourges Cathedral,
several apostles are beardless; none is mustachioed.
Admittedly, evidence has been lost from Angers, Saint-Ayoul
in Provins, Ivry-la-Bataille and even Étampes. Some
reservation should therefore be maintained.

25. See Chapter V.

26. R. Adams, "The Virtues and Vices at Aulnay Re-
examined," in The Twelfth Century, Acta, II, Binghamton,
1975, pp. 53-73, esp. pp. 63-65.

27.   The present trumeau in the Saint-Anne portal is a copy.   The original, today preserved in the north tower of the cathedral, was itself restored by Romagnesi in 1818 (See Sauerländer, 1972, pp.405-406, ill. 26) but surely still reflects its medieval arrangement if not its medieval detail. Given the proliferation of frankish patron saints, these two images must reflect a monumental tradition of a scope far larger than one can now imagine.   See also n.31 below.

28.   On ecclesiastical costume in the Middle Ages, see J. Braun, Die Liturgische Gewandung im Occident und Orient, Freiburg-im-Breisgau, 1907.   A useful handbook for the English terms is, H. Norris, Church Vestments, their origin and development, London, 1949.

29.   The mitre, which is damaged in the front, origi- nally had the points (or horns) placed in the front and at the back.   "Bull-horned" mitres, that is, mitres with the horns on the sides, occur on the second, third and fifth voussoirs of the left side of the outer archivolt (cf. figs. 48, 50, 54).

30.   As indicated above the body is disposed in a frontal fashion.   Movement is manifested only in the arms and head.   With the right shoulder destroyed it is impossible to say whether or not there was even a slight contrapposto arrangement reflecting such motion as is given.   The rigid frontality of the lower body and feet strongly suggests the contrary.

31.   There are, of course, few preserved twelfth-century trumeaux with which to compare the figure at Saint-Loup. But, it appears exceptional that the priory's sculpted figure

extends as far as it does beyond the rectangular limits of the pilaster block behind it. Enough remains at Notre-Dame-en-Vaux, at Corbie, at Paris (Portail-Sainte-Anne), as well as in the later trumeaux at Sens, Meaux and Chartres, to suggest that the Saint-Loup-de-Naud figure stands somewhat apart.

The so-called trumeau from the nearby Saint-Thibault-de-Provins, now in the Grange-aux-Dîmes in Provins, may reflect a parallel to Saint-Loup. It is however so badly damaged that one cannot be certain as to what type of architectural member it was attached. At the head and neck area parts of a column are still extant. Whether these are part of a half-column attached to a pilaster as at Saint-Loup or part of the full cylindrical shaft of a column figure simply cannot be resolved. The old drawings are also not conclusive. (Maillé, 1939, pp. 191 and 198-199). If the trumeau in the engraving of the portal at Vermenton represents a twelfth-century sculpture and not a later interposition, this would constitute another, related example. The Plancher engraving of Saint-Bénigne makes clear that the trumeau as we see it there is not in a strictly twelfth-century (?) context and thus hard to judge.

32. Precisely what meaning with respect to the antique world such "tetrarchan" forms may have had is not at all clear. Whether it is a now meaningless formal tradition, or part of a specific or general medieval renascence--itself a dubious commodity for many art historians (see, for example

W. Sauerländer, 1970, p. 32)--remains to be thoroughly investigated. The type is certainly not restricted to Saint-Loup-
de-Naud. Other examples include the bishop of the Sainte-
Anne portal tympanum in Paris (see n. 27 above) and the head
(so-called) of Ogier the Dane from Meaux.

33. Bourquelot, 1840/41, p. 251, first correctly
identified the holy archbishop using costume and the dedication of the priory as criteria.

34. The drilling on the neck of the creature on the
right side may have been part of an intention to distinguish
them.

35. Distinctions between various stylised animals is
difficult, if not impossible except when the creatures are
accompanied by a recognizable iconographic context or an
identifying text--e.g., bestiaries. Even in the bestiaries
the form of any given creature may vary from manuscript to
manuscript. On the asp and dragon (and on the bestiaries in
general) see F. McCullogh, Medieval Latin and French Bestiaries, rev. ed., Chapel Hill, 1962 (UNC Studies in the Romance
Languages and Literatures, 33), pp. 88-91, 112-113 and pls.
I and III. See also n. 34.

36. Bourquelot, 1840/41, p. 251, qualified by noting
the serpents' tails; Salet, 1933, p. 162; Lefevre-Pontalis,
1902, p. 84, curiously, "deux colombes".

37. Aufauvre and Fichot, 1854-1858, p. 141, followed
by most subsequent authors.

38. Lapeyre, 1960, 137 and n. 6.

39. The likelihood of an intended evil symbolism
finds confirmation in the probability that the crozier
held by the saint extended to the head of the creature on
the left. There are ample parallels for such a placement--
the Saint Marcel trumeau in Paris being the most obvious
example (cf. n. 27 above).

40. Grésy, 1867, p. 70, quoted part of the psalm
passage and called the beasts "...l'emblème des victoires
remportées sur le paganisme..." and "...le personification
du démon..."

41. Traces of a painted nimbus appear to exist
behind the saint's head on the right.

42. The pallium, insignia of archiepiscopal rank,
has not been represented. It is not clear whether the
stole is independently articulated. The top and front of
the mitre are damaged.

43. The figure may represent a deacon who also
assists at mass. The alb, regalia of subdeacons,is a full
length, loose-fitting, tight-sleeved garment; that of dea-
cons is the dalmatic. This latter is a mid-calf, loose-
sleeved garment which is usually richly embroidered. (Dea-
cons also retain the alb beneath the dalmatic.) While the
garment worn by the kneeling figure here conforms to the
alb, in the area of the right arm there appear to be two
sleeves, one tight-fitting and the other loose and embroidered. See also fig. 57 (WM3-n/6) where subdeacon
and deacon are represented side by side in
the representation of a similar scene.   See also

n.28 above.

44.   See n.43 above. The figure wears an undergarment which corresponds to an alb, but the outer garment which appears to be draped over the shoulders and arms, gathered at the waist and to hang down over the thighs, clearly is not a deacon's dalmatic. The figure does, however, bear a book (the Gospels?) as a deacon would. See fig. 57 (WM3-n/6).

45.   Over the chest and arms, the figure appears to wear a priest's chasuble. However, the garment does not hang down the center where it should end in a loop as does the chasuble worn by the saint. Instead it appears to hang almost to the ankles and is perhaps gathered up in the hand which also holds a book. Possibly the figure should simply be termed an ecclesiastic without any designation of rank.

46.   One must also point out that the "weight" of the drapery and the restrained gestures and movement, particularly in the upper bodies of all but the kneeling figure, give at least a certain appearance of naturalistic concern, even if, on close inspection, the conception is ultimately additive.

47.   The kneeling figure has weathered rather more than the others so that it is harder to tell in which "direction" his folds originally lay.

48.   Weathering may have softened the contours somewhat, but probably not enough to mislead.

49.   Bourquelot, 1840/41, p.251, first correctly

identified the scene, quoting from the text of the vita found in Acta Sanctorum, 1 September, p. 262. It is doubtful whether this same miracle is repeated in the archivolts of the portal (WM3-n/6, WM2-n/6 and keystone). See below, pp. 455-457.

50. The perfectly smooth, regular shape of the stone precludes the possibility of its being a damaged Manus dei, an iconographic alternative.

51. A glance at any of the apostle lintels of the "Early Gothic" portals (e.g., at Saint-Loup itself, apostle s/2--significantly the only figure with an open book) indicates the meaning of the gesture and the context confirms the extension of the meaning. Pointing to books or scrolls, or other attributes held, does not seem to have received detailed study. See O. Holl, "Handgebarden," LCI, II (1970), cols. 214-217.

52. Perhaps the figure is to be understood as the author of the vita.

53. Salet, 1933, p. 163, states that the feet of these column figures "...reposent presque à plat sur des consoles...". This interpretation of the figures' poses is encouraged by the damage to the toes of several figures. Enough remains, however, to conclude that the feet curved over the edges of the consoles. One should rather say, with Aubert, 1929, p.16, that the figures' feet are "...posés d'oblique sur une terrasse inclinée...". As seemingly unimportant as these observations may appear, it must be borne

in mind that the relative "naturalism," or the lack of it, in details such as these take on great weight in the insistent struggle among absolute chronologists over 'vers 1160' or 'vers 1170.'

54. A.Katzenellenbogen, The Sculptural Programs of Chartres Cathedral, New York, 1964 (1st ed., 1959), pp. 27-36, considers the possibility of a double layer of meaning for figures such as these. Recently, J. van der Meulen, "Chartres: Die Weltschöpfung in historischer Sicht," Francia. Band 5 (1978), n. 15 has called for a reconsideration of this question.

55. These lines are analogous to the handling of individual folds. They are neither strictly incised nor strictly modelled. Similar lines exist beside the nose on the left as stylizations of sagging flesh.

56. Comparison of this head to that of 3-n--to which it is very close--suggests that the nose would have been straight and quite prominent.

57. Bourquelot, 1840/41, p. 252 first recognized the figure as Saint Paul, while Fleury, 1902 (1903) pp. 482 and 485, stressed the bald head, the bare feet and the book as criteria. Aufauvre and Fichot, 1854-58, p.142, first cited the book as an attribute, which Aubert, 1929, p. 16, went so far as to identify as a book of Acts. Salet, 1933, p. 163, called it a book of Epistles. The costume provides another criterion, as does the obvious pairing of the figure with Saint Peter opposite in the right embrasure (see below, p. 415).

58. A rather more random curvilinear rhythm is established in the drapery of the cloak and the undulating braid of hair, especially on the left side (compare the same area on figure 1-n). The rotulus may well have echoed this curving pattern.

59. The crown is a circlet type which once had three fleurons: on the front and both sides at the back. Traces of all three remain. Identical in essentials to that worn by the male figure 2-s opposite, the crown is decorated with an alternating pattern of elliptical and diamond-shaped gems.

60. It is impossible to tell for sure what effect, if any, weathering may have had in blunting a sharper, more linear distinction at the brow.

61. Admittedly there are suggestions of cheekbones, but the lack of any articulation in the flesh, either below the eye or in the cheek itself, mitigates the naturalistic effect their appearance would otherwise have.

62. See n. 54 above.

63. First suggested by Aufauvre (and Fichot) 1854-58, p. 142, although he included Bathsheba as an alternative. Lefevre-Pontalis, (1902) 1903, p. 84, limited the identity to Sheba. Bourquelot and several others, including Sauerländer, most recently, offer no identification at all.

64. See Chapter IV, pp. 171, 173.

65. This type of headgear, which consists of a narrow fillet at the base and "pleats" which cover the top and run from front to back, is common enough among the Early Gothic

"Old Testament" column-figures. Examples of it found on sculptures conclusively identifiable as Moses by the tablets which the figures hold [Chartres West, north portal, col. fig. 2-s (the only one remaining in this embrasure); Bourges, south portal, col. fig. 3-s] would at first seem to suggest an Old Testament context for all figures wearing mitres of similar form. However, one clear exception refutes this interpretation: the "jewish-mitred" trumeau image of Saint Bénigne from Dijon which is known to us from Plancher's engraving which corresponds to the surviving head now in the city archeological museum. This enigma may perhaps be explained by the (former) presence in the left embrasure at Dijon of a figure which like the trumeau saint, also wears priestly garb and the jewish mitre. Pendant to a horned Moses bearing tablets in the opposite embrasure, this figure is probably correctly identified as Aaron (see Sauerländer, 1972, pp.389-390). The similarity in costume and mitres between Aaron and Saint Bénigne, together with the presence of Moses strongly suggests that part of the theme of the destroyed Dijon portal dealt with the concept of continuity between the Old Testament priesthood and the New, particularly in the position of Christian bishops. The tympanum figures of Ecclesia and Synogoga also would have formed part of this theme. On this concept and the mitre in general, see R. Mellinkoff, <u>The Horned Moses in Medieval Art and Thought</u>, Berkeley, 1970, pp.94-106.

66. The position of the figure's right arm might be

taken to indicate that his right hand once held some object like a staff. This possibility appears to be increased by the presence of what seems (in photographs) to be the fragment of a connecting strut on his right shoulder. However, on-site inspection reveals this "node" to be simply a stain or discoloration on the surface of the stone. Since the position of the arm requires that the figure held something in that hand, the mostly probable conclusion is that the rotulus once curved up to it.

67. The sculptor at first appears to have confused tunic and mantle at the waist. The clarifying fold, however, is simply hidden behind his left hand when viewed from the front.

68. Aufauvre and Fichot, 1854-1858, p. 142. Presumably following Aufauvre, A. Heimann, "Jeremias," L.C.I., II, cols. 387-392, lists Saint-Loup-de-Naud among the monuments which possess an image of Jeremiah.

69. See Chapter IV, pp. 173-174.

70. Bourquelot, 1840/41, p. 251, recognized the key and stressed the "petite barbe". He also described "un double nimbe autour de la tête", evidently in reference to the concentric incisions which form the rim of the figure's nimbus.

71. In fact the only interruption at all is the upper end of the rotulus.

72. See Chapter III, n. 23 and Chapter V, n. 18.

73. In contrast the knee area is articulated, but

through emphasis of an abstract swirled incision which bears no relationship to bone structure.

74. As on the queen's crown, two other fleurons once existed at the point of intersection between crown and nimbus. Parts of these also still exist.

75. Since Aufauvre (and Fichot), 1854-58, p. 142.

76. For example, Lefevre-Pontalis, 1903, p. 84; Salet, 1933, p. 164f and Lapeyre, p. 137, n. 3.

77. See Chapter IV, pp. 171, 173.

78. See the discussion under state of preservation concerning the Le Secq photograph of 1851 and the Fichot engraving, probably of 1855, in Appendix A.

79. Before the damage to the hem of his right sleeve, that side was probably more deeply undercut than the corresponding sleeve of Saint Peter. It is, however, more thoroughly decorative in its 'S'-shaped-curving swirl. Neither sleeve is as deeply undercut as that of the corresponding arm of the trumeau figure. It should also be mentioned that while the peripheral hems of the figure undulate gently, they, too, are little undercut and compare closely to the other column-figures.

80. They are, however, so abraded that only a close on-site inspection revealed their original form.

81. The left eyebrow is less weathered and rather more sharply handled than the other side or any of the other figures. It may be closer in form of the original state than any of the column-figures.

82. Aufauvre (and Fichot), 1854-1858, p. 142.
Lefevre-Pontalis, 1903, p. 84, followed the earlier hypothesis uncritically. Apparently unaware of the rotulus
fragments visible in early images of the portal, Aubert,
1929, p. 37, argued that the position of the hands (which
is very similar to the position of the hands of the figure of Saint Paul) indicated that the lost attribute was
a tablet and that the figure represented Moses. The evidence given by the early images (see Appendix A, p.
287 and n. 18) precludes this possibility. Salet, 1933,
p. 166, seems to have sensed the problem when he wrote
that the figure was "...peut-être Moise, portant sans
doute un phylactere...". However, Salet also seems unaware of the early images, because he further states that
"...la droite semblait benir."

83. This impression of coarseness must be qualified by recognizing that the damage to the mouth area and
the absence due to weathering of linear incisions around
the eyes--neither of these conditions is original.

84. See Chapter IV. pp. 173-174.

85. The configuration of the base with its
"double torus" at the top is not uncommon. The same form
appears at Chartres West, at Étampes and at Provins,
Saint-Ayoul. It may also have appeared at Saint-Germain-
des-Prés and Dijon, Saint-Bénigne.

86. The beast on the inner face of the capital
clearly has a spiralling serpent's tail. For the beast on
the outer face the tail evidently merges with the foliation.

87.   See n. 35 above.

88.   See McCullogh, 1962, pp. 113-115, and 158-160, and pls. III.5 and VII.1 respectively. The vulture (see pp. 184-186 and pl. X.2) is another possibility. Van der Meulen has rightly cautioned that stylised representations of birds over the whole of Late Antiquity and the Middle Ages all resemble each other sufficiently closely as to make it impossible to distinguish between them.

89.   The tail of the outermost creature extends beneath the inner one, echoing the rhythm of the latter's upraised foreleg. This motif also links the two sides of the capital.

90.   See McCullogh, 1962, pp. 122-123.

91.   This composition reflects the rectangular shape of the capital. See Chapter III, pp. 102-103.

92.   See D. Jalabert, "De l'art oriental antique à l'art roman, II, sirènes," Bulletin Monumental, 95 (1936), pp. 434ff and McCullogh, 1962, pp. 166-170. The siren evolved into three not always distinct forms: siren-fish, siren-bird and siren-serpent, to which category the Saint-Loup creatures would seem to belong. In discussing this capital, Mâle, 1924 (2nd ed.), p. 336 and n. 5 and subsequently, Adhémar, 1939, p. 183 identify (presumably only) the right figure as a "sirène-oiseaux." However, this identification ignores the serpent's tail which the creature clearly possesses.

93.   See nn. 35 and 92 above.

94.   F. Salet, 1933, p. 160 remarked that this pair of creatures, "curieusement," hold hands, but "curieusement," he

made no reference to the cowl or veil.

95. See D. Jalabert, "De l'art oriental antique à l'art roman: recherches sur la faune et la flore romanes, I, le sphinx," Bulletin Monumental, 94 (1935), pp. 71-104, esp. pp.102-104 on Saint-Loup. The sphinx is not a part of the bestiary vocabulary (cf. McCullogh, 1960). Mâle, 1924 (2nd ed.), p.353f associates the creatures at Saint-Loup with oriental art and insists unnecessarily on transmission through Islamic tapestries (cf J. Beckwith, "Coptic Textiles," CIBA Review, 12, no.133 (1959), pp.2-26). Van der Meulen has drawn attention to the fact that sphinxes formed part of the symbolic vocabulary of Gaul since the sixth century B.C. with the Greeks of Marsilia and that through Cisalpine Gaul, the entire range of "etruscan" creatures was known long before the Roman Empire united Gaul to the eastern Mediterranean-- a period which terminated only at some time after 600 A.D. when Gregory of Tours refers to "Syrian" being spoken on the streets of that city.

96. This figure apparently still retained its head in the nineteenth century, cf. fig. 111.

97. A careful glance at the area of the left knee, for example, reveals it to be isolated both above and below.

98. On this long, narrow vestment which is today also worn by the celebrant at the mass, see Braun, 1907, pp.228-231 and J. Braun, "Humeral Veil," Catholic Encyclopedia 7 (1910), pp.542-543.

99. The poor state of preservation, which often makes distinctions between pieces of drapery all but impossible to

see, requires that little can be said with certainty about the possibility of other humeral veils held by angels in comparable portals. None of the angels in the voussoirs at Bourges, South; Provins, Vermenton, or Le Mans appear to carry the humeral veil. Two angels at Chartres (WM1-s/5 and WS1-s/3) appear to carry the humeral veil, but these also appear to hold a disk (wafer? or astrolabe?) and censer respectively. In Plancher's engraving of Saint-Bénigne, the angel in WM1-n/7 may carry the humeral veil alone. Possibly the attribute was unique to the angels at Saint-Loup.

100. Presumably the connection would have been in metal. The completeness of the drapery, in front of which it would have passed, precludes its having been carved from the block of the figure.

101. The degree of the forearm's freedom from the torso suggests that it held an incense boat as do figures s/1 and s/2.

102. C. Maines, "A Figure of St. Thomas Becket at Chartres," Zeitschrift für Kunstgeschichte, 36 (1973), pp.163-173, establishes a more comprehensive methodology for the identification of holy personages than has been followed here. The absence of the requisite local liturgical texts, of comparable "local" image cycles and of rigorous distinctions in ecclesiastical costume in the figures in question has made the practical application of that methodology impossible. However, the vitae of the homonymic episcopal saint, Lupus of Troyes, the important archiepiscopal saint

Savinianus of Sens (whose relics the parent abbey Saint-Pierre-le-Vif possessed) and the only episcopal saint (other than Saint Loup) mentioned in a document for Saint-Loup-de-Naud (see Appendix B, Doc. X, sect. B, text), Nicolas of Bari, have each been investigated. None of these vitae contain episodes which can be related to the scenes and figures in the voussoirs of Saint-Loup-de-Naud. Some degree of caution must, however, still be maintained.

103. The sloping bench-type throne is articulated with colonnettes at the front corners and closely resembles the throne of the Virgin on the lintel.

104. If the thickened band along the base of the veil just above the brow were a crown, it would have been thicker still, more horizontally placed on the head and show evidence of break marks where fleurons once existed. Cf. the veils of the two women in the adjacent voussoir and the crown worn by the lintel Virgin (figs. 78, 138).

105. First correctly identified by Aufauvre, 1854-1858, p.142. Earlier Bourquelot, 1840/41, p.255, suggested that the scene represented a sick person imploring the intercession of Saint Loup. On Annunciation types, see D. Robb, "The Iconography of the Annunciation in the Fourteenth and Fifteenth Centuries," Art Bulletin, 18 (1936), esp. p.481f.

106. Aufauvre, 1854-1858, p.141, first correctly recognized the scene. Earlier, Bourquelot, 1840/41, p.254, thought the scene might represent an embrace between Saint Loup and one Verosia, a woman of whom he was spiritually fond.

107. A survey of comparable monumental Visitation scenes at Chartres WS, Paris WS, Le Mans, La Charité and Bourges S reveals that a crown (Chartres WS) or a nimbus (La Charité) is necessary to differentiate the two women. Later, of course, physiognomy indicates the difference, as it does, for example, at Chartres NE. For the earlier period there is no left/right preference in the placement of the figures. Neither does the embrace give any clue. At Le Mans, where Mary is crowned, Elizabeth touches the Virgin's sleeve at the level of the abdomen but not the abdomen itself as happens at Saint-Loup. Paris WS is identical to Le Mans but both figures are veiled only. At Bourges S the figure on the right points dramatically at the other's abdomen, but both heads are broken off.

108. On the bull-horned mitre, see Mellinkoff, 1970, pp.94-106.

109. The upright fingers of the blessing hand have been broken off. However, those drawn over to touch the thumb remain, so that the interpretation of the gesture cannot be questioned.

110. This is curiously formed. Knotted below the abdomen, the wide bands flow around the figure to a large flat oval piece which covers the small of the back.

111. Bourquelot, 1840/41, p.255, correctly identified the devil in the vase on the basis of a passage in the Golden Legend of James of Voragine. In the adjacent figure of Saint Loup he saw, however, "...une femme couronnée,

assise, montrant un livre ouvert...".

112. Aufauvre, and Fichot, 1854-1858, pp. 141-142, extended the episode in the Golden Legend version of the saint's life to both voussoirs. Although he nowhere articulates the idea separately, it is clear from his description of the voussoirs that Aufauvre understood the pairing. Curiously, he followed Bourquelot in calling the rectangular object with rounded corners a book. It is thicker in the center than at the edges and, surprisingly, depresses where the saint's thumb pushes on it. Lapeyre, 1960, p. 228, first correctly followed the latin and called it a pillow (plumacio).

113. Acta Santorum, 1 September, p. 262. See also, Introduction, n. 3.

114. The two outermost fingers are broken off, but they must have been held upright so that the gesture could have been one of blessing.

115. Bourquelot, 1840/41, p. 254.

116. Aufauvre and Fichot, 1854-58, p. 141.

117. Lapeyre, 1960, p. 288 and n. 4., based on J. Corblet, Hagiographie du diocèse d'Amiens, IV, Paris, 1874, p. 399 rather than on the vita directly. Mâle, 1924 (2nd ed.), p. 224 identified the crownless figure kneeling before the saint as King Clotaire; it would seem that Mâle confused this voussoir with the one above it, where a crowned figure does occur.

118. Acta Santorum, 1 September, p. 259.

119.   Ibid.   "Dumque Vir Domini ad eum pervenisset locum, frucbatur de peregrinatione solatio patriarcharum priorum exemplo, recordans sancti Joseph in Aegypto, cujus servierunt manus in cophino Gaudebat quippe in Domino sentiens se ab eo missum ad populum incredulum instruendum, ibique quemdam caecum illuminans,...".   As a result of this latter miracle, the local pagan duke was converted and baptised by the saint.   This event is represented in the next pair of voussoirs.   Perhaps the proximity (causal connection) of the two events in the text and the baptism scene in the next voussoir underlie Lapeyre's interpretation of this scene?

120.   One cannot apply narrative sequence systematically to the voussoirs on this side of the portal, so that the relationship between the two scenes in question may be only coincidental.   The vita as it survives offers no other obvious possibilities.

121.   The saint is not regaled as an archbishop, which rank he held, because the pallium has been omitted.   It--or a variation of it--is present on WM2-n/6 where the saint is also represented.   Evidently precision of ecclesiastical costume was not a consistent concern for the designers of this portal.

122.   Aufauvre and Fichot, 1854-1858, pp.141-142.

123.   Lapeyre, 1960, p.288 and n.4.

124.   Acta Santorum, 1 September, p.259.   See also n.119 above.

125.   Bourquelot, 1840/41, pp.253-254, recognized the "church" on the right voussoir, but, apparently not able to

see the left voussoir adequately, identified the figure only
as "...un personage à genoux..." (254).

126. Aufauvre and Fichot, 1854-1858, pp. 141-142.

127. Acta Sanctorum, 1 September, p. 257.

128. Given the precision of liturgical costume on
the adjacent voussoir, the confusion here is curious and perhaps reflects a model-tradition. This holy archbishop wears
an alb, dalmatic (visible at the ankles beneath the altar and
at the wrists) a simple amice and a chasuble. A maniple
hangs from the wrist on the right and he wears a mitre with
lappets and horns placed in front and behind. The costume
of rank, however, the pallium, has been confused with decoration down the center of the chasuble. The former is a
'Y'-shaped garment, decorated with crosses (as on the trumeau
figure); the latter is a simple band running from the amice
to the bottom of the chasuble. On this voussoir the two
have been fused into one so that the ornament of the pallium
occupies the position of the chasuble's decorated band.

129. Cf. the chalice on the altar represented on
the trumeau capital.

130. It becomes impossible to state, therefore,
whether the shape is that of a right hand or a left hand.

131. The figure wears two garments: an undergarment
visible at the ankles (alb) and a loose sleeved, ankle-
length outer garment (tunicelle).

132. The deacon wears full liturgical attire. The
alb is visible at the ankles and is covered by a dalmatic with

an embroidered hem and cuffs. A maniple hangs from the wrist on the right and the neck is accentuated with a large, decorated amice.

133. The only obvious instance appears on the left forearm of the subdeacon, who is, decoratively, the most active of the three figures.

134. There exists some evidence in the slight forward swelling and the grouping of folds to indicate legs within the drapery of the deacon. However, the real emphasis resides in a nearly planar, hipless conception of the anatomy.

135. Aufauvre and Fichot, 1854-1858, pp. 141-142. Bourquelot, 1840/41, pp. 251 and 253-254, who had correctly recognized the capital scene, was apparently unable to see this one clearly enough to recognize it. On the trumeau capital, see above, pp. 399-402.

136. Lapeyre, 1960, p. 288. Aufauvre (and Fichot), 1854-1858, p. 142 associated the two assistants with "...la porte Saint-Aignan, au baptême et aux sujets places vis-a-vis." Part of the reason for this interpretation, if not all of it, lies in the physical relationships of the voussoirs. See text fig. 14, p. 177. See also the discussion of archivolt composition in Grésy, 1867, p. 69. In spite of the fact that "laterally adjacent" voussoirs were paired iconographically had been recognized for about seventy-five years, Salet, 1933, p. 161, attempted to link these two figures (WM3-n/6) with the image of the saint at prayer below (WM3-n/5) and with the two figures one voussoir further down

(WM-n/4). For Salet, the upper and lower figure pairs represented licentious clerics whom Saint Loup rescued from the sinful desires through his prayers (Acta Sanctorum, 1 September, p. 262f). Salet evidently was unable to see that one of the "licentious clerics" on WM3-n/4 is the saint himself.

137. Acta Sanctorum, 1 September, p. 262. In any case, the two scenes represent different moments. On the capital, the saint approaches the altar bearing the paten of the host. Here, the gesture of the saint indicates a later moment in the mass, after the host has been consecrated.

138. Aufauvre and Fichot, 1854-1858, p. 141, first did so ("Une petite main céleste, placée au-dessus, indique l'origine de la pierre."). Lapeyre, 1960, p. 288, accepted this interpretation. Other authors who discuss the scene omit mention of this form.

139. Lapeyre, 1960, p. 288, (the voussoir represents) "...la messe dite par saint Loup tandis que la pierre précieuse descend dans le calice; la petite main céleste sculptée au-dessus révèle l'origine divine de la pierre." If this form is in fact the falling stone, it makes a sharp contrast with the far more three-dimensional, "suspended" stone on the trumeau capital.

140. (H. Jursch), "Hand Gottes," L.C.I., II, cols. 211-214 and Réau, II, 1. p. 7.

141. While hardly a satisfactory conclusion from the point of view of what the scene represents, this conclusion does eliminate the problem of duplication of icono-

graphy with the scene on the trumeau capital.

142. Grésy, 1867, p.69 and n.1.

143. Acta Sanctorum, 1 September, p.264. Both
Grésy, 1867, p.69 and Lapeyre, 1960, p.288 would have the
saint "...se penche sur sa selle (the horse) pour écouter
les voix des anges...". While it is true that one hand (his
left) of the saint rests on the horse's neck, the leaning is
as much a function of available space as it is iconographically motivated. Since the bottom edge of the block
was cut away to allow the horse's legs both to be longer and
to have a "ground" to rest on, it is clear that the designer
was aware of his problems.

144. A strut mark, which is broken off the hem of
the outer mantle between the knees of the king on the left,
confirms this interpretation.

145. The mark on the right knee may not be a support
strut for a staff. There is also a large chip missing from
the head.

146. The left sleeve of the third king hangs loosely
to reveal a tight-sleeved garment at the wrist. At no
other point on the figure are these pieces of costume clari-
fied.

147. Aufauvre (and Fichot), 1854-1858, p.141, first
correctly identified the scene. Earlier Bourquelot, 1840/41,
saw (on the left block) a bishop exhorting another (headless)
figure (p.253) and (on the right block) two "vieillards qui
semblent nimbés" (p.254).

148.   Bourquelot, 1840/41, p.253 and n.1.

149.   Acta Sanctorum, 1 September, p.259.

150.   Ibid. p.262.

151.   Ibid.

152.   Bourquelot, 1840/41, p.253 and n.1.

153.   Aufauvre and Fichot, 1854-58, p.141; Grésy, 1867, pp.67-69; Lefevre-Pontalis, 1902, pp.84-85; Mâle, 1924, p.223; Aubert, 1829, p.15; and, Droulers, 1934, p.3.

154.   Salet, 1933, p.160, "cette scène reste obscure..."; Lapeyre, 1960, p.290.

155.   This directionality serves to isolate the figure from the surrounding iconographic context.

156.   It is not clear whether the object was ever longer.

157.   The exception is Grésy, 1867, p.69, "...le musicien qui joie (sic) de la viole me parait fêter la réconciliation du roi Clotaire et de S. Loup qui occupent une division inférieure." The reconciliation to which Grésy refers must be the scene below which Aufauvre had already correctly identified as the Magi before Herod.   In any event there is no basis for Grésy's hypothesis.

158.   Bourquelot, 1840/41, p.254.

159.   The form resembles the altar on the trumeau capital; equally, it could be a draped funeral bier.

160.   Aufauvre and Fichot, 1854-1858, p.141.   Earlier Bourquelot, 1840/41, p.253, suggested that she knelt before "une porte."

161. Below equals inside, the part synecdochally substituting for the whole. The structure appears never to have had a cross surmounting one of the peaks, but the two towered, gabled center reads as a plausible shorthand for church facade.

162. Acta Sanctorum, 1 September, p. 264, "Sed cum levatus in grabato ad Sancti fuisset deportatus sepul-chrum, qui venerat ex fide, recepit medicinam depulvere."

163. A comparison with the veiled, cloaked female ecclesiastic who wears a garment with similar sleeves found to the left of God on the tympanum at Sainte-Foy in Conques (B. Rupprecht, Romanische Sculptur in Frankreich, Munich, 1975, pl. 116) suggests that this figure might be a religious. However, the presence of equally long-sleeved garments on the unveiled female figure above in the inner archivolt (WM2-n/6) and on the Queen in the left embrasure (2-n) render the possibility extremely tenta-tive.

164. Bourquelot, 1840/41, p. 254.

165. Acta Sanctorum, 1 September, p. 264, "Nam quaedam mulier curriculo triginta annorum lumen perditum oculorum, dum ibidem advenisset cum fide, sana recessit cum lumine."

166. It should also be remarked that the phrase ex or cum fide is not limited to this miracle but is reprised in most. It seems a more central element in

this episode, however. Perhaps one should see in this figure a more general level of meaning: that all who come to Saint Loup <u>ex fide</u> shall find succor.

167. The doubling up of folds at the neck hardly constitutes an amice as a comparison with either WM2-n/6 or WM3-n/4 reveals.

168. No point of attachment is evident on the right side of the voussoir where the staff might have terminated.

169. Bourquelot, 1840/41, p. 253.

170. Lapeyre, 1960, p. 289, described the figure simply as "un évêque."

171. The exception is the scene on WM3-s/6 and s/7.

172. See n. 159 above.

173. Traces remain on the background to the left of the figure's head which indicate where the object attached. Aufauvre (and Fichot) 1854-1858, p. 141, thought the object was "un manuscript"--which its form precludes. He also thought the figure was a woman. Perhaps the object was a crucifix.

174. Bourquelot, 1840/41, p. 254.

175. Bourquelot, 1840/41, p. 253, "...une femme agenouillée...c'est sans doute une malade implorant les secours de Saint Loup...". Bourquelot also thought that the figure seemed to "pleurer".

176.   Aufauvre and Fichot, 1854-1858, p. 141,
"Une femme sur un lit, invoquant sa guérison."

177.   Lapeyre, 1960, p. 289. Salet, 1933, p. 160,
adheres to the incorrect description of her pose as
kneeling.

178.   Acta Sanctorum, 1 September, p. 264, "Mulier
quaedam a nativitate soluta tota paralyti, dum a parenti-
bus deferretur ad locum sepulchri...coeperunt membra
inculta vigere, gluttinum solidita restaurare."

179.   Matt. 9:2; Mark 2:3 and Luke 5:18.

180.   The crozier has broken at the top where it
probably curled free of the ground. There are also other
areas of minor breakage; the fingers of the left hand,
the hem of the cloak, the mantle at the center of the
chest.

181.   Bourquelot, 1840/41, p. 254.

182.   Acta Sanctorum, 1 September, p. 260,
"...quatenus sanctum Lupum de exilio revocaret, et ad
pristinam dignitatem remitteret, ne plebs sine pastore
lupinus saucibus deperiret.

183.   The lexica which make reference to the fact
give no sources or dates. See: Réau, 1958, III/2,
p. 286; Cahier, 1867, p. 621.

184.   Bourquelot, 1840/41, p. 253.

185.   Aufauvre and Fichot, 1854-1858, p. 141.

186. Bourquelot, 1840/41, p. 254.

187. Aufauvre and Fichot, 1854-1858, p. 141, "Des prisonniers (Saint Loup, en revenant à Paris, delivra plusieurs prisonniers)." Actually, Bourquelot had also suggested this episode as a possibility, but he clearly preferred to interpret the scene as a conversion of pagans since that was the episode he stressed with a footnote. (Bourquelot, 1840/41, p. 254, n. 4).

188. Acta Sanctorum, 1 September, p. 261-262.

189. Acta Sanctorum, 1 September, p. 262, "Cumque tunc sanctus Lupus per Parisius transiret, multa incarceratorum turba, ostiis per se apertis, fractisque vinculis..."

APPENDIX D

PRELIMINARY REMARKS CONCERNING THE
ICONOGRAPHY OF THE "INTERMEDIATE" PORTAL AT THE
PRIORY OF SAINT-LOUP-DE-NAUD

Today, amid the plethora of sculpture which fills
the western portal at Saint-Loup, it is difficult to
imagine the much more simplified "intermediate" portal
which preceded it.[1] In the embrasure zone, the richly
decorated capitals would have stood out strongly as
the only decorated element in the starkness of the
architecture (fig. 22). Presumably the archivolts
were undecorated, as they are in the lateral portals
of nearby Provins (fig. 116).[2] The tympanum, if there
was one, may have been carved, or painted, or even
bare, but of these parts of the portal we can never
hope to know anything with precision.

While little enough has been said about the
iconography of the capitals individually,[3] there are
a number of features about them which urge us to go
beyond individual iconographies and consider them as
a group.

Each of the three capitals in the right embrasure
possesses clear moralizing content (fig. 34). Capital
(1/s) contains a pair of composite creatures whose
male and female human heads are positioned sufficiently
close together to suggest physical intimacy. While the
male figure raises one cloven hoof toward his partner,
the female raises her right hand and extends the index
finger in a gesture of admonishment or discourse.
This theme is reprised on capital (3/s) where winged,

human-headed quadrupeds which clasp forelegs have the cowl and veil of a monk and a nun respectively. Between these two on the intermediate capital (2/s) another composite creature with a tonsured head raises his leg in response to an asp-like, devilish creature who touches him on the neck. As a group these capitals make reference to temptation and sin, to the consequences of yielding to the sensual or "bestial" side of human nature and it is interesting to note that these images refer to both communities of worshippers at Saint-Loup.[4] We know from documentary sources that the church was used by seculars as well as monks after the late tenth century,[5] and the need felt to address both audiences finds clear expression here.

In contrast, the capitals in the left embrasure contain no obvious moralizing content (fig. 33). Capital (1/n) bears antithetically paired composite beasts posed amid acanthus foliage and vines. Capital (2/n) is virtually identical save that the creatures are birds. The outermost capital (3/n) contains griffins set against a background of acanthus. Here the composition varies in that both griffins face away from the portal but they, like the four other creatures, each turn their heads to gaze upward.

It is important to note that the two groups of three are related across the portal. The four inner capitals contain bird-like creatures; the outer pair contains quadrupeds. In contrast to the up-turned gazes of the six beasts in the left embrasure, the heads of the creatures in the right embrasure hold their heads horizontally and, as a result of the curve of the capital core, appear to gaze toward the spectator below. Finally, the creatures in the left embrasure capitals possess a stricter heraldic arrangement[6] than those in the right embrasure and they are unencumbered by any anecdotal, moralizing element.

There is, of course, a paradisal connotation associated with the peaceful depiction of animals in a plant-surrounded setting which has its origins in the Genesis description of Eden[7] and its early visual formulation in Early Christian and Carolingian _fons vitae_ imagery.[8] Caution has rightly been expressed in regard to the over-interpretation of symbolic import in images such as these,[9] but even Saint Bernard, in his well-known diatribe against such imagery in cloisters, hints that such sculptures did contain a message.[10] Moreover, symbolic interpretations are common to Physiologus and bestiary texts and, we may conclude by extension, to medieval man's thinking about animals.[11]

The contrast between the peaceful, harmonious

vision of intermingled animal and plant life found in
the embrasure capitals and the explicitly moralizing
group on the right seems to indicate a symbol-laden
contrast between salvation and perdition. During the
Middle Ages positive, allegorical meanings were
assigned to at least one of the three types of beasts
represented in the left embrasure. Griffins (represented on the outermost capital) were related to the
resurrection and were understood as symbols of the two
natures of Christ.[12] It is not certain how the birds
on the second capital were intended to be interpreted,
but a positive connotation for them was certainly
possible.[13] Neither asps nor dragons (probably represented on the innermost capital) ever seem to have
been given an analogous positive interpretation, in
all likelihood because of the explicitness of the
passage in Psalm 91:13 and because of the negative
interpretation they each received in Christian exegesis of it.[14] This need not, however, affect our
contextual interpretation of the beasts at Saint-Loup.
In a later twelfth-century Beatus manuscript, now in
the John Rylands Library, Manchester,[15] the Ark of
Noah is represented with small compartments containing
more than thirty antithetically paired beasts among
which can be recognized owls, peacocks, griffins and

asps (or dragons).[16] The eschatological interpretation
given to the Noah story in the gospels of Matthew and
Luke[17] assures that, in spite of the specifically negative interpretation given to the asp (and the dragon),
a contextual interpretation in which one or the other
is seen in a positive light--the harmony of living
creatures on the ark or, in a paradisal setting--is
certainly possible. The presence of a tympanum with
some simple paradisal image like an _Agnus_ _Dei_ or a
cross, toward which the beasts in the left embrasure
could be said to turn, would confirm this. While we
cannot reconstruct the complete iconographic intention
of the "intermediate portal," we can be reasonably
certain that the remains of it seen in the capitals
represent a theme sufficiently generalized to be
incorporated easily and successfully into the present
portal program.

APPENDIX D

FOOTNOTES

1.   See Chapter III, pp. 118-119. That the
"intermediate" portal may have evolved elsewhere than
at Saint-Loup (and parts of it imported at the same
time as the other spoils) need not concern us here.
Its probable composition and meaning would be the same
regardless.

2.   The side portals of the west facade of
Saint-Ayoul in Provins each have an iconographically
analogous set of capitals in their embrasures but
neither portal appears to maintain the groupings
within each embrasure which we find at Saint-Loup (on
which, see immediately below). A similar situation
may also occur in the capitals of the lateral portal
at Notre-Dame-en-Vaux where again the state of preservation precludes certainty.

3.   See Appendix C, pp. 426-429.

4.   Jalabert, 1936, p. 456 and n. 1, suggested
a moralizing theme for capital 1/s on the basis of
the bestiary tradition in which the siren is described
as a temptress (see F. McCullogh, Medieval Latin and
French Bestiaries, rev. ed., Chapel Hill, 1962, pp.

166-169). It is unlikely that the intended theme was ever as specific as Roblot-Delondre, 1913, p. 122, would have it. She suggested that the clasped hands made "...allusion aux scandales qui eurent lieu dans les couvents et qui furent réprimés par saint Loup."

5. See Appendix B, Doc. X, esp. Section C, Comments.

6. On heraldic arrangement, see F. Klingender, Animals in Art and Thought to the End of the Middle Ages, edited by E. Antal and J. Harthan, Cambridge, Mass., 1971, p. 267.

7. Specifically, the second chapter of Genesis.

8. See P. Underwood, "The Fountain of Life in Manuscripts of Gospels," Dumbarton Oaks Papers, 5 (1950), pp. 41-138, which includes a discussion of the Early Christian period.

9. A convenient resumé of the question is provided by Klingender, 1971, pp. 328-336. See also V.-H. Debidour, Le Bestiare sculpté du Moyen Age en France, Paris, 1961, pp. 295-300.

10. Saint Bernard of Clairvaux, "Apologia ad Guillelmum Sancti-Theoderici Abbatem" in Migne, P. L., 182, cols. 914-916. Saint Bernard speaks of monks being more tempted to read in marble than in books, clearly implying the presence of something to "read"

in the sculpture. One thinks of the passage in which
Job, seeking to demonstrate the hand of God active in
all things, says "But ask now the beasts and they shall
teach thee; and the fowls of the air, and they shall
tell thee:..." (12:7). Saint Gregory the Great, in
his commentary on Job which enjoyed wide and continued
popularity in the Middle Ages, extends the meaning of
the text by seeing the beasts and birds as respectively, symbols of dullwitted men and theologians who by
their examples teach us to recognize God (Migne, P. L.
75, cols. 955-956).

11. See McCullough, 1962, pp. 78-192, passim.
To the specific interpretations quoted by McCullough
one might append the passage quoted in translation by
Debidour, op. cit., p. 279, from an unidentified early
thirteenth-century Picardan bestiary: "Toutes les
créatures que Dieu créa en terre, il les créa pour
l'homme, et pour prendre exemple en elles de foi et
de créance"--almost a paraphrase of Job 12:7!

12. L. Charbonneau-Lassay, Le Bestiare du Christ,
La mystérieuse emblématique de Jésus Christ, Bruges,
1940, pp. 368-369 and pp. 371-372 respectively.
Neither of these interpretations seem to have been
part of the bestiary tradition (cf. McCullough, 1962,
pp. 122-123).

13.   If the birds were intended to represent eagles or phoenixes, they would have been understood as symbols of Christ. See L. Charbonneau-Lassay, 1940, pp. 71-87 and 410-421 and McCullough, 1962, pp. 113-115 and 158-160, respectively. If the birds were intended to represent vultures, they could have been interpreted as figures of the Virgin. Although not discussed by McCullough, 1962, Cambridge University Library Ms. 11.4.26, edited by M. R. James for the Roxburghe Club, 1928 and published in translation by T. H. White, The Book of Beasts, New York, 1960 (1st ed., London, 1954), contains this passage (cf. White, 1960, p. 109).

14.   See Chapter IV, pp. 175-176.

15.   Ms. 8, fol. 15r. The ms. is no. 18 in the list of twenty-two Beatus mss. given by W. Neuss, The Miniatures of the Gerona Codex in the Light of other Illuminated Mss. of the Beatus Apocalypse (Urs Graf Facsimile of the Gerona Apocalypse, vol. 2), Olten, 1962, pp. 47-55. The folio is illustrated in Klingender, 1971, p. 228 (fig. 137).

16.   Surprisingly there is even a pair of seven-headed beasts which resemble the form given to the Beast of the Apocalypse.

17.   Matt. 24:37 and Luke 17:26 which both compare the "days of Noah" to the coming of the Son of Man.

SELECTED BIBLIOGRAPHY

Abbreviations of titles cited:

D.T.C.   Dictionnaire de Théologie catholique, 15 vols., ed.
         A. Vacant, E. Mangenot and E. Aman, Paris, 1930-
         1950.

L.C.I.   Lexikon der Christlichen Ikonographie, 8 vols., ed.
         E. Kirschbaum, Freiberg-im-Breisgau, 1968-1976.

N.C.E.   New Catholic Encyclopedia, 15 vols., ed. by the staff
         of the Catholic University of America, New York, 1967.

P.L.   Patrologiae cursus completus, series latina, ed. J.-P.
         Migne, Paris, 1878-1890.

Réau   L. Réau, Iconographie de l'art chrétien, 3 vols.,
         Paris, 1958.

Anonymous, "Vita sancti Lupi senonensi," Acta Sanctorum,
         1 September, pp.255-267.

Adams, R., Chartres Cathedral: The Eastern Portal of the
         North Transept Facade; An Initial Study Towards
         Defining the Original Sculptural Program of the
         Cathedral Design of 1194, unpublished disserta-
         tion, The Pennsylvania State University, 1974.

Adhémar, J., Influences antiques dans l'art du moyen âge
         français: recherches sur les sources et les
         thèmes d'inspiration (Studies of the Warburg
         Institute, 7), London, 1939.

Alp, E., Die Kapitelle des zwölften Jahrhundert im Ent-
         stehungsgebiete der Gotik, Freiburg, 1926.

Andrieu, M., Le Pontifical romain au moyen âge, tome I:
         le pontifical romain du XIIᵉ siècle, (Studi
         e Testi, 86), Vatican City, 1938.

Anfray, M., L'Architecture normande, son influence dans le
         nord de la France aux XIᵉ et XIIᵉ siècles, Paris,
         1939.

Appellof, M., Gothic Sculpture: The Iconography of the Beau Dieu, unpublished Honors thesis, Wesleyan University, 1977.

Aspinwall, W., Les écoles épiscopales monastiques de l'ancienne province ecclésiastique de Sens du VIe au XIIe siècle, Paris, 1904.

Aubert, M., French Sculpture at the Beginning of the Gothic Period, 1140-1225, Florence, 1929.

_____, La Sculpture française au moyen âge, Paris, 1946.

Aufauvre, A. and C. Fichot, Les monuments de Seine-et-Marne, Melun, 1854-1858.

Baltrusaitus, J., "Villes sur arcatures," Urbanisme et Architecture, études écrites et publiées en l'honneur de Pierre Lavedan, Paris, 1954.

Barre, H., Prieres anciennes de l'Occident à la Mere du Sauveur, Paris, 1963.

Barsch, V., The Church of St. -Trophîme, Arles: Architectural and Iconographical Problems, unpublished dissertation, Northwestern University, 1971.

Beaulieu, M., "Les anciens portails de Saint-Bénigne de Dijon," Bulletin Monumental, 115 (1957), pp.293-295.

Benoit, F., L'Occident médiéval, du romain au roman, Paris, 1934.

Berger, K., "Der traditionsgeshichtliche Ursprung der 'Traditio Legis'," Vigiliae Christianae, 27 (1973), pp.104-122.

Bloch, P., "Christus, Christusbild, III: Das Christusbild der karolingischen, ottonischen und romanischen Epoche, L.C.I. I, cols. 399-414.

Blumenkranz, B., Les auteurs chrétiens latins du moyen âge sur les Juifs et le Judaisme, La Haye and Paris, 1963.

_____, Le juif médiéval au miroir de l'art chrétien, Paris, 1966.

Bouillart, dom J., Histoire de l'abbaye royale de Saint-Germain-des-Préz, Paris, 1794.

Bournazel, E., Le gouvernement Capetien au XIIe siècle (1108-1180): structures sociales et mutations institutionnelles, Paris, 1975.

Bourquelot, F., Histoire de Provins, 2 vols., Provins, 1839-1840.

_____, "Notice historique et archéologique sur le prieuré de Saint-Loup-de-Naud," Bibliothèque de l'École des Chartres, 2 (1840/41), pp.244-271.

_____, Études sur les foires de Champagne...aux XIIe, XIIIe, et XIVe siecles (Mémoires de l'Académie des Inscriptions et des Belles-Lettres, 2nd ser., V, ptie. 1-2), Paris, n.d.

Bouvier, H., "Histoire de Saint-Pierre-le-Vif," Société des sciences historiques et naturelles de l'Yonne-Bulletin, 45 (1891), pp.5-212.

_____, Histoire de l'église et de l'ancien archdiocèse de Sens, Paris and Amiens, 1906.

Branner, R., Burgundian Gothic Architecture, London, 1960.

Braun, J., Die Liturgische Gewandung im Occident und Orient, Freiburg-im-Breisgau, 1971.

Brenk, B., Tradition und Neuerung in der christlichen Kunst des ersten Jahrtausends (Wiener Byzantinistische Studien, 3), Vienna, 1966.

Brullée, L., Histoire de l'abbaye royale de Sainte-Colombe-lez-Sens, Sens, 1852.

Cahn, W., "The Tympanum of the Portal of Saint-Anne at Notre-Dame de Paris and the Iconography of the Division of Powers in the Early Middle Ages," Journal of the Warburg and Courtauld Institutes, 32 (1969), pp.55-72.

Chartraire, E., La cathédrale de Sens, Paris, n.d. (1921).

Chenu, M.-D., Nature, Man and Society in the Twelfth Century,
        trans. from the French by J. Taylor and L.
        Little, Chicago, 1968.

Christe, Y., Les grands portails romans, études sur l'icon-
        ologie des théophanies romanes, Geneva, 1969.

_____, La vision de Matthieu, origines et développe-
        ment d'une image de la deuxième parousie,
        (Bibliothèque des Cahiers archéologiques, 10),
        Paris, 1973.

_____, "Les representations médiévales d'Apocalypse
        IV (-V) en visions de la seconde parousie:
        origines, textes et contexte," Cahiers arch-
        éologiques, 23 (1974), pp.61-72.

_____, "Apocalypse IV-VIII, 1: de Béde à Bruno de
        Segni," Mélanges E.R. Labande, Poitiers, 1974,
        pp.145-151.

_____, "Apocalypse et Traditio Legis, Römische Quartel-
        schrift für christlichen Altertumskunde und
        Kirchengeschichte, 71 (1976), pp.42-55.

Clemen, P., Die romanische monumental Malerei in den Rhein-
        lande, Dusseldorf, 1916.

Coathalem, H., "Le parallelisme entre la Sainte Vierge et
        l'église dans la tradition latine jusqu'a
        la fin du XIIe siècle," Analecta Gregoriana,
        LXXIV, Rome, 1954.

Crozet, R., "Apropos des chapiteaux de la façade occidentale
        de Chartres," Cahiers de civilisation médiévale,
        XIV (1971), pp.159ff.

Davis-Weyer, C., "Das Traditio-Legis Bild und seine Nach-
        folge, Münchener Jahrbuch für Bildende
        Kunst, 3, (1961), pp.7-45.

Debidour, V., Le Bestiare sculpté du moyen âge en France,
        Paris, 1961.

Deichmann, F., "Die Spolien in der spätantiken Architektur,"
        Bayerische Akademie der Wissenschaften,
        Sitzungberichte, 6, 1975, pp.3-101.

Delahaye, H., _Sanctus: Éssai sur le culte des saints_,
  Brussels, 1927.

Delius, W., _Geschichte der Marienverehung_, München and
  Basel, 1963.

Demus, O., _Romanesque Mural Painting_, trans. from the German
  by Mary Whitall, London, 1970.

Deschamps, P., "Les deux tympans de Saint-Bénigne de Dijon
  et de Til Châtel," _Bulletin monumental_, 81
  (1922), pp.380-386.

d'Hubert du Manoir, ed., _Maria: études sur la sainte vierge_,
  2 vols., Paris, 1952.

Droulers, C., _Saint-Loup-de-Naud_, Provins, 1934.

Duru, L.-M., _Bibliothèque historique de l'Yonne_, 2 vols.,
  Auxerre and Paris, 1850-1863.

Durwell, F., "Lamb of God," _N.C.E._, 8, pp.338-340.

Emminghaus, J., "Verkundigung an Maria," _L.C.I._, IV, cols.
  422-437.

Enlart, C., _Manuel d'archéologie française, depuis les temps
  merovingiens jusqu'à la Rénaissance, I, architecture religieuse_, 2nd ed., Paris, 1919-1924.

Evans, J., _The Romanesque Architecture of the Order of Cluny_,
  Cambridge, 1938.

Fairweather, E., ed. and trans., _A Scholastic Miscellany:
  Anselm to Ockham_, Philadelphia, 1956.

Fawtier, R., _The Capetian Kings of France, Monarchy and
  Nation_, trans. from the French by L. Butler
  and R. Adams, London, 1960.

Fleury, G., " Le portail de Saint-Ayoul de Provins et
  l'iconographie des portails du XIIe siècle,"
  Congres archéologique, 69 (1903), pp.458-488.

_____, _Études sur les portails imagés du XIIe siècle_,
  Mamers, 1904.

Focillon, H., L'art des sculpteurs romans, recherches sur l'histoire des formes, Paris, 1964 (1st ed., 1931).

Forsyth, I., The Throne of Wisdom, Wood Sculpture of the Madonna in Romanesque France, Princeton, 1972.

Fourrey, R., Sens, ville d'art et d'histoire, Lyon, 1953.

Francastel, G., Le Droit au trône, Paris, 1973.

Gall, E., Die gotische Baukunst in Frankreich und Deutschland, Teil 1, Brunswick, 2nd ed. 1955.

Gerson, P., The West Facade of St.-Denis, an Iconographic Study, unpublished dissertation, Columbia University, 1970.

Grabar, A., "The Virgin in a Mandorla of Light," Late Classical and Medieval Studies in Honor of A.M. Friend, Jr., Princeton, 1955, pp.305-311.

Graef, H., Mary: A History of Doctrine and Devotion, 2 vols., New York, 1963-1965.

Greisennegger, W., "Ecclesia," L.C.I., I, cols. 562-569.

_____, "Ecclesia und Synagogue," L.C.I., I, cols. 569-578.

Grésy, E., Iconographie de Saint Loup, empruntée principalement aux monuments de l'art local, Meaux, 1867.

Gripkey, M., The Blessed Virgin Mary as Mediatrix in the Latin and Old French Legend prior to the XIVth Century, Washington, 1938.

Grodecki, L., "La 'première sculpture gothique', Wilhelm Vöge et l'état actuel des problèmes," Bulletin monumental, 117 (1959), pp.265ff.

Guldan, E., "'Et verbum caro factum est'--Die Darstellung der Inkarnation Christi im Verkundigungsbild," Römische Quartelschrift für christliche Altertumskunde und für Kirchengeschichte, 63 (1968), pp.145-169.

_____, *Eva* und *Maria*, Cologne, 1966.

Hamann, R., "Ottonische Kapitelle im Chor der Kathedrale von Sens," *Festschrift* *für* Hans Jantzen, Berlin, 1951, pp.92-96.

Hamann-MacLean, R., "System einer typographischen Orientierung im Bauwerken," Jahrbuch des Marburger Universitätsbund, 1965, pp.1-35.

Heimann, A., "The Capital Frieze and Pilasters of the Portail Royal, Chartres," *Journal* of *the* Warburg and Courtauld Institutes, 31 (1968), pp.73ff.

_____, "Jeremias," *L.C.I.*, II, cols. 387-392.

Held, M., "Apostle: 1. in the Bible," *N.C.E.*, I, pp.679-691.

Herrad von Landsberg, *Hortus Deliciarum*, commentary and notes by A. Straub and G. Keller, ed. and trans. A. Caratzas, n.d., New Rochelle, N.Y.

Hofmann, H., *Die heiligen drei Könige*, zur Heiligenverehung im kirchlichen, gesellschaftlichen und politischen Leben des Mittelalters, Bonn, 1975.

Holl, O., "Handgebärden." *L.C.I.*, II, cols. 214-217.

Hollander, H., "Isaiah," *L.C.I.*, II, cols. 354-359.

Hubert, J., *L'art pré-roman*, Paris, 1974 (1st ed. 1938).

_____, "Les 'cathédrales doubles' de la Gaule," *Genava*, 11, n.s. (1963), pp.105-125.

Jalabert, D., "Recherches sur la faune et la flore romanes, II, les sirènes, *Bulletin* monumental, 95 (1936), pp.433-471.

James, M., *The Apocryphal New Testament*, Oxford, 1960 (1st ed., 1924).

Jullian, R., "Évolution des thèmes iconographiques: le couronnement de la Vierge," *Le siècle* de Saint Louis, Paris, 1970, pp.153-160.

Julliot, G., Chronique de l'abbaye de Saint-Pierre-le-Vif...
        redigée vers la fin du XIIIe siècle par Geof-
        froy de Courlon, Sens, 1876.

Julliot G. and M. Prou, Geoffroy de Courlon, le livre des
        reliques de l'abbaye de Saint-Pierre-
        le-Vif-de-Sens, publié avec plusieurs
        appendices, Sens, 1887.

(Jursch, H.) "Hand Gottes," L.C.I., II, cols. 211-214.

Katzenellenbogen, A., The Sculptural Programs of Chartres
        Cathedral, Baltimore, 1959.

_____, "Iconographic Novelties and Transforma-
        tions in the Sculpture of French Church
        Facades, ca. 1160-1190," Studies in
        Western Art, Princeton, 1963, Vol.1,
        pp.103ff.

Kauffman, C., A Survey of Manuscripts Illuminated in the
        British Isles, III, Romanesque Manuscripts,
        1066-1190, London and Boston, 1975.

Kehrer, H., Die heiligen drei Könige in Literatur und Kunst,
        Leipzig, 1909.

Kelly, C., "Agnus Dei," N.C.E., I, pp. 209-210.

Kerber, B., Burgund und die Entwicklung der französischen
        Kathedralskulptur in zwölften Jahrhundert,
        Recklinghausen, 1966.

_____, "Salomo," L.C.I., IV, cols. 15-24.

Klingender, F., Animals in Art and Thought to the End of the
        Middle Ages, ed. E. Antal and J. Harthan,
        Cambridge, Mass., 1971.

Kunze, H., Das Fassadenproblem der französischen Früh- und
        Hochgotik, Leipzig, 1912.

Lapeyre, A., Des façades occidentales de Saint-Denis et
        Chartres aux portails de Laon, Paris, 1960.

de Lasteyrie, R., Études sur la sculpture française au
        moyen âge, (Monuments Piot, 8), Paris, 1902.

——————————, L'Architecture religieuse en France à l'époque romane, 2nd ed., Paris, 1929.

Laurentin, R., Maria, Ecclesia, Sacerdotium, éssai sur le développement d'une idée religieuse, Paris, 1953.

Lawerence, M., "Maria Regina," Art Bulletin, 7 (1924/25), pp.150-161.

Lefevre, L.-E., Le portail royal d'Étampes (portail méridional de l'église Notre-Dame), XIIᵉ siècle, 2nd ed., Paris, 1908.

Lefevre-Pontalis, E., "Église de Saint-Loup-de-Naud," Congrès archéologique, 94 (1903), pp.82-85.

Lechner, M., "Johannes der Evangelist," L.C.I., VII, cols. 108-130.

Leroy, G., "Une visite à Saint-Loup-de-Naud," Bulletin de la Société archéologique de Seine-et-Marne, 1867, pp.125-128.

Levi d'Ancona, M., The Iconography of the Immaculate Conception in the Middle Ages and Early Renaissance, (CAA Monographs, 7), New York, 1957.

Livius, T., The Blessed Virgin in the Fathers of the First Six Centuries, London, 1893.

de Lubac, H., Exégèse médiévale, 2 vols., Aubier, 1959-1963.

de Maillé, M., Provins, les monuments religieux, 2 vols., Paris, 1939.

Mâle, E., L'art religieux du XIIᵉ siècle en France, étude sur les origines de l'iconographie du moyen âge, Paris, 2nd ed., rev. et cor., 1924.

Maudit, F.-J., Histoire d'Ivry-la-Bataille et l'abbaye de Notre-Dame d'Ivry, ed. anon., Evreux, 1899.

Mayeux, A., "Les grands portails du XIIᵉ siècle et les bénédictines de Tiron, Revue Mabillon, 1906, pp.97-122.

_____, "Essai de classification méthodique des grands portails sculptés du XIIᵉ siècle, Bulletin de la Société nationales des Antiquaires de France, 1924, pp.291-296.

McCullogh, F., Medieval Latin and French Bestiaries, Chapel Hill, rev. ed., 1962.

Meer, F. van der, Maiestas Domini: Théophanies de l'Apocalypse dans l'art chrétien, Paris and Rome, 1938.

_____, "Maiestas Domini," L.C.I., III, cols. 136-142.

Melinkoff, R., The Horned Moses in Medieval Art and Thought (California Studies in the History of Art, 14), Berkeley, 1970.

Messerer, W., "Mandorla," L.C.I., III, cols. 147-149.

Meulen, J.van der, "A Logos Creator at Chartres and its Copy," Journal of the Warburg and Courtauld Institutes, 29 (1966), pp.82-100.

_____, "Recent Literature on the Chronology of Chartres Cathedral," Art Bulletin, 49 (1967), pp.152-172.

_____, "Schöpfer, Schöpfung," L.C.I., IV (1972), cols. 99-123.

_____, Über die Kathedrale von Chartres, a pirate edition of three articles published by the Société Archéologique d'Eure-et-Loir, Chartres, 1974.

_____, Notre-Dame de Chartres: die vorromanische Ostanlage, Berlin, 1975 (I).

_____, "Sculpture and Its Architectural Context at Chartres around 1200," The Year 1200: a Symposium, New York, 1975 (II).

_____, "Die Abteikirche von Saint-Denis und die Entwicklung der Frühgotik," Kunstchronik, 30, no. 2 (1977), pp.60-61.

_____, "Chartres: Die Weltschöpfung in his-
          torischer Sicht," Francia, V (1978),
          pp.81-126.

Mielke, U., "Konigin von Saba," L.C.I., IV, cols. 1-3.

Muller, A., Ecclesia-Maria, Die Einheit Marias und der
          Kirche (Paradosis: Beiträge zur Geschichte
          der altchristlichen Literatur und Theologie,
          V), Freiburg, 1951.

Musset, L., Normandie romane, la Haute-Normandie (la nuit
          des temps, 41), La Pierre-Qui-Vire, 1974.

Myslivec, J., "Apostel," L.C.I., I, cols. 150-173.

New-Smith, A., Twelfth-Century Sculpture at the Cathedral
          of Bourges, unpublished dissertation, Boston
          University, 1975.

Nilgen, U., "Evangelistensymbole." Reallexikon zur deutschen
          Kunstgeschichte, fasc. 64-65, Stuttgart, 1970,
          cols. 517-572.

Oakeshott, W., The Mosaics of Rome, Greenwich, Ct., 1967.

Porée, C., "Les architects et la construction de la cathédrale
          de Sens," Congrès archéologique, 74 (1907),
          pp.559-598.

Pressouyre, L., "Quelques vestiges sculptés de l'abbaye de
          Nesle-la-Reposte," Bulletin de la Société
          nationale des Antiquaires de France, 1967,
          pp.104-111.

_____, "Un Tombeau d'abbé provenant du cloître de
          Nesle-la-Reposte," Bulletin monumental,
          125 (1967), pp.7-20.

_____, "Une tête du Louvre prétendue dyonisienne,"
          Bulletin de la Société nationale des
          Antiquaires de France, 1967, pp.242-250.

_____, "Réflexions sur la sculpture du XIIe siècle
          en Champagne," Gesta, IX/2 (1970), pp.16-32.

Quantin, M., Cartulaire générale de l'Yonne, 2 vols. Auxerre,
          1854-1860.

Quarré, P., "La sculpture des anciens portails de Saint-
      Bénigne de Dijon," Gazette des Beaux-Arts,
      1957, pp.177-194.

Rademacher, F., Die Regina Angelorum in der Kunst des
      frühen Mittelalters, Dusseldorf, 1972.

Robb, D., "The Iconography of the Annunciation in the Four-
      teenth and Fifteenth Centuries," Art Bulletin,
      18 (1936), pp.480-526.

Roblot-Delondre, L., "Saint-Loup-de-Naud," Monuments Piot,
      21 (1913), pp.111-144.

_____, "Notes sur l'église de Saint-Loup-de-
      Naud," Revue archéologique, 1929,
      pp.58-63.

Rosenbaum, E., "Dialog," Reallexikon zur Deutschen Kunst-
      geschichte, III, Stuttgart, 1954, cols. 1400-
      1408.

Rupprecht, B., Romanische Skulptur in Frankreich, München,
      1975.

Salet, F., "Saint-Loup-de-Naud," Bulletin monumental, 92
      (1933), pp.129-169.

_____, "Voulton," Bulletin monumental, 102 (1944),
      pp.91-115.

_____, "Un chapiteau venant de Saint-Pierre-le-Vif de
      Sens," Bulletin de la Société Nationale des
      Antiquaires de France, 1960, pp.143-146.

_____, "La cathédrale de Sens et sa place dans l'architec-
      ture médiévale," Comptes rendus de l'Académie des
      Inscriptions et Belles-Lettres, 1955, pp.182-187.

Sauer, J., Symbolik des Kirchengebäudes, Freiburg, 2nd ed.,
      1924.

Sauerländer, W., Von Sens bis Strasbourg, Berlin, 1966.

_____, "Sculpture on Early Gothic Churches: the
      State of Research and Open Questions,"
      Gesta, IX/2 (1970), pp.32-43.

_____, Gothic Sculpture in France, 1140-1270, trans. from the German by J. Sondheimer, New York, 1972 (orig. ed. 1970).

Saxl, F., "Frühes Christentum und spätes Heidentum in ihren Kunstlerischen Ausdrucksformen I: Der Dialog als Thema der Christlichen Kunst," Wiener Jahrbuch für Kunstgeschichte, n.s., II (1923), pp.64-77.

Scaccia Scarafoni, E., "Il mosaico absidale di S. Clemente in Roma," Bolletino d'Arte, 29, 1935, pp.44-68.

Schapiro, M., Selected Papers on Romanesque Art, New York, 1977.

Scher, S.K., The Renaissance of the Twelfth Century, Providence, R.I., 1969.

Schlink, W., Zwischen Cluny und Clairvaux, die Kathedrale von Langres und die burgundische Architektur des 12 Jahrhundert, Berlin, 1970.

Schmitz, P., Histoire de l'ordre de Saint Benoît, 6 vols., Liège, 1949.

Schrade, H., La peinture romane (version française), Paris, 1966.

Schuhmacher, W., "Dominus Legem Dat," Römische Quartelschrift für christlichen Altertumskunde und Kirchengeschichte, 54 (1959), pp.1-39.

_____, "Traditio Legis," L.C.I., IV, cols. 342-351.

Schurenberg, L., "Spätromanische und frühgotische Plastik in Dijon und ihre Bedeutung für die Skulptur des Strassburger Munsterquerschiffs," Jahrbuch der preussischen Kunstsammlungen, 1937, pp.13-25.

Schwartz, S., "Symbolic Allusions in a Twelfth-Century Ivory," Marsyas, 16 (1972-1973), pp.35-42.

Seiferth, W., Synagogue and Church in the Middle Ages, trans. from the German by L. Chadeayne and P. Gottwald, New York, 1970.

Sejourné, P., "Saints (culte des)," D.T.C., 14, cols. 870-978.

Severens, K., The Cathedral at Sens and its Influence in the Twelfth Century, unpublished dissertation, The Johns Hopkins University, 1968.

Simson, O. von, The Gothic Cathedral, New York, 1956.

Smalley, B., The Study of the Bible in the Middle Ages, Oxford, 1952.

Spicq, C., Esquisse d'une histoire de l'exégèse latine au moyen âge, Paris, 1944.

Staniforth, M., Early Christian Writings, Baltimore, 1968.

Sticca, S., The Latin Passion Play: its Origins and Development, Albany, 1970.

Stoddard, W., The West Facades of Saint-Denis and Chartres, Sculpture in the Ile-de-France from 1140 to 1190, Theory of Origins, Cambridge, Mass. 1952.

Suau, J., "Les débuts de la sculpture gothique dans l'Eure, I: L'abbaye Notre-Dame d'Ivry," Nouvelles de l'Eure, 49 (1973), pp. 48-71.

Summerson, J., Heavenly Mansions and Other Essays on Architecture, New York, 1963.

Swarzenski, H., Monuments of Romanesque Art, The Art of Church Treasures in North-Western Europe, 2nd ed., London, 1967.

Thirion, J., "Les plus anciennes sculptures de Notre-Dame de Paris," Comptes rendus de l'Académie des Inscriptions et Belles-Lettres, 1970, pp.85-112.

Vaudin-Bataille, E., Fastes de la Sénonie, 2nd ed., rev. and cor., Paris, 1898.

Vezin, G., L'Adoration et le cycle des Mages dans l'art chrétien primitif, étude des influences orientales et greques sur l'art chrétien, Paris, 1950.

Vloberg, M., La Vierge et l'enfant dans l'art française, Grenoble, 1933.

_____, La Vierge, notre médiatrice, Grenoble, 1938.

Vöge, W., Die Anfänge des monumentalen Stiles im Mittelalter, eine Untersuchung über die erste Blützeit französischer Plastik, Strasbourg, 1894.

Vöretzsch, A., "Stab," L.C.I., IV, cols. 193-198.

Watson, A., The Early Iconography of the Tree of Jesse, London, 1934.

Wessel, K., "Regina Coeli," Forschungen und Fortschnitte, 32 (1958), pp.11-16.

Wienand, A., ed., Die heiligen drei Könige, Cologne, 1974.

Wilmart, A., Auteurs spirituels et textes dévots du moyen âge latin: études d'histoire litteraire, Paris, 1932.

Young, K., The Drama of the Medieval Church, 2 vols., 2nd ed., Oxford, 1962.

Fig.1 View West from the
Crossing.

Fig.2 View East from the
Crossing.

Fig.3 North Nave Wall in Bays
WI and WII.

Fig.4 South Side-Aisle from
the East.

Fig.5 View of the Central Vessel from the West.

Fig.6 South Side-Aisle from the West.

Fig.7 View of the Crossing Vault
from the Southwest.

Fig.8 Crossing Pier en.

Fig.9 View of EINI and ANI
from the West.

Fig.10 Western Tower Porch.

Fig.11 Southern End of the West Facade.

Fig.12 Juncture of the Nave and Tower Porch on the North Side.

Fig.13 Porch Pier w7n from the Southeast.

Fig.14 Eastern Massing from the Southeast.

Fig.15 Eastern Massing from the Northeast.

Fig.16 Sens
Cathedral Pier
ws from the
Southwest.

Fig.17 Pier
w4n from the
Southwest.

Fig.18 Sens
Cathedral Pier
w6n from the
Southwest.

Fig.19 Bases of
Piers w4s and
w3s from the
Southeast.

Fig.20 Sens
Cathedral Pier
e1n1, East
Side.

Fig.21 Sens
Cathedral
Pier e1s from
the Southeast.

Fig.22 Western Portal (WM).

Fig.23 Tympanum and Lintel

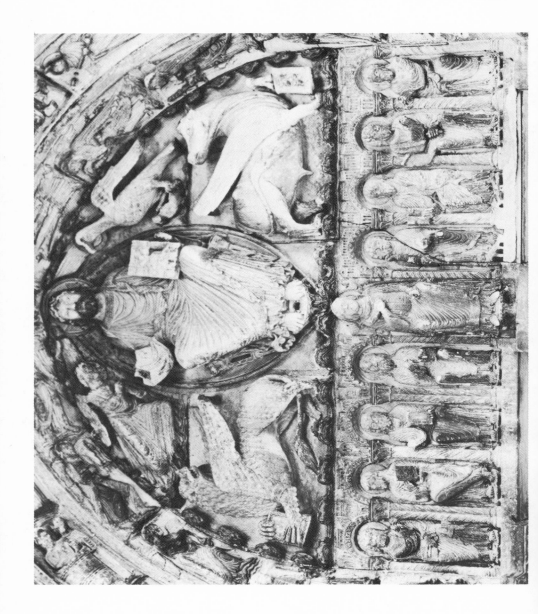

Fig.24 Lintel (M).

Fig.24a Lintel (M) Detail
Showing the Veil of the Temple.

Fig.25 Lintel (M) North Side.

Fig.26 Lintel (M) South Side.

Fig.27 Trumeau.

Fig.27a Trumeau, Detail.

Fig.28 Trumeau Capital.

Fig.29 Trumeau Capital
North Side.

Fig.30 Trumeau Capital
South Side.

Fig. 31 North Embrasure Column- Figures

Fig.32 South Embrasure Column-Figures.

Fig.33 North Embrasure Capitals.

Fig.34 South Embrasure Capitals.

Fig.35 WM1 - n/1.

Fig.36 WM1 - n/2.

Fig.37 WM1 - n/3.

Fig.38 WM1 - n/4.

Fig.39 WM1 - n/5.

Fig.40 WM1 - Keystone.

Fig.41 WM1 - s/1.

Fig.42 WM1 - s/2.

Fig.43 WM1 - s/3.

Fig.44 WM1 - s/4.

Fig.45 WM1 - s/5.

Fig.46 WM3 - n/l.

Fig.47 WM2 - n/l.

Fig.48 WM3 - n/2.

Fig.49 WM2 - n/2.

Fig.50 WM3 - n/3.

Fig.51 WM2 - n/3.

Fig.52 WM3 - n/4.

Fig.53 WM2 - n/4.

Fig.54 WM3 - n/5.

Fig.55 WM2 - n/5.

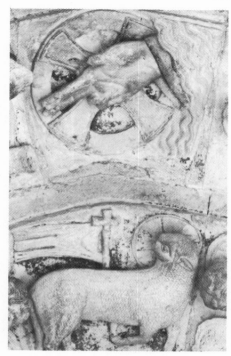

Fig.56 WM1 and WM2 –
Keystones.

Fig.57 WM3 - n/6.

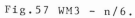

Fig.58 WM2 - n/6.

Fig.60 WM3 - Keystone.

Fig.59 WM3 - n/7.

Fig.61 WM2 - s/1.

Fig.62 WM3 - s/1.

Fig.63 WM2 - s/2

Fig.64 WM3 - s/2.

Fig.65 WM2 - s/3.

Fig.66 WM3 - s/3.

Fig.67 WM2 - s/4.

Fig.68 WM3 - s/4.

Fig.69 WM2 - s/5.

Fig.70 WM3 - s/5.

Fig.71 WM3 - s/7.

Fig.72 WM2 - s/6.

Fig.73 WM3 - s/6.

563

Fig.74 Apex of
Tympanum Where
Undulant Cloud
Border Is Inter-
rupted by Nimbus
of Christ Figure.

Fig.75 Detail of
S. Side of Tym-
panum Where Un-
dulant Cloud
Border Ends Be-
neath Eagle.

Fig.76 Detail of
S. Side of Tym-
panum Showing
Gap in Undulant
Cloud Border Be-
hind Ox.

Fig.77 Detail of N. Side of Tympanum Showing Continuity of Cloud Border Along Bottom and Side of Upper Left Block.

Fig.78 Lintel (M) Detail of Figure Showing Repositioning of Head.

Fig.79 Lintel: Three-Quarter Capital at n/4.

Fig.80 Lintel: Cropped Double Capital at n.

Fig.81 Lintel: Cropped Double Capital at s.

Fig.82 Lintel: Double and Three-Quarter Capitals at s/3 and s/4.

Fig.83 Column-Figure 1-n: Relationship
Between Figure, Shaft, and Capital.

Fig.84 Column-Figures 1-n and 2-n:
Relationship Between Figures and Arris.

Fig.85 Column-Figures 3-n and 2-n:
Inward Cant of Column-Figure 2-n.

Fig.86 Column-Figures 3-n and 2-n:
Relationship Between Figures and Arris.

Fig.87 Column-
Figure 2-n: Rela-
tionship Between
Halo and Astragal
(shaft hidden from
 view).

Fig.88 Column-
Figure 2-n: Junc-
ture Between Shaft
and Capital (right).

Fig.89 Column-
Figure 2-n: Axial
Deflection Between
Figure and Impost.

Fig.90 Column-Figure 3-n:
Cropping of Halo to Ac-
comodate Figure to Capital.

Fig.91 Column-Figure 3-n:
Left Side Showing Relationship Between Shaft and Capital.

Fig.92 Column-Figure 1-s:
Relationship Between Shaft
and Capital (left).

Fig.93 Column-Figure 1-s:
Relationship Between Ring-
Console and Base.

Fig.94 Column-Figure 1-s:
Relationship Between Shaft
and Capital (right).

Fig.95 Column-Figures 1-s and
2-s: Abutment of Figures.

Fig.96 Column-Figure 2-s:
Relationship Between Ring-
Console and Base.

Fig.97 Column-Figure 2-s:
Relationship Between Shaft
and Capital (left).

Fig.98 Column-Figure 2-s:
Relationship Between Shaft
and Capital (right).

Fig.99 Column-Figure 3-s:
Relationship Between Shaft
and Capital (left).

Fig.100 Column-Figure 3-s:
Relationship Between Shaft
and Capital (right).

Fig.101 Column-Figure 3-s:
Relationship Between Ring-
Console and Base.

Fig.102 Voussoirs
North Side: Showing
Projection of WM3 -
n/1 and WM2 - n/1
Beyond the Vertical
Plane of Their Imposts.

Fig.103 WM3 - n/1:
Detail Showing Pro-
jection of Voussoir
Beyond Plane of Impost.

Fig.104 Voussoirs
South Side: Showing
Projection of WM2 -
s/1 and WM3 - s/1
Beyond the Vertical
Plane of Their Imposts.

Fig.105 View of South Side Voussoirs from Below Showing
Projection of WM2-s/1 and WM3-s/1 Beyond the Plane of Their
Imposts.

Fig.106 Juncture Between Porch
Pier w6n and Portal Embrasure
at the Socle Zone (corresponds
to Text Fig.10, p.92).

Fig.107 Juncture Between
Porch Pier w6n and Portal
Embrasure at the Capital Zone.

Fig.108 Juncture Between
Porch Pier w6s and Portal
Embrasure at the Socle Zone
(corresponds to Text Fig.
10, p.92).

Fig.109 Juncture Between
Porch Pier w6s and Portal
Embrasure at the Capital
Zone.

Fig.110 Fichot Etching (1855).

Fig.111 Buval Drawing (1844).

Fig. 112 Lintel: Detail Northern Lateral
Block Showing Stone Repair to Upper Edge.

Fig. 113 Lintel: Detail Northern Lateral
Block Showing Stone Repair to Lower Edge.

Fig.114 Châlons-sur-Marne,
Notre-Dame-en-Vaux, Southern
Lateral Portal, West Embrasure.

Fig.115 Châlons-sur-Marne,
Notre-Dame-en-Vaux, Southern
Lateral Portal East Embrasure.

Fig.116 Provins, Saint-Ayoul Western Portals.

Fig.117 Provins, Saint-Ayoul
WM Column-Figures 4-n--1-n.

Fig.118 Provins, Saint-Ayoul
WM Column-Figures 1-s--4-s.

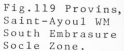

Fig.119 Provins,
Saint-Ayoul WM
South Embrasure
Socle Zone.

Fig.120 Provins,
Saint-Ayoul WM:
Detail Showing
Relationship Be-
tween Ring-Con-
sole 3-s and
Base 3-s.

Fig.121 Provins,
Saint-Ayoul WM:
Detail Showing
Relationship
Between Shaft
4-s and Base 4-s

Fig.122 Provins, Saint-Ayoul WM Column-
Figure 1-n: Relationship Between Shaft
and Capital (left).

Fig.123 Provins, Saint-Ayoul WM Column-
Figure 1-n: Relationship Between Shaft
and Capital (right).

Fig.124 Provins, Saint-Ayoul WM Column-
Figures 2-s and 3-s: Detail Showing the
"Scalloping" Behind 3-s.

Fig.125 Provins, Saint-Ayoul WM: Detail
Showing Difference in Voussoir Profiles
and Figure Consoles Between Archivolts
WM1 and WM2.

Fig.126 Lintel: Detail of the Head of
Saint John (apostle s/1).

Fig.127 Dijon, Musée Archéologique
Last Supper Tympanum from Saint-Bénigne:
Detail of the Head of Saint John.

Fig.128 Lintel: Apostle n/1.

Fig.129 Dijon, Musée Archéologique
Last Supper Tympanum from Saint-Bénigne:
Detail of the Legs of the Second Apostle
to the Left of Christ.

Fig.130 Dijon, Musée Archéologique
Last Supper Tympanum from Saint-Bénigne:
Detail of the Head of the Second Apostle
to the Left of Christ.

Fig.131 WM3-s/1 (first Magus and Herod).

Fig.132 Dijon, Musée Archéologique
Last Supper Tympanum from Saint-Bénigne:
Detail of the Head of the First Apostle
to the left of Christ.

Fig.133 WM3-s/1: Detail of the Head of
the First Magus.

Fig.134 Sens, Musée Municipale
Capital (?) from Saint-Pierre-le-Vif
Rex Robertus (Robert the Pious).

Fig.135 Sens, Musée Municipale
Capital (?) from Saint-Pierre-le-Vif
Saint Peter and Saint Paul.

Fig.136 Sens, Musée Municipale
Capital (?) from Saint-Pierre-le-Vif
Saint Peter.

Fig.137 Sens, Musée Municipale
Capital (?) from Saint-Pierre-le-Vif
An Ecclesiastic.

Fig.138 Embrasure Capital 1/n. Fig.139 Embrasure Capital 1/s.

Fig.140 Sens, Palais Synodale
End Capital from the Dado Zone
Arcade of the Cathedral.

Fig.141 Sens Cathedral, AIINI
Dado Zone Arcade Capital.

Fig.142 Embrasure Capital 2/s.

Fig.143 Sens, Palais Synodale
Capital from the Dado Zone
Arcade of the Cathedral.

Fig.144 Embrasure Capital 3/s.

Fig.145 Detail of Fig.143.

Fig.146 Detail of Fig.139.

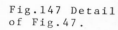

Fig.147 Detail
of Fig.47.

Fig.148 Sens
Cathedral, AINI
Detail of Dado
Zone Arcade
Capital (Vint-
ner's Capital).

Fig.149 Detail
of Fig.144.

594

Fig.150 Sens Cathedral, AINI
Dado Zone Arcade Capital
(Vintner's Capital).

Fig. 151 WM3-s/6.

Fig.152 Chartres Cathedral
WN S. Jamb, fig.5.

Fig.153 Sens, Musée Municipale
Fragment of a Capital (?).